merry Christmas,
Ken and Kathy,
Kenny and Kristine,

"Let's go adventuring together"

Fondly,
Ed & Nancy

Andy Alpine, *Co-publisher*
Steen Hansen, *Co-publisher*
Risa Weinreb, *Editor*
Lisa Carolan Alpine, *Associate Editor*

SIMON AND SCHUSTER
NEW YORK

The ADVENTURE VACATION CATALOG

BY THE PUBLISHERS OF
SPECIALTY TRAVEL INDEX

ISBN 0-671-50770-2

In Appreciation

We would like to thank the enthusiastic, dedicated people who worked hard to make this book informative and accurate.

In particular, we'd like to thank John Leland, Kate Miller and Kay Potter for the many hours they devoted to researching and writing this book. We also appreciate the contributions made by Nancy Fezell, Neil Klotz and Barbara Zalaznick.

We're grateful to the many tour operators who provided the huge quantities of information needed to put together this book. And we owe special thanks to Carol Knapp for her invaluable work in preparing the manuscript.

Finally, we'd like to thank you, the adventurous vacationer, for continuing the spirit of learning and discovery. May your wanderlust lead you to wonderful places.

Contents

Introduction

Looking for "something different" in a vacation?

- Dive into another world . . . where gaudily-colored fish swim languidly in the warm waters off Australia's Great Barrier Reef.
- Bounce across a dusty savanna in a Land Rover. Suddenly, you come across the only watering hole within miles . . . where elephant, zebra, eland, oryx and giraffe all converge to drink.
- For hundreds of years, Sherpas have led travelers through the mountains of Nepal. Today, they are guiding you 17,500 feet up . . . to the base camp of Mt. Everest.
- In a chateau nestled in the Loire Valley, you are seated at an oaken table where three kings have dined. You are about to sample some of the great wines of France. The first selection is an exquisite Chateauneuf du Pape.

Wildlife safaris, trekking, scuba diving, wine tasting . . . all these varied activities are known as "adventure travel" or "special interest travel."

If you are looking for a unique vacation, *The Adventure Vacation Catalog* is a comprehensive source book of adventure travel opportunities throughout the world. It contains facts about over six hundred different activities worldwide and lists almost four hundred tour operators. You will find up-to-date information about dates, costs and itineraries . . . everything you need to make your dream trip a reality. Quite literally, we've covered our subject from A to Z—archeology to zoology, from Alaska to Zimbabwe. In between, you'll find such off-the-beaten-path opportunities as caving, villa rentals, photography tours and camel expeditions. Because this book covers such a wide range of activities, it can give you lots of good vacation ideas—for this year and years to come.

The Adventure Vacation Catalog has been compiled by the publishers of *Specialty Travel Index*. For nearly four years, travelers and travel agents have relied on *Specialty Travel Index* as their leading sourcebook for adventure vacations. Now with *The Adventure Vacation Catalog,* complete planning information about unusual trips is directly available to you, the adventurous vacationer.

Adventure travel is for everybody. Whatever your level of skill or accomplishment—from complete beginner to seasoned expert—*The Adventure Vacation Catalog* has a trip that's right for you. All the trips in this book are guided adventure vacations under skilled leadership. The tour operator and outfitters have the knowledge and expertise to give you an exciting but safe vacation. You'll be able to relax and enjoy your trip—knowing that your guides possess advanced skills in their fields.

Importantly, adventure travel is safe—when undertaken with an experienced trip organizer or outfitter and if you realistically evaluate your own knowledge, ability and limitations. Age is no barrier—many of these excursions have been enjoyed by enthusiastic kids and energetic eighty-year-olds. The only requirements are general good health and a sense of adventure.

The Adventure Vacation Catalog can help you plan that once-in-a-lifetime vacation you've always dreamed of. But a lot of adventures listed are great escapes too—for weekend getaways in your own area or region. Because of the tremendous diversity and size of the United States, you can find plenty of extraordinary travel opportunities right in your own backyard. Do you live in New York? You can dive for sunken treasure just a few thousand yards off the shore of Long Island. California? How about trekking through the Shasta Mountains with llamas? There's dog sledding in Minnesota, mountaineering in New Hampshire, bicycle touring in Florida . . . and they are all included in *The Adventure Vacation Catalog.*

Sometimes adventure travel is an adventure for the body. But always, it is an adventure for the mind—whether it involves mastering ice climbing on the sheer face of the Cascade Mountains or studying the traditions of native art in the lush highlands of Papua New Guinea. Although adventure travel demands more effort and commitment than, let's say, lounging by a hotel pool, it also gives you more rewards.

Adventure travel offers you a unique opportunity to observe spectacular scenery, fascinating cultures, the incredible power and majesty of nature—while participating, accomplishing and learning for yourself. As one adventurer explained: "I'd always been intrigued by the Grand Canyon, but I wanted to do more than just look at it. So I spent ten days rafting down the Colorado River. I swam in the river and learned to steer through rapids. And every night, the stars were so incredible I didn't want to go to sleep. It's an experience I'll always remember."

ABBREVIATIONS

In listings, we have abbreviated the various American states as follows:

TWO-LETTER STATE AND TERRITORY ABBREVIATIONS

Alabama	AL	Kentucky	KY	Oklahoma	OK
Alaska	AK	Louisiana	LA	Oregon	OR
Arizona	AZ	Maine	ME	Pennsylvania	PA
Arkansas	AR	Maryland	MD	Puerto Rico	PR
American Samoa	AS	Massachusetts	MA	Rhode Island	RI
California	CA	Michigan	MI	South Carolina	SC
Canal Zone	CZ	Minnesota	MN	South Dakota	SD
Colorado	CO	Mississippi	MS	Tennessee	TN
Connecticut	CT	Missouri	MO	Trust Territories	TT
Delaware	DE	Montana	MT	Texas	TX
District of Columbia	DC	Nebraska	NE	Utah	UT
Florida	FL	Nevada	NV	Vermont	VT
Georgia	GA	New Hampshire	NH	Virginia	VA
Guam	GU	New Jersey	NJ	Virgin Islands	VI
Hawaii	HI	New Mexico	NM	Washington	WA
Idaho	ID	New York	NY	West Virginia	WV
Illinois	IL	North Carolina	NC	Wisconsin	WI
Indiana	IN	North Dakota	ND	Wyoming	WY
Iowa	IA	Northern Mariana Islands	CM		
Kansas	KS	Ohio	OH		

PROFESSIONAL ASSOCIATIONS

AAMWG	Alaska Association of Mountain & Wilderness Guides
ACA	American Canoe Association
ARRA	American River Recreation Association
ASTA	American Society of Travel Agents
BITOA	British Incoming Tour Operators Association
EPRO	Eastern Professional River Outfitters
IATA	International Air Transport Association
PATA	Pacific Area Travel Association
PSIA	Professional Ski Instructors of America
RMSIA	Rocky Mountain Ski Instructors Association
TIAA	Travel Industry Association of America
USFS	United States Forest Service
USTOA	United States Tour Operators Association
WRGA	Western River Guides Association

HOW TO CHOOSE A TOUR OPERATOR

The operators and outfitters listed have been selected because of their professionalism, experience and reliability. When it comes to adventure travel, they're the experts . . . and they can pass along the skills and know-how necessary for you to become an expert yourself.

Although we have evaluated tours to the best of our ability, we have not personally visited or inspected all these operators. Here are some guidelines for choosing the tour that's right for you:

1. First, use the Table of Contents to pick out the tour(s) you are interested in.
2. Write or call the operators asking for their brochures. A stamped, self-addressed envelope—or international postal response coupon for foreign organizations—speeds the process.
3. Now that you have received brochures from the tour operators, which one to pick? Here are some tips:

- Ask for references. Most tour operators will refer you to national clubs, associations or past passengers, who can vouch for the quality of their trips.

- Check with various trade organizations, state fish and game commissions or the area Chamber of Commerce yourself. Many activities and sports have associations supervising their participants, such as the Appalachian Trail Conference for backpackers or the Professional Association of Diving Instructors for scuba diving. For activities such as horsepacking, backpacking, mountaineering, river rafting, fishing and hunting, many states in the United States require outfitters and guides to be licensed and/or bonded. Licensing and bonding, administered by state fish and game commissions, will generally assure you that a tour operator has extensive knowledge about the activity and area, including knowledge of relevant safety techniques, and is backed by sufficient financial resources to provide the services promised to the public.

For your information, a list of various activity associations starts on page 368. To check on foreign operators, contact that country's National Tourist Office. A list of addresses begins on page 361.

- Ask how long the operator has been around. Experience counts when it comes to travel. If an organization has run tours for several seasons, they must be doing something right!
- Analyze the brochure itself. A good brochure is well-written, informative, and answers most of your questions. Is previous experience required for the trip? What's included—meals? transfers? What will the trip be like?
- Finally, analyze yourself a bit. What kind of vacation do you really want? Are you happy tacking up, feeding, grooming and hobbling a packhorse in the Sierra Nevadas—or would you prefer to hand Ol' Paint over to a wrangler at the end of the day? On an archeological dig in Italy, do you actually want to put hand to shovel . . . or do you want to learn about Etruscan pottery in the shelter of a cool, cosmopolitan museum?
- Honestly evaluate your skill level. Adventure travel is safe so long as you don't exceed your own capabilities. If you've never done whitewater river rafting, pick an operator geared to first-timers. On the other hand, if you're a "river rat" who paddled before you could walk, avoid a tour that announces: "Leisurely runs in quiet waters—great for novices."

Depending on the activity, there may be other factors to consider when choosing a tour operator. You'll find some general information about each activity—as well as specific pointers for planning your trip—in the introduction to each chapter.

ABOUT TRAVEL AGENTS

To help you plan your trip, an experienced travel agent can save you a lot of time. Travel agents can assist you in evaluating a tour operator, find the best airfares and provide you with useful background information. Using a travel agent doesn't cost you any money, since their commissions are paid by the tour operator, hotels and airlines.

TOUR DATES

We've listed tour dates or seasons for each operator. However, these dates may change because of weather and other conditions. Please check the individual tour operator for information about changes, additions and cancellations.

RATES

As we all know, prices change rapidly. Particularly with foreign tours, costs will fluctuate along with the exchange rate for the U.S. dollar. All prices quoted are for one person unless otherwise stated. Please verify rates with the individual tour operator.

When evaluating how much a tour costs, it's important to consider what a given rate includes. On safari, will you be housed in a luxury game lodge, dining off fine china and silver—or do you need to bring your own tent? How many meals are included? What kinds of meals—gourmet or canned? Does the tour operator provide transfers from the airport to tour starting point? Are taxes included? (Sales tax runs as high as 8¼% in the United States; arrival and departure taxes in foreign countries can cost a tidy sum.) How about tips—which can add up to 25% to your bill?

Finally, the major item—does the price include airfare? For many tours in this book, it won't.

ABOUT AIRFARES

Recent moves towards airline deregulation in the United States have brought travelers both good news and bad news.

First the bad news: Rates change constantly, and it's pretty tough to figure out who's offering the best deal to where.

Now the good news: It's probably cheaper than ever before to get where you want to go . . . if you shop around.

Shopping around means checking the daily papers to see which airline has a special deal. It means consulting a travel agent—or sitting down yourself with a book called the *Official Airline Guide* (you may get a copy from your travel agent), which lists airlines flying to various destinations.

Also useful is the *World Directory,* published annually by *Travel Weekly* magazine and available at libraries. The *World Directory* has a complete listing of the world's airlines (along with United States phone numbers), as well as cruise lines, hotel chains and lots more.

Foreign tourist offices are another important source of information about traveling abroad. Tourist offices can fill you in about which airlines (scheduled and charter) fly to their countries, ferry connections, car rental, train and bus service. Our list of foreign tourist offices begins on page 361.

When calling the airlines, check these points carefully:

- Are you flying peak season—or low season? Sometimes, you can save money by changing your flight dates.
- Is it cheaper to fly at night? Midweek?
- Are APEX (Advance Purchase Excursion) fares available?

• How about baggage allowances? (Some special interest activities—most notably mountaineering and hang gliding—require equipment that boggles the mind of your average airline baggage handler . . . so plan ahead!)

Look into charter flights. Today, charter flights are completely respectable and passenger payments are protected. All charter flight operators must put funds from passengers in an escrow account—and these funds are not released to the charter company until the flight(s) has been completed. To make sure your charter payment is protected, make out your check to the charter escrow account—*not* the tour operator. You or your travel agent can get the correct escrow account name from the charterer. Some good sources of charter flight information are:

Jens Jurgen's Charter Flight Directory
    and Guide to Other Air Travel Bargains

Travel Information Bureau
P.O. Box 105
Kings Park, NY 11754

The Travel Company
501 5th Avenue, Suite 3314
New York, NY 10017

Traveling to faraway places—via Europe? Then investigate certain low airfares available only through retail firms in Europe. In England, such companies are called "bucket shops." Here's how they work.

The British "bucket shops" buy plane seats in bulk, then resell them to individuals. Cheap. The price is substantially less than that available from airlines or authorized travel agents. There is a catch—since bucket shops are not licensed or regulated, the traveler has to check a firm's references and reputation carefully. A good source of information about the variety of cheap flights from England to other parts of the world is *Time Out,* a guide to what's going on in London. Americans can get *Time Out* by sending £1.50 to:

TIME OUT, Ltd.
Tower House
Southampton Street
London WC2
England

DEPOSITS—PAYMENTS—CANCELLATIONS

Tour operator's policies regarding deposits, final payments and cancellations vary—so check individual operators for details.

To protect yourself against cancellation penalties, you can buy low-cost trip cancellation insurance—available through insurance companies or your travel agent.

On occasion, operators cancel or change departure dates. You should be aware that in such cases, you may be liable for certain airfare penalties—even though the alteration wasn't your fault. Once again, low-cost trip cancellation insurance can protect you.

WHEN TO GO

Since this book covers the whole world, there's no one answer about the best season to travel. It will vary from one country to another—and also vary according to what you want to do there. Although January is a terrible month for skiing in Australia, it's the height of the windsurfing season. Do a little research on your own—and use your common sense.

WHAT TO WEAR/BRING

The tour operator will provide you with very detailed packing lists about equipment and clothing—even how many pairs of socks you'll need. Contact the tour operator if you have any other specific questions.

Now get ready for some great adventuring!

How to Use This Book

We think you'll find that *The Adventure Vacation Catalog* is the most comprehensive guide to unusual vacations around the world. To get the most out of this book, however, it's important to know how to use it.

FORMAT

As you'll see in the Table of Contents (page 7), *The Adventure Vacation Catalog* is arranged by activity, and the activities are listed alphabetically. Within each activity, we have listed tour operators alphabetically.

TO FIND A SPECIFIC ACTIVITY OR PLACE

If you want to find out about an activity in a specific place (let's say bicycling in China), turn to the "Bicycle Touring" section. You can read through the section to see which tours operate in China. Or you can consult the geographical index under "China" to see which bicycle tours are listed there. Although most of the listings for a given activity will appear in the appropriate section, some might appear elsewhere in the book. For example, a trip in Colorado that combines two days of horsepacking with four days of river rafting will appear in the river rafting section—but will be listed in the geographical index under both "Colorado—river rafting" and "Colorado—horsepacking." Similarly, a university research project about whales might appear with the research expeditions—but might be indexed under both "Research Expeditions" and "Whalewatching." To make sure you find all the listings for an activity in a given locale, use the geographical index at the end of the book.

TO FIND A SPECIFIC TOUR OPERATOR

An alphabetical listing of all tour operators included in this book starts on page 370.

Archeology •

—What is the meaning of the lines of Nazca—huge outlines of monkeys, spiders, birds and other animals built into the Peruvian mountainsides hundreds of years ago—yet visible only from above, in modern-day airplanes?

—Who built the pyramids of Egypt—and how had they obtained a scientific and mathematical understanding so advanced, that they could incorporate the precise circumference of the earth and length of the year (correct to several decimal places) into their design?

—As capital of Akbar the Great, Moghul emperor, Fatehpur Sikri was a glittering city filled with silks, rubies and diamonds. Why was it abandoned only fourteen years after its completion?

Archeology embraces mysteries more compelling than those found in any detective story, for it seeks to retrace and illuminate the course of human existence.

The word "archeology" literally means "the study of old things," coming from the Greek *archios*—"old"—and *logos,* a discourse or study. While history concerns itself with all aspects of the past—political, artistic and social—archeology concentrates on man's physical remains—humble dwellings and lavish funerary temples . . . weapons and farming implements . . . jewelry, cooking utensils and burial sites. The time frame is a vast one: although written history reaches back a scant five thousand years, pre-history covers everything that has happened since man's first appearance on earth . . . twenty million years ago.

The programs which follow offer you a wide choice of archeological adventures—from guided visits at famous sites to hands-on digs where you yourself join in the fieldwork. You can stroll through the fabled Minoan palace of Knossos, deeply associated with Greek mythology . . . help excavate burial mounds in Illinois . . . see the brooding statue of Chac-Mool, crucial icon of Mayan sacrificial rituals . . . explore the ruins of Carthage or the Great Zimbabwe.

And as you walk along a passageway worn smooth by centuries of pilgrims . . . run your hand over a stone wall perfectly fitted together without use of mortar . . . or pause to view an exquisite urn that last carried water 2,500 years ago, you'll be linked to the very beginnings of human civilization.

SECTIONS OF RELATED INTEREST

> *Art/architecture*
> *Culture/history*

 Aitken Spence Travels, Ltd.
P.O. Box 5
Colombo, Sri Lanka
(01) 36735/36755
Telex 21142 AITKEN CE 21598   *Sri Lanka*

Tour the exciting ancient cities of Sri Lanka. This trip will give you a chance to visit famous Anaradhapura, a city over two thousand years old and filled with exotic ruins and artifacts. Here you can stroll through the Royal Pleasure Gardens and stand before the famous Bo-tree—grown from the original tree under which the Buddha attained enlightenment. In Polonnaruwa you'll explore the rare rock sculptures and tour the century-old King's Palace. Then see Dambulla—famous for its rock cave temples and colossal statue of the recumbent Buddha cut from solid rock. Member of Pacific Area Travel Association. Includes: Visits to all archeological sites. Dates: Year-round. Length of trip: 8 days. Group size: Maximum 15 persons. Cost: From $300 per person.

Ancient Mexico
Nature Expeditions International
474 Williamette Avenue
Box 11496
Eugene, Oregon 97440
503-484-6529   *Mexico*

On this special cultural expedition, you'll experience the incredible variety of Mexico, from cosmopolitan Mexico City and colonial cathedrals to colorful Indian markets and the mysterious ruins of some of the world's greatest civilizations. Your adventure begins in Mexico City where a visit to the renowned National Museum of Anthropology provides an ideal introduction to Mesoamerican culture. Next you'll explore the ancient ruins around Mexico City, Oaxaca and the Yucatan peninsula, including Teotihuacan, Palenque, Uxmal and Chichen Itza—with its sacred cenote. In business for over ten years, faculty of thirty teachers as guides. Includes: All land accommodations, transportation, meals except in Mexico City, entrance fees, tips. Dates: December through February. Length of trip: 17 days. Group size: Maximum of 20. Cost: $1,590.

Cedok
10 East 40th Street
New York, NY 10016
212-689-9720   *Czechoslovakia*

Cedok, the official Czech Travel Bureau, offers a tour of the full archeological circuit in Czechoslovakia. The sites include Karlstejn, the famous fourteenth-century castle built by Charles IV and the depository of the Holy Roman Empire; Zavist, a large complex of medieval fortifications; Levy Hradec and Kourim, ruins of Slavonic fortresses; and Pavlov, with ancient remains of the early Stone Age. The tour will cover archeological and folklore museums throughout the region. There will be sightseeing in Prague, Bratislava and Brno. Evenings will be spent at musical and cultural events, night clubs, and brasseries. Includes: Accommodations, full board, guides, ground transportation, sightseeing and entrance fees. Dates: All year. Length: 8 days. Group size: 15–35. Cost: $366–$423.

Colorado Institute
P.O. Box 875
Crested Butte, CO 81224
303-349-5118   *Southwest United States*

Come discover a world of ancient Indian culture while climbing the cliff dwellings of Mesa Verde National Park. Shop for authentic Indian artifacts in Durango, and ride a famous narrow-gauge railroad through the mountains to Silverton, and then enjoy a rustic chuckwagon dinner. Next stop is the San Luis Valley and a visit to Sand Dune National Monument. Sightseeing options include the Hopi reservation, Canyon de Chelley, Monument Valley and the Grand Canyon. As part of this program, you'll get background information on prehistoric Indian culture, and an institute anthropologist will accompany you to various sites. Fifteen years' experience. Includes: Transportation, lodging, meals and instruction. Dates: June through September. Length of trip: 5–7 days. Group size: 10–20. Cost: $60 a day per person.

Cross Cultural Adventures
P.O. Box 3285
Arlington, VA 22203
703-243-7194
Telex 440283 ACI UI   *Tunisia*

Over the centuries the Berbers, Phoenicians, Greeks, Carthaginians, Romans, Vandals, Byzantines, Arabs and French all came and made their home in this northernmost African land. It is here that Ulysses encountered the lotus eaters and here that Hannibal fought his last battle. During this thorough two-week journey you'll explore both Tunisia's layers of ancient civilizations and its present-day delights: the well-preserved ruins of Carthage, Utica, Dougga; El Djem's awesome amphitheater; Kairoan, one of Islam's holiest cities; the fascinating Tunis medina; and the thermal spas of Cap Bon. Turning south to the Sahara desert, you'll stay in underground dwellings in Matmata and explore the Nefta oasis, where the world's best dates are grown. Before flying home, you'll have a well-deserved rest on the serene Island of Djerba. Tour leader is an art and archeology scholar. Includes: Accommodations in deluxe or first-class hotels, meals, transportation, tour leader and escorts. Dates: December. Length of trip: 2 weeks. Group size: Maximum of 15. Cost: $1,200. Special requirements: $300 deposit with reservation, balance 6 weeks prior to departure.

Crow Canyon Campus
Center for American Archeology
1911 Ridge Avenue
Evanston, IL 60201
312-492-5300   *Southwest United States*

Ten miles from Mesa Verde National Park in southwestern Colorado, Crow Canyon lies at the crossroads of the overlapping histories which make up the American Southwest. The Four Corners area (Colorado, New Mexico, Arizona and Utah) surrounding the canyon has been home to the prehistoric Anasazi, as well as Utes and Navajos, Spanish conquistadors, miners, authors and homesteaders. Crow Canyon projects need research associates to assist archeologists in rescuing data and cultural materials. Current projects examine archeoastronomy (the relation between natural features, man-made structures and the sun), the rock art along the San Juan River, and the health and habitat of the desert bighorn sheep. The tax-deductible contribution of $300 helps meet the cost of conducting the research expedition. Affiliated with Northwestern University since 1968. Includes: Instruction, all meals, local transportation, overnight accommodations in a lodge first and last nights of session. The rest of the session is camp-out; you supply your own camping gear. Dates: Summer and fall. Length of trip: 3, 5 or 7 days. Group size: 15–20. Cost: $300 (tax-deductible contribution).

Forum Travel International
2437 Durant Avenue #208
Berkeley, CA 94704
415-843-8294   *Bolivia*

The Andes of Peru and Bolivia offer two of the most impressive experiences imaginable—the Inca mountaintop citadel Machu Picchu, and vast Lake Titicaca, the highest navigable lake in the world. On this exploration of the realm of Inca, you'll also visit Arequipa, with its many colonial buildings; and Cuzco, ancient Inca capital. For shopping, it's on to Pisac and its lively native market and then a rest at a delightful, restored convent containing priceless colonial relics. Then you'll drive past fishermen in reed boats to Tiahuanaco, to see the massive stone statues, semi-subterranean palace and the "Portal of the Sun." You can also extend your journey to include: the Galapagos Islands, an enchanting world of lava, exotic plants and strange animals; Nazca Plains, with its strange lines and the Valley of the Grumbling Giants; and Easter Island. Operating since 1965. Includes: Land price, accommodations, transportation by land and water, most meals, sightseeing, excursions, entrance fees, guiding. Escort for groups of 15 or more. Dates: Year-round. Length of trip: 17 days. Group size: 2–20 people. Cost: $1,298.

GEO Expeditions
P.O. Box 27136-STB
Oakland, CA 94602
415-530-4146   *Galapagos Islands, Peru*

This expedition combines the rich Inca ruins of Peru with the unique natural history of the Galapagos Islands. You'll spend the first part of the trip exploring the ruins of Pisac, Ollantaytambo, and fabulous Machu Picchu, and visit the Sunday market at the village of Chincheros. Then enjoy a week of cruising among the Galapagos Islands aboard chartered auxiliary-powered sailing yachts with first class accommodations. Travel between the islands will be at night, leaving the days available for hiking a different island each day, examining the numerous plant and animal species unique to the Galapagos. The Galapagos itineraries are flexible to take advantage of the best weather conditions and visit islands where the wildlife and vegetation are at their peak. Optional extensions to Lake Titicaca, the Ballestas Islands and Nazca lines are also available. Includes: All inclusive—Accommodations, land transportation, cruise, most meals, expert leadership. Dates: August. Length of trip: 21 days. Group size: 15 maximum. Cost: $2,295. Special requirements: $200 deposit.

Great Expeditions, Inc.
2956 West 4th Avenue
Vancouver, B.C., Canada V6K 1R4
604-734-4948   *Peru*

It's Sunday in Chinchero and the market is pulsing with activity, but it swirls around you unnoticed because you are intent on getting a piece of Indian art you've fallen in love with—and you're practicing the newly discovered art of bartering. Still ahead of you on this adventure in Peru are two days of rafting the Urubamba River through the Sacred Valley of the Incas, exploring the magnificent ruins of Cuzco, and experiencing the thrill of coming face-to-face with the mighty Machu Picchu. Member of Pacific Area Travel Association; established in 1977. Includes: Accommodation, guide, some meals, transport (land only), river raft. Dates: July and August. Length: 10 days. Group size: 10 maximum. Cost: $950. Special requirements: $300 deposit.

Kampsville Archeological Center
Center for American Archeology
1911 Ridge Avenue
Evanston, IL 60201
312-492-5300   *Illinois*

In the Illinois River Valley sixty miles north of St. Louis, the Kampsville Archeological Center is the focus for one of the most ambitious archeological programs in the United States. Excavations at the famous Koster site have revealed evidence of settlements spanning ten thousand years. The Center needs associates—special friends of archeology who give of their time and money to assist directly in on–going research. Current Kampsville projects include the Stone House Survey, examining the nineteenth-century history of Greene County; and the Elizabeth Mounds, burial sites over five thousand years old. The tax-deductible fee goes to supporting the cost of the research. Affiliated with Northwest University since 1968. Includes: Instruction, tools, local transportation, room and board. Dates: Spring, summer and fall. Length of trip: 1–2 weeks. Group size: 15–20. Cost: $500 (tax-deductible).

Lindblad Travel, Inc.
P.O. Box 912
Westport, CT 06881
203-226-8531
Telex 221412 *Egypt*

Kharga and Dakhla oases lie approximately one hundred and fifty miles southwest of Assiut and eighty miles due west of the Valley of the Kings. This area known as the "New Valley" conceals an incredible wealth of interesting places to visit and has only recently had its "restricted area" status removed. You will view great temples still half buried in sand; cross a "river" of the Great Sand Sea and the "Plain of the Pyramids" with its Stone Age petroglyphs and painted desert; visit the two-thousand-year-old necropolis of Begawat; see underground streets in an old Islamic settlement, fields of wheat . . . even rice paddies and a duck farm in the midst of the Sahara. There are hot springs and cold springs, some with mineral-laden water reputed to benefit arthritis sufferers. Operating tours in Egypt for 25 years. Includes: Full breakfast Cairo; all meals Kharga for four days; specially guided by Adam Hassoune, Archeological Researcher; air transportation between Cairo and El Kharga. Dates: September through April. Length of trip: 5 days. Group size: Maximum of 21 persons. Cost: $3,100.

Serenissima Travel, Ltd.
2 Lower Sloane Street
London, England SWIW 8BJ
(01) 730-7281 *Crete*

Home of the great and mysterious Minoan civilization, Crete is full of archeological sites. This tour combines visits to the most important of them with breathtaking scenery and monuments of Crete's Roman, Byzantine and Venetian past. Highlights include Knossos, the great Minoan palace deeply associated with mythology . . . Gortyna, the ancient Roman capital . . . the Minoan palace at Mallia . . . and the Byzantine Church of Panayia Kera with outstanding frescoes dating from the fourteenth and fifteenth centuries. All Serenissima tours are accompanied by a noted expert in each field plus a tour manager. Eleventh year operating world-wide tours. Includes: All inclusive. Dates: April. Length of trip: 8 days. Group size: Varies. Cost: £635.

United Touring Company
P.O. Box 2914
Harare, Zimbabwe
793701
Telex 2173 *Zimbabwe*

This thirteen-day archeology tour begins in Inyanga with accommodations at the Troutbeck Inn. During the three days here, you'll visit Diana's Vow and Ruins on Harleigh Farm,

Rhodes Museum, Nyagwe Fort and pit structures, Worlds View, St. Catherine's Church, Van Niekerk Ruins and Nyahokwe. After a day in Harare and a visit to Markwe Cave, you'll fly to Victoria Falls, where highlights include a tour of the falls and Crocodile Ranch, an afternoon "Sundowner Cruise," and an evening of "African Spectacular" tribal dancing. The next four days will be spent in the Bulawayo area with trips to Matopos and Mswatugi Caves, Khami Ruins, Naletale Ruins, Ohlo Ohlo and Regina Ruins. The tour ends in Harare, where you'll visit the Great Zimbabwe Ruins as well as see rock paintings in Kyle National Park. Includes: Accommodation and table d'hote meals throughout, airport transfers and porterage, sightseeing, all ground transportation, local guides and entry fees. Dates: Year-round. Length of trip: 13 days. Group size: 16. Cost: Z$783.55, single supplement: Z$117.20.

Unitrex
1043 E. Green Street
Pasadena, CA 91106
800-421-5744
Then dial I.D. #90-80-707   *Mexico*

None of the early explorers visited as many sites as you will on this Mexican archeological adventure. You'll cover the modern Mexican states of Tabasco, starting with the Olmec culture, and continue on to Chiapas, Campeche, Quintana Roo, and of course, Yucatan. Some of the sites you will visit include La Venta, Comalcalco, Palenque, Tonina, Edzna, Tohok, Dzibalchen, Hochob, Uxmal, Mulchic, Sayil, Labna, Xlapak, Mayapan, Acanceh, Dzibilchaltun, Izamal, Chichen Itza, Old Chichen, Balancanche, Coba, Tulum, Rio Bec, Chicanna, and Becan among others along the way. Other Unitrex expeditions in Mexico focus on the Easter ceremonies of the Taralnumara Indians, Daxaca, and the State of Chiapas. Includes: Accommodations, some meals, entrance fees, guide. Dates: March through July, November. Length of trip: 16 days. Group size: Varies. Cost: $1,163 (single supplement $345).

University of California Santa Cruz Extension
Santa Cruz, CA 95064
408-429-2761   *Mexico*

An opportunity to tour the land of Kukulcan, Mayan god of the feathered serpent. This program highlights both history and artifacts of the ancient Maya people, whose magnificent civilization collapsed so abruptly four hundred years ago, and the amazing diversity of birds and other wildlife present in the Yucatan. You'll explore the Caribbean coast and the southern tropical jungle rain forest near Chetumal on the Belize border. Based on the coastal community of Xelha, you will visit Mayan ceremonial centers of Tulum and Coba, plus the island of Cozumel, where you'll snorkel in crystalline water of the National Park. You will then move south through the jungle to Chetumal, spending time at Laguna de Bacalar, and the partially restored Rio Bec-style sites at Kahunlich and Rio Bec itself. College credits may be available. For almost twenty years, University Extension has offered worldwide study tours for adults on such diverse topics as the arts, education and natural history. Includes: Tuition, airfare, land transportation, accommodations and some meals. Tour is conducted by a highly knowledgeable naturalist fluent in Spanish. Dates: New Year's holiday (Dec. 27–Jan. 5). Length of trip: 10 days. Group size: Limited to 24. Cost: $1,250.

Art •
Architecture •

After the artist or builder moves on, the art and the architecture remain—as a permanent reminder of how a beautiful thought was interpreted.

Art and architecture—the glory of a people leaving their aspirations for future generations to see. The grace and beauty of the works draw gasps of admiration and have left millions in awe at their magnificence.

The selection of art and architecture programs which follow is wide-ranging; from chances to visit the world's greatest masterpieces, to contemporary exhibitions, to programs where you can learn to paint or sculpt your own.

Whatever the art form is, it will be special—the ancient rock-art pictures of the Bushmen in the caves of South Africa's Drakensberg mountains; spirit-objects created by the isolated natives of New Guinea, the soaring brilliance of the Piazza di San Marco, Doge's Palace, Galleria Deglia Uffizi and Michelangelo's Campidolio in Italy.

To make sure you get the most out of your trip, instructors are crucial, so find out as much as possible about their background. Also check what's included in your tour—hotels, entrance fees, meals, etc. Academic credit may also be available.

SECTIONS OF RELATED INTEREST

Culture/History Expeditions.

Art Explorer's Tours
P.O. Box 26689
San Francisco, CA 94126
415-921-7677

New Guinea

Untouched by modern trends, almost one thousand different tribes in Papua New Guinea dwell isolated from the "outer world," as well as from one another. Highlanders live amidst sheer granite mountains, cloaked by jungles so impenetrable as to defy extensive contacts. Using wood, horn, features, shells and whatever else was at hand, these isolated peoples turned collectively to the creation of what they saw as spirit-objects—and we call "art." No less than 750 distinct artistic styles developed, perhaps the most divergent in Asia. Many have declined in recent decades, along with worship of the ancestors that inspired them. Others, however, remain as living monuments to the spiritual tradition, historical evolution and artistic brilliance of the communities explored by this tour. Hank Baum, B.A., president of Art Explorer's Tours and member of the art faculty of the University of California Berkeley extension, is a noted lecturer and tour leader. Includes: First class hotels and ship, round-trip economy airfare, all transportation, tips and transfers, most meals. Dates: March. Length of trip: 2 weeks. Group size: 10–15. Cost: $4,500 (approximate).

Art Explorer's Tours
P.O. Box 26689
San Francisco, CA 94126
415-921-7677   *Italy*

The oldest and best known of all the International Art exhibitions, the Venice Biennale is presented in a lovely garden park just a short vaporetto ride from the Piazza San Marco. Nestled among the trees are thirty-six pavilions constructed by different nations to house their exhibitions. The purpose of the Biennale is to show the most interesting art being created in a country at that time. The tour continues on to Paris and London, as well as to one other city (which is different each time), and includes the DOCUMENTA (Germany) when that event is held the same year as the Biennale. Hank Baum, B.A., president of Art Explorer's Tours and member of the art faculty of the University of California Berkeley extension, is a noted lecturer and tour leader. Includes: First class hotels, round trip economy airfare, all transportation, tips and transfers, most meals. Dates: September—even years. Length of trip: 2 to 3 weeks. Group size: 10–20. Cost: $3,500 (approximate).

Art Explorer's Tours
P.O. Box 26689
San Francisco, CA 94126
415-921-7677   *Brazil*

The Sao Paulo Biennale is the oldest, largest and most important international exhibition of contemporary art held in South America. Highlighting the most important artistic developments occurring throughout the world, the Biennale provides an opportunity for South American audiences to see and study these current expressions. The tour includes visits to Rio de Janerio, Brasilia, Lima, the ancient Inca cities of Cuzco and Machu Picchu, Caracas and one other city (different each time), and features a three-day cruise of "the showcase of evolution" to the Galapagos Islands, on the M/V Santa Cruz. Hank Baum, B.A., president of Art Explorer's Tours and member of the art faculty of the University of California Berkeley extension, is a noted lecturer and tour leader. Includes: First class hotels, round trip economy airfare, all transportation, tips and transfers, most meals. Dates: November—odd years. Length of trip: 3 weeks. Group size: 10–20. Cost: $4,500 (approximate).

Art Explorer's Tours
P.O. Box 26689
San Francisco, CA 94126
415-921-7677   *West Africa*

Visit capital cities . . . meet village elders . . . and witness tribal dances by firelight on this artistic and cultural adventure in West Africa. The program includes visits to Dakar and Thies (Senegal); Lomo and Kpalime (Togo); Abomey (Kingdom of Dahomey); Contonou, Ganvie, Lake Nocoue (Benin); Abidjan, Korhogo, Upper Volta, Senoufou country, Fakaha, Waranien, Boundiali, Koni, Kassaoumbara (Ivory Coast). An optional seven-day extension to Mococco visits Casablanca, Rabat, Tangier, the Caves of Hercules, Fes, Larache, and the Ruins of Volubilis, the Holy City of Moulay Idriss, Meknes, the Atlas Mountains, Moulay Ismail, the Bab El Mansour Gateway, Beni Mallal, Marrakesh, Saadian Tombs and the Bendi Palace. The program will include visits with native artists, woodcarvers, weavers, potters, and gold and silversmiths. Museums and native dance programs will be featured. Hank Baum, B.A., president of Art Explorer's Tours and member of the art faculty of the University of California Berkeley extension, is a noted lecturer and tour leader. Includes: First class hotels, round trip economy airfare, all transportation, tips and transfers, all meals. Dates: August. Length of trip: 2 to 3 weeks. Group size: 10–20. Cost: $3,000 (approximate).

**Art-in-Action
45 Griffin Avenue
Scarsdale, NY 10583
914-725-3480**   *Northeast United States*

Discover the art of America in the mansions of Philadelphia and the lofts of Soho. Whether you're an antique collector, or someone fascinated by early twentieth-century architecture, an art tour along the Eastern seaboard is sure to open your eyes. You can visit the studios of well-known artists . . . meet the curators of outstanding museums . . . or study "ikebana"— Japanese floral arranging—right in New York City. Examine eighteenth-century arts and crafts, or browse through antique jewelry. A wide range of programs, all utilizing interesting leaders from the world of art, literature and education, are available. Includes: Guided tours. Dates: Mid-September through mid-December, mid-March through mid-June. Length of trip: Varies: half day, full day, several days. Group size: Minimum of 6, maximum of 100–200. Cost: Varies.

**Country Homes and Castles
138A Piccadilly
London, WIV 9FH
England
(01) 491 2584
Telex 24609**   *Italy*

Experience the beauty of Renaissance art through the eyes of members of the Florentine aristocracy. The Baroncino de Piro, a member of the ancient Knights of Malta, will accompany this special tour to show you the personal side of Florence, art center of Italy. During your week in Florence, you'll view the beauty of Italian art in famous galleries such as the Uffizi and the Pitti Palace. In addition, the Baroncino has arranged for you to visit with some great Italian aristocrats, who open their private palazzos and art collections and offer you a warm welcome that should remain a special memory. Includes: Breakfast and some meals; flight London–Pisa–London; accommodations. Dates: October. Length: 10 days. Group size: 20. Cost: £1,500. Special requirements: $250 deposit.

**Cross Cultural Adventures
P.O. Box 3285
Arlington, VA 22203
703-243-7194
Telex: 440283 ACI UI**   *Italy*

A showcase of Romanesque and Renaissance art, especially of the paramount Quattrocento period, Northern Italy is equally well-renowned for its fine wine and cuisine. Starting in Milan, where you can see Da Vinci's Last Supper for inspiration, you will explore the region's most important artistic, architectural, and cultural sites with British art historian Peter Higginson. In between, you will take time for wine tasting at some of the area's best known wineries, producers of Asti, Barbaresco, Barbera, Freisa, and vermouths. Accommodations are mostly in family inns, where you can indulge in local culinary delights. Includes: Accommodations, meals, transportation, wine tasting, expert tour leader, guide. Dates: Early June. Length of trip: 2 weeks. Group size: Maximum of 15. Cost: To be determined. Special requirements: Deposit with reservation; balance six weeks prior to departure.

Dillman's Sand Lodge, Inc.
P.O. Box 98
Lac du Flambeau, WI 54538
715-588-3143   *Wisconsin*

Artists of all levels can improve their skills at Dillman's Sand Lake Lodge. Located in Wisconsin's Northwoods, Dillman's is a comfortable, family-centered resort, which offers instructional painting workshops. In an informal studio environment, you can study watercolor, oil and acrylic painting with well-known, professional instructors. Learn to paint landscapes and portraits—or carve realistic waterfowl, in some of the many courses offered. A one-day seminar is also available on "Marketing Your Art." For non-artists, Dillman's offers an array of recreational facilities including golf, tennis, swimming and horseback riding along with good food and comfortable accommodations. Includes: Accommodations, breakfast and dinner, tuition, instructor's fee, use of all recreational facilities. Dates: May through October 15. Length of trip: 6 days. Group size: 25. Cost: $375–$425.

Fun Safaris, Inc.
P.O. Box 178
Bloomingdale, IL 60108
312-893-2545
800-323-8020
Telex 910-291-3542   *South Africa*

This deluxe program is designed for the traveler who wants an in-depth view of the art and ancient cultures of Southern Africa. You'll visit the lovely cities of Johannesburg, Cape Town and Durban in South Africa and the capital city of Harare in Zimbabwe, then go back in time to the fabulous rock-art pictures of the Bushmen people in the caves of the Drakensberg mountains—"Mountains of the Dragon." You'll visit great Zimbabwe—magnificent ruins dating back to 500 to 700 A.D. Also included is game viewing at Wankie National Park, a visit to a gold mine, and of course a view of the splendid Victoria Falls. Specialist in these areas for the past ten years. Includes: Round trip airfare, best hotels, most meals, sightseeing. Dates: September to November annually. Length: 22 days. Group size: Maximum of 30 persons. Cost: $4,300.

International Summer Schools
Warnborough College
Boar's Hill
Oxford, OX1 5ED England
0865 730901   *Great Britain*

Gain a first-hand knowledge of art and antiques on this Oxford-based study course. Visits to Blenheim Palace, the Ashmolean Museum, the Iveagh Bequest, the Wallace Collection, Ascott Park with the de Rothschild collections, and Woburn Abbey are among the field trips that, in addition to lectures and discussions, make this course valuable to both amateurs and professionals. Three hours of college credit may be earned. Includes: Accommodations, breakfast and dinner, lectures, field trips and excursions, and course examination and transcript. Dates: June through August. Length of trip: 2 weeks. Group size: Varies. Cost: $895.

Paris American Academy
9 Rue Des Ursulines
Paris, France 75005
325-3509   *France*

Paris—a place for lovers, is also a place for learners and has captured the hearts and minds of people like Gertrude Stein, F. Scott Fitzgerald and Ernest Hemingway. At the Paris American Academy, located in the heart of the Latin Quarter, students choose their own course of study from a variety of subjects, all taught in well-equipped studios. Classes also venture into museums, galleries and fashion houses for a close-up look at the subject being learned, whether it's making use of France's unique heritage in art history; exposing the budding artist to the wide range of French paintings; or delving into the French fashion scene. Founded in 1965 by an American graduate of Carnegie-Mellon Institute, Columbia University and the Paris Conservatory of Music. Associated with the University of Paris (Sobonne) and the Louvre. Includes: Full-time classes in painting, sculpture, ceramics, drawing, printmaking, art history, French, fashion design, illustration and draping. Dates: Mid-October through May. One-month workshops also available. Length: 7 months or 1-month workshop. Group size: Varies. Cost: 28,000 Francs. 6,500 Francs for 1-month workshop. Special requirements: 18 years of age, equivalent U.S. high school diploma, portfolio of work.

TEMPLE
UNIVERSITY

Art History Department
Temple University
1912 Park Mall
Philadelphia, PA 19122
215-787-7837   *Italy*

Spend three weeks with Professor Glenn Benge in Italy studying the masterpieces of Rome, Florence and Venice. In Rome, highlights include Michelangelo's Campidolio, the Borghese Gallery, St. Peter's and the Vatican Palace. In Florence, you'll explore the Galleria deglia Uffizi, Loggia dei Lanzi and the Duomo. Venice, a miraculous city of waterways, offers art students such magnificent sights as the Piazza di San Marco, Doge's Palace and San Giorgio Maggiore. All tours are accompanied by in-depth lectures. May be taken for undergraduate, graduate or auditor credit. A professor of art history at Temple University, Glenn Benge lived in Rome with his family for four years while teaching at Temple University abroad. Includes: Air fare, rail travel in Italy, accommodations and lectures. University summer school tuition is additional. Dates: July. Length of trip: 3 weeks. Group size: 30 or less. Cost: $1,600.

Travel by Design
2260 Market Street
San Francisco, CA 94114
415-864-6604   *Europe*

These tours for lovers of design concentrate on contemporary and historical sources of architecture, interiors and furnishings, graphic design and advertising art, industrial and product design, textile art, etc. Meetings are arranged with colleagues, and there are also visits to design studios, professional offices, special collections and exhibitions, private homes, manufacturers and showrooms. In addition, the programs include ample free time and the usual vacation touring activities. Among the upcoming tours scheduled: "Graphic Impressions—Paris/Amsterdam/Zurich," and "Color, Texture, Form—Greece and the Islands." Also planned: a design tour of Scandinavia and "Italy—A World of Design." For design professionals, business-related portions of the itinerary may qualify trip as a tax-deductible business expense. Travel by Design was founded by George DeWoody, award-winning graphic designer and art director. Includes: Air fare, first-class hotels, transfers, porterage, tips, sightseeing, visits to design studios, showrooms, private homes, special exhibits, etc. Continental breakfast, plus welcome and farewell dinners, tour escort throughout. Dates: Year-round. Length of trip: 2–3 weeks. Group size: 30 maximum. Cost: $2,000–$3,000.

**Tour Designs
713 6th Street, S.W.
Washington, DC 20024
202-554-5820**   *Russia*

Here's a chance to explore the USSR—not just Russia, but the Baltic and Caucasian states as well. You'll see the cathedrals and art collections of Moscow and tour the Kirov Theatre in Leningrad, and you'll also have the unique opportunity to visit the churches and castles of Lithuania, Latvia and Estonia. Discover the romantic flavor of Tallinn, Estonia's capital and a major seaport. Learn about classical architecture in Riga, capital of Latvia. You'll be greeted by fiery, high-jumping folk dancers in the Transcaucasian republics of Georgia, Azerbaijan and Armenia. Or travel to the Ukraine—encompassing the blue slopes of the Carpathian Mountains, the woods and valleys of the forest-steppe and the lavish beauty of the Black Sea Coast. Member of American Society of Travel Agents; Intourist-appointed agent. Includes: All inclusive. Dates: May through November. Length of trip: 11–18 days. Group size: 7–20. Cost: $1,789–$2,549. Special requirements: USSR visa processed by Tour Designs.

**Wonder Bird Tours
500 Fifth Avenue
New York, NY 10036
212-840-5961**   *Trinidad, West Indies*

The annual, two-week Drawing and Painting from Nature seminar held at the Asa Wright Nature Centre in Trinidad, takes place in late July/early August. Leaders Wayne Trimm and Lucien Harris III teach design; wildlife and plant anatomy; and how to use nature as a medium of artistic expression. Students receive individual guidance in problem areas and are instructed how to critique their own, and each other's work. The diversity of plant and animal life on The Centre's grounds provides inexhaustible subject matter (there are forty-five to fifty species of birds). Live birds, plants, and insects are brought to class for sketching purposes. Night walks are taken around the trails to collect nocturnal specimens. Included in the workshop is a trip to Tobago, for underwater sketching around the exquisite coral gardens of Buccoo Reef. Includes: Private bath, three meals daily, transfers, field trips with transportation (including two days in Tobago), boat trips, gratuities to household help, personal feedback from seminar leaders. Dates: Last week July and first week August. Length of trip: 15-day seminar—14 nights. Group size: 20 participants. Cost: $725. Special requirements: Suitable for amateur and professional students of tropical ecology. Deposit of $50.

Backpacking •

Backpackers are a self-sufficient breed. Trekking into the wilderness, they carry their food, clothing, and shelter with them—on their backs.

This self-sufficiency makes for extreme mobility. Backpacking programs cover everything from gently rolling woodlands to the foothills of Mt. Everest. Whatever level of strenuousness and excitement you're ready for, a program will outfit you and put you on the trails, accompanied by an experienced guide.
You can:

- learn basic backpacking and camping skills, and try them out along a stretch of the Appalachian Trail.
- become a "desert rat," exploring the remote canyons and mesas of Texas' Big Bend country.
- combine disciplines for a glacier backpack/raft expedition through the wilds of Alaska.
- climb the towering peaks of the Grand Tetons, and set camp in the rich forest wilderness of northwest Wyoming.

For this book, we've differentiated between hiking/trekking and backpacking expeditions. On a hike/trek, someone or something else—porter, packhorse, or overland jeep—totes along your gear. On these backpacking expeditions, you do it yourself, carrying everything you need for survival—from food to sleeping bags—right on your back.

Although self-sufficiency is one of the charms of backpacking, the experience and expertise of outfitters make organized expeditions more fulfilling. Different terrains pose different sets of challenges. Your tour operator will know all the inside secrets of the areas—what gear to bring, how far to try to hike in a day, how the weather changes, and how and where to get the most spectacular views. The operator will also be familiar with the wildlife of the region, and can enrich your journey by providing background on the sights you see.

Although backpacking can be hard work, it's incredibly satisfying. Traveling on foot, you get an insider's view of the wilderness. There's no better way to appreciate the richness and variety of the forest than to hike through it and camp out under it. You'll experience the grandeur of its mightiest trees and the preciousness of its most delicate wildflowers. And you'll get a feel for the terrain, crossing streams, stepping over roots, and climbing up and down hills. The uphill climbs are the most difficult, but also the most rewarding: from lofty precipices you'll look out over miles of verdant forest landscape.

Explorations come in all sizes and degrees of difficulty. As a general rule, the greater the number of days you pack at a stretch, the more weight you'll have to carry. Lightweight food and scientifically designed equipment, however, greatly reduce the strain on backpackers.

In their brochures, you'll find that many outfitters grade their programs as to their degree of difficulty and strenuousness. For example, one operator classifies expeditions as follows:

Trips are ranked by both a letter and a numerical grade. The numerical grade (1, 2 or 3) takes into account "subjective" factors (length of daily walks, physical exertion, trail conditions, or extremes of temperature).

1: Easy   2: Moderate   3: Strenuous

The letter grade (A,B,C,D,E) denotes "objective" distinctions, such as the altitude reached on the trip or any special experience required.

GRADE A: These non-hiking trips can be undertaken by almost anyone who is in good health and enjoys a moderately active life.

GRADE B: Hiking, below fifteen thousand feet. Average six to ten miles per day. These trips are for people who enjoy excellent health and who, in the normal course of their lives, spend most of their weekends hiking, running, skiing or in other active outdoor sports.

GRADE C: Hiking and altitudes above fifteen thousand feet. These trips are for people truly in top condition.

GRADE D: In addition to assuming that you are in excellent condition, this rating requires that you have practical experience in basic use of climbing equipment (ropes, ice axe, crampons) and some general mountain knowledge.

GRADE E: These trips require at least three years of solid experience in the skills appropriate to the expedition.

Each operator should explain its own grading system; some may be less stringent than others. Check descriptions or contact the operator before you finalize your tour plans.

In choosing a trip, consider the distance of daily hikes, difficulty of the terrain, and the amount of weight you'll be carrying. Some advanced programs require special skills—like rock climbing or canyoneering—or extensive backpacking experience. In the mountains and deserts, climate tends toward extremes, which can take its toll on hikers. Check what weather conditions prevail in the area you consider. Also, if the trip involves high altitudes, you'll need time to acclimate yourself to the elevation.

On almost all backpacking trips, you'll camp out in the wilderness. Many programs teach basic camping and fire-building skills that could benefit even experienced trailblazers. The tour operator will send you a very specific list of what gear and clothing to bring. Most operators will outfit you with all necessary wilderness equipment; you may have to bring your own sleeping bag or backpack. If you have to buy gear, take weight into consideration; on the trail, every ounce counts.

Everyone tells you this, but it's so important that we'll toss it one more time. Break in new boots thoroughly well in advance. Neet's foot oil will soften stiff new leather; but the only sure way to break in boots is to give them repeated small doses of actual wilderness terrain. Go on short hikes—load your pack too so your legs and shoulders get in shape at the same time. The most comfortable sock set-up is a cotton pair with a woolen pair over it. This absorbs moisture, keeping your feet cool and dry.

Backpacks themselves come in various designs, suited to different purposes. Your tour operator will either provide an appropriate one for you, or suggest a design. In general, external frame packs carry the most with the best support. A hip belt takes much of the strain off of your shoulders; padded hip belts and shoulder straps make your load more comfortable to bear. When packing your pack, put the bulk of the weight in the bottom—it will be more stable and easier on your upper body muscles.

Backpacking adventures offer many non-hiking pleasures as well. In the forests, you'll have unique opportunities to study and photograph the flora and fauna. If you want to observe the wildlife, check migratory patterns to see what animals frequent a region during specific seasons. Also, pick a program whose pace allows you time to study the animals.

Backpacking is an inexpensive, rewarding vacation offering a myriad of possibilities. And a valuable lesson in self-sufficiency.

SECTIONS OF RELATED INTEREST

Llama/Mule/Camel Expeditions
Hiking/Trekking/Walking
Horseriding/Packing
Outdoor Skills/Wilderness Survival

Alaska Discovery
P.O. Box 26
Gustavus, AK 99826
907-697-3431   *Alaska*

This adventure takes you backpacking across the wildest, most scenic area in Alaska, the outside coast of Glacier Bay National Park. Completely outfitted, it's ten days of wilderness backpacking at its best with the waves of the Gulf of Alaska on one side and the grandeur of 15,300-foot Mt. Fairweather on the other. This is a fairly rugged, sixty-mile coastal hike with numerous river crossings which are forded or, when necessary, crossed by raft. This experience affords a little bit of everything, from sandy beaches to boulder-strewn capes to bear trails through moss-carpeted forests, not to mention the glaciers, mountains, and ocean swells that make Alaska's outside coast famous. Twelve years' experience, charter member of Alaska Association of Mountain and Wilderness Guides, certified outfitter. Includes: Completely outfitted, all camping and cooking gear, all food, all ground and charter air transportation, guides and insurance. Dates: June and July. Length of trip: 10 days. Group size: 6–10. Cost: $950. Special requirements: Good health for ten-day, moderately rugged backpacking.

American Wilderness Experience
P.O. Box 1486
Boulder, CO 80306
303-444-2632   *Colorado*

Over forty miles of on- and off-trail backpacking takes conditioned hikers through a remarkable region of high peaks, thick forests, and towering sand dunes. Starting with a four-wheel drive high into the Sangre de Cristo Mountains, camp is established at the base of several thirteen- to fourteen-thousand-foot peaks. Moving to a new campsite every night, you'll explore the wonders of the jagged Sangre de Cristo. At night and along the trail your guide takes time to demonstrate survival techniques, wildlife and plant identification, shelter building, and wilderness first aid. By a secret trail known only by a few guides you wind your way out of the mountains and into the back side of the Great Sand Dunes National Monument. You'll spend one day exploring these giant hills of sand. Guide and outfitter Ernie Wilkinson has over thirty-eight years of back country experience. Includes: Airport pick-up, trailhead transportation, all gear, all meals, guide, camphands, wilderness instruction. Dates: August. Length of trip: 6 days/5 nights. Group size: 4 to 10 guests (crew of 2). Cost: $350. Special requirements: Guests must be in good condition. $100 deposit.

American Youth Hostels—Metropolitan N.Y. Council
132 Spring Street
New York, NY 10012
212-431-7100   *Vermont*

American Youth Hostels offers special introductory trips designed to teach newcomers the art of backpacking. On this trip you'll have the chance to learn wilderness skills while exploring scenic Vermont. Trek through the forests and meadows of Merch Forest . . . swim in Birch Pond . . . backpack to Bromley Mountain and hike a portion of the Appalachian Trail. Along the way, you'll learn to build a fire, pitch a tent and identify wild plants. Most of the terrain on this trek is fairly moderate, but there will be some difficult stretches. Separate adult and teen departures offered. American Youth Hostels has thirty years' experience in outdoor travel programs. Includes: Food, transportation per trip itinerary, leadership fee and group equipment rental fee, individual equipment rental and instruction as per itinerary. Dates:

Mid-July through August. Length of trip: 8 days. Group size: 8 group members and 1 leader. Cost: $329 per person.

Arctic Treks
P.O. Box 73452
Fairbanks, AK 99707
907-455-6502   *Alaska*

Backpack and raft in the vast arctic wilderness of the Brooks Range of Alaska. Starting from Summit Lake at the crest of the Arctic Divide, you'll backpack through the dramatic canyon of the upper North Fork of the Koyukuk River. You'll have a chance to hike up Bombardment Creek at the base of Mt. Doonerak—an area of jagged peaks, hanging valleys and waterfalls. From here, you'll take to the river in rafts, floating through the grand peaks, Frigid Crags and Boreal Mountain, which gave Gates of the Arctic National Park its name. All during the twenty-four-hour daylight of arctic summer, a golden glow fills the sky even at midnight. Backpacking trips at Lakes Schrader and Peters also available. The trips in the Gates of the Arctic National Park and the Arctic National Wildlife Range offer spectacular scenery and the chance to view abundant wildlife—caribou, beaver, moose, dall sheep and grizzlies, to name a few. A family-run business, Arctic Treks is in its fifth year of guiding in the Brooks Range. All guides Alaska Wilderness Guides Association certified. Includes: Round-trip airfare from Fairbanks, food and cooking gear, rafts, paddles, life jackets, guide. Dates: Mid-June through Mid-September. Length of trip: 11–15 days. Group size: 8 to 10. Cost: From $1,390. Special requirements: $200 deposit.

Brooks Range Expeditions
Bettles Field, AK 99726
907-692-5333
907-692-5444   *Alaska*

This backpack and float trip through the scenic Brooks Range begins with backpacking (full packs) through the magnificent "Gates of the Arctic." There will be hiking along mountainside game trails to Red Star Lake, where canoes await for a leisurely float down the North Fork of the Koyukuk River. During this float portion, through mountains, valleys and Arctic taiga, you'll have ample time for fishing and optional side treks. Member Alaska Association of Mountain and Wilderness Guides. Includes: Everything except sleeping bags, packs, and personal gear. Meals will be full and hearty. Round-trip airfare Fairbanks–Bettles Field also included. Dates: Mid-August through Mid-September. Reservations should be made well in advance due to the shortness of the season. Length of trip: 14 days. Group size: 6–8. Cost: $1,500 per person. Special requirements: $250 deposit and full payment 60 days in advance.

Colorado Adventure Network
194 South Franklin Street
Denver, CO 80209
303-722-6482   *Colorado*

These trips are organized for people who would rather carry a camera than an ice axe and climbing rope. Trips are moderately paced so that you'll have time to thoroughly enjoy your excursion through the San Juan Mountains of southwestern Colorado—riding an historic "narrow gauge" railroad back to Durango; catching fish for dinner in the Wind River Range (home of Sacjawea); or finding a secluded hot spring in Montana's Brooks Range. The guides provide information on geology, wildlife, camping skills, and most importantly, how to have a great time outdoors. Tour operator/guide has climbed nearly every major peak in Colorado; organized expeditions throughout the world. Includes: All necessary gear—tents, packs, rain gear, sleeping bags, cooking and eating utensils, two nights of lodging; and surface travel round trip from Denver to the trailhead and back. Dates: July through September. Length of trip: 8, 9, or 10 days. Group size: 8 people maximum. Cost: $375–$400/trip. Special requirements: Novice hiking ability; reasonably good physical condition. Deposit: 25%, balance due 60 days prior to departure date.

Kichatna Guide Service
Chugiak, AK 99567
907-688-3256   *Alaska*

Kichatna Guide Service offers three different trips into the Alaskan wilderness, all geared to the hiking enthusiast and photography buff. A trip to remote headwaters of Johnson Creek Glacier in the Alaskan Mountain Range provides opportunities to observe wildlife ranging from grizzly bears and moose to bald eagles. An expedition into the Kichatna River region features the Cathedral Spires, an area of pristine, rugged and strange beauty. For sea-loving adventurers, there's a journey to Kodiak Island's Uganik Bay. The scenery is mountainous and provides the chance to see and photograph Kodiak brown bear, fox, otter, seals and whales. An Alaskan resident for twenty-seven years and a registered guide for nine, operator Harold Schetzle has had photographs on exhibit in Canada's Museum of Man and the Royal Scottish Museum. His work has appeared in Alaska Magazine, Field and Stream and other publications. Includes: Food, camping gear, guide; campers must bring own sleeping bags and backpacks. Dates: Spring, summer, fall. Length of trip: 3–15 days. Group size: Maximum of 5. Cost: Varies, depending on length of trip. Special requirements: One-third deposit; some experience necessary for backpacking trips.

Liberty Bell Alpine Tours
Star Route
Mazama, WA 98833
509-996-2250   *Washington*

Hundreds of brilliant flowers carpet your path as you hike along Devils Ridge, spotting elusive sheep and shy mountain goats . . . where mountain passes provide breathtaking views and magnificent sunsets and sunrises. Backpacking the North Cascades and Olympic National Park, with hikes lasting up to six hours a day, provides a rare opportunity to sample a land seldom explored. Visit small alpine villages serviced via boat and plane or boat only with names like Porcupine Creek, Cutthroat Pass and Devils Park Shelter. Eighth year of operation. Includes: Meals, lodging, equipment, experienced guide. Dates: May through September. Length: 5–14 days. Group size: 4–10 persons. Cost: $200–$600. Special requirements: You will be expected to carry your share of the food and group gear, but your pack shouldn't weigh over 35 pounds.

Mountaineering School at Vail, Inc.
P.O. Box 3034
Vail, CO 81658
303-476-4123   *Colorado*

Learn the art of backpacking while enjoying the world-famous scenery of Vail, Colorado. You'll cover everything from cooking and setting up tents to trekking and orienteering. There's also plenty of time to get acquainted with various forms of wildlife. The Gore Range and New York Peak provide a perfect backdrop of granite cliffs, pine forests and raging rivers. This is a tour that will teach you to appreciate and preserve the untouched wilderness. Founded in 1970. Includes: All inclusive, except sleeping bags and backpacks. Dates: June through September. Length of trip: 6–10 days. Group size: 8 students. Cost: $245.

Rick Horn Wilderness Expeditions
1090 South Highway 89
Jackson, Wyoming 83001
307-733-7503   *Wyoming*

Enjoy the wilderness away from civilization. Rick Horn Wilderness Expeditions is a guide service for foot travel or climbing excursions into the Tetons, Gros Ventre and Wind River Ranges of northwest Wyoming and the Yellowstone area. Expeditions include backpacking, mountaineering, rock climbing, ski touring, trout fishing, camping, map reading, survival and conservation of the wilderness. During the trips, you can visit beautiful alpine lakes, meadows, streams, valleys and peaks. Actual distances vary according to your ability, inclination, weather and terrain. Twenty years' mountaineering, rescue, instructing and guiding experience. Includes: Guides only. Dates: Winter and summer. Length: Up to 14 days. Group size: 1–10. Cost: $100 per day. Special requirements: Any skill level; $100 advance deposit.

Southwest Wilderness Center
P.O. Box 2840, Dept. T
Santa Fe, NM 87501
505-982-3126   *Texas*

The Big Bend Country along the Rio Grande in southeastern Texas is one of continental America's last frontiers. It is a place where the flavor of the West as it was a century ago can be sensed in the burning sky, sculptured canyons and isolated peaks. As part of a small group of fellow desert rats, you will backpack through the canyons and across the mesas of the Big Bend country. Participants learn the art of competent desert travel, including basic rock-climbing and canyoneering (technical descents and ascents of canyons using roped systems) which will enable you to travel into the remote and beautiful section of this lost land. All staff are expert desert travelers, climbers and knowledgeable about the natural history of Big Bend. Includes: Transportation from Alpine, Texas; food, all camping and technical gear, instruction in desert travel, basic rock climbing and canyoneering. Dates: October through March. Length of trip: 9 or 14 days. Group size: 5 to 10. Cost: 9 days—$425; 14 days—$600. Special requirements: No prior experience necessary.

Wild Horizons Expeditions
P.O. Box 2348
Jackson, WY 83001
301-733-5343   *Wyoming*

Wild Horizons offers a variety of backpack adventures into the spectacular beauty of northwest Wyoming. You can climb the majestic Tetons, their peaks towering seven thousand feet above the famous valley of Jackson Hole. Or hike and fish in the Gros Ventre Range, keeping a look out for bear, moose, deer and bighorn sheep. In the Absaroka Range, you'll get a chance to explore volcanic buttes topped by sweeping expanses of alpine tundra. Abundant wildlife, steaming geysers, clear, cold lakes and sparkling waterfalls await you in Yellowstone—America's first national park. Perhaps visit the Wind Rivers Range—with some of the most rugged country in the Rockies, known for Gannet Peak, Wyoming's highest. Ten years' experience, licensed. Includes: Transportation to and from trailheads, food, gear. Dates: March through September. Length of trip: 5–10 days. Group size: Maximum of 8. Cost: $45 a day/per person and up. Special requirements: Good physical condition.

**Wilderness: Alaska/Mexico
Bissel Road, Dept. STB
Hunters, WA 99137
509-722-3263**   *Alaska*

Sheer granite walls, rushing streams and snow capped peaks greet you on this combination backpack/kayak adventure into Northern Alaska. First, you'll cover thirty-five miles over ten days of strenuous hiking into the Arrigetch Peaks, an area located at the Gates of the Arctic National Park. After the backpacking, you'll spend a leisurely four days kayaking down the peaceful Alatna River, surrounded by spruce and birch forest amid the valley walls of the Brooks Range. You may participate in one or both of the trips, which are timed to coincide with the splendid autumn color displays. Five years' experience. Includes: Air charter transportation from Bettles to start of trip and return, food, tents, camping equipment, kayaking gear; sleeping bags can be rented. Dates: Late August to September. Length of trip: 10–15 days. Group size: 6–12 people. Cost: $855–$1,231. Special requirements: Basic backpacking experience.

**Yukon Mountain and River Expeditions, Ltd.
P.O. Box 5405
Whitehorse, Yukon Y1A 4Z2
Canada
403-668-2513
403-399-3131 Home**   *Canada*

Kluane Park, Canada's largest National Park, is dominated by spectacular ice fields, glaciers and 19,500-foot Mt. Logan. The area also offers the backpacker a different experience with high alpine tundra, spruce-lined valleys and a wide variety of wildlife. On this trip you will gain easy access to the high alpine tundra up Burwash Creek and walk through an area inhabited by a herd of caribou, as well as sheep and mountain goats. With good weather, you will be able to see ninety miles into the glaciers and mountains of the St. Elias Range. Then descend into the Donjek Valley, and walk along grassy benches adjacent to the huge, seven-mile-wide snout of the Donjek Glacier. Your circular trip will be completed by recrossing the tundra and meadow, descending the rocky gorges, and then following moose and game trails back to Kluane Lake. Nineteen years' guiding experience. Includes: Transportation, food, camping equipment; guiding and naturalist service. Hikers bring pack, pad, clothing. No hotel accommodations. Dates: July and August. Length of trip: 11 days. Group size: Maximum of 10. Cost $795 (Canadian). Special requirements: Intermediate hike in mountainous terrain, with some steep ascents and descents. $200 deposit.

Ballooning •

In 1783, the Montgolfier brothers loaded a sheep, duck and rooster into a large wicker basket attached to a balloon made of paper and silk. Up and away the balloon floated over Paris.

The sport of hot air ballooning was officially launched.

If you crave a real bird's-eye view of the countryside, if you want to live life with your head—or heels—in the clouds, then hot air ballooning is the pastime for you. Climb into the basket and listen as the blast of the burner breathes life into the colorful dome overhead. As you softly lift off, the trees seem to drop away and waving friends shrink in size. Your progress is gentle—you can only judge your speed (generally about eight to ten miles per hour) relative to the landmarks below. There's magic in the air as you waft above neat farms ... bustling villages ... shimmering lakes ... all appearing as perfect miniatures. And since your balloon drifts at exactly the speed of the surrounding air, you'll never tip or sway. The calm is hypnotic.

Today most "aerostation" (the art of lighter-than-air flight) is by hot air balloon. Gas balloons (filled with helium) are generally reserved for long-distance flights: the *Double Eagle II,* which in 1978 became the first manned balloon to cross the Atlantic, was a helium balloon.

Hot air ballooning applies the principle that warm air rises. A propane burner heats the air temperature within the balloon to about one hundred degrees centigrade. Fully inflated, a balloon can stand seventy feet tall. Firing of the burners controls altitude but not direction, which depends on the wind. However, knowledgeable balloonists made use of the fact that wind direction varies fairly predictably at different altitudes—so pilots can "steer" their craft by catching wind currents at different elevations.

The balloon itself (called the "envelope") is generally made of nylon or dacron. Although modern technology has improved envelope and burner design over the last two hundred years, the wicker basket in which balloonists ride has remained virtually unchanged since the eighteenth century.

In the United States, balloons are regulated by the Federal Aviation Authority (FAA), which registers and inspects the craft and licenses pilots. To learn to fly a balloon yourself, you have to pass both written and oral exams, and log in ten flying hours under instruction.

The balloon companies that follow offer wonderfully scenic introductions to the magic of ballooning. Most balloon trips take off at either sunrise or sunset, when wind and visibility conditions are optimal. Flights generally last one to two hours.

An important part of any balloon flight is the ground crew who help unload, lay out and inflate the balloon—and also assist in retrieving the craft after it lands miles away. While the aeronauts (balloon passengers) drift contemplatively with the wind currents, the chase crew has a more zany and rowdy time—scurrying across country roads and tracks, trying to decipher maps as they detour around rivers and bounce along unpaved roads.

After landing, all participants enjoy another ballooning tradition which has remained blessedly unchanged for two hundred years—the champagne brunch.

Balloon Aviations of Napa Valley
P.O. Box 3298
520 Ornduff Street
Napa, CA 94558
707-252-7067   *California*

Looking for the ultimate California experience? How about a sunrise Champagne Balloon Flight over the wine country of famous Napa Valley? Guests gather for pre-flight coffee and introductions and can watch or assist in inflating the colorful balloons. The balloons are flown by certified FAA pilots and drift lazily over beautiful Napa Valley for over an hour. After setting down in a meadow or field, the balloons are met by the chase crew for return to the starting point. The trip culminates with a champagne brunch featuring the area's best labels. Each guest receives a framed plaque to commemorate the trip. Tenth year in operation. Includes: Ground transportation, balloon flight, champagne brunch, and plaque. Dates: All year. Length of trip: Approximately 2½ hours, 1 hour in the balloon. Group size: 1–40. Cost: $95.

Hot air ballooning gives a bird's-eye view of the countryside.
(PACIFIC ADVENTURES COMPANY)

Colorado Adventure Network
194 South Franklin Street
Denver, CO 80209
303-722-6482   *Colorado*

Champagne breakfast flights as well as Continental Divide flights offer you high adventure in the Colorado Rockies. Trips last approximately one to one-and-one-half hours; the Continental Divide trip lasts about two-and-one-half hours. All flights begin early in the morning, helping assure beautiful clear sailing and gentle winds. According to the operator, "The ride is very gentle, not unlike riding in a very calm sea, only in a sea of air." Lodging can be arranged, as well as other vacation adventures such as raft trips, horseback riding, or hiking. Tour operator has been a balloon pilot in Colorado for seven years; participates in balloon races, instruction, sales and maintenance; pilots are certified with the FAA. Includes: Balloon, pilot, champagne, lunch (on longer flight). Dates: Year-round. Length of trip: 1 and 2½ hours. Group size: Maximum of 3 people. Cost: $100–$224 per person. Special requirements: Payment due 15 days prior to trip.

Pacific Adventures
P.O. Box 5041
Riverside, CA 92517
714-684-1227   *California*

Hot air ballooning with Pacific Adventures means getting involved: learning about the equipment, inflating the balloon, ascending and flying over the rolling hills of Rancho California and Perris. The balloons skim on the air, never hurrying, gliding soundlessly wherever the wind directs them. The flights last between one-half and three-quarters of an hour. Those waiting to fly will take part in the "great chase"—often as madcap an adventure as the flight itself. Following your flight, enjoy a generous champagne brunch. Includes: Ground transportation, chase vehicle, 45-minute flight, instruction and champagne brunch. Dates: September through June. Length of trip: 1 day. Group size: 9. Cost: $99. Special requirements: 25% deposit.

RANGE TOURS

Range Tours
1540 South Holly Street
Denver, CO 80222
303-759-1988
800-525-8509   *Colorado*

Range Tours offers a three-day hot air balloon excursion in the Colorado Rockies. You'll be lodged at the Rockies Condominiums and treated to a complimentary bottle of wine upon check-in. The balloon trips include a gondola ride to the top of Mt. Werner and ten hydrotube rides around the area. Guests are also allowed free admission to Steamboats Hot Springs for a relaxing soak in the natural sulfur springs. Includes: 2 hours of hot air ballooning, 2 nights lodging, admission to Steamboat Springs hot springs. Dates: April through November. Length of trip: 3 days, 2 nights. Group size: 6–10. Cost: $259 double occupancy.

Bed & Breakfast •
Homestay •

Chances are the major chain hotel in your home town is pretty much the same as the same major hotel in Australia or Hawaii. The rooms are comfortable and clean, and the color TV a late model, but there's often nothing to convey the character of the exotic vacation spot you've traversed oceans and mountains to explore.

You have an alternative. The Bed & Breakfast (B&B). Bed & Breakfast travel is an inexpensive way to experience the charm and personality of the places you visit. You'll be a welcome guest in the home of a hospitable host. And you'll almost always save money in the bargain.

Bed & Breakfast travel can bring you into homes as varied as the terrain you're stalking. You can choose to stay at . . .

- A New Zealand farm, where you'll be welcomed into the rhythms of the bucolic life—without having to help with the chores . . .
- A classic English home, where you can take tea and scones like a true blue-blooded Briton . . .
- A Hawaiian home, where you'll get to know the islands and the islanders . . .
- Or any number of charming country inns, historic guest houses, antique-filled homes, and quaint cottages around the world.

More and more travelers are turning to Bed & Breakfast arrangements for the personal touch of the homes and the lighter touch on the wallet. Originally an English idea, Bed & Breakfast homes now provide appealing accommodations throughout the USA and Europe, and in many other areas of the world.

As a Bed & Breakfast traveler, you'll find your host to be an invaluable source of information. Want to know where the shopping bargains are? Where to get a mouth-watering meal? How to get across town? Your host will know. He or she can steer you clear of tourist traps, and point you toward regional highlights that only a native would know about. When in Wales, why not see the sights the Welsh are most proud of?

And don't forget the second B—breakfast. You'll always receive at least a continental breakfast (juice, coffee or tea, and a roll or pastry). Often you'll be treated to a more elaborate spread, including regional treats, old family recipes . . . maybe a surprise wedge of melon. There's no substitute for the imagination and pride that a homemaker puts into the family meals.

Variety is the spice of Bed & Breakfast travels. You can find all sorts of situations and conditions—look for an arrangement that best suits your needs and private neurosis. Here are some points to keep in mind as you scour the B & B circuit and compare referral associations.

1. Are the homes checked out by the referral association? Bed & Breakfast organizations are often loosely-knit umbrella groups. A referral association that inspects all its lodgings is better able to tell you just what sort of bed—and breakfast—to expect.
2. Location. Unlike the major chains, which have to be centrally located to accommodate the business traveler, Bed & Breakfast hotels can be scattered throughout cities, as well as in suburbs and even more remote wildernesses. If you take a room in an outlying area, make sure there's public

transportation accessible. Consult a map to see how far an inn is from any sights or attractions you absolutely have to see. The referral association should be able to provide information on the schedules and routes of available transportation.

3. House rules. Every Bed & Breakfast hotel—like every home—has its own eccentricities. It's best to know what house rules and regulations await you before you lug your bags across the doorstep. Breakfasts can be either social—often in the family dining room—or private, with the luxury of breakfast in bed. You may have to share a bathroom. Some inns won't brook late hours; others are unrestricted. You may not be permitted to smoke. If you suffer from allergies, ask whether there are pets in the home.

4. Freedom of choice. Some referral organizations will, on request, send you a listing of their hotels, and you can pick the inn that inspires the heartiest appetite and strongest wanderlust. Other associations simply assign lodgings based on where you want to go.

5. On bookings and reservations. Various policies apply. Generally you'll have to put up the first night's rent in advance as a deposit. How far in advance also varies—check the individual referral association.

6. Some organizations offer prepaid vouchers which you can exchange for any associated Bed & Breakfast lodging. This system allows you complete freedom to route your vacation on the spur of the moment. Just call the B & B where you want to stay to make sure there's room, present your voucher upon arrival, and you're all set.

Bed & Breakfast International
18 Oxford Street
Woollahra, Sydney, NSW 2025
Australia
(02) 33-4236
Telex AA27229   *Australia*

Meet the Australians and the place they call home on a homestay visit. Homestays are available in all cities around Australia and also in many beach, mountain and rural areas; all accommodations are well serviced by public transport. Each home has been inspected personally by Bed & Breakfast International staff, and you are free to book accommodations in advance or travel on an open voucher system. Each location has been placed into one of three price categories—Economy, Quality or Superior—so you are able to choose the one most suited to your needs. In addition to the private home accommodations, a number of selected private hotels and self-catered apartments and houses are also available. Operated nationally for four years. Includes: All homestays based on B & B; however, dinner, bed & breakfast or full board are available on request. Dates: Accommodations available all year. Length of trip: Dates as requested. Group size: No limitations. Cost: From AU$18 per person.

Britain Your Way
Eurolanguage, Ltd.
P.O. Box 6735
San Jose, CA 95150
408-255-1044   *Great Britain*

On Eurolanguage's "Britain Your Way" program, you'll enjoy the warm hospitality of selected British homes, where you'll live as a member of the family. There are welcoming hosts in many parts of Britain. From your home base, you can plan a program of sightseeing assisted by your hosts. By living with the British, you'll gain a better understanding of a country whose heritage is so closely linked to our own. Eurolanguage has operated for fifteen years in Great Britain. Local agent, Donna Harris, has twenty-one years' background with Sister Cities programming. Specialist in people-to-people exchange programs. Includes: Private home hosts, including bed, breakfast, dinner, hospitality. Dates: Year-round. Length of trip: Minimum of 2 weeks. Group size: Varies. Cost: Approximately $100 per week. Special requirements: Over 18 years of age. No maximum age limit.

Go Native-Hawaii, Ltd.
130 Puhili Street
Hilo, HI 96720
808-961-2080   *Hawaii*

For a memorable vacation in Hawaii, malihinis (newcomers) can try real-life island living hosted by native islanders in a native Hawaiian home! Go Native-Hawaii specializes in Bed & Breakfast accommodations in Hawaii. Carefully selected resident island hosts provide you with bed & breakfast in their private homes, all distinguished by their special locations and high standards of comfort, and for their affable, hospitable native hosts. A membership fee of $4 entitles you to a directory of guesthomes, quarterly up-dates, membership card and Hawaii travel information. Owned/operated by appointed Air Traffic Conference travel counselors. Included: Bed & Breakfast accommodations. Dates: Year-round. Length: 1 night or more. Group size: 1 or more. Cost: $25–$45 per day.

Homemade Holidays
"Bankside" Cox Green, Rudgwick
Horsham, W. Sussex, England RH12 eDD
01144 40371 2579   *Great Britain*

Try scones at tea time and chintz wallpaper on an English homemade holiday beginning at the airport when your hosts pick you up and drive you to their home. *You* will have chosen the type of home you want, from quaint cottages and grand country homes to tidy suburban places, all within easy reach of London, restaurants, discos, antique markets to browse in and the English pub. Every home has been personally visited and checked for friendliness and comfort. This service, run by Joy and Moira Buchanan-Banks, a mother and daughter team, allows you to pick the style your vacation will be . . . and whatever it is, a warm English welcome awaits you. In operation since 1979. Includes: Room and private bath, full English breakfast, 3 course dinner, car from and back to airport. Dates: Year-round. Length: As long as you like. Cost: $275 per week. Special requirements: $25 deposit.

International Friends
5819 Green Oak Drive
Los Angeles, CA 90028
213-465-8331   *California*

Are you looking for the unusual in a vacation—but with a personal touch to make you feel right at home? Then try a sunny Californian homestay. This central booking service will line you up with an available home in California suited to your needs and travel desires. Stay two hours or as long as you wish. This is a chance to make new friends, integrate yourself into the California lifestyle, see the sights and share your experiences right then and there with a California family. Operated since 1978. Includes: Room and breakfast, sightseeing arrangements. Dates: Year-round. Length: Varies. Cost: Varies.

New Zealand Home Hospitality, Ltd.
P.O. Box 309
Nelson, New Zealand
(54) 85-727
Telex NZ. 3697 attn HOMEHOSP   *New Zealand*

Get to know New Zealand by living on farms, in country homes, in city houses. Go as you please and meet the people as you stay with families throughout the country. New Zealand Home Hospitality will provide you with pre-purchase vouchers plus a list of hosts you can call ahead day-by-day for reservations. There are 350 friendly families, all personally selected. You'll come away with friends for life and a deep, warm feeling for the country and its people. Allied member—Travel Agents Association of New Zealand. Member—New Zealand National Travel Association. Includes: Varies—bed and breakfast only; dinner, bed and breakfast; or full board—usually best for farm holidays. Dates: Year-round. Length of trip: Individual itineraries arranged. Group size: Varies. Cost: $25–$40 per day.

PT International
1318 SW Troy Street
Portland, OR 97219
800-547-1463
503-245-0440
Telex 277311 PTI UR   *Worldwide*

Searching for accommodations in a charming, tiny country inn . . . an interesting bed & breakfast hotel . . . secluded resort . . . a historic guest house . . . or friendly family residence? PT International specializes in unique, hard-to-find lodging for individual or group travel, representing more than twenty-five thousand bed & breakfast rooms in several countries, including the Unites States, Canada, Australia, New Zealand, England, Scotland, Wales, France, Ireland, Puerto Rico and St. Thomas. Includes: Bed and breakfast accommodations. Dates: All year. Length: 1 night or more. Group size: 1 or more. Cost: Varies. Special requirements: Prepayment in full.

Bicycling •

The bicycle is the most efficient complex machine known to man. It will carry you more miles per unit of energy expended than any other means of travel—including walking. And next to walking, it's the most inexpensive form of travel. It can take you anywhere that paved roads go. The bicycle is safe, quiet, and utterly non-polluting. And the exercise is good for you.

As you can see, bicycling has a lot to recommend it. But the points above are only its tangential virtues. The real reason to go on a bicycle tour is . . . it's fun.

Bicycling takes you across the countryside at a gradual sightseeing pace. You won't be racing to put hundreds or thousands of miles behind you before nightfall so that you can finally begin your vacation. You'll savor every mile you cover, and take delight in all of its idiosyncrasies: a gentle curve through a peach orchard, an unusual tree or a castle by the side of the road, a surprise view of a great mountain range on the horizon.

On bicycle tours, you and your fellow pedal pushers will have time to point out to one another the intricacies of the scenery, as you make your way through it. If a member of your group spots an august eighteenth-century farmhouse while traveling along a quiet New England back road, you can all stop to investigate. Take a minute to eat an apple or drink some cool water in the shade of an oak nearby. Then, legs refreshed after the brief pause, you're on the road again, delighting in the continuous panorama of roadside attractions.

Where can you go by bicycle? Virtually anywhere that paved roads exist. And unlike car travelers, you're not compelled to stick to major highways. Since you can't go 55 mph anyway, you'll make just as good time exploring back roads and country lanes. There, the traffic is light and the diversions heavy. You can see how people live in the regions you travel through—what sort of homes they have, how their towns are designed, what they do for sport. If you're hungry, you can even taste the local delicacies or have a favorite snack.

Cycling is not limited to your own home town. Each year, hundreds of enthusiasts pedal their ten-speeds from New York to California, or vice versa—over thirty-five hundred miles. As they watch the American landscape gradually transform itself, its vegetation, and its wildlife from one area to the next, they'll cover up to one hundred miles per day—a rigorous daily regimen.

Not all cycle adventures are this extensive, or this strenuous. Trips range from mild day outings centered on a common home base to full-scale, cross-country migrations, with virtually every graduation in between. If you're a healthy beginner, you should have little trouble pedaling across twenty to forty miles of plains and gentle hills per day. Intermediate cyclists might want to try their legs on forty to sixty miles per day of varied landscape.

An advantage to less strenuous trips is that you have time—and energy—left after your ride to pursue other pleasures. Pair up with a fellow rider for a set or two of tennis. Relax your muscles with a swim in a pool or lake. Take in a round of golf. Put your bike aside for some in-depth local sightseeing. Or swap road stories (legends in the making) with your cycling companions. Another virtue of short trips is that you can schedule your cycling for the most comfortable riding hours. This generally means the morning, when the dew rises from the country grass, and the sun illuminates the hills and trees, casting long shadows across the fields.

Intermediate trips offer a balance of on- and off-the road activities, and show you more of the countryside. By logging in those few extra miles each day, you'll be able to observe subtle transitions in the scenery. As you begin the long, graceful descent from the last of a series of hills, you'll be able to see—and feel—the level plains stretching out before you. You'll notice, during the course of a day's ride, that the forests have thickened or thinned. Or that the evergreens of the morning have given way to oaks in the afternoon. You'll enter and pass through rich farmlands or rolling orchards, or travel quietly through populous deer country.

Advanced trips—sixty to eighty average miles per day, or rigorous terrain cycling—are for the ardent two-wheel enthusiast. The eager pedaler who wants to see all that (s)he can, to transcend the limits of motorless travel. On these expeditions you'll eat up vast stretches of road, and enjoy intense and empathetic sightseeing over great chunks of the American—or other national—landscape.

Cycling trips cover the world over. You can ride the winding back roads of New England ... tour Europe by cycle ... take on the foothills and even the peaks of the Himalayas ... pedal around parts of China, where bicycle travel is a way of life ... or explore the country lanes of Ireland. Terrain varies from the most demanding (mountains) to gentle level plains. Mountain riding often requires a special fifteen-speed bike; rough rock riding on unpaved passes also requires special equipment—fat tires and a frame-and-wheel configuration designed to take a beating. Many tour operators rate their expeditions for difficulty as well as distance.

The main difference between bicycle treks within any level is the accommodations. Cyclists who wish to continue their rolling romance with the outdoors into the night may sleep out under the stars in tents. This is economically advantageous, and appeals to the bicyclist's sense of independence. It also allows you complete flexibility about where you decide to curtail a day's travels.

Hotels offer a more comfortable night's sleep. Many tours that cover back roads stop at quaint centuries-old country inns—totally consistent with the flavor of your sightseeing. Many hotels have pools or other facilities for post-ride activities. Youth hostels are another inexpensive but reliable alternative.

Even if you plan your evening stops in advance, many tours allow you to improvise the path and pace in between. Sometimes you have to stick with the group; sometimes you can leg it at your own speed. If you intend to break from the pack, make sure the tour operator provides maps. In tours that don't set daily end points, the group is often free to plan the itinerary as it pedals. Then you can make hay while the sun shines, and not be committed to a full day's ride if it rains.

At any level of strenuousness, you really rely on your bike. Good equipment is essential. If you own a good lightweight cycle that you're comfortable with, take it with you. You can fly it most places in the United States for about $25. Before the trip, oil all moving parts, true the wheels, and consider new brake shoes and tires. If your machine isn't up to snuff, you can usually rent one from the tour operator. Make sure it's in good running shape, and—above all—that it fits you. A wrong-sized frame strains or cramps your legs.

Other equipment? Pick up a hard-shell riding helmet, or rent one from the operator. Next, the saddle. You and your seat are going to be on intimate terms for long hours during your ride, so make sure you're compatible. The most comfortable saddle is an anatomic seat, which molds to your contours and eases saddle soreness. Other good accessories include a water bottle, tire pump, carrying racks, and a repair kit. This should include a tire patch kit, spare tubes and spokes, pliers, and a spoke wrench.

You can make things easy on yourself by choosing the right clothing. Shorts are de rigeur—and special wool touring shorts, with a leather shammy in the crotch, can make the saddle-rider relationships even better. Bicycle shoes are optional. Your shirt should be close-fitting and light-colored—to reflect the sun. Bicycle hats or painter's caps will keep the sun off your head. You may want to bring suntan lotion and sunglasses.

The best turn you can do yourself is to ride at home before your trip. This will get your legs—and rump—in shape for the long rides. If you're going on a tour that requires you to carry all of your gear—and maybe some communal tents plus pots and pans—practice riding your bike, fully loaded, near home.

Many operators lug your gear for you. A "sag wagon" follows the group, carrying all supplies and an assortment of tools and spare parts. The sag wagon also gives weary road warriors a needed lift. In other programs, the group leader brings up the rear, handling any problems that might arise.

A sag wagon may also carry a special treat—lunch. A picnic lunch break is a precious respite in any day. You can also carry your lunch yourself, and stop under a shady tree whenever your appetite stirs. Or you can break for lunch in restaurants, individually or en masse. Operators' lunch policies differ. Some don't even include it in the tour cost.

Final considerations are group size, the amount of off-bike sightseeing included, and the amount of free time you'll have to explore on your own. The great thing about bicycle touring is that, with the variety of programs offered, almost anyone can do it.

All-Outdoors Adventure
2151 San Miguel Drive
Walnut Creek, CA 94596
415-932-8993 *Hawaii*

Tour the beautiful Hawaiian Islands of Maui and Kauai by bicycle. Pedalers will enjoy the natural splendor of the Islands, learn some history and language, and experience magnificent sun and water, snorkel with certified instructors, help prepare Hawaiian meals and still have time for activities of personal interest. The group camps out except for a few nights in modern-day "grass shacks." Sites of interest include Hanelei Bay, the South Pacific's waterfall slide, ten thousand-foot Haleakala crater, Lahaina and much more. A vehicle will carry luggage and tired travelers. Fifteen years' experience. Includes: Park fees, group food, admissions, excursions, land transportation. Dates: July through August. Length of trip: 15 days. Group size: 10–18. Cost: $695. Special requirements: Riders supply their own bicycle and tents (tents may be rented for nominal fee).

American Youth Hostels—Metropolitan N.Y. Council
132 Spring Street
New York, NY 10012
212-431-7100 *China*

Experience the adventure of cycling through China. Pedal past thriving banana trees, rice paddies and peasants working in fields. After an overnight cruise from Hong Kong to Canton, you'll explore the lush tropical vegetation, friendly people and unusual scenery of the Guandong (Canton) province. Cycle to Foshan, where you'll visit a workshop where the art of Chinese papercutting is practiced. Later, tour a local commune and school. In Seven Star Crags, you'll have time to explore the caves and lakes of the region, and stop for lunch in a Buddhist monastery. Then bathe in the famous hot springs of Conghua, to soothe those hard-worked biking muscles. Next, fly to Peking for four days' sightseeing—including the Great Wall, Ming Tombs and the Temple of Heaven. American Youth Hostels has run outdoor travel programs for thirty years, and was the first organization to plan a bicycling trip to China. This trip is part of their adult program. Includes: All-inclusive land rate, as per their itinerary, including hotel accommodations throughout. Air fare to and from China not included. Dates: Year-round. Length of trip: 21 days. Group size: 15 people. Cost: Land only—$1,799.

American Youth Hostels—Metropolitan N.Y. Council
132 Spring Street
New York, NY 10012
212-431-7100 *United States Coast-to-Coast*

Cycle thirty-five hundred miles across the American continent. Challenge yourself to face the mental and physical demands of a truly rewarding experience. Expect to cycle seventy to eighty miles a day, with occasional one hundred-mile days on a route you and your group choose. You'll cross the Great Plains . . . zigzag through the mysterious Badlands of South Dakota . . . climb the Rocky Mountains and the Continental Divide. Celebrate your achievement with a swim in the mighty blue Pacific ocean. A former trip leader summed up the journey: "Going from coast to coast was as demanding as it was enriching. In just ten weeks I cycled across a continent, experienced a myriad of emotions, witnessed a land of great contrasts, and was made to feel welcome everywhere I went." Separate adult and teen departures are offered. American Youth Hostels has over thirty years' experience in outdoor travel programs. Includes: Daily food budget, overnights, transportation as per the trip itinerary, group equipment rental fee, activities as per itinerary. Dates: End of June to beginning of September. Length of trip: 73 days. Group size: 10 people and 2 trip leaders. Cost: $1,969. Special requirements: Qualifying pre-trip weekend ride.

Backroads Bicycle Touring Co.
P.O. Box 5534
Berkeley, CA 94805
415-652-0786   *Western United States*

From the California coast and wine country to the Colorado Rockies; from the Canadian Rockies to the Grand Canyon . . . Backroads Bicycle Touring gives you a wide choice of cycling vacations in the West. See the San Juan Mountains, Bryce and Grand Canyon, Death Valley, Yellowstone, the Grand Tetons, Puget Sound and more! Bikers may choose between camping out or staying in historic and charming country inns. Tours are easy to challenging, for both adults and families. Ride as fast or slow as you prefer—in small groups or alone—it's entirely up to you. A complete set of maps, written directions and guide sheets noting scenic points, landmarks and interesting side trips is given to each rider, while a support van serves as a mobile repair and refreshment center. Member Bicycle Touring Group of America and Bikecentennial. Equipment rental is available. Includes: Lodging, 3 meals daily, entrance fees and a support van. Dates: April through November. Length of trip: 2–7 days. Cost: $137–$629.

Bicycle Detours
535 Cordova Road, Suite 463
Sante Fe, NM 87501
505-984-0856
                                        Arizona

Explore the "Old West" by bicycle. Starting from Tucson, Arizona, you'll ride through the majestic Sonora Desert scenery of Saguaro National Monument. Visit the Cochise Stronghold and Chiricahua Mountains before walking in Wyatt Earp's footsteps in Tombstone, "the town too tough to die." In picturesque Bisbee, stay in the lovely and historic Copper Queen Hotel and then ride along the Mexican border to Nogales, Sonora—passing through the majestic San Rafael Valley. Bird watchers, historians, and nature lovers of all riding abilities find this "detour" most enjoyable. Average daily cycling distance—twenty miles, more or less as desired. All gear transported for you, and the support van and chuckwagon will be your combined magic carpet and base camp. Includes: 15-speed, lightweight mountain bike, support van and chuckwagon, professional guides, hostess, 3 nights' lodging, all meals, camping gear (except sleeping bag), entrance fees, singing cowboys. Dates: Winter, spring, fall. Length of trip: 1 week. Group size: 12. Cost: $730.

Bicycle Detours
535 Cordova Road, Suite 463
Santa Fe, NM 87501
505-984-0856   *Paraguay*

Bicycle Detours offers a program cycling through one of the world's most remote and fascinating areas—the Paraguayan Gran Chaco. You'll visit the new two-million-acre Defensores Del Chaco National Park, home to an incredible variety of mammals. Jaguar, puma, ocelot, tapir, peccary, fox, monkey, armadillo and giant anteater are but a few of its exotic species. Starting from Paraguay's capital, Asuncion, you'll ride into the countryside to view local arts and crafts and meet the friendly Paraguayans. Accompanied by American and Paraguayan wildlife biologists and naturalists, you'll travel by jungle bus and mountain bike into the Chaco. Each day participants divide into small groups to explore, birdwatch, photograph, and study wildlife management. Your adventure concludes with a visit to famous Iguazu Falls. Includes: Rugged 15-speed mountain bike and accessories, camping gear (except sleeping bag), all meals, all in-country transportation costs, deluxe hotel and best available lodging, American and Paraguayan guides. Dates: July and August. Length of trip: 20 days, 19 nights. Group size: 15. Cost: $1,800 (in-country).

Bicycle Detours
535 Cordova Road, Suite 463
Santa Fe, NM 87501
505-984-0856   *Peru*

The magnificent setting of Peru and the cultural remnants of the Inca Empire offer you the opportunity to participate in an ultimate cycling adventure—mountain biking the Inca Trail! You'll spend several days exploring the Lima area, visiting weaving centers and cycling into the back country for fishing and camping. Then fly to Cuzco, ancient capital of the Inca Empire, and get acclimatized while touring this culturally rich city. You'll bike the trails and roads built by the Incas to one of the wonders of the world, Machu Picchu—perched on a ridge overlooking the Urubamba River Valley two thousand feet below. You also traverse slopes on narrow foot-paths, ride around alpine lakes and cross high meadows where alpacas and llamas graze. Each day new cycling groups are formed according to physical level and individual interest. While visiting Arequipa, energetic guests may ride up the slopes of Mt. Misti or Mt. Chachani, both nineteen thousand-foot mountains. Includes: Rugged 15-speed, fat-tired mountain bike and accessories, camping gear (except sleeping bag), all meals, in-country transportation costs, deluxe hotel and best available lodging, American & Peruvian Guides. Dates: May and June. Length of trip: 20 days, 19 nights. Group size: 15. Cost: $2,045. Special requirements: Good physical condition.

Bicycle Detours
535 Cordova Road, Suite 463
Santa Fe, NM 87501
505-984-0856   *New Mexico*

Thrilling whitewater rafting and a ride on one of America's most spectacular steam-powered railroads highlight this adventure. Mountain bikes take you along forgotten roads and trails between Santa Fe and Taos. You'll spend a day rafting the famous "Taos Box" on the Rio Grande, considered one of the most exciting day-long whitewater trips in the West. In Taos, you'll visit the oldest inhabited village in the United States, the Taos Pueblo, and meet its friendly residents. You'll then cycle sections of backroads into Colorado where you board the Cumbres-Toltec train for a very scenic ride into San Juan Mountains to Chama, N.M. Returning to Santa Fe, you'll visit archeological museums, centuries-old Spanish communities and take in the majestic scenery of Northern New Mexico. Average daily cycling distance—twenty miles, more or less as desired. All gear is transported for you. Bicycle Detours also offers a two-week exploration of the Four Corners area and the prehistoric Anasazi Indian culture, including Monument Valley, Canyon de Chelly and Chaco Canyon. Includes: 15-speed mountain bike and accessories, support van and chuckwagon, professional guides and boatmen, 4 nights' lodging, camping gear, all meals, river and train trip fees, museum fees. Dates: June and July. Length of trip: 1 week. Group size: 12. Cost: $750. Special requirements: Trip designed for recreational riders of all abilities.

Bicycling West, Inc.
P.O. Box 15128
San Diego, CA 92115
619-583-3001   *Western United States*

Get off the beaten track and bicycle through rural areas and small towns where roads are lightly used and the scenery is unspoiled. Bicycling West offers one- and two-week tours in the Western United States for the intermediate (twenty-five to fifty miles a day) bicyclist. The Baja Peninsula tour runs from San Diego through the Baja Desert to La Paz, Mexico. The San Diego tour loops through San Diego County on rural roads and mountain passes and through several desert spring areas. The Napa Valley tour circles the wine region, then pedals southeast to the Russian River. The Monterey to Los Angeles trip travels down the spectacular Pacific coast along scenic Highway 1 and includes a tour of the Hearst Castle. The Oregon coast tour and the Central Oregon tour encompass the Willamette Valley, Siuslaw National Forest, the Oregon coast and Mackenzie Pass. On tour, the accommodations are campgrounds, with one night per week spent in a motel. Operating bicycle tours since 1977. Includes: Campground fees and motel accommodations, all meals and a support vehicle. Dates: March through August. Length of trip: 7 days. Group size: 25. Cost: $35 per person per day. Special requirements: Sleeping bag and tent; participants should be able to cycle 40 miles a day (intermediate bicyclist).

Bike Virginia
P.O. Box 203
Williamsburg, VA 23187
804-229-4046   *Virginia*

Discover the geographic diversity and beauty of Virginia—the riverside plantations, hills and valleys of the Piedmont Mountains; historic Williamsburg; famous Chesapeake Bay; and lovely Shenandoah Valley. Bike Virginia tours some of the oldest towns and historical sites in the United States. Travel back into time to explore Yorktown, Jamestown, Lexington and Williamsburg. Visit Stratford Hall, ancestral home of the Lees, that's still a working plantation; and Wakefield Plantation, birthplace of George Washington. Each day you can choose from a variety of routes designed to accommodate novices . . . and historic seventeenth-, eighteenth-, and nineteenth-century hotels and inns provide lodgings and fine food—ranging from haute cuisine to hearty home cooking. Member of Bikecentennial and the Virginia Bicycle Federation. Includes: Lodging, 2 meals daily, and a support van. Dates: April through October. Length of trip: Weekends, 5 days, or 2 weeks. Group size: 10–25. Cost: $115–$690.

British-American Cycle Tours
P.O. Box 236
Claremont, CA 91711   *Great Britain*

Meet the British as you ride through charming villages and farms, past castles, cathedrals, manors and pubs on this two-week bicycling holiday. The tour cycles through southern England and Wales with stops in Winchester and Salisbury, both famous for their grand cathedrals; and Bath, the beautiful Georgian city of Jane Austen and Thomas Hardy. Then you'll enter Wales through the Wye Valley, passing the ruins of Tintern Abbey, immortalized by the poet, Wordsworth. Crossing back into England, the tour pedals through Tewkesbury and Stratford-on-Avon, Shakespeare's birthplace. Next on to Oxford and Windsor, home to Oxford University and Eton College, respectively. A support van accompanies the tour to carry luggage, weary cyclers and spare parts in case of mechanical problems. Member Cyclists' Touring Club of Great Britain and Bikecentennial. Includes: Nightly lodging at Bed and Breakfast inns, tour escort and support van, transfers to and from airports to the tour starting point. Only breakfast is included. Dates: June through early September. Length of trip: 2 weeks. Group size: 10–15. Cost: $50–$75 a day. Special requirements: Good health, children under 18 must be accompanied by an adult.

China Passage, Inc.
302 Fifth Avenue
New York, NY 10001
212-564-4099
800-223-7196
Telex 668916   *China*

With China Passage, you'll travel as close to the earth as possible—on bicycle, also using boats, trains, and small vans, putting you in the best possible vantage point to observe China and its people. You'll be moving along at a leisurely pace with leeway for individual exploration, and stay in first-class hotels and enjoy the best Chinese cuisine available throughout the tour. Bicycle tours are available in: South China; Yangtse Valley; East China. China Passage also offers a unique cycling excursion through the Ordos region of Inner Mongolia, homeland of the pre-Mongol Huns and the base area for Ghengis Khan's thirteenth-century conquest of China. Founded 1980. President, Fredric M. Kaplan is Chairman of U.S.-China Peoples Friendship Association. Includes: All transportation, accommodations and meals in China. Dates: All year. Length: 18–26 days. Group size: 10–20. Cost: $995–$1,950 land.

China Sightseeing, Inc.
58 Second Street, 4th Floor
San Francisco, CA 94105
415-896-1906
Telex 67511 CHINAINC   *China*

Bicycle touring with China Sightseeing enables cycling enthusiasts to sample incredible sights along the almost fourteen-hundred-year-old Grand Canal, the largest man-made waterway in the world. Most importantly, it allows you many opportunities to observe what life is like for rural inhabitants. You'll be able to set your own pace, leisurely or swift, through the rice paddies and lush bamboo groves of rural China. China Sightseeing, Inc. has specialized

Bicycling gives travelers the best vantage point to observe China and its people.
(CHINA PASSAGES)

in tours to China since the normalization of diplomatic relations. Includes: Round-trip airfare from California; all accommodations, transportation, meals, transfers, and porterage in China; daily sightseeing in China with English-speaking guides; visa fee and admission fees to cultural exhibits and events. Dates: March through September. Two departures each month beginning in March and ending in September. Length of trip: 14 days. Group size: 15–30. Cost: $2,181. Special requirements: Reservations based on $250 deposit per person with final payment due no later than 60 days before departure.

**Churchill House Inn
RD #3
Brandon, VT 05733
802-247-3300**

Vermont

Bike from inn to inn in scenic Vermont. During the day, explore unspoiled country vistas with rolling farmlands, narrow valleys and quaint vistas. At night, settle into charming inns from the 1800's, known for their excellent cuisine. Cyclists have the choice of either ten-speed bicycles or stumpjumpers—bicycles designed for rough terrain touring. The self-guided tours are routed away from traffic on back roads and trails, and the distances can be adjusted to the cyclist's ability. Overnight stops are spent at delightful old country inns along the way. Includes: Individualized planning for tours, maps, lodging, meals, stumpjumper rental. Dates: May through October. Length of trip: 10-speed bicycle trips—2 days to 2 weeks; stumpjumper trips—4 nights, 3 days to 6 nights, 5 days. Group size: 10-speed bicycle trips—up to 12; stumpjumper trips—up to 6. Cost: 10-speed bicycle trips—$45–$55 per day; stumpjumper trips—$72–$80 per day. Special requirements: Advance reservations and deposits required; must be 18 or older unless with parent.

Colorado Adventure Network
194 South Franklin Street
Denver, CO 80209
303-722-6482   *Colorado*

Inn-to-inn bicycle trips provide an excellent way to travel through the spectacular scenery of Colorado. Cyclists may set their own speed, traveling in groups or alone. Maps, plus information about places of scenic or historic interest and best lunch stops are provided. A rear leader provides additional information and help along the way. A support van carries luggage from one lodge to the next and is available to help out tired cyclists. All roads are paved and little-traveled. At night, enjoy accommodations at comfortable inns, lodges and hotels. Fuji 10-speed bikes and helmets are available for rental. Six years' experience. Includes: Lodging, 2 meals daily, support van. Dates: June through September. Length of trip: 3-, 5-, and 7-day trips. Group size: 10–20. Cost: $200–$425. Special requirements: Good health.

Colorado Bicycle Tours
P.O. Box 45
Pitkin, CO 81241
303-641-4240   *Colorado*

Peaks, mountainside streams, flower-carpeted valleys and the ghostly remnants of nineteenth-century mining camps—see the spectacular Colorado mountain country by bike. With Colorado Bicycle Tours, you can pick from several length rides every day. Detailed maps with easy directions, plus notes on local attractions, are provided so that cyclists may travel in groups or alone. At night, you'll stay at comfortable inns, lodges and hotels—many with historic flavor. (Swimming, sauna and spa facilities are sometimes available too.) Colorado Bicycling offers several routes. Vail Pass Bike Path rides past Copper Mountain and into Vail village and on to Camp Hale and Leadville, Colorado's leading town during the 1880 silver boom. The Gold Rush Tour pedals through the Arkansas River Valley to Leadville, Pike, Arapaho and other boom towns of the Gold Rush era. The San Juan Mountain trip rides over Slumgullion Pass, the Continental Divide and into Durango before crossing Red Mountain Pass. Middle Park Tour heads through the Victorian mining community of Georgetown, down into Rocky Mountain National Park, along famous Trail Ridge Road and through Arapaho National Forest. The Central Colorado route circles the Elk and Sawatch ranges, visits Crested Butte and Aspen, passing through Gunnison, White River and San Isabel National Forest. On all routes, a support vehicle carries luggage and provides assistance. Riders may rent Fuji twelve-speed bikes and helmets or bring their own. Third year of operation. Includes: Lodging and 2 meals daily. Dates: June through September. Length of trip: 3, 5, and 7 days. Group size: 8–24. Cost: $199, $349 and $419. Special requirements: Intermediate or advanced ability, advance deposit.

Country Cycling Tours
167 West 83rd Street
New York, NY 10024   *Northeast*
212-874-5151   *United States*

Bicycle touring with Country Cycling Tours allows you to see the world at a natural pace, with plenty of time for exploring. Country Cycling Tours offers an extensive program of one-day, weekend and extended inn-to-inn bicycle tours for adults and families. One-day excursions explore surprisingly quiet country roads just beyond the borders of New York City. Weekend tours in New York State, Massachusetts, Vermont, New Hampshire, Pennsylvania and Maryland encompass some of the best bicycling these regions have to offer. Five- and seven-day inn-to-inn tours enable cyclists to intimately explore entire regions of Massachusetts (including Cape Cod and Martha's Vineyard), Vermont and New Hampshire. International vacation tours to Nova Scotia, England, Ireland, France (both the Loire and Dordogne valleys), and Israel offer unique opportunities to discover the beauty and people of faraway places. More than a decade of professional bicycle touring experience in the Northeastern U.S. and Europe. Membership in Bicycle Touring Group of America, Bikecentennial and League of American Wheelmen. Includes: Country Cycling Tour leaders, who are experienced mechanics, accompany every tour. A fully-equipped support van is used to carry luggage and spare parts, and to give a hand to cyclists in need. Days begin and end with homecooked meals in the informal ambience of a traditional country inn. Tennis, swimming, theater, antiquing and historical sites. Bicycle rental; round-trip transportation available from New York City. Dates: April through November. Length of trip: 1–14 days. Group size: 20–30. Cost: $15–$929 excluding airfare.

Directions Unlimited
344 Main Street
Mt. Kisco, NY 10549
914-241-1700 (Collect)   *France, Germany*

Imagine the pleasure of cycling through the scenic wonders of the French countryside, never taking the same road twice. Linger in market towns, historic villages and castles. See the details and appreciate the tranquility of a lifestyle that moves no faster than the pumping of a pedal. Directions Unlimited has been in operation for fourteen years. Includes: Bikes, transportation of luggage, hotel, breakfast, tips, taxes, transfers, escort. Dates: April through October. Length: 1 week. Group size: 20. Cost: $395–$495. Special requirements: Excellent physical condition.

Freewheeling Adventures
84L Durand Drive
Rochester, NY 14622
716-266-7224   *New York*

Freewheeling Adventures leads tours through the beautiful Niagara, Finger Lakes and Erie Canal regions of upstate New York. The "Champagne Country Tour" follows routes through the famous Finger Lakes wine country, with stops at two or three vineyards to observe the wine-making process. The tour continues past Waneta, Seneca, and Keuka Lakes and the sparkling waterfalls of the Watkins Glen State National Park. The "Noble Niagara Tour" winds along the Niagara River to one of the seven wonders of the world, Niagara Falls. See Fort Niagara, preserved as it stood before the American Revolution, and Fort George in beautiful Niagara-on-the-Lake in Ontario, Canada. The tour pedals on to Goat Island, Three Sisters Island and Grand Island, largest natural fresh-water island in the world. Beginners and veterans are welcome on these and other tours Freewheeling offers. Ten years' experience planning and leading bicycle tours. Includes: Lodging, dinner and breakfast, support vehicle for luggage and tired bikers. Dates: Spring, summer and fall. Length of trip: Weekend or 5-day trips. Group size: 10–25. Cost: $130–$360. Special requirements: Riders may bring their own bikes or rent from Freewheeling.

Gerhard's Bicycle Odysseys
4949 S. W. Macadam
Portland, OR 97201
503-223-2402   *Ireland*

The old song claims "It's a long way to Tipperary" but it won't be for you on your bike trip through the country lanes of Ireland. Taste the salty air of the Atlantic as you bike past thatched-roofed cottages, wandering sheep and roving gypsies. The smell of the Irish countryside will linger with you—turf fires, drying kelp, freshly baked soda bread and blooming heather. You'll start at Limerick, Ireland's oldest town, pass through and savor the age-old city of Cork, and discover the beauty of Killarney ... all the while being charmed by the friendly people. And if your legs should tire there is an escort vehicle available. Average daily distance is thirty-three miles. Ten years' experience. Includes: Hotels, most meals, escort vehicle (sag wagon), 2 leaders/mechanics, maps, airport/hotel transfers and special parties. Dates: June and July. Length: 2 weeks. Group size: 20 maximum. Cost: $1,195.

Gerhard's Bicycle Odysseys
4949 S.W. Macadam
Portland, OR 97201
503-223-2402   *France, Germany*

Let the backroads of Germany and France lead you to unforgettable sights and special times as you wine, dine and bicycle through the Mosel and Rhine Valleys, and the Alsace region of France. The countryside will be a procession of colorful villages and crumbling castles as you bike from Trier with its famous Roman baths to the Mosel River, where vineyards with familiar names dot the route. You'll see Pfalz castle sitting on a small island in the middle of the river—a toll house in medieval times. You'll visit the beautiful cities of Strasbourg and Comar—complete with old painted and sculptured houses. All along the route, the wines of the regions will help wash down the local cheese, freshly baked bread and the peasant specialties. Average daily distance is thirty-seven miles. Ten years' experience operating bicycle tours. Includes: Hotels, most meals, escort vehicle for bicyclers who tire, 2 leaders/mechanics, maps, airport/hotel transfers and special parties. Dates: June through August. Length: 2 weeks. Group size: 20 maximum. Cost: $1,195.

Gerhard's Bicycle Odysseys
4949 S.W. Macadam
Portland, OR 97201
503-223-2402   *Germany*

As you glide past a castle going 15 mph on your bike or swoop down a backroad heading for a remote village to sample the local homemade sausages and sauerkraut, Wiener schnitzel or spaetzle, you know you have become part of a world that is impossible to witness from inside a car. On this bicycle tour of southern Germany and Austria, you'll see ancient city walls, their outlines barely visible under the moss of centuries ... picturesque half-timbered medieval houses ... the castle-dotted countryside of the Neckar Valley ... monasteries from the twelfth century ... silent forest land where shy deer make their home ... and the Alps, towering over everything. Average daily distance traveled is thirty-six miles. Starting in Heidelberg, your route includes Rothenburg and Munich before finishing up in Salzburg. Born in Heidelberg, director Gerhard Meng has ten years' experience organizing bicycle tours. Includes: Hotels, most meals, escort vehicle if you tire, 2 leaders/mechanics, maps, airport/hotel transfers and special parties. Dates: June through August. Length of trip: 2 weeks. Group size: 20 maximum. Cost: $1,195.

Gerhard's Bicycle Odysseys
4949 S.W. Macadam
Portland, OR 97201
503-223-2402   *New Zealand*

New Zealand is a bicycling paradise—a world of diverse sights, sounds and sensations changing mile by mile ... majestic glaciers ... deserted beaches ... awesome mountain ranges surrounding gem-like lakes ... and fast-flowing rivers full of fish. On this bicycling adventure, you'll visit Queenstown—nestled in the Remarkable Mountains ... Cromwell— an old goldmining center ... Fox Glacier—with its magnificent sweeps of rocky coastline and awe-inspiring mountains. Each person can set his own pace through the country if desired, with detailed maps and route outlines to smooth the way. Average daily distance is forty-nine miles. Ten years' experience. Includes: Hotels, most meals, escort vehicle (sag wagon), 2 leaders/mechanics, maps, airport/hotel transfers and special parties. Dates: February. Length: 3 weeks. Two-week program also available. Group size: 20 maximum. Cost: $1,295.

Gerhard's Bicycle Odysseys
4949 S.W. Macadam
Portland, OR 97201
503-223-2402   *Austria, Germany*

The Heart of Europe awaits you on this slow and easy bicycle tour from Munich to Vienna. Your path will follow the lovely Danube as its winds its way through the Austrian landscape, with a rich pageant of history unfolding on either bank. Along the way, you'll see tiny villages with their distinctive onion-topped Baroque churches ... medieval fortresses with ramparts half a mile around ... wide valleys covered with a dark green carpet of forest ... the medieval town of Freistadt with its massive gateways and moats. Then refresh yourself at a charming coffee house with delicious strudel fresh from the massive oven and oozing with goodness. Average daily distance is thirty-seven miles. Born in Heidelberg, director Gerhard Meng has ten years' experience organizing bicycle tours. Includes: Hotels, most meals, escort vehicle for cyclists who tire, 2 leaders/mechanics, maps, airport/hotel transfers and special parties. Dates: July and August. Length of trip: 2 weeks. Group size: 20 maximum. Cost: $1,195.

Cyclists pedal through the quaint cobblestone streets of Bad Wimpfen in Germany.
(GERHARD'S BICYCLE ODYSSEYS)

Greater Boston Council/American Youth Hostels
11 Shepard Lane
Shrewsbury, MA 01545
617-842-2343   *New England, New York*

As you bike through the color-rich country roads of New England on your way to sun-splashed Cape Cod, Martha's Vineyard or Nantucket, you'll see what makes this part of the country so special. Or try biking the stretch from Coastal Maine and the Acadia National Park to the wonders of the Adirondacks and Niagara Falls . . . or go a little further afield to unspoiled Nova Scotia, a favorite site for bike camping. For the super ambitious biker, there's a seventy-day extravaganza tour that starts in Boston and ends in glorious San Francisco covering thirty to sixty miles per day. Includes: Food, lodging, camping equipment for camping trips, recreational fees, insurance, T-shirts. Dates: Late June to Labor Day. Length: 6–70 days. Group size: Varies. Cost: $197–$1,100. Special requirements: Most trips are planned to meet the needs and interests of adolescents although there are tours for adults available.

Jamaica Camping & Hiking Association
P.O. Box 216
Kingston 7, Jamaica
809-927-5409   *Jamaica*

Savor the beauty and excitement of Jamaica on a self-guided bicycle tour around the island. You'll have plenty of time to stop and swim in the sparkling waters, or relax and enjoy the exotic scenery and the friendly people. The roads are easy-going and you can bicycle at your own pace—and if you crave a little adventure there's always the high mountains to explore for a strenuous side trip. Accommodations are spaced an easy ride apart from each other—and include simple rooms, cabanas and some tents . . . but each property recommended has its own restaurant so there's no lugging pots and pans along with you. So come to Jamaica!! Includes: Accommodations in rooms only. Dates: All year. Length: 2 weeks. Group size: Varies. Cost: $152. Special requirements: Good health, 50% deposit. Bring your own bicycle.

Journeys and Vermont Bicycle Touring
Box 711-SN
Bristol, VT 05443
802-453-4811   *Sri Lanka*

Few Western cyclists have enjoyed the island paradise of Sri Lanka. This tour is an opportunity to see and participate in Sri Lankan life on an intimate level. Your route leads through ancient Buddhist ruins, lush tea plantations, tropical forests . . . along coral coasts and through some of the friendliest and most fascinating communities in South Asia. You might share the road with wandering elephants, or catch sight of a leopard or wild buffalo. Accommodations are in Western-style hotels with private baths or British-built, Sri Lankan-style rest houses. The group is accompanied by American and Sri Lankan guides and 2 sag wagons for luggage and weary riders. Twenty-five to thirty easy miles will be covered each day, suitable for beginners. Cycling will be from dawn until noon each day to avoid the afternoon heat, maximizing free time for sightseeing and other activities. Over ten years' experience.

Includes: Lodging, sag wagons, most meals. Dates: December through March. Length of trip: 16 days. Group size: 15. Cost: $1,195. Special requirements: Personal repair kit.

**Kashmir Himalayan Expeditions
Boulevard Shopping Complex
P.O. Box 168
Srinagar, Kashmir, India
78698/73913**   *Kashmir*

While cycling through some of the most magnificent scenery in Kashmir, you'll explore remote villages and see a variety of Himalayan birds. Starting from the capital, Srinagar, you'll make your way past holy mosques, temples, paddy fields and orchards; visiting schools, local bazaars and camping out in tents. Highlights include Mansbal Lake; Lolab Valley and Wular Lake, a major Asian reservoir. A tonga (victoria) will carry all the equipment and a car will accompany the group throughout. There'll be plenty of time to explore en route; check out some of Kashmir's fine crafts—carpet weaving, intricate wood carvings and delicate papier-mâché. In operation since 1970. Dates: March to December. Length of trip: 14 days; 8 days cycling. Cost: $400.

**Liberty Bell Alpine Tours
Star Route
Mazama, WA 98833
509-996-2250**   *Washington*

Your legs keep up a steady rhythm of pedaling ... the wind blows through your hair ... you're amazed by the spectacular beauty of the North Cascades as you cycle through wide flat valleys shimmering with the early morning dew. On this trip, you'll spend two weeks bicycling through the heart of Washington's mountain and lake country. Along the way, there's plenty of time to enjoy a quick dip in a lake and some fresh Washington apples or juicy ripe peaches from a local fruit stand—then continue through narrow winding mountain passes where the air is pure and sweet. You'll take a break from cycling with an exciting day river rafting at Mazama—the tingling spray will keep you cool as you ride out the river! Cyclists will carry their own equipment, covering four hundred miles in fourteen days. Liberty Bell Alpine Tours also has a San Juan Island bicycle trip available. Eighth year of operation. Includes: Meals, lodging, group camping equipment. Dates: May through September. Length of trip: 5–14 days. Group size: 4–10 people. Cost: $200–$600.

**Lucullan Tours
402 29th Street
Des Moines, IA 50312
515-243-4089**   *France*

Lucullan offers tours of three of the most bikeable regions in France—the Loire Valley, Burgundy and Normandy. All three trips are designed for pleasure, not endurance. On the Loire Valley tour, you'll cycle through river and stream valleys, passing gently rolling hills, spectacular chateaux and walled towns. During the trip, you'll stay for two or three nights at each major site to allow for in-depth exploration of the region. Also scheduled: several tastings of Loire Valley wines. Or combine your love of biking with fine food and wine on a luxury tour of celebrated Burgundy. Lodgings and restaurants (Michelin-starred establishments) have been chosen to complement the quality of the wines you will enjoy at ten wine tastings. The Normandy Coasts tour covers the promentories and beaches of the coast and the rolling countryside. Hard cider and brandy from the many apple orchards covering the region will be sampled en route. The operators of the tour are Julian Archer, a professor of French, European and Ancient History at Drake University; and his wife Jane, a former restaurant critic. Includes: Transportation to and from airports to start and end points of the tours, hotel and inn accommodations, wine and brandy tastings, continental breakfasts, mechanic and a support vehicle. Dates: June and July. Length of trip: 10–17 days. Group size: 25. Cost: $595 for the Normandy Coast, $795 for the Burgundy Vineyards, and $975 for the Loire Valley.

Michigan Bicycle Touring, Inc.
3512 Red School Road #TI-4
Kinsley, MI 49649
616-263-5885   *Michigan*

Michigan Bicycle Touring's weekend or week-long trips provide an excellent introduction to bicycle touring. More than twenty different tours are offered throughout northern Michigan. The trips encompass Lakes Huron, Michigan and Superior; Sugar Loaf Mountain; Skull Cave; "Copper Country"; and other unique and interesting areas. One trip is devoted to "Hemingway's Michigan"—visiting many of the places described in his novels and short stories. Riders stay overnight at comfortable inns, ski resorts, or motels, each near a pool or refreshing lake. Tennis, golf, canoeing and hiking are also available. The tours are on back-country roads with minimal traffic, and are suitable for all ages and abilities. Michigan Bicycle Touring has offered bicycle tours since 1978. Includes: Lodging, 2 meals daily, luggage transport, canoe and ferry fees. Dates: May through October. Length of trip: 2, 3, or 5 days. Group size: 25. Cost: $125–$330. Special requirements: Advance deposit; 10-speed Motobecan or Lotus bikes are available for rental.

Pacific Adventures
P.O. Box 5041
Riverside, CA 92517
714-684-1227   *Bali*

Explore the island kingdom of Bali in the Sea of Java. Pacific Adventures allows you to tour this paradise by bicycle, as the Balinese themselves do, meeting and mixing with them along the way. This exciting expedition is steeped in the Balinese culture; you will lodge at native losmen (guest houses), eat spicy and exotic Balinese meals, visit ancient stone temples still in use today, and wander through the dusty streets and colorful markets of ageless and exotic villages. Seven years' experience leading bicycle tours. Includes: Most meals, accommodations, ground transportation, guides. Dates: All year. Length of trip: 2 weeks. Group size: 10–12. Cost: On request. Special requirements: Riders must supply their own bicycles; 25% deposit.

Pacific Adventures
P.O. Box 5041
Riverside, CA 92517
714-684-1227   *California*

Pacific Adventures offers two very special bike tours in California—through the beautiful wine country and incredible Death Valley National Monument. Each tour is led by experienced guides and is accompanied by a sag wagon for luggage. The wine country trip cycles through the famous Napa and Sonoma Valleys, past the vineyards of Christian Brothers, Inglenook, Mondavi and more. One winery will be chosen for a complete tour of cellars, casks, vineyards and processing rooms. Bikers will ride along the Silverado Trail across Napa and into Sonoma to the "Valley of the Moon." The Death Valley tour is on a gentle downhill and rolling terrain, through Scotty's Castle, Furnace Creek, the Devil's Golf Course and Badwater. Riders will cross the lowest point in the continental U.S. and still see snow on top of Telescope Peak just twenty miles distant. Seven years' experience leading bicycle tours. Includes: Ground transportation, all meals, accommodations, guidance and instruction, and a support van. Dates: April through October. Length of trip: 3 days. Group size: 9–20. Cost: $179–$189. Special requirements: Riders must supply their own bicycles; 25% deposit.

Pacific Adventures
P.O. Box 5041
Riverside, CA 92517
714-684-1227   *Hawaii*

Maui Bicycling is the perfect way to savor the beauty of this tropical island paradise. You'll visit the grottoes of Wainapanapa Caves . . . hike and picnic at Waimoku Falls . . . bicycle the Hana Highway to Seven Pools National Park to camp and swim. In addition, you'll spend afternoons on warm beaches, snorkel on tropical reefs and ascend, by car, to the volcano of Haleakala for a spectacular sunrise. At night sleep beneath the stars in Maui's beautiful campgrounds. Seven years' experience leading bicycle tours. Includes: All on-island expenses, meals, "sag-wagon" support, mechanical assistance with bikes, campground reservations and fees, tents and guidance. Dates: July and August. Length of trip: 2 weeks. Group size: 9–20. Cost: $695 per person. Special requirements: Riders must supply their own bicycles; 25% deposit.

Pathfinder Bicycle Tours
RD 1, Box 266
Rexford, NY 12148
518-399-0123   *New York*

Pathfinder offers unusual biking adventures for adults and families in New York State's magnificent Adirondack and Cooperstown regions. Weekend tours operate out of a single inn, with day excursions to places like historic Warrensburg in the Adirondacks; the Hudson and Schroon River Valleys; the pastoral villages of Cherry Valley, Pleasant Brook, and Roseboom; and Huckleberry, Craine and No. 9 Mountains. The trip through Cooperstown spotlights the Baseball Hall of Fame, the Farmer's Museum, and the Fenimore House. The Great Pathfinder five-day tour is designed for advanced-beginner, intermediate, and advanced cyclists. Each night is spent at a different family-oriented lodge or inn. Days are spent touring the Schroon River Valley, the Adirondacks, beautiful Long Lake, Buttermilk Falls and more. A bonus day of bicycling at no extra cost is offered to those who arrive before 11:00 a.m. of the first day of either the weekend or weekday excursions. Third year of operation. Includes: Lodging, 2 meals daily, and a support vehicle. Dates: May through October. Length of trip: 2 or 5 days. Group size: 12–25. Cost: $130 for weekends, $330 for week trips.

RANGE TOURS

**Range Tours
1540 South Holly Street
Denver, CO 80222
303-759-1988
800-525-8509**   *Colorado*

Explore Colorado by bicycle! Range Tours offers two extensive tours of Colorado's Middle Park and Gold Rush areas. The Middle Park tour begins in Lake Dillon and cycles up and through the Rocky Mountain National Park. Each night is spent in a different mountain lodge with an extra night at the Grand Lake Lodge to allow more time for biking in the park. Hiking and swimming are also available. The tour continues through the Arapaho National Forest offering rugged mountain peaks, broad valleys, alpine tundra and beautiful lakes. The Gold Rush tour also begins in Dillon and cycles through Breckenridge, a gold boomtown; the Arkansas River Valley; Leadville, a silver town; the Vail Pass Path; and Copper Mountain. Experienced leaders and support vans accompany both tours. Includes: 6 nights' lodging, all breakfasts and dinners, round-trip transportation for Lake Dillon to tour start and end points, support van, leaders and mechanics. Dates: June through September. Length of trip: 7 days, 6 nights. Group size: 6–10. Cost: $419. Special requirements: Good physical condition.

**Vermont Bicycle Touring
P.O. Box 711-AN
Bristol, VT 05443
802-453-4811**   *Vermont*

Carefree bicycling for people who like the comfort of country inns. Experienced guides lead cyclists throughout scenic Vermont, stopping now and then for a swim or photography. At night, travelers rest, relax and enjoy good food with fellow adventurers at comfortable country inns. A support van specially outfitted for bicycle touring accompanies five-day tours. Bicycles and helmets can be rented. Since 1972. Includes: Lodging, breakfasts and dinners, gratuities, taxes, leaders, maps and complete written directions. Dates: May through October. Length of trip: 2, 3, and 5 days. Group size: 15–40. Cost: Approximately $75 per person per day. Child, group discounts. Special requirements: $50 deposit for 2- and 3-day tours, $100 deposit for 5-day tour.

Vermont Country Cyclers
Box 145
Waterbury Center, Vermont 05677

**Vermont Country Cyclers
P.O. Box 145-2
Waterbury Center, VT 05677
802-242-5215**   *Vermont*

"Biking with class"—that's what *McCall's* Magazine called Vermont Bicycling Touring. Run by Bob and Cindy Maynard, the company aims to offer the best in adult bicycle touring, featuring small, friendly groups and accommodations in the finest country inns. The tours cycle through New England's covered bridges and corridors of maple trees . . . past sweeping views and along cool mountain streams. Each day leaves ample time for dipping in secluded swimming holes, relaxing on the village green, visiting historic sights or browsing through Vermont's unique shops and galleries. Bikers can explore the hills and valleys of the Green Mountains from which the state receives its name. Other trips tour the Lake Region of southwestern Vermont, including Lakes Champlain and Bomoseen; Sugarbush Valley; the Mad River; Warren Falls; and Joslin Round Barn, one of the last standing round barns in the country. Lodging is at the best country inns featuring excellent cuisine, cosy country charm—maybe even a hot tub. Tours are rated for distance and difficulty. Operating quality bike tours since 1979. Includes: Accommodations, 2 meals daily, mechanic, and a support van. Rentals are available. Dates: May through October. Length of trip: 2, 3, or 5 days. Group size: 18–25. Cost: $148–$389.

Birdwatching •

Sweeping the tree branches with your binoculars, you spy a brief movement and spot of color. You shift your position slightly for an unobstructed view, and focus on the gaily feathered crest. A Blue-backed Manakin! Pointing the bird out to your Tobagan guide, you reach a steady hand for your camera. Focus. A nearby rustling captures the Manakin's attention. Profile. Click. It opens its wings and begins to lift itself off the branch. Click. Later, you learn that you caught the bird at full wing extension, and your slide captures the rich saturation of color on the plumage. Examining it proudly, you think you can even almost detect a glimmer of anticipation in the Manakin's face. A bounteous treasure, reaped from your birdwatching holiday in the British West Indies.

Ornithological tours give bird lovers the chance to play peeping tom in the far corners of the world, lurking in the foliage while exotic birds soar overhead. You'll go into the wilderness, and quietly observe rare species frolicking in their own natural habitat—birds that you otherwise could see only in zoos.

Get up early and see mothers feeding their young; and have your patience pay off when before your eyes a male eagle courts his mate.

A big advantage to organized birdwatching trips is that your guides will be experts in the ecology of the terrain. They know where the birds roost. They will point out and identify exotic species, and tell you the characteristics of the birds you see. Familiar with the habits of the area's avifauna, they'll teach you the subtleties of birdwatching peculiar to that region: what seasons and times of day are best, which birds scare easily, how best to see the young, and which trees to scour for the most precious rarity. Most tour operators use qualified ornithologists as guides. Check with the individual operator for guides' credentials. In an activity as quiet as birdwatching, large groups can be unwieldy and overly noisy. Look for small group sizes, or high ratios of guides to participants.

Birdwatching is a seasonal activity, geared to the birds' migratory patterns. Again, the tour operator will be familiar with the flocks' coming and goings, and time its trips accordingly. Ask the operator to provide information on migratory patterns. You might even happen to see unexpected birds, not indigenous to the region, passing by overhead or stopping for a drink of water en route to a distant destination.

Every region offers its own set of challenges and rewards, so you should study the choices carefully before picking a tour. In some cases, light hiking will take you up to the nesting areas. Other regions require more strenuous hiking, or even exploring by canoe or raft. Depending on how deeply into the wilderness you want to get, you can either camp out or stay in a hotel. Camping offers more convenient early morning and twilight birdwatching opportunities; hotels are more comfortable. On the subject of comfort, pick an area with a climate that suits you. Birdwatching combines periods of relatively strenuous activity with stretches of inactivity, so extreme climates on either end of the scale can be uncomfortable.

On birdwatching trips, you can count on spending your vacation with kindred spirits— avid aviophiles. Some will have hidden in bushes in areas you've always wanted to try; others will express healthy envy for your experiences. You can swap stories, and even swap slides. After all, birds of a feather . . .

SECTIONS OF RELATED INTEREST

Nature Expeditions

64

Earthwatch
10 Juniper Road
P.O. Box 127 H
Belmont, MA 02178
617-489-3030
Telex 951404   *China*

Earthwatch invites you to join an ornithological survey of the Zha Lung Preserve located northeast of Beijing. One of the world's largest fresh-water wetlands, this sanctuary is home to over 280 different species of birds (including four exceedingly rare species of crane). Earthwatch is a nonprofit organization which offers people the opportunity to participate in field research expeditions around the globe. Over the past decade, they have matched the interests of over five thousand volunteers with the scientific objectives of some of the world's top researchers. Includes: Accommodations, meals and daily travel from arrival at staging area until the end of the project. Dates: Year-round. Length of trip: 2–3 weeks. Group size: 4–14. Cost: $2,480. Program expenses as well as transportation costs to and from the staging area are tax-deductible, since the participant is performing a volunteer service.

Echo: The Wilderness Company
6529 Telegraph Avenue
Oakland, CA 94609
415-652-1600   *Idaho*

Each year well over one thousand eagles, falcons, hawks, and other birds of prey return to an eighty-one mile stretch of the Snake River Canyon in southwestern Idaho, to court, mate, and rear their young. Here, a unique ecosystem has attracted the densest-known population of raptors in North America. Fifteen species, including golden eagles, kestrals, four species of hawks, six species of owls, and around five percent of the world's prairie falcons annually nest here. Echo's five-day, leisurely float trips down this calm reach of the Snake are designed primarily for the spotting and photographing of these birds. Twelve years of commercial, professional river running. Includes: Guides, gear, food, shuttle from Boise and return; naturalists accompany many of the trips. Dates: Late April through May. Length of trip: 5 days. Group size: 6–20. Cost: $475. Special requirements: Reasonable physical condition, camping skills. Deposit of $100 per person required, full payment due 60 days before trip starts.

Lyon Travel Services
1031 Ardmore Avenue
Oakland, CA 94610
415-465-8955   *Florida*

Interested in a unique nature photography and birdwatching experience? Lyon Travel offers two ten-day expeditions in the Everglades National Park and the Sansibel Islands. The Everglades offers more than three hundred species of birds and fascinating flora. The leisurely-paced trip explores the exciting world of the "River of Grass," taking you to within ten feet of the most exotic birds in North America. You'll also see sawgrass prairies, mangrove swamps, alligator holes, and tidal flats. Also on view . . . tropical hardwood hammocks, virgin stands of bald cypress, and an array of colorful shells from the Gulf. Accommodations are in motels and inns. Lyon Travel has been in operation since 1975. Includes: All meals, lodging, ground transportation. Dates: February. Length of trip: 10 days. Group size: 5. Cost: $1,150. Special requirements: $250 deposit.

United Touring Company
P.O. Box 2914
Harare, Zimbabwe
793701
Telex 2173   *Zimbabwe*

United Touring Company's ornithological tour begins with a day and an overnight stay in the capital city of Harare, before moving on to Lake McIlwaine National Park, home of Zimbabwe's third largest lake. Here the combination of woodland and lake-side environments has encouraged an unusually wide variety of bird life—counts of over two hundred species in a single day have been known. A trip to the Inyanga Mountains follows, with intermittent stops at the Vumba Botanical Gardens, Mtarazi Falls, Honde View, and Pungwe Falls. You'll spend two days in Inyanga, with plenty of time to pursue bird watching. After a day in Harare, with visits to the Pit Structures, Fort Inyangwe and Trout Research Centre, you'll continue on to Hwange National Park, where game viewing and bird watching abound. The tour comes to an end after visiting the Victoria Falls area. Includes: Accommodation and table d'hote meals throughout, airport transfers and porterage, sightseeing, all ground transportation, local guides and entry fees. Dates: Year-round. Length of trip: 15 days. Group size: 16. Cost: Z$897.35, single supplement: Z$111.75.

Wonder Bird Tours
500 Fifth Avenue
New York, NY 10036
212-840-5961   *Trinidad, West Indies*

The annual, two-week seminar on Ornithology held at the Asa Wright Nature Centre in Trinidad, takes place in late June/early July. Leaders Fred Sibley and John Yrizzary discuss speciation, distribution, the interrelationship between birds and their habitat, how the ecology and food sources of tropical birds influence behavior, and altitudinal variation among forest species. The avifauna of Trinidad and Tobago totals four hundred species and amateur birders can expect to spot one hundred and fifty to two hundred species during their two-week stay, including hummingbirds, manakins, toucans, parrots, trogons, bellbirds and crested oropendolas. Riding the thermals above the nearby slopes are white and black hawks, ornate hawk-eagles, bat falcons, and other raptors. At dusk, semi-collared nighthawks, spectacled and pygmy owls, and flocks of swifts make their appearance. In addition, there are field trips to a variety of habitats. A two-day trip to Tobago provides both birdwatching and snorkeling opportunities around the Buccoo Reef. A short boat trip away is Little Tobago Island, the only place outside of New Guinea where the great bird of paradise exists in its wild state. Includes: Private bath, three meals daily, transfers, field trips with transportation (including two days in Tobago), boat trips, gratuities to household help, personal feedback from seminar leaders. Dates: Last week June and first week July. Length of trip: 15 days. Group size: 20. Cost: $725. Special requirements: Suitable for amateur and professional students of tropical ecology.

Botany •
Horticulture •
Garden Tours •
Foliage Tours •

Exquisite flowers whose blooms are a precious rarity in North America flourish in wild abundance in other parts of the world. A host of flora-oriented tours takes you to see rare specimens as well as elegantly manicured formal gardens throughout the world.

- Tour the rich wildflower area of South Africa's Cape and Eastern Transvaal, where eighteen thousand plant species grow.
- Bring ample supplies of color film to capture the splendid gardens and grounds of England's Castle Howard, setting for the TV-film adaptation of Evelyn Waugh's *Brideshead Revisited.*
- In the virgin wilderness of Brazil's Mountain Cloud Orchid Forest, see an incredible 112 orchid species flowering in what has been called the closest thing to a permanent natural orchid garden.
- Or view colorful fields of Australian wildflowers on a six-day spring rail cruise through the continent's lushest areas.

Tour operators add color to the flowers by identifying species and providing background information. They'll teach you how to distinguish an epiphytic orchid, or a bromeliad. Some tour guides are expert botanists and horticulturists—check the qualifications of the guides for each operator.

Botanical tours should be timed to coincide with nature's most vivid floral displays. In New England, you can see the chromatic richness of the foliage on autumn tours. The American Southwest reveals its true colors in spring, when hundreds of varieties of wildflowers paint the desert with brilliant hues. In any area, ask the tour operator what flowers will be in bloom in the season of your travels.

SECTIONS OF RELATED INTEREST

Nature Expeditions

Brazilian Views, Inc.
201 East 66th Street, Suite 21G
New York, NY 10021
212-472-9539   *Brazil*

As Charles Darwin wrote of Brazil after the historic voyage on the HMS Beagle: "The land is one great wild, untidy, luxuriant hot house, made by Nature for herself." There is no doubt that the diversity of Brazil's fauna and flora is staggering: for example, of the fifty species of Calatheas listed in TROPICA, over half are Brazilian. You can spend two exciting weeks discovering the orchids, roses, coffee plantations, waterfalls, and butterflies of this lush tropical world. The trip concentrates on the southeastern part of Brazil (Parana, Sao Paulo and Rio) and includes Iguassu Falls which is situated in the National Park, home of rare species of birds and exotic tropical plants. Brazilian Views also offers a ten-day botany trip to Brazil's Mountain Cloud Orchid Forest—virtually a virgin forest of trees, ferns, palms and mysteriously and obsessively fascinating wild orchids. Includes: Round-trip airfare US/Brazil; air and ground transportation in Brazil; accommodations; breakfast daily plus several other meals; transfers; guides. Dates: September and October. Length of trip: 14 days. Group size: 15 to 36. Cost: From under $3,000 (including air).

Fun Safaris, Inc.
P.O. Box 178
Bloomingdale, IL 60108
312-893-2545
800-323-8020
Telex 910-291-3542   *South Africa*

South Africa, with its diversity of climatic conditions and ever-changing landscape, is truly the "Rarest Garden on Earth," with over eighteen thousand species of flowers. This program takes you to the splendid wildflower areas of the Cape and Eastern Transvaal, and to the magnificent Victoria Falls. You will spend time viewing and photographing the great variety of wild animals and birds at the exclusive Mala Mala Game Reserve. Also included are the National Botanical Garden in Pretoria and the Kirstenbosch Botanical Gardens in Cape Town, which contains as many of South Africa's eighteen thousand species as will grow there. Includes: Transportation, accommodations, sightseeing, entrance fees, most meals. Dates: August through October. Length: 18 days. Group size: Maximum of 30 people. Cost: Approximately $3,800 per person.

Lyon Travel Services, Inc.
1031 Ardmore Avenue
Oakland, CA 94610
415-465-8955   *Southwest United States*

From the carpets of primroses, asters, yellow tackstems and a hundred other flowers exploding in vibrant hues . . . to the sprawling cacti, forming beautiful shapes as they twist upwards towards the sun . . . the desert blooms in springtime with the wonders of nature. On this twenty-one-day adventure, you'll explore the Sonora and Mojave Deserts, and adjacent areas. Highlights include Death Valley; Joshua Tree National Monument; Oak Creek Canyon and the ruined cliff dwellings of Tonto National Monument. You'll also drive along the scenic Apache Trail rich with wildflowers . . . pass ghost towns . . . and have ample time to photograph, sketch, press, identify and admire the amazing wildflowers of the desert. Includes: All-inclusive except air fare to Phoenix from Las Vegas. Dates: April. Length of trip: 21 days. Group size: 5 people. Cost: $2,200. Special requirements: $250 deposit. Participants should be in good health.

R & I Country Tours
138A Piccadilly
London W1V 9FH England
1-491-2584   *Great Britain*

Tour some of the loveliest and most stately homes in Britain and Scotland. R & I Country Tours gives you an opportunity to visit some very special gardens in the company of the owners or their gardeners. A major highlight of this trip is the tour of the sublime gardens and grounds of Castle Howard, seen as the family seat on the PBS presentation of Evelyn Waugh's Brideshead Revisited. Besides Castle Howard, the tour also covers the grounds and gardens of Harlow Car, an all-season garden; Thorp Perrow, sixty acres of landscaped grounds and an arboretum; Priorwood Gardens, specializing in dried and wild flowers; Carolside, an eighteenth-century "Cottage" garden; and Ayton Castle, known for its extensive grounds and hot-houses. Includes: Accommodations, meals (often with the owners of the gardens or in private historic homes), ground transportation, guide, porterage, tips and taxes. Dates: July and August. Length of trip: 7 days. Cost: £635.

Western Australian Government Railways
P.O. Box 51422
Perth, West Australia, Australia 6001
(09) 326-2811   *Australia*

Waving fields of exquisite, golden colored wildflowers gently sway in the breeze—waiting for you to discover them in one of the world's last frontiers—Australia . . . a mecca for enthusiasts with over seven thousand species of unique wildflowers to dazzle the eye and tingle the nose. Westrail (the Western Australian Government Railways) operates a variety of tours from Perth throughout some of the most scenic areas. On this six-day train journey during the Australian spring (August through October) you'll criss-cross the country and savor the beauty of Australia's wildflowers, as much a treasure as the goldmines and kangaroos. Westrail has provided public transport service since 1879 and operated tours for forty years. Includes: Hostess, botanist, motel accommodations, all meals. Dates: August through October. Length of trip: 6 days. Group size: 40 people. Cost: From $AUS 440. Special requirements: $30 deposit.

Canal Cruising •
Canal Barging •

Imagine yourself floating past the wooded countryside of Brittany down grand old canals built by Napoleon ... slipping past the great chateaux of the Loire River Valley while savoring an exquisite French burgundy that explodes with taste ... planning a day of sun-bathing while watching the grandeur of the English countryside of Yorkshire, Wales or the Midlands slowly weave by ... steeping yourself in the beguiling enchantment of Ireland from the rivers Shannon and Barrow ... or savoring Scotland on Caledonian Canal and the remote West Coast Inner Hebrides.

The possibilities are limitless when you pick the unhurried pace and tranquility of canal barging for your next vacation. You can attempt every type of voyage from a totally independent pilot-yourself boat to fully-crewed and serviced cruises on actual "floating hotels."

The mellow charm of going by canal barge is addictive. For this singularly different vacation idea, there are many different types of canal barges—everything from old working canal boats fully equipped with galley, bathroom, shower, beds, heating and a full six-foot-two-inch headroom to deluxe, luxurious canal barges where gourmet foods and wines are served—you'll taste all the local delicacies from creamy seafood dishes to ambrosial desserts.

There are two basic types of barge travel available: The "floating hotels" with captain and crew, or self-charters where you are the pilot.

THINGS TO ASK:

If you pick a self-charter, inquire whether previous boating experience is necessary. It usually isn't—the boats are very easy to handle.

On a self-charter, ask the tour operator for maps and suggested routes.

What amenities are on the boat ... TV? Radio? Bicycles for on-shore excursions?

Find out if they stock the boat with provisions (food, linen, etc.) or whether you'll have to do it yourself.

Ask about accessibility of shore activities—are they right near where you tie up, or will you have to rely on public transportation?

On a "floating hotel" ...

Are shore excursions included or will you have to pay extra?

Sometimes different special interest sailings are available (history, gastronomy, etc.)—check with tour operator for details.

The following canal barge cruises encompass a wide variety of tastes and adventures. Read all the choices and pick the one suited for you.

Canals Europe
220 Redwood Highway
Mill Valley, CA 94941
415-388-7908

Europe

From the rippling waters of the River Shannon in Ireland to mysterious depths of Loch Ness and Greece's turquoise Saronic Gulf—watch as Europe unfolds. Canals Europe offers canal adventures in five countries aboard modern self-drive cruisers. In France, explore the Canal Du Midi to the south, built during the reign of Louis XIV, or the eighteenth-century Canal Du Nivernais along the open countryside of Burgundy. To the north, the Canal de Bourgogne weaves through Dijon, gastronomic capital of Burgundy, and the famous vineyards of Cotes de Beaune such as Nuit-St.-Georges. Cruise the Loire Valley to Sancerre or sail and power along the Cote D'Azur near Monaco. In Britain, explore the Thames, Severn, and Avon rivers, visiting Shakespeare's birthplace at Stratford-on-Avon. Enjoy the ancient system of English narrow canals which take passengers through the Midlands, Yorkshire, and Wales. Or perhaps go barging up Norfolk broads, fenlands near Cambridge, Scotland on the Caledonian Canal and the West Coast Inner Hebrides. In Ireland, enjoy a lazy, picturesque voyage along the rivers Shannon and Barrow, and the Grand Canal. Tours of Holland feature South Holland and Friesland, and in Greece feature flotilla sailing in the Saronic Gulf. Includes: Fully-equipped boats with refrigerators, hot and cold running water, showers, electric lights, all kitchen utensils and linens. Optional bicycles and T.V. available. Dates: March through October. Length of trip: From 1 week. Group size: 2–10 and up. Cost: $150 per week and up. Special requirements: Fuel security deposit of $150 and up. Some boat-handling experience desirable but not required.

Continental Waterways
11 Beacon Street
Boston, MA 02108
617-227-3220   *Europe*

Hotel barges are an innovative, unique way to explore England and France. Look at beautiful stretches of European countryside from the water; savor the ancient castles and the modern food; toast to good times with a fine bottle of burgundy. All this can be done when you cruise by hotel barge. It's a luxurious ride into the grandeur of Europe—with plenty of stops along the way to satisfy even the most curious of travelers. Includes: Meals, unlimited table wine, tours conducted by Continental Waterways, transfers in the barge's minibus to and from hotel and barge, all excursions in the barge's minibus and use of barge's bicycles. Dates: April through November. Length: 6 days. Group size: 6–24 passengers. Cost: $1,300. Special requirements: $500 deposit required 10 days after booking.

Esplanade Tours
38 Newbury Street
Boston, MA 02116
617-266-7465
800-343-7184
Telex 940421   *France*

These cruises combine the tranquility of a barge holiday with an extensive sightseeing program. Each centers on a seven- or ten-day cruise of the three-hundred-year-old Canal du Midi aboard the "Athos," a thirty-meter barge converted to sleep twelve in six double cabins. Built especially for Esplanade's France programs and clientele, the "Athos" features a roomy salon/dining room and ample deck space for sunning and canal-watching. All cruise-tours are escorted and provide a varied look at the highlights of France's Languedoc region: the walled city of Carcassonne, the Toulouse-Lautrec museum in Albi and several private chateaux. Some programs also offer extensions in chateaux-hotels in the Pyrenees and Provence. The "Athos" is also available for charters (cruises without escorted sightseeing). Other France programs include weekly departures through the Champagne and Burgundy vineyards. Thirty years' experience in specialty tours and cruises for small groups. Includes: Accommodations aboard barge and (on some departures) in deluxe/first class hotels, all meals, sightseeing, special receptions, transfers, porterage and services of an Esplanade tour expert.

Dates: April through October. Length of trip: 7–14 days. Group size: 12. Cost: From $1,725 per person. Special requirements: $350 deposit due on confirmation.

European Canal Cruises (Romsey), Ltd.
79, Winchester Road
Romsey, Hants SO5 8JB
England
(794) 514412   *France*

Anna and Norman Riddle aim to combine first-class service, individual attention and the highest standards of comfort possible afloat . . . with cuisine your tastebuds will never forget. On their barge cruises, you can see the wooded country of Brittany from the canals built by Napoleon . . . travel past the great chateaux of the Loire River Valley . . . or glide through sweeping locks and the delightful vineyards of Charente. Along the way, you'll sample the best local wines and feast on mouth-watering regional specialties such as salt-marsh lamb, crepes, seafood . . . with perhaps a tempting sabayon for dessert. Anna Riddle's cooking has figured twice in *Gourmet* Magazine and has received an entry in *Gourmet's France*. European Canal Cruises has been operating for thirteen years. Includes: Accommodations, all meals, wine, excursions. Dates: April through October. Length of trip: 6 days. Group size: 8–12 persons. Cost: $990 per person. Special requirements: $350 deposit per person to confirm reservation, balance 8 weeks prior to departure.

Flot' Home S.A.R.L.
B.P. 151
34300 Agde
France
(67) 949420   *France*

Sip fine wine and dine on gourmet meals while traveling the canals and rivers of Burgundy and Southern France. With Flot' Home, you can enjoy cruises aboard hotel barges as well as self-drive charters throughout the region. Splendid sightseeing excursions by chauffered minibus are included to chateaux, wine caves and historic sites. Though cruises run primarily through the lovely waterways of France's Burgundy and southern regions, trips to the Champagne and Camargue areas can also be arranged. A special cruise from Paris to Amsterdam is also available. Flot' Home has been operating in France for over ten years. Includes: All meals, wine, twin berth cabins with shower and toilet, side trips. Dates: March and April. Length of trip: 1–2 weeks. Group size: 6. Cost: $6,000 for 6 people.

Inland Waterway Holiday Cruises, Ltd.
Preston Brook
Runcorn, Cheshire WA7 3AL
England
09286 376   *Great Britain*

Explore Britain's delightful and historic inland waterways aboard genuine "narrowboats" converted into comfortable floating hotels. These boats retain the gay "roses and castles" decoration of the working canal boat and are resplendent in glittering brasswork and scrubbed white ropes. The boats navigate most rivers and canals between Oxford and Liangotten. For the energetic there are locks to be worked, swing bridges to be opened, and canalside villages and inns to be explored. For those preferring complete relaxation, the well deck provides a comfortable viewpoint from which to contemplate canal and countryside. Inland Waterway Holiday Cruises has been operating in Great Britain for twenty-six years. Includes: All meals, services on boat, house wine, taxes. Bar purchases extra. Dates: April through October. Length of trip: 1 week. Group size: 12 maximum. Cost: £160.

Mayflower Charters, Ltd.
Maison Eclusiere 6l
Mailly le Chateau
Chatel Censoir 89660
France   *France*

Laze along the waterways and rivers of France's Burgundy region. A refurbished cargo barge, the "Nymphea" provides a comfortable floating home for a family or a group of six friends. The Canal Royal du Nivernais, built around 1800, winds gently through the green heartland of Burgundy—from the cathedral city of Auxerre to the River Loire at Decize. Enjoy the unhurried pace of the barge as you pass through small villages, forests, lakes, lush river plains, and steep-sided rocky cuttings. Gourmet food, wine and this magnificent landscape all combine to make the trip a memorable vacation. Mayflower Charters is now in its seventh year of operation. Includes: All meals, wine, excursions in ship's minibus, transport to and from rendezvous towns to barge, services of crew, use of ship's bicycles. Dates: Every Sunday, April through October. Length of trip: 1 week. Group size: 6. Cost: $4,800 for 6 persons.

SUNDOWNER
BOAT COMPANY

Sundowner Boat Company
30 Longport Wharf
Stoke-On-Trent, Staffs ST6 4NA
England
(0782) 812674/813831   *Great Britain*

Take a step back in time and explore portions of England almost untouched by the twentieth century. Over two thousand miles of canals connect Britain's major rivers, flowing through cities, villages and beautiful countryside. Aboard a modern narrowboat, you'll pass two-hundred-year-old wrought iron, stone and brick bridges, tunnels, aqueducts and locks. You can cruise to Stratford-on-Avon and moor beside the Shakespeare Theatre or enjoy a visit to Oxford. Many other local points of interest lie within easy reach of your floating home—including Warwick, the Wedgewood Potteries and Peak Forest National Park. Sundowner, with seven years' experience, provides a wide variety of easy-to-handle narrowboats fully equipped with galley, bathroom, shower, beds, heating, and a full six foot, two inch headroom. Includes: Boat, fuel, gas for heating and cooking, bedding, many consumable domestic items. Dates: March through October. Length of trip: 3 days to 3 weeks. Group size: 2 through 12. Cost: from £22–80 per person for the first 72 hours depending on season and number in group; children under 10 free.

UK Waterway Holidays, Ltd.
Penn Place
Rickmansworth, Herts WD3 1EU
England
(0923) 770040   *Great Britain*

Spend an idyllic holiday along Britain's historic inland waterways. UK Waterway Holidays offers both a totally independent "skipper-yourself" boat and fully serviced cruises aboard a

Canal barging provides leisurely sightseeing. Cruise aboard a floating hotel, or skipper your own boat—they're easy to operate. (U.K. WATERWAY HOLIDAYS, LTD., DEREK PRATT)

floating hotel. A good choice of starting places is provided throughout England and on Scotland's Caledonian Canal. From there, you travel at leisure, exploring the countryside, villages and popular tourist sights of Great Britain. The boats are simple to operate and no previous experience is needed. Designed as comfortable, floating homes, they have beds, well-equipped kitchens, heating, and bathroom with shower. UK Waterway Holidays Limited is part of the British Waterways Board. Includes: Boat rental (with service of skipper if chartered), taxes, insurance, all domestic items (linens, towels, etc.), engine fuel, bottled gas for cooking and heating, local cruising guide, navigation tuition. Dates: April through October. Length of trip: 1 week minimum. Group size: Charter: 12. Solo: 2 through 12. Cost: Charters: £395–455 per group. Solo: £33–150 per person per week depending on season and group size. Special requirements: 50% deposit to confirm reservation.

Canoeing •
Kayaking •

The river. It has long been a source of excitement and fascination to the adventurous spirit. Coursing feverishly through craggy gorges or stretching out gracefully into open lengths, the river creates an endless variety of physical challenges and visual spectacles. It is an untamed, untameable force.

The river is a powerful emblem of the wilderness, just as the highway is an emblem of development. Rivers have cut paths through the most rugged terrain, allowing you to enter a world you could never see by roads.

To enter this world, you need a boat: either a canoe or kayak. These sleek, maneuverable crafts will take you along waterways where motor- or sailboats cannot go. Both offer myriad opportunities for the expert; both can be handled competently and safely by novices, after a little instruction.

In either craft, you can choose river running or touring, or make your way along lakes or oceans. The majority of excursions concentrate on rivers, but there are plenty of rewarding programs on the more open bodies of water.

THE RIVER

River running offers two discrete charms: what you see and what you do. There are the athletic thrills—racing pulsing whitewater through a serpentine course of exhilarating rapids. And a more contemplative, gentler side—the magnificent scenery and unspoiled wilderness along the river.

We tend not to think of river expeditions as sightseeing tours. This is a mistake. Except when the few feet of whitewater immediately before the bow demand your complete attention, you'll get your greatest satisfaction from observing the flora and fauna along the banks.

Since your craft makes virtually no sound, you'll get close-up views of undisturbed wildlife. See a crimson-breasted frigate bird spread its wings in the supple elegance of flight. Or photograph a giant Alaskan caribou unconcernedly dipping its head for a cool drink from the river. River trips are a bird-, plant-, or animal-watcher's fantasy come true. In lush swamp forests like the bayou or the Everglades, a canoe is the only way to observe the rich ecology of the interior.

Great as these charms are, one cannot ignore the allure of whitewater . . . the thrill of running narrow gorges . . . hitting tell-tale downstream "V's" between rocks and shooting through in a blur of spray and hope.

Rapids are classified according to their degree of difficulty by the American Whitewater Affiliation. Ratings range from I to VI, as follows:

I. Easy. Suitable for any level adventurer.
II. Moderately difficult, with some small riffles or rapids. You'll have to be able to avoid occasional minor obstacles.
III. Medium difficult, with high-wave rapids, rocks, and other obstacles. A novice should not attempt rapids of Grade III or higher unless accompanied by a whitewater expert.
IV. Difficult—only for experienced whitewater adventurers. Extended rapids, strong waves, boils, eddies. The course is tough to follow. A kayak navigates these waters more advantageously; for canoes, spray covers are essential.

V. Extremely difficult. Rougher than IV. Even experienced whitewater enthusiasts should study the course and characteristics of the river before
attempting it.

VI. Dangerous, even for top experts.

KAYAKING OR CANOEING?

The kayak, a seemingly more exotic craft, is no more difficult to learn to operate than a canoe. Kayaks are generally shorter and shallower than canoes, and are better suited to the really rough water. They are partially enclosed. The kayaker sits with his or her upper body protruding from an opening in the hull. Paddles with blades at both ends are used, held transversally across the beam of the boat.

Because most of the hull is covered, kayaks are less susceptible to splashing or spraying than are open canoes. They can also rock a bit without filling with water. The kayaker sits on the floor of the boat, giving kayaks a low center of gravity. These two factors make them extremely stable, even in rough water. They won't tip and the water can't splash or overflow into them.

Kayaks maneuver like a dream. The two-bladed paddle, worked in short, quick strokes, gives its operator almost instantaneous access to either side of the boat. There's no need to switch grips and heave your paddle from port to starboard. So kayakers can handily execute sharp turns to avoid rocks or to veer into the whitewater.

The maneuvers? Advanced or expert kayakers have developed their own vocabulary of river mastery. Besides the basic strokes, which will get you through most situations, kayak clinics teach the subtleties of the sport. Like high and low braces, which bring the boat sharply around. Or eddy turns, a necessary move on whitewater. You'll learn the science of the river, techniques for ferrying and surfing, and—when you're ready for it—the coveted Eskimo roll.

Canoes are somewhat more comfortable than kayaks in less torrid rapids. You can sit up straight and move your legs around. Canoe paddles are lighter and allow you more rest between strokes. Canoes also carry more gear, and allow easier access to it. If, as you glide soundlessly down a river, you should spot a deer gracefully loping along the banks, you'll be able to get out your camera and capture the moment—if you're in a canoe. In a kayak, access to gear is a trickier matter.

LAKES AND OCEANS

Canoeing and kayaking aren't restricted to rivers. Some of the most scenic and relaxing waters are found in lakes and oceans. The open waters offer brilliant sightseeing opportunities and a chance to combine other pursuits.

Like fishing. Imagine paddling smoothly through the tranquil lakes surrounding Alaska's Admiralty Island, drawing your line on the salmon- and trout-filled waters. Or animal watching. Admiralty Island boasts the largest concentrations of brown bear and bald eagles in North America. Kayaking on Baja's Sea of Cortez, you'll see a dazzling assortment of birds, and possibly sight a Pacific gray whale.

Open water touring is more relaxing than river running. You'll be able to talk quietly with your partner, or just gather your thoughts as you paddle smoothly over the still waters.

CHOOSING A CANOEING/KAYAKING TRIP

Programs are available for all levels of canoers and kayakers. Many operators structure their expeditions so that you start with short daily runs on gentle waters and work your way up to longer distances and more challenging rapids. These programs allow even beginners to develop and apply the techniques of advanced river running.

In the listings which follow, the tour operator will indicate how strenuous a trip is, and whether any special skill or experience is necessary. In most cases, you don't even need to know how to swim. Key factors influencing difficulty include grades of rapids, length of daily runs, and water levels during the season of the trip. In high water seasons—generally during and after the rainy season, and after the spring thaw—rapids boil more furiously. Also, beginners should consider water temperatures—warmer waters make spills less treacherous.

High grade rapids generally require special instruction. Check the qualifications of the guides or instructors, and the ratio of students to instructors. If you are a raw beginner tackling rough whitewater, you may want your instructor in your canoe with you.

An advantage to less strenuous trips is that they allow you time—and energy—to pursue other activities. The wilderness is full of possibilities—after your river run, you may want to go hiking or take photographs in the woods. Or go fishing along the banks of the river.

On any level of expedition, you'll need a good boat. The tour operator generally supplies this—you don't need to bring your own. In addition, the outfitter should also supply you with paddles and life jackets. If the tour involves camping out, you'll need basic camping equipment. The operator will send you a list of essential gear, telling you what you need to bring, and what you can rent. Add any rental fees to the tour price when calculating the cost of the trip.

Whether you choose a canoe or kayak, still water or rapids, you'll enjoy a new perspective on the outdoors—from the water, looking onto the land.

Alaska Discovery, Inc.
P.O. Box 26
Gustavus, AK 99826
907-697-3431

Alaska

On this quiet water kayak adventure, you'll explore the most remote beaches and inlets of Glacier Bay National Park—site of some of the most active glacial systems in the world. Eagles, brown and black bear, coyotes and mountain goats are among the many types of wildlife to be found on land, while in the waters are seal, whales and porpoises. Time is spent kayaking along the cliffs of a large bird rookery, where such exotic species as puffins, murrelets and kittiwakes all nest. A one-week itinerary skirts the entire West Arm of Glacier Bay; but if you only have four days to spend kayaking, a shorter program is also available. Twelve years' experience, Alaska Association of Mountain and Wilderness Guides certified outfitter. Includes: Completely outfitted, kayaks, all camping and cooking gear, all food, ground and air charter transportation, insurance and guides. Dates: June through August. Length of trip: 1 week or 4 days. Group size: 8–12. Cost: $750 or $475. Special requirements: None—tour kayaking, not white water. Instruction included.

Alaska Discovery, Inc.
P.O. Box 26
Gustavus, AK 99826
907-697-3431

Alaska

This trip offers you canoeing, on both salt water and fresh water lakes, through the beautiful mature hemlock and spruce rain forests of Admiralty Island National Monument. Admiralty Island boasts the largest concentrations of brown bear and bald eagles in North America. In July and August, fishing for both salmon and trout is excellent. On this one-week, completely outfitted canoe outing, you can cross the island from east to west, beginning and ending on salt water, but traversing a series of seven lakes and connecting portage trails. For a shorter experience, dates are also scheduled for canoeing and fishing the Mitchell Bay Area of Admiralty Island. Twelve years' experience, Alaska Association of Mountain and Wilderness Guides certified outfitter. Includes: Completely outfitted, canoes, all camping and cooking gear, all food, ground and air charter transportation to and from Admiralty Island, insurance, guide. (Fishing gear not provided.) Dates: June through August. Length of trip: 7 days or 4 days. Group size: 6–12. Cost: $725 or $450. Special requirements: None. Instruction included, beginners welcome.

Alaska Float Trips
P.O. Box 8264
Anchorage, AK 99508
907-333-4442
                                                                          Alaska

Experience the outstanding wildlife and scenic grandeur of Alaska from the North Slope to the Aleutian Peninsula by canoe or raft. Groups, generally limited to ten, are led by Alaskan guides/residents, knowledgeable in an area's natural history. Watch for bald eagles, falcons, caribou, moose and grizzly bear while learning about the unique Alaska ecosystem. If you like, cast your favorite fly or lure for five species of Pacific salmon, rainbow trout, grayling, arctic char, sheefish or pike. Custom paddle experiences and discounts can be arranged for special groups; exploratory and wilderness skill development experiences also available. Members of Alaska Association of Mountain and Wilderness Guides. Includes: Guides, rafts, life-jackets, food, tents, transportation from Anchorage to area and return to Anchorage, and natural history information about destination. Dates: May through October. Length of trip: 1–14 days. Group size: 3–10. Cost: $30–$2,000. Special requirements: Minimum age 10; 25% deposit with reservation; balance due 60 days before departure.

Canoe Canada Outfitters
P.O. Box 1810T
Atikokan, Ontario
Canada P0T 1C0
807-597-6418
                                                                          Canada

Quetico Park is a two-thousand-square-mile wilderness area of crystal clear lakes in northwestern Ontario. Canoe Canada Outfitters prepares people of all ages and abilities for exciting self-adventure trips. Guests are lodged in Atikokan the first night for organizing, orientation and trip planning. The next morning canoers are equipped with first-class, ultralight camping gear, custom-packed deluxe meals, canoes and instructions for their week-long excursion in Quetico. Canoe Canada Outfitters has been one of Canada's leading outfitters for ten years. Includes: Overnight accommodations in Atikokan, one week's complete outfitting (all food and equipment), and park fees. Fishing licenses are extra. Dates: May through September. Length of trip: 8 days, 7 nights. Group size: 2–8. Cost: $245.

Ecosummer Canada Expeditions, Ltd.
1516 Duranleau Street
Granville Island
Vancouver B.C., Canada V6H 3S4
604-669-7741
                                                                          Canada

As you kayak along the North coast of Somerset Island, you'll cross the migration route for white whale, walrus, harp seal and bearded seal. The towering cliffs of the island offer ideal nesting places for thousands of exotic birds, while the waters attract Arctic cod and the beluga whale. Or put your kayak in the waters of the Northwest Passage and spot frolicking polar bears, white whales and nesting Thayer gulls along the spectacular coastline. Seven years' experience. Includes: Tents, stoves, cooking equipment, food and any technical gear necessary. Dates: July. Length: 11 days. Group size: 8. Cost: $2,150. Special requirements: $500 deposit, balance due 60 days prior to departure. Moderate to strenuous.

Everglades Canoe Outfitters
39801 Ingraham Highway
Homestead, FL 33034
305-246-1530   *Florida*

The Everglades invites you to explore its mysteries. Canoe and camp along winding trails through creeks, rivers and open bays in the mangrove wilderness of the park. Your naturalist guide will lead you through areas few people have seen and explain how the plant, marine and animal life interact. Spot scarlet ibis, spoonbill, herons, egrets and storks. See alligators and watch for the elusive Everglades mink. You will also find such tropical plants as orchids, bromeliads, buttonwood, and giant leather fern. Everglades Canoe Outfitters schedules seven-day and twelve-day trips to let you completely immerse yourself in this rare and endangered area. These are trips for doers—folks who'd rather paddle than ride, who enjoy working together and sharing the camp chores. Everglades Canoe Outfitters operates under a contract with Everglades National Park. Includes: From arrival at Outfitters, double-occupancy at hotel. Dates: November through May. Length of trip: 7, 9, or 12 days. Group size: Maximum of 9 people per guide. Cost: $439–$695 per person. Special requirements: Some experience in canoeing and camping is helpful but not necessary. $100 per person deposit.

Hugh Glass Backpacking Company
P.O. Box 110796
Anchorage, AK 99511
907-243-1922   *Alaska*

Let Hugh Glass Backpacking Company take you on a journey back into the Ice Age. Hugh Glass Backpacking offers a variety of trips on the spectacular rivers of the Alaskan wilderness. Float trips in road-accessible areas are conducted in aluminum canoes, while durable Klepper kayaks are used for air-accessible areas. Kleppers are used in the Kenai Fjords National Park, where the deep blue North Pacific meets and the wildlife exists as it has for the past one thousand years. Canoes are used on the 125-mile Wild River in Central Brooks Range. The absence of demanding stretches of whitewater make this a relaxing canoe trip. Daylight is a twenty-four-hour phenomenon, so there is plenty of time to fish, hike and photograph. The Hubbard Glacier trip offers an opportunity to witness the great glacier as it thunders seaward. The Noatak River begins as meltwater high up in Brooks Range and gradually courses its way through canyons and forests to the Bering Sea four hundred miles distant. Entirely above the Arctic Circle, this trip is best traveled by Klepper. Forested with birch and spruce, the Swanson River and lakes system offers a wonderful canoe adventure. The waters are clear and support a population of rainbow trout and Dolly Vardon char. Hugh Glass Backpacking has been in business for ten years and is a certified member of the Alaskan Wilderness Guides' Association. Includes: Round-trip transportation from Anchorage, boats, tents, group gear, meals and guides. Dates: June through September. Length of trip: 5–14 days. Group size: 2–6. Cost: $375–$1,500. Special requirements: 20% deposit.

Jamaica Camping and Hiking Association
P.O. Box 216
Kingston 7, Jamaica
809-927-5409   *Jamaica*

Imagine sunrise over the spectacular Blue Mountains—or the crystal clear waters of a river surrounded by lush, exotic beauty. This is Jamaica—a jewel-like setting for a canoe trip, with plenty of places to swim, or just cool off, after an exciting run over one of the many breath-taking rapids to be conquered. Birds and butterflies accompany you on your water journey and play in the sun as you relax by a secluded waterfall—an idyllic spot for lunch. Back at campsite around sunset, your evening can be spent in Kingston—full of restaurants and reggae. The Jamaica Camping & Hiking Association, with the cooperation of SOBEK Expeditions, has pulled together the first-ever River Canoe Trips of Jamaica—the land of many rivers. Includes: Transport, 2 nights' camping, all equipment, 3 meals and 2 guides. The choice of the river depends on the group's interest and weather conditions. There are 2 rivers on which the canoeing can be combined with a leisurely 2½ hour bamboo raft trip on the lower reaches—for this option there is an additional $15 per person. Dates: Year-round. Length: 2 days. Group size: 4–20 people. Cost: $95. Special requirements: Participants must be swimmers, 50% deposit.

Karpes and Pugh Company
P.O. Box 5152
Whitehorse, Yukon
Canada Y1A 2S3
403-668-4899   *Canada*

Retrace the paths of the nineteenth-century adventurers who journeyed the Yukon water-ways in search of fur and gold. The Yukon still counts more caribou, moose and bear among its population than people, and the Teslin, Yukon and Big Salmon rivers offer the adventure of a lifetime. Karpes and Pugh offer a ten-day excursion over 250 miles of the Teslin and Yukon rivers, from Johnson's Crossing to Carmacks, and a separate eleven-day trip on 150 miles of the Big Salmon River. There is ample time to visit abandoned Gold Rush villages like Hootalinqua, Teslin Crossing, Big Salmon Village and more. However, fishing is the order of the day: for Arctic grayling, northern pike and more. Gus Karpes and Irene Pugh have been in the wilderness business for over ten years and are steeped in the lore and history of the Yukon. Includes: Meals, transportation to and from start and end points, canoes, tents and group equipment. Dates: May through September. Length of trip: 10 and 11 days. Group size: 4–15. Cost: $1,100 (Canadian).

Mainstream Outfitters
P.O. Box 51
Canton, CT 06019
203-272-8053   *Connecticut*

Tired of doing the same old thing with your weekend? Then a canoe trip along the Connecticut River could be the answer. It's a special way to get away from it all and relax as you paddle from Middletown to Old Saybrook along a scenic route, passing lush foliage, green rolling hills in the distance and famous Gillette Castle. The waters are quiet throughout the trip and an expert guide will provide instruction for those who wish. Tour operator has ten years' experience. Includes: Canoes, tents, paddles, life-jackets, guide instructor, meals.

Dates: Every weekend, May through October. Length of trip: Friday evening to Sunday afternoon. Group size: 20–25. Cost: $55. Special requirements: No canoeing experience needed. Guide will provide instruction.

Pacific Adventures
P.O. Box 5041
Riverside, CA 92517
714-684-1227   *California*

Return to a more primitive era—canoe on California's mighty Colorado River. Enjoy a slow drift through the canyonlands, reedy marshes and still backwaters as did your Indian predecessors. Pacific Adventures' California excursion is a two-and-one-half day trip through the volcanic canyonlands of the Topock Gorge and the backbays of the the Havasu Wildlife Refuge. A leisurely pace of nine miles a day will be punctuated with stops to play beach volleyball, hike, swim, visit Indian petroglyphics, and enjoy Pacific Adventures' famous outdoor barbeque. Includes: Round-trip transportation from Riverside, outdoor gourmet meals, canoes, and recreational gear. Dates: April through October. Length: 2½ days. Group size: 8–20. Cost: $169. Special requirements: 25% deposit.

Pacific Adventures
P.O. Box 5041
Riverside, CA 92517
714-684-1227   *Utah*

Pacific Adventures offers a spectacular canoe trip through the canyons and river valleys of the Colorado plateau in Utah's Canyonlands National Park. The trip begins in Riverside with an air-conditioned ride across the desert, through Las Vegas and on to Zion National Park for the first night of camping. A short driving tour of Zion will precede the trip to Green River State Park where canoeing and safety instruction will begin. The group, limited to fifteen, will spend ten leisurely days covering 120 miles of the Green River. There will be plenty of time for fishing, volleyball and relaxing, and stops to visit Navajo and Moki Indian dwellings, petroglyphics, outlaw hideouts and secret canyons. The canoeing ends at the confluence of the Green and Colorado rivers with a four-hour return trip by jet boat to Moab, Utah. Includes: Round-trip transportation from Riverside, three outdoor gourmet meals each day, canoes and canoe gear, jet boat pickup, tents and group gear. Dates: April through October. Length: 12 days. Group size: 15. Cost: $695. Special requirements: 25% deposit.

Pacific Adventures
P.O. Box 5041
Riverside, CA 92517
714-684-1227   *Alaska*

Take a canoe trip along the very backbone of the Continental Divide! Pacific Adventures' ten-day Alatna River excursion covers over two hundred miles of the majestic river, running right alongside the divide. You'll glide past the spectacular Endicott Mountains and the awesome Arrigetch Peaks, 150 miles north of the Arctic Circle. You will encounter moose, black bear and maybe even the magnificent Dall mountain sheep. Meals will be enhanced by salmon and pike pulled fresh from the river and bread baked right in camp. There will be day hikes and treks into the mountains to explore and photograph Arctic flora and fauna. The trip flows through the Brooks Range area with its panoramic views and fast-moving water.

White water will add additional excitement and move you rapidly toward the Eskimo village of Allakaket, where the expedition comes to a close. Includes: Flight from Fairbanks to Bettles, bush flight from Bettles into the Brooks Range and from Allakaket to Fairbanks, 2 nights' lodging in Fairbanks, gourmet meals, tents, canoes and canoe gear. Dates: Summer. Length: 10 days. Group size: 8–20. Cost: $1,795. Special requirements: 25% deposit.

Pacific Adventures
P.O. Box 5041
Riverside, CA 92517
714-684-1227   *Wyoming*

Variety is the spice of life, and Pacific Adventures' combination canoe/backpacking/raft Wyoming expedition offers a lively blend of activities. First, there is an air-conditioned two-day drive from Riverside, through Nevada and Utah to Yuma Lake, Salt Lake City, Wasatch National Forest and Teton National Park. Morning and afternoon canoeing begins on the Snake River and continues through Oxbow Bend to Jackson Hole, Wyoming. The trip continues with backpacking in the Cascade Canyon to set up camp in the south fork at the base of Grand Teton. The next few days are spent in fishing, day hikes, and relaxing around scenic wilderness spots like Alaskan Basin, Death Canyon, and Phelps Lake. The final stage is an exciting whitewater raft trip down the rapids of the Snake River. The return trip to Riverside features rest and relaxation stops in Salt Lake City and Las Vegas. Includes: Round-trip transportation from Riverside, 3 meals each day, canoe and raft gear, tents, campground fees and reservations. Dates: April through October. Length: 10 days, 9 nights. Group size: 8–20. Cost: Upon request. Special requirements: $100 deposit.

Pacific Rim Expeditions
P.O. Box 2474
Bellingham, WA 98227
206-676-8550   *Washington*

Located on Washington's inner coast, the lush San Juan islands provide a perfect setting for kayak touring. As you glide along the clear waters, dazzling wildflowers wave in the breeze ... seals clap their welcome ... birds such as loons, bald eagles and great blue herons soar overhead. No experience is necessary; Pacific Rim will teach you everything you need to know. They also offer kayak/whale watching expeditions to Baja's Sea of Cortez, calving ground for the Pacific gray whale; plus Alaska and British Columbia to observe humpback whales and the British Columbia killer whale. Includes: Kayaks, guides, dinners, and breakfasts, some transportation, camping equipment. Dates: All year. Length of trip: 2–16 days. Group size: 10 people. Cost: $85–$750. Special requirements: $100 deposit.

Quetico
Canoe
Adventures

Quetico Canoe Adventures
194 South Franklin Street
Denver, CO 80209   *Colorado,*
303-722-6482   *Montana, Utah, Wyoming*

Quetico Canoe Adventures provides quiet water canoe trips on six beautiful rivers in the Rocky Mountain West: The Yampa in northwestern Colorado, the North Platte in southeastern Wyoming, the Colorado River as it crosses from Colorado into Utah, the Gunnison in western Colorado, the Green in eastern Utah and the Missouri in Montana. The journeys offer the opportunity to view spectacular canyons, abundant wildlife, and Indian pictographs . . . learn about the history of the American West . . . and enjoy wilderness camping, good food and great company. Quetico Canoe Adventures also runs other trips across the country, including Missouri's Current River, and Florida's Everglades. Ten years' experience as rafting and canoeing guide and instructor. Includes: Two experienced guides, canoes, paddles, life jackets, cooking and eating utensils, tents, canoe practice, meals. Dates: May through October. Length of trip: 2 to 7 days. Group size: 10 to 20. Cost: $105–$425. Special requirements: No canoeing experience or conditioning requirements.

Quetico Canoe Adventures
194 South Franklin Street
Denver, CO 80209
303-722-6482   *Minnesota, Ontario*

Ontario's Quetico Provincial Park and Minnesota's Superior National Forest form a huge wilderness area of thousands of interconnected lakes, streams and waterfalls. Quetico Canoe Adventures currently uses outfitters in Ely, Minnesota and on the Gunflint Trail on the southern and eastern edges of the Quetico. The complete package includes canoe practice prior to all trips, making them appropriate even for rank beginners. Each trip has a different emphasis—fishing, laid-back, strenuous, family, fly-in, etc. Fantastic fishing and fresh blueberry-picking are other highlights. Been running safe and successful canoe trips in the Boundary Waters since 1976. Includes: Experienced guides, complete outfitting (including tents and sleeping bags), canoe practice prior to trip, arrangements for airport pick-up and lodging, boat tow or pontoon plane to the Canadian border. Dates: June through September. Length of trip: 5 to 10 days. Group size: 9, but can take up to 3 groups. Cost: $45–$75 per day. Special requirements: No previous canoeing experience or conditioning requirements, but participants should be prepared to sign on as "crew," not "passengers."

RANGE TOURS

Range Tours
1540 South Holly Street
Denver, CO 80222
303-759-1988
800-525-8509   *Utah*

Have fun kayaking the whitewaters of Utah's Green River. On early spring and summer trips the water volume of the Green often exceeds that of the Colorado River! The scenery is spectacular—sheer white cliffs overhang the water, shorelines are covered with box elder and wildlife is abundant. This trip runs through Dinosaur National Monument and the famous Warm Springs. Designed for the hardy adventurer, the weather can be fairly cool and the water is "wild." Includes: 6 days' kayaking, 5 days' camping; round-trip transportation from Moab, Utah to the Green River; all meals, group equipment, supplies. Dates: May, July and

August. Length of trip: 6 days, 5 nights. Group size: 8–10. Special requirements: Good physical condition.

River Roam, Inc.
367 Maple Street
Ashland, OR 97520
503-482-4776   *Oregon*

Although Zane Grey wrote about and made famous Oregon's Rogue River, he used the lesser-known Umpqua as his own personal retreat. No river holds more magic; its bedrock shapes strangely from bend to bend, steelhead flash deep in its pools, and the river falls steadily through a seemingly endless progression of rapids. Too small for rafting, the Umpqua is ideal for River Roam's inflatable canoes. Open on top like standard canoes, they have multiple air chambers for safety and buoyancy. River Roam also offers trips on the Rogue River, which provides both action-packed rapids and long stretches of calm water for extensive paddling. Includes: Deluxe meals, individual canoes, complete river equipment, instruction, guides, van support, round-trip transportation from Ashland. Dates: June through September. Length: 2 days on the Rogue, 3 days on the Umpqua. Group size: 12. Cost: $140 for the Rogue, $250 for the Umpqua. Special requirements: $50 deposit for the Rogue, $100 deposit for the Umpqua. Minimum age is 12.

River Roam, Inc.
367 Maple Street
Ashland, OR 97520
503-482-4776   *California*

River Roam believes that the right way to experience a river is through intimate involvement with it, and their paddle-yourself inflatable canoes offer just that kind of personal contact with the river. This trip runs the mighty Klamath River, flowing 175 miles from the Shasta Confluence to the Pacific Ocean. It offers every kind of water, from beginner sections to some of the wildest white water on the West Coast. The Klamath starts in Sage Brush Flats, pours through deep canyons and stands of redwoods to the salt flats. Bear, deer, elk, otter, mink and coyote frequent its shores, as do osprey, heron, eagles and smaller birds. The river also hosts one of the largest runs of salmon and steelhead. Thirty-two to forty miles will be covered in inflatable canoes which provide an exciting but stable ride. The Trinity and Salmon rivers, tributaries of the Klamath, may also be run. River Roam has eight years' experience on Oregon and California whitewater rivers. Both Robin Carey and Reider Peterson, tour operators, are licensed Commercial River Guides. Includes: Deluxe meals, individual canoes, complete river equipment, van support, pre-trip instruction, expert guides, round-trip transportation from Ashland. Group size: 12. Cost: $235–$250. Special requirements: Minimum age is 10 on shorter trips, 12 on longer. $100 deposit.

Saco Bound/Northern Waters Whitewater School
P.O. Box 113
Center Conway, NH 03813
603-447-2177   *Maine, New Hampshire*

Saco Bound offers canoe trips on the forty-three-mile stretch of the Saco River from Center Conway, New Hampshire to Hiram, Maine. This stretch is renowned for its crystal clear water and smooth sandy beaches. The Saco meanders through forests and farmlands, bound by stands of white pine, meadows, silver maple and studded marshes . . . all beneath the majestic White Mountains. In addition, Saco Bound has whitewater trips on the Androscoggin and flat water outings on the Magalloway River and Lakes Umbagog and Aziscoo. All areas are abundant with bear, deer, moose, fox, beaver, crane and eagles. Salmon and trout fishing is excellent. Saco Bound also runs the Northern Waters Whitewater School on the Androscoggin River, offering class II and III rapids. The School teaches both novice and advanced canoers and kayakers the techniques of paddling safely—and with style. The School also offers a five-day Junior Camp Session for children. Many of the staff are professional racers. Includes: Canoes and gear. School tuition covers gear, instruction and campsite. Dates: April through October. Length of trip: 1–7 days. Group size: Variable. Cost: $18.50 a day per canoe. School tuition is $40–$250. Special requirements: Deposit to reserve space.

Salmon River Outfitters
P.O. Box 307
Columbia, CA 95310
209-532-2766   *Idaho*

Go kayaking on Idaho's Salmon River! Owner-guided Salmon River Outfitters specializes in quality trips on their favorite river. Moments of excitement alternate with long periods of serenity, as you float through the majestic mountain landscapes. This evergreen river canyon is rich with history and wildlife, occupying the largest wilderness area in the continental United States. The Main Salmon trip is six days and eighty miles, with shorter options available. For hard-shell kayakers, Salmon River Outfitters also offers support trips, rental, and instruction. Twelve years' experience guiding trips on the Salmon and other western rivers. Includes: Guides, all boating equipment, inflatable and hard-shell kayaks, meals, some tents, naturalist guides, even a portable sauna. All you need is everyday clothing. Dates: April through October. Length of trip: six days, five days, three days. Group size: Maximum of 20. Cost: Varies.

Slickrock Kayak Adventures
P.O. Box 1400
Moab, UT 84532
303-963-3678   *Mexico*

Looking for a new winter vacation experience? Accompany Slickrock Adventures on a kayak trip down the fabulous Jatate River, deep in the jungles of Chiapas, in southern Mexico. The region, once a center of Mayan culture, is a mountainous area carved by the "Agua Azul" or turquoise waters. The Jatate is renowned for its warm waters (70°–80°), travertine formations, dams and cascades, which turn the rapids and drops into a fantasy land of slides, pools, chutes and waterfalls. Monkeys and macaws are often sighted among the banana and mahogany trees along the river's banks. The trip also includes a run through the famous Colorado Canyon of the Usumacinta River and the waterfalls and whitewater of the Santo Domingo River. Slickrock has been in operation since 1977. Includes: Everything except airfare. Dates: February through March. Length of trip: 18 days. Group size: 10. Cost: $1,350. Special requirements: $250 deposit. Beginners welcome.

Slickrock Kayak Adventures
P.O. Box 1400
Moab, UT 84532
303-963-3678   *Nepal*

Kayak the high-caliber rivers of exotic Nepal! Slickrock offers fascinating trips into this land of majestic mountains, ancient cultures and wide ranges of climates, flora and fauna. Several tours designed exclusively for kayakers are offered, and will be arranged according to the ability of the group members. Short two- and three-day runs will be complemented by longer raft-supported trips. Numerous scenic treks to the base of some of the most awesome peaks in the world are also available. Other options include expeditions to wild and remote river basins never explored by boaters. Slickrock Kayak Adventures has been in operation since 1977 and Cully Erdman, owner and operator, has been kayaking since 1971. Includes: Meals, accommodations, expert guides, kayaks and support rafts. Dates: February, March, September and November. Length: 21 or 28 days. Group size: 10. Cost: $1,495 and $1,950. Special requirements: 25% deposit.

Slickrock Kayak Adventures
P.O. Box 1400
Moab, UT 84532
303-963-3678   *Costa Rica*

Join Slickrock and explore beautiful Costa Rica in Central America. Costa Rica provides world-class rivers, pristine beaches, twelve thousand-foot active volcanoes and an internationally-heralded park system. Slickrock Kayak Adventures' regular eleven-day tour reaches deep into virgin jungle to explore the astonishing variety and abundance of flora and fauna. The whitewater is both challenging and warm. Slickrock Kayak Adventures' second option will be an exclusive expedition into unexplored territory, where several runs down completely new rivers will be attempted. This trip is for hardy, adventurous experts only. There will be strenuous hiking, portage and self-support, accompanied by extreme isolation. The reward is a chance of a lifetime, discovering some of the rare pockets of unexplored wilderness left on this planet. Slickrock Kayak Adventures also offers a twelve-day beginners' trip starting on flat waters, rivers and lakes and gradually progressing up to Class III waters. Slickrock Kayak Adventures has been in operation since 1977. Includes: Meals, kayaks, ground transportation, hotel accommodations, guides and porters. Dates: November through February. Length: 11–21 days. Group size: 10. Cost: $695–$769. Special requirements: 25% deposit.

Slickrock Kayak Adventures
P.O. Box 1400
Moab, UT 84532
303-963-3678   *Colorado*

Operating in the heart of Colorado's canyon country, Slickrock Kayak combines instructional clinics with the adventure of a river trip. Emphasis is on instruction and safety; the carefully structured program allows you to progress at your own speed. Trips are offered on the Dolores River, which drains the western slope of the San Juan Mountains through lush meadows and forests as it gradually cuts its way deep into a desert canyon; and on the Arkansas, nationally known for outstanding whitewater and mountain scenery. Beginning in the fourteen-thousand-foot Collegiate Range, the Arkansas contains over one hundred miles of rapids before entering the plains, where there are mellow stretches of easy water and the one-thousand-foot-deep Royal Gorge. Clinics are also run on Utah's Green River. Slickrock Kayak Adventures has been running these rivers since 1977. Instructors are American Canoe Association certified, with Utah Boatmen's licenses. Includes: Raft support, transportation, instruction, kayak equipment and meals. Dates: May through August. Length of trip: 5–6 days. Group size: 5–20 depending on the river trip. Cost: $295–$485. Special requirements: Minimum age is 13, beginners welcome, 25% deposit.

Sun Valley Trekking Company
P.O. Box 2200
Sun Valley, ID 83353
208-726-9595   *Alaska, Idaho*

Take an exhilarating ride on the Salmon River—or explore the waterways of Alaska—and do it in a kayak, the unique boat used by the Eskimos. You can learn how to handle this graceful, sliver-thin water craft in a special kayak school that tailors individual instruction according to experience and ability. So get ready to paddle your kayak through some unbelievably exciting waters! All personnel licensed by the Idaho Outfitters and Guides Board. Includes: Varies according to trip planned—everything from guide services and instruction only, to deluxe trip with all equipment, food and a French chef. Dates: June through September. Length: 1–5 days. Group size: 2–8 people. Cost: $50–$500. Special requirements: $150 non-refundable deposit, balance 30 days in advance of trip.

Sundance Expeditions, Inc.
14894 Galice Road
Merlin, OR 97532
503-479-8508   *Oregon*

Sundance Kayak School features one of the most comprehensive hardshell kayak programs available in the West. The basic nine-day program on the wild and scenic Rogue River is designed for beginners and teaches wilderness knowledge and whitewater skills. The Rogue can be demanding yet has ample stretches of easy, warm water, perfect for instructing novices. The beautiful canyons, beaches, forested hills and creeks are filled with a variety of wildlife. The first four days of the clinic are spent on day-long outings on increasingly difficult sections of the Rogue (Class I and II water). You will learn dry and wet exits, basic strokes, high and low braces, the Eskimo roll, eddy turns, ferrying, hydrology, surfing, kayak etiquette, safety and rescue. The fifth day is spent in Class III water to test skills and warm up for the final outing—a three-day trip covering forty miles of challenging whitewater. One instructor accompanies every five students and a support raft carries food, camping gear and safety equipment. Ten years' experience instructing kayaking. Includes: Instruction, kayak and gear, 5 days' and nights' lodging at Sundance Riverhouse, all meals, and group camp gear. Dates: June through September. Length of trip: 9 days. Group size: 10. Cost: $675. Special requirements: Average physical condition, minimum age is 14, 25% deposit.

Sunrise County Canoe Expeditions, Inc.
Cathance Lake
Grove Post, ME 04638
207-454-7708

Canada

Rising off the remote Labrador Plateau, cutting a spectacular glacial canyon through the Quebec North Shore, the Moisie River ranks among the world's finest wilderness whitewater trips. The river landscape is characterized by towering headlands and sheer cliffs up to two thousand feet tall; waterfalls cascade off the northern taiga above. A steady, dropping gradient provides the canoeist with many long, open, but navigable rapids (some portages). In September the climate is similar to fall in New England; bugs are gone, water level is ideal—providing an excellent opportunity to develop technical whitewater and tripping technique. Seventeen years' experience. Registered Maine Guides; member Eastern Professional River Outfitters, American Canoe Association. Includes: Services of professional guiding staff (all Registered Maine Guides), all food, canoes, gear, and float plane into river, railroad back out. Basically everything but personal clothing and sleeping bags. Dates: September. Length of trip: 10 days. Group size: Up to 10. Cost: $1,100, $1,900 for 2. Special requirements: Prior experience with extended river camping trips. At least some whitewater experience.

Rising off the remote Labrador Plateau, the Moisie River offers a spectacular setting for learning whitewater skills. (SUNRISE COUNTRY CANOE EXPEDITIONS, INC.)

Sunrise County Canoe Expeditions, Inc.
Cathance Lake
Grove Post, ME 04638
207-454-7708   *Maine*

Known and respected for combining the best of traditional northwoods guiding and canoe-manship with modern whitewater technique, Sunrise County Canoe has attracted some of the finest professional Maine Guides and canoeists in the northeast. Trips are run with integrity; with respect to aesthetics, instruction, and service. Although Sunrise County Canoe specializes in the handling of a canoe with both pole and paddle, people also come for flyfishing, duck hunting, and most popularly, just plain "river touring" on Maine's thousands of miles of canoeable waterways—from isolated lakes and streams to challenging whitewater rivers. Seventeen years' experience. All Registered Maine Guides. Member Eastern Professional River Outfitters and American Canoe Association. Includes: Services of Registered Maine Guide(s), hearty cuisine, all canoes, camping gear, and incidentals, transportation to and from river. Basically everything except personal clothing and sleeping bags. Dates: May through October. Length of trip: 4–12 days. Group size: 4–10. Cost: $70 per day (child and group rates available). Special requirements: Difficulty level of various rivers vary; there are itineraries suitable for novices to experts.

Ultrasports
P.O. Box 581
Lotus, CA 95651
916-626-8250   *California*

Learn to kayak and raft on California's wild and scenic rivers. Ultrasports is family-owned and operated, so hospitality is not forgotten. Also the very best equipment is used, including color video taping with instructional films. All classes are flexible with instruction at all levels. The company has its own on-river location, with a three-to-one, student-to-instructor ratio. Courses vary from one- to five-day duration with monthly specialty trips to various rivers such as North and Middle forks of the American, the Klamath, California's Salmon, Carson and others. Ten years of kayaking experience. Includes: Instruction, transportation, camping on river and all meals from breakfast the first day to lunch the last day. All equipment provided. Dates: May through September. Length of trip: 2–5 days. Group size: 6–25. Cost: $130–$350. Special requirements: ½ deposit is required to hold reservations.

Wilderness: Alaska/Mexico
Bissel Road, Dept. STB
Hunters, WA 99137
509-722-3263   *Alaska*

Kayak Alaska's Noatak River in the awe-inspiring Brooks Range, far north of the Arctic Circle. With its headwaters in the granite peaks of Mt. Igikpak, the unspoiled Noatak flows west through tundra and forests for over four hundred miles to Kotzebue Sound. The trip begins with a thirty-mile, one-week backpack trip in the Gates of the Arctic National Park. Although no trails exist, the backpacking is moderate; since packs weigh thirty-five to fifty-five pounds, good physical condition is necessary. Upon reaching the headwaters of the

Noatak, you'll continue with an eighteen-day float trip. Kayaking the Noatak is moderately easy; no previous experience is necessary and instruction will be provided on the river. You can join this trip for the backpack portion, kayak portion (one or two weeks) or both. Wilderness Alaska/Mexico also offers a very easy trip for young and old alike floating the Yukon River. You'll explore abandoned gold towns and trapper colonies, fish for salmon and pike, and photograph a variety of Arctic wildlife. Four years' experience. Includes: All meals in the field, tents, group gear and kayaks. Dates: July and August. Length of trip: 7–25 days. Group size: 6–12. Cost: $661–$1,838. Special requirements: Rafting or canoeing experience is helpful for the Noatak trip, although no kayaking experience is necessary for either trip.

Wilderness Expeditions
P.O. Box 755 Cooma
NSW 2630 Australia
(0648) 21 587   *Australia*

Australia offers some of the most beautiful whitewater country in the world. Wilderness Expeditions has chosen a number of rivers that will fill you with anticipation, concentration and ecstatic relief. The inflatable canoes and kayaks are virtually unsinkable and require no previous experience. You are taught to read rivers and manage your craft in even the roughest waters. Trips include the Thredbo, offering easy and exciting canoeing; the Mitchell River, Victoria's best-kept whitewater secret; and the Shoalhaven River, which has spent millions of years carving a spectacular whitewater route through coastal mountains. Includes: All boating gear, meals, camping equipment, guides, and instructors. Dates: September through April. Length of trip: 1–8 days. Group size: 3–8. Cost: $55 per day. Special requirements: Swimming ability.

Caving •

Picture this: You descend from the bright light of day into the grassy mouth of a chosen grotto. As you advance into the underground wilderness, your guide in the fore, the gentle glow from the entrance gives way to total darkness. There is absolute still silence in the air. Not even a wind whisper.

You become aware of two unfamiliar smells. The first is the acetylene smell emanating from the carbide lamp on your hard hat. The second, richer aroma is the deep smell of the subterranean world around you. You are breathing the smell of the inside of the earth.

As your eyes adjust, you begin to make out shapes in the darkness. The cavern glistens palely with the bewitching geometry of centuries-old speleothems: soda straws, canopies, stalagmites and stalactites.

The tunnel opens into a huge cavern: a natural rock enclosure the size of a basketball court. Giant stone formations spiral effortlessly upward toward the cavern's jagged ceiling. A good sized lake, its taut surface utterly unrippled, fills a far corner of the great hall.

Welcome to the world of caving, or spelunking. A magical world totally different from the experiences of the surface. Here, the standard sensations which we take for granted are suspended or distorted. Light and sound are conspicuously absent. Spelunkers' well-intended accounts of distances and lengths rival those of fishermen in their inaccuracy. Within the slow evolutionary rhythms of caves, sense of time evaporates—what are the spelunker's few subterranean hours compared with the thousands of years helectites take to form?

It's easy and relatively inexpensive for even dedicated surface dwellers to enter this strange world of the traglodytes.

1. Getting started. Even if you think soda straws are only found in drug stores, you can go on an exciting and vigorous spelunking expedition. Caving can be risky, so you should engage the services of experienced guides before you go down into the darkness. They'll outfit you and show you the ropes (literally), and make sure all members of your party find their way back topside. No experience is necessary for most trips, and you don't have to be a prime physical specimen—although it doesn't hurt.
2. Gear. Check whether the tour operator will provide key equipment—or if you should bring your own. You'll need at least a hard hat with a carbide or electric light on it. This will fill you with the pioneering spirit of exploration and help you see in the dark. Wear sturdy boots with lug soles for traction. Just as you won't ever be the same again after your first spelunking expedition, neither will your clothes. Cave dirt and mud permeate everything. Wear old clothes or clothes set aside for underworld. Clothing should be unrestrictive, and free of loose cloth that can get caught on projections. Woolen long underwear is a good idea. You'll also want a flashlight (this should hook onto your belt), extra carbide or batteries (ditto), candles, and matches in a waterproof container. Ask the operator for advice.
3. Safety. By thinking ahead, you'll minimize most caving hazards. You should only cave with an experienced guide. Avoid mine shafts—their decaying supports make them death traps. If you are separated from your group, stay where you are and yell to them. Your guides will come and get you. Finally, make sure all of your equipment is in good shape before you start. Don't wait until you are in the bowels of Mother Earth to discover a weak battery or a frayed rope.
4. What you'll see. Knowing the difference between a stalagmite and a stalactite creates a favorable first impression. The former rises from the ground; the latter hangs from the ceiling. Soda straws are hollowed stalactites. Col-

umns are the union of stalagmites with stalactites. Helectites are gravity-defying speleothems which spiral upward. You'll also see underground lakes, springs, and streams, in all shapes and sizes.

5. Photography. You can capture the beautiful eccentricities of caverns and speleothems using an ordinary camera equipped with a flash. Subterranean photos tend to have an other-worldly feel and striking color combinations. On film, caves show off their fragile intricacy.

6. The options. Expeditions can be relatively easy or grueling. You can go down for a few hours or you can spend the day chasing tunnels farther and farther beneath the earth's surface. With some experience, you can try your hand at vertical caving: rapelling down "chimneys" or along sheer rock faces. The possibilities are numerous—read up on the subject before you cement your plans.

Czechoslovakia Travel Bureau
10 East 40th Street
New York, NY 10016
212-689-9720
Telex 62467 AUW   *Czechoslovakia*

Visit the most famous of Czechoslovakia's caves. Various programs include the Harmanecka, an abyss cave; Gombasecka, Dobsinka ice cave; and Demanovska, known for its small lakes, stalactites and stalagmites. Or tour the caves of Bohemia and Moravia, including Koneprusy, a significant archeological site; the three-story Zlaty Kun cave; and Moravian Karst, famous for its variety of ravines, canyons, abysses and underground rivulets. Includes: Accommodations, all meals, transfers, guides and cave visits. Dates: Year-round. Length: 6 days. Group size: 15–35. Cost: $243–$309.

Sierra Nevada Recreation Corp.
P.O. Box 78
Vallecito, CA 95251
209-736-2708   *California*

California Caverns at Cave City is an extensive limestone cavern of unsurpassed beauty. Located in the heart of the Mother Lode, Cave City was a rich mining town in the days of the California Gold Rush when every adventurous soul "headed west." This spelunking tour is lead by experienced guides who relate the rich historical and geographical information about this area and provide expert instruction. No previous caving or mountain experience is necessary. You will spend five hours exploring, crawling and climbing slopes with ropes and ladders through the many challenges of this totally natural cavern. By raft, cross deep, crystal-clear lakes to go deeper into new passages and rooms that have only recently been discovered. Viewing the spectacular beauty of the crystalline formations, the deep lakes, large chambers and "jewel box" grottoes is an experience you'll always remember. Includes: Coveralls, gloves, helmets with lights. Qualifications: 16 years of operation in commercial caves, Western Regional Director of National Caves Assn. Dates: August through October. Length: 5 hours. Group size: 10. Cost: $49. Special requirements: Over 12 years old, good health. Reservations recommended.

Cooking •
Gourmet •

Certain aromas linger from childhood—the garlicky zing of fresh tomato sauce on the stove . . . rich golden crackle of a roasting chicken . . . warm melt of chocolate chip cookies just-emerged from the oven.

Although cooking has always been part of everyone's life, only in the last twenty years or so has cooking for fun become something of a reality. Now you'll find amateur cooks hotly debating the best way to glaze a duck, carve a turkey or sauce a fish. Food and its preparation has become an important ingredient in people's lives—not out of necessity, but for pure pleasure.

Because of this tremendous interest in fine food, there has been an increase in the quality and variety of cooking courses available for all levels of chefs—from novice to expert. The programs vary widely in content—from visits and meals at famous restaurants; to hands-on cordon bleu classes; to courses concentrating on one type of cuisine. You can experiment with French novelle cuisine or try your hand at the many sauces of China, delve into the exotic herbs and spices of Middle Eastern cooking or master the subtle elegance of Japanese sushi.

Whether you try a cooking course in New York or Normandy, oftentimes where the course is held will be as interesting as what's simmering on the stove. Many courses are conducted in old castles with fascinating histories, or in stately homes with remarkable stories hidden behind the walls.

When choosing a gourmet program, keep a few questions in mind:

1. What kind of a tour is it? Visits and tastings at world-famous restaurants or participatory, learn-to-cook lessons?
2. If it's a cooking class, do you participate or observe? What level of cook is it geared to—novice or pro? How many sessions/hours a day? How many students in each session? Will everyone be able to observe/participate easily? What is the cooking background of your instructor?
3. Will you receive copies of the recipes worked on? Are notebooks provided?
4. Check what the tour price covers—are the featured meals in famous restaurants included or do they cost extra? If it's a cooking class, do you get to sample what's been prepared? Will there be an entire meal at the end of each lesson?
5. Where will you be staying? What is the availability of other recreational activities nearby? Are there any activities available for non-cooks with whom you may be traveling? Do non-cook travel companions get reduced rates?

The following cooking courses offer a wide range of tastes and levels for you to choose from.

93

A Taste of the Mountains Cooking School
P.O. Box 381
Glen, NH 03838
603-383-4414   *New Hampshire*

Here's a perfect vacation for those who love to cook, love good food and want to expand their cooking repertoire. The course is designed to broaden practical knowledge of classical French cooking and nouvelle cuisine. Emphasis is on the basic building blocks of French cuisine—sauces and pastries—as well as fanciful garnishes and cake decorating. You'll learn the step-by-step preparations of delicacies like duckling with olives, smoked fish crepes, herbed cheese tartlets and Chocolate Marquis. Both the five-day course and the weekend course feature intensive lessons, gourmet picnics, luncheons and dinners. The setting is the lovely three-star (Mobil) Bernerhof Inn, in the heart of Mount Washington Valley. Steven Raichlen, instructor, is the food critic for *Boston Magazine* and is a graduate of both Cordon Bleu and La Varenne. Includes: Lodging, all meals, wine and tuition. Dates: September and May. Length: Weekends (Friday–Sunday) and midweek (Sunday–Friday). Group size: 8–10. Cost: $200–$500. Special requirements: $50–$100 deposit.

Art-in-Action
45 Griffen Avenue
Scarsdale, NY 10583
914-725-3480
914-698-0080   *New York*

See New York in a new light. Join Mimi Livingston, Director of Art-in-Action, for a gourmet tour of the Big Apple's ethnic enclaves, art and antique districts, and chic residential areas. Art-in-Action lets you sample, snack, nosh and nibble with the makers and bakers, cookers and caterers, smokers and stuffers in their shops, schools, homes and restaurants. The company can also arrange meals and tastings in many of the city's two- and three-star bistros, brasseries and restaurants; gourmet cooking lectures and demonstrations with renowned chefs; and combinations of gourmet dining with art, antique and architectural tours. Includes: Meals with wine, lectures, demonstrations and tours. Dates: All year. Length of trip: Half day, full day, evening, lunch and dinner hour. Group size: 8–100. Cost: Variable.

Association
des amis
de la cuisine
et des traditions
provençales

Association des amis de la Cuisine
et des Traditions Provençales
Les Megalithes
84220 Gourdes
France
16.90 72.23.41   *France*

Enjoy a sunny gourmet holiday in the heart of Provence, the culturally rich region in the south of France. You'll stay and cook at the Megalithes—a charming stone country house set among pine trees in the villages of Gourdes, near Avignon. Learn the secrets of the famous provençal specialties, such as daube de boeuf or bouillabaisse. In summer, have a cooling swim in the pool and in fall and winter, enjoy the warmth of the fireplace. Includes: Private room with bath, all meals and tuition. Dates: All year, except August. Length of trip: 1 week. Group size: 5–6. Cost: 1,400 French Francs.

Catercall Cookery Courses
109 Stephendale Road
London SW6 2PS England
1 731 3996   *Great Britain*

Catercall Cookery runs half-day to two-week-long sessions throughout the year in stately homes in and near London. The homes are as interesting as the classes and include Blackdown House, a stone-built Cromwellian mansion in Surrey; Winslow House, a privately-owned seventeenth-century home; Darney Court, a Tudor Manor house, home to the Peregrine Palmers for over four hundred years; and Mentmore Towers, the Buckinghamshire home of the Rothschilds. The cookery courses change every three months but certain basics are always covered: English cooking from the Middle Ages to the present; contemporary French, Italian, Middle-Eastern and Chinese cuisine; wine appreciation; game preparation; baking; entertaining; and flower arrangement. Michele Berriedale-Johnson, Catercall Cookery Courses' owner and director, is an English food expert who writes, lectures and broadcasts regularly in the U.K. and U.S.A. Includes: Tuition, food, demonstration/participation and accommodations. Dates: All year. Length: ½ day to 2 weeks. Group size: 8–100. Cost: Approximately $30 a day. Special requirements: 10% deposit, full payment 3 weeks before class.

Cook 'N' Tour
Johnson & Wales College
8 Abbott Park Place
Providence, RI 02903
401-456-1120   *Rhode Island*

Cook 'N' Tour invites you to Rhode Island for a long weekend of gastronomical adventure. You are welcomed Friday evening with a gala cocktail and dinner party. Saturday begins with a hearty breakfast at the Plantation Room of the Rhode Island Inn, then on to classes at the Culinary Center. Cook 'N' Tour's weekend themes feature Italian Festa, Alfresco buffets, lavish but light entertaining, seafood cookery, classical cuisine, and festive buffets. You'll also learn some advanced bartending—how to whip up drinks, and how to stock, set-up and estimate quantities for your home bar. The day ends with a lavish classical banquet, in the Old World tradition of white-gloved service. Sunday includes another complete breakfast and a tour of the southern coastal area of Rhode Island. Smith's Castle, the harborside village of Wickford, and Newport are among the highlights. Includes: Accommodations, meals, classes, tours and instruction material. Dates: Spring and summer. Length: Friday through Sunday. Group size: 15–40. Cost: Approximately $250.

EXPLORE

Forum Travel International
2437 Durant Avenue, #208
Berkeley, CA 94704
415-843-8294   *France*

Forum Travel offers a delightful traditional cooking course in Quercy, France. The five-day program covers the essentials of French cuisine from a simple tourin (soup) to a complicated daube (stew). You also learn to make pâté, sausage, cassoulet, pork confit (preserved in its own fat), and many pastries and desserts. Classes run from nine a.m. to twelve-thirty p.m., followed by lunch from twelve-thirty to two-thirty. Afternoons are filled with visits to neighboring vineyards; *Bastides*—fortified villages dating from the twelfth and thirteenth centuries; museums, chateaus and prehistoric caves. Accommodations are in the school's seventeenth-century manor house or two- and three-star hotels. Includes: Accommodations, breakfast, lunch, dinner for hotel residents, lessons and ground transportation. Dates: Summer and fall. Length: 1 week and up. Group size: 2–20. Cost: From $438.

Giuliano Bugialli's Cooking in Florence
2830 Gordon Street
Allentown, PA 18104
215-435-2451 *Italy*

Cooking in Florence was the first cooking school in Italy to be taught in English. Founded in 1973, the school combines the finest cooking instruction with an immersion in the life and culture of Italy. Florence is known as the "mother of modern European culture" and the classes are centered here; however, there are also trips to Piemonte, Veneto, Umbria and Montcatini. Each dish is authentic and taught so that it may be reproduced at home. They range from a little-known "torta" of Genoa to a classic fish dish of Sardinia and other delicacies. Lectures, demonstrations and student participation takes place in the airy elegance of the Florentine teaching kitchen. Classes are scheduled in the morning and are followed by lunch and a tasting of wines from the school's cellar. Dinners are in elegant restaurants and rustic trattories. Other activities include market and vineyard visits, sightseeing tours, concerts and ballets. Autumn classes specialize in game and truffle preparation. Includes: Tuition, field trips, special dinners, art tours, sightseeing and accommodations. Dates: June through October. Length: 6–11 days. Group size: 15–20. Cost: Variable. Special requirements: Basic knowledge of cooking. Companion may accompany students at a reduced cost.

Guides for All Seasons

Guides for All Seasons
P.O. Box 97
Carnelian Bay, CA 95711
917-583-8475 Call Collect *Japan*

Martin and Chizuko Waller bring together their expertise in cooking and knowledge of Japan to create a tour that will delight the most discriminating palate and entertain any gourmet cook. Chizuko, native Tokyo resident and English interpreter, and Martin, an accomplished San Francisco Bay Area chef, are a dynamic team. You'll tour Tokyo, Kyoto, Kanazawa Peninsula and Kobe to learn about and sample some of Japan's best regional dishes. Though the cuisine varies significantly throughout the country, it is all characterized by the gentle handling of fresh ingredients and simple elegance of presentation. Most people are aware of the tempura, sushi and sukiyaki so popular in Tokyo. Less widely known and equally interesting are the traditional Kaiseki cuisine of the historical capitol Kyoto, the beef of Kobe, and seafood of the coastal regions. The simple, nutritious soba noodles of Tokyo and hearty udon of the Kansia area are also of gastronomical interest. From visits to the local fish and produce markets to demonstrations from expert chefs (with English explanations) you will gain a practical knowledge of Japanese food preparation. All demonstrations will end with a meal of what has been prepared. Includes: All lodging, ground transportation, demonstrations of Japanese cuisine preparation, translators, bi-lingual guides, most meals. Dates: May, October, February. Length of trip: 12 days. Group size: Maximum of 16. Cost: $1,800.

The Grange Cookery School
The Grange, Beckington
Bath, Avon BA3 6TD England
(0373) 830607   *Great Britain*

The Grange occupies the central part of historic Beckington Abbey, which dates from the early Tudor period. Three courses are offered. Course I: The four-week "Basic to Béarnaise" program covers how to prepare everything from hors d'oeuvres to desserts, including sauces, soups, and breads. Course II: A four-day, "self-preservation" course for people with little or no knowledge of cooking. Everyday methods are demonstrated and simple recipes are demonstrated and practiced. Course III: "Food with Flair." Also four days, this course is designed for those with some practical knowledge. Lessons cover tried-and-true shortcuts, basic techniques, and "everyday" French cooking. Specialties include gratin dauphinois, Italian seafood salad, gnocchi, rough puff pastry, and creme brulee. Includes: Food and wine with dinner, tuition and accommodations (weekends are extra). Dates: All year except June. Length of trip: 4 days or 4 weeks. Group size: 1–7. Cost: £125–£500.

Unravel Travel
660 Market Street
San Francisco, CA 94104
415-398-8330   *California*

This is a tour of San Francisco and the nearby Napa and Sonoma Valleys for those who enjoy fine eating and good wines. Tour members are given an insider's view of the city and surrounding areas, dining in several of the most outstanding restaurants of the Bay Area and visiting several exceptional wineries. In San Francisco, you'll stay at the charming Bedford Hotel, and in Wine Country at the glamorous Sonoma Mission Inn. Among the restaurants where the groups dine are the California Culinary Academy, Chez Panisse in Berkeley, and the Mandarin Restaurant. In the Napa Valley there is a lunch at Auberge du Soleil and another at the Depot Hotel in Sonoma. In business fourteen years. Martha Nell Crow, co-owner, has written books on San Francisco and the area. Includes: Hotel, several special meals; transportation. Dates: May and October. Length of trip: 7 days. Group size: 15 to 20. Cost: $795.

Unravel Travel
660 Market Street
San Francisco, CA 94104
415-398-8330   *Italy*

This tour centers on cooking classes at Lo Scaldavivande Cookery Club in Rome. Classes are conducted by American-born Jo Bettoja, who published "Italian Cooking in the Grand Tradition" in 1983. In addition, one day Jo Bettoja takes the group to visit the famous food market at Piazza Vittorio, and another day she hosts a luncheon at her country home in Caprarola. The group stays at the Hotel Mediterraneao, which is owned and operated by the Bettoja family. Leading the group is Sharon Shipley, San Francisco Bay Area cooking teacher. Includes: Cooking classes (four) with sightseeing and several special meals. Dates: Spring. Length of trip: Week. Group size: 10. Cost: $900 (approximately).

Voyages Sans Frontieres, U.K.
Travel Concepts
191 Worcester Road
Princeton, MA 01541
617-464-2933   *Europe*

The Cooking Class is a fifteen-day program that includes three nights each in Europe's two major capitals, London and Paris, plus a full week at a French cooking school near Mont-Saint-Michel in Normandy. In London and Paris, you'll enjoy guided sightseeing and special behind-the-scenes "kitchen visits" to some of these cities' best restaurants. Then you'll travel to the beautiful Normandy region of France for a week of lectures, demonstrations and classes at an exclusive cooking school, as well as included excursions to Caen, Bayeux, St. Malo, Mont-Saint-Michel, and the Normandy beaches. Fifteen years' experience in speciality group travel. Includes: Transatlantic air transportation; first-class accommodation; meals; transfers; lectures, demonstrations and classes at the Cooking School; kitchen visits in London and Paris; full-time courier; sightseeing. Dates: Year-round. Length of trip: 15 days. Group size: 10–15. Cost: $1,500.

Crafts •

Captivating the eye of the beholder is the aim of the craftsperson—whether engaged in weaving tapestries in Brazil, dollmaking in Japan, glassblowing in Italy or needlework in England. If you have a favorite hobby—sewing, embroidery or carpentry—why not make it the center of your next vacation? As you travel, you'll discover how far along other peoples and cultures are in their knowledge and expertise of the same craft you pursue with such relish. It's fun and informative to swap tidbits and share information with a variety of people from around the world. At the same time, your appreciation and love for the beauty of a fine handicraft can help you understand a widely divergent culture, and make you feel more at home in a foreign country.

Many cultures have highly-developed folk arts which are vanishing—there are not enough people to pursue the making of a craft, and not enough people interested in buying. But your interest and enthusiasm can help keep alive some of the painstaking skills that have been passed down for generations.

The following craft tours provide an opportunity to pursue and appreciate folk arts from every corner of the globe.

Brazilian Views, Inc.
201 East 66th Street, Suite 21G
New York, NY 10021
212-472-9539   *Brazil*

The transformation of fibers for practical use and artistic expression has been prevalent throughout Brazil for centuries. Among this tour's highlights is a visit to Madeleine Colaco's house/studio outside of Rio de Janeiro. One of the foremost tapestry artists in the world, her work combines the technical perfection and patience of Europe and North Africa with the brilliant tropicalism of Brazil. You'll also tour a workshop in Salvador, Bahia that gives courses in needlework, lacemaking, weaving and ceramics. Other features include a schooner trip to the Island of Mare to see lace makers at work; an Afro-Brazilian folkloric show; a visit to Tracunhaem, outside of Recife, Pernambuco, famous for its folk clay sculptors and potters. Includes: Round-trip airfare US/Brazil; air and ground transportation in Brazil; accommodations; breakfast daily plus several other meals; transfers; guides. Dates: May through October. Length of trip: 15 days. Group size: 15–36. Cost: Around $3,000.

**Country
Homes
&
Castles**

Country Homes and Castles
138A Piccadilly, London W.1
London, England
(01) 491 2584
Telex 24609   *Great Britain*

Cherish the past, adorn the present, create for the future—needleworkers can claim success in carrying out this motto, and you'll understand why on this specialized tour to England.

Highlights include: fun-filled London; a private visit to Gawthorpe Hall, home of an extensive collection of delicate needlework and crafts dating from the seventeenth century to the present day; needlepoint sessions where you'll pick up new ideas and new stitches while studying needlework in British country houses; private lunches with experts in the crafts field. In addition, there's plenty of sightseeing to savor ... the magnificent walled city of Chester ... the shores of Loch Lomond ... the remote island of Gigha, home of wildflowers and tranquility ... and the scenic drive to the city of Edinburgh. Seven years' experience. Includes: Bed and breakfast in London, all meals on tour, lectures and tuition on needlepoint, visits to private collections and a day at Gawthorpe Hall, Royal School of Needlework, Embroiderers Guild. Dates: September. Length: 15 days. Group size: 20 persons. Cost: £1,465. Special requirements: $250 deposit.

Directions Unlimited Travel
344 Main Street
Mt. Kisco, NY 10549
914-241-1700   *Japan*

Join Shay Pendray and Directions Unlimited for a rich and exciting tour of the crafts and needle arts of Japan. The trip begins in Tokyo where you have the choice of attending one of three seminars: Japanese doll-making, gold and silk embroidery, or traditional Rosashi. The trip goes on to include an exclusive tour of the renowned Kurenai Kai School of Traditional Japanese embroidery, plus visits to silk and textile mills, puppet-makers and potteries. You'll also visit the seven-hundred-year-old Daibutsu ("Great Buddha"), relax in hot spring baths within sight of Mt. Fuji; participate in traditional Japanese tea ceremonies and enjoy sightseeing in Kyoto, Nara, Kurashiki and Kagoshima. In operation over fifteen years. Includes: Accommodations, most meals, ground transportation, bilingual guides, seminars, sightseeing, taxes and tips. Dates: Spring, summer and fall. Length of trip: 17 days. Group size: 15–25. Cost: From $1,598.

Directions Unlimited Travel
344 Main Street
Mt. Kisco, NY 10549
914-241-1700   *Italy*

Directions Unlimited offers this connoisseur's tour of Italy specially designed for embroiderers and those interested in the crafts of Italy. The tour features visits to private workshops, homes, and museums not usually open to the general public. You will visit the beautiful and charming cities of Milan, Stresa, Venice, Bologna, Florence, Assisi and Rome. The program also includes trips to La Scala Opera House, the Duomo, Basilica San Marco, Saint Mark's Square, Pantheon, Colosseum, Roman Forum and much, much more. Special crafts highlights include trips to a traditional lacemaking school and museum, a glass-blowing factory, textile and leather centers, and needlework and antiques throughout the region. This tour is led by Vima Micheli, a noted teacher and lecturer on needlework and embroidery. In operation over fifteen years. Includes: Accommodations, most meals, lectures, museums, and sightseeing, guides, taxes and tips. Dates: Spring, summer and fall. Length of trip: 15 days. Group size: 15–25. Cost: From $1,598.

Forum Travel International
2437 Durant Avenue, #208
Berkeley, CA 94704
415-843-8294   *China*

Forum Travel has constructed this three-week tour of Mainland China to cover the two principal categories of the indigenous textile design of the country: folk art patterns, mainly produced in Southern and Western China by peasants and minority nationalities; and traditional weaving and embroidery produced for export in the major textile centers of Eastern China. This itinerary permits extensive exploration of China's immense textile arts production, as well as some other crafts. Major historical and natural sites will also be visited, with ample free time for individual exploration in cities like Beijing, Xi'an, Shanghai, Suzhou, Hong Kong and more. You'll also tour the Forbidden City, Palace Museum, the Great Wall, National Art Gallery and other interesting sites. In operation since 1965. Includes: All air and land transportation from San Francisco, accommodations, meals, sightseeing, bilingual guides, visas, taxes and tips. Dates: Once every year, usually September. Length of trip: 22 days. Group size: Up to 32. Cost: $3,488.

Forum Travel International
2437 Durant Avenue, #208
Berkeley, CA 94704
415-843-8294   *Peru*

Peru nurtured the greatest golden age of textile arts the world has ever seen. Forum Travel explores textile and folk arts, costumes, villages, dances, handicrafts, foods, ruins, music and peoples of the ancient Peruvian culture. You will stay overnight in the "Lost City of the Incas," Machu Picchu; meet with local artisans; visit outstanding private and public collections of Incan and pre-Incan artifacts; visit archeological ruins; and tour Cuzco, Lima and other sites of interest. One need not be a weaver textile artist to enjoy this trip into one of the world's oldest cultures. An optional six-day extension visiting Lake Titicaca and the archeological sites of Taquile Island is also available. In operation since 1965. Includes: Accommodations, most meals, all land costs, ground transportation, sightseeing, taxes and tips. Dates: Spring, summer and fall. Length of trip: 16 days. Group size: 2–20. Cost: $1,717.

Cruises •

In this book, we've taken a special point of view about cruises. We think they should be very unique, very intense vacation experiences. That's why you'll find no gigantic ocean liners listed here. Instead, you'll find more thoughtful and unusual voyages, where you'll be able to savor the stark beauty of a glacier, watch a whale, or explore an enchanted isle of Greek mythology.

Adventure cruises are only limited by your imagination—you can pick from:

- Journeying along the mighty MacKenzie in Canada's Northwest Territories—one of the world's longest rivers.
- Passing remote jungle villages as you cruise the Amazon from Peru to Colombia.
- Island-hopping in the Aegean.
- Taking a traditional Indian barge ride past ageless shrines and ancient villages along the Ganges.

There are cruises for everyone, on every type of boat, from luxury ships with air conditioning, heating and private facilities to fifty-seven-foot sleek yachts to small sturdy boats equipped to sail around the world.

The best thing about cruises is their all-inclusive feature. You know what your trip will cost before you leave home. (Just check whether shore excursions are included in cost.)

Some Points to Remember

Find out precisely what the accommodations are and what kind of ship you'll be traveling on. Perhaps the ship is slightly less pretty but sturdier for rough waters, or perhaps the ship travels faster than others doing the same route and therefore can include more stops in the same amount of time.

If a cruise is for special interests (nature trip, archeology) ask if an expert guide will be on board to give information about what you're seeing.

Get an idea about how loose or structured the voyage is—are all stops scheduled, or will the captain play it by ear?

How do you get to and from the ship at beginning and end of cruise? Are transfers included?

If this is a combination cruise/land excursion, find out about sleeping arrangements at night . . . tents? Who supplies the camping gear?

Alaska Travel Adventures
200 N. Franklin Street
Juneau, AK 99801
907-586-6245
800-227-8480 Toll free   *Alaska*

Alaska Travel Adventures offers a varied cruise/hike/river raft adventure. First, board your ship in Vancouver, B.C. and cruise Alaska's spectacular Inside Passage with ports of call at Ketchikan and Juneau. At Juneau, two hike and float options are available—along the historic Chilkoot Trail or in Denali National Park. Those who choose the Chilkoot Trail will follow the footsteps of the Gold Rushers of '98—hiking, viewing artifacts and reading Robert

Service poetry around the campfire. To cap the trip, paddle a raft from Lake Lindemann to Lake Bennett. If you choose Denali National Park, you'll camp out within sight of Mount McKinley, breathe the fresh mountain air, raft the Nenana River's famed whitewater and spend a night in a rustic cabin after a moonlit hot tub soak. Founded 1979. Includes: One-way cruise aboard cruise ship, all meals, guide services, camping gear, group equipment and connecting transportation. Dates: June through August. Length of trip: 9–10 days. Group size: 12–16 people. Cost: from $1,475. Special requirement: Good health. Advance deposit to confirm reservations.

Alaska Travel Adventures
200 N. Franklin Street
Juneau, AK 99801
907-586-6245
800-227-8480 Toll free
Telex 090-45380   *Alaska*

Experience the many facets of Southeast Alaskan culture, activities and natural history when you take a cruise along this breathtaking region. The round-trip cruise begins and ends in Vancouver, B.C., with diversified ports of call. During a stop in Ketchikan, you'll learn about the native Indian culture and try to master the art of paddling the awesome Indian war canoes. In Sitka, you'll explore the spectacular inland waterways teeming with marine life. In Juneau, you can tackle whitewater rafting and feel the surge of excitement as the wet spray hits you in the face. And in Skagway, you'll get the feel of the Gold Rush days when fortunes were made—and lost—overnight! Includes: 7-night round-trip cruise with all meals and shore excursions, guides, special equipment, local transportation. Dates: June through September. Length of trip: 8 days, 7 nights. Group size: 24 maximum. Cost: Starts at $1,300. Special requirements: Good health. Deposit required to confirm reservation.

Australian Travel Service
116 So. Louise Street
Glendale, CA 91205
213-247-4564   *Australia*

In the land of kangaroos and koalas, here's a chance to cruise through the Whitsunday Passage and see and feel the beauty and grandeur of the Great Barrier Reef. There will be fascinating looks at Hayman, South Molle, Brampton, Happy Bay, Lindeman and Dent Islands . . . and your ship comes equipped with glass-bottom boats for coral viewing like you've never seen before. You'll also travel to the Atherton Tableland with its tobacco plantations, exquisite rain forests and the Crater Lakes district. Includes: Cabin; all meals on cruise; flight Mackay—Cairns; land transportation; hotels, guides, transfers. Length: 1 week. Cost: $830 per person double occupancy.

Cebu Cruises
1017 168th Avenue S.E.
Bellevue, WA 98008
(206) 746-3414   *Washington*

These relaxing cruises through the Northwest Passages are offered for non-smokers only. The eleven-day cruise aboard the fifty-two-foot diesel yacht "Cebu" starts in Seattle's Lake

Union. From here, you'll head north to the beautiful San Juan Islands of Washington. Cruising forty to fifty miles per day, you journey through the picturesque Gulf Islands lying just east of Vancouver Island, then across the Strait of Georgia to the mainland. Jervis Inlet leads you through Malibu Rapids into the breathtakingly beautiful Princess Louise Inlet. Returning on Jervis Inlet you'll see changing vistas at every turn. En route to your northern terminus at Cortes Bay, you will treasure the solitude of Desolation Sound, the unspoiled Redonda Islands, and rugged Toba Inlet. After a night at Cortes Bay, a chartered seaplane will take you back to Lake Union in Seattle. Eight-day cruises from Cortes Bay to Lake Union also available. Includes: All meals, lodging aboard, shore tours, scenic 2-hour float plane flight. Dates: Mid-May through late September. Length of trip: 8 or 11 days. Group size: 8 guests, 4 crew. Cost: 1983: $760, $1,045. Special requirements: Non-smokers only, no alcoholic beverages aboard, $150 deposit per person.

Esplanade Tours
38 Newbury Street
Boston, MA 02116
617-266-7465
800-343-7184 (outside Mass.)
Telex 940421   *Mediterranean*

Set sail on a two-week cruise from Lisbon to Copenhagen aboard the comfortable, seventy-five-passenger m.s. "Lindblad Polaris." All thirty-eight cabins are outside, with private bath and air conditioning. The ship's compact size and exceptional maneuverability allow calls in small ports denied to larger ships. Highlights of this cruise include visits to Santiago de Compostela in Spain, La Rochelle and Belle Ile in France, a sail up the Seine River to Rouen, canal passages to both Bruges and Amsterdam and special calls in the Danish archipelago before arrival at Copenhagen. This voyage is part of a series of spring and fall departures planned and operated by Esplanade Tours aboard the "Lindblad Polaris" which include cruises in the Aegean, Adriatic and western Mediterranean. All cruises accompanied by an expert lecturer and experienced cruise staff. Thirty years' experience in specialty tours and cruises. Office and tour staff equipped to handle individual requests. Includes: Price includes Main Deck cabin on m.s. "Lindblad Polaris," all meals aboard and special meals ashore, all sightseeing, transfers, porterage, services of a cruise manager, tour manager and guest lecturer. Dates: May and September. Length of trip: 2 weeks. Group size: 75 passengers maximum. Cost: From $3,990 to $5,990 per person twin (air extra). Special requirements: $500 deposit due upon confirmation of space.

ITG International Travel Group, Inc.
175 Fifth Avenue
New York, NY 10010
212-475-7773
Telex 238763   *Russia*

Manned by today's Volga boatmen, your luxurious cruise ship the "M/S Alexandr Pushkin" will bring you to areas seldom seen by tourists along the fabled Volga and Don Rivers. You will see Rostov-on-Don, originally an eighteenth-century Cossack outpost and now renowned for its museums and botanical gardens. Another stop is Cossack Island, an unspoiled area of sandy beaches and forests of wildflowers and wildlife. Then it's on to thoroughly modern Volgograd, which provides a total contrast to Kazan, a city with many sights reminiscent of its thirteenth-century beginnings—like the striking seven-tier Syumbeka Tower. Ashore, you'll also tour Moscow and Leningrad, Erevan, Tbilisi and Helsinki. Includes: All meals, first class hotels, 9-day cruise, sightseeing, transfers, tips, taxes. Dates: June through September. Length of trip: 22 days. Group size: Varies. Cost: $1,495–$1,995.

ITG International Travel Groups, Inc.
175 Fifth Avenue
New York, NY 10010
212-475-7773
Telex 238763   *Yugoslavia*

The crystal-blue waters of the Southern Adriatic Islands are waiting for you after you board your sleek yacht, the fifty-seven-foot "Radoslav Tomas." Let the sails fill with wind and take you to exotic ports of call. There's Makarska, with its famous Museum of Shells . . . and Korcula, birthplace of Marco Polo. Enjoy sunny, peaceful days at sea as you cruise to Dubrovnik. Dating back to the seventh century, this famous walled town features charming palaces, bistros and churches. Then dip into the warm waters for a refreshing swim before you get ready to attend the Captain's dinner—looking healthy, tanned and satisfied. Includes: Yacht accommodations, all meals. Dates: May through September. Length of trip: 8 days, 7 nights. Group size: 20 people. Cost $399.

Ladatco Tours
2220 Coral Way
Miami, FL 33145
305-854-8422   *Brazil*

The Amazon holds a special mystique for all—and as the reality of the river unfolds during a four-day cruise from Manaus to Belem in Brazil, you'll be rewarded with a lifetime of memories. As your cruise begins, there's already excitement as you cross the "Meeting of the Waters" where the muddy Amazonas and the black Rio Negro meet and travel side by side for miles. The halfway point of your cruise is the city of Santarem, founded in 1661 and perfect for exploring. Then it's on to the Narrows of Breves where the jungle seems to touch the boat as natives paddle out to greet you in their ubas (dugout canoes). Cruise can be combined with five days in Rio. Ladatco Tours has specialized in South American tour programs for the last seventeen years. Includes: Accommodations, all meals, river transportation, on-board activities and ports of call. Dates: Year-round. Length of trip: 4 days. Group size: Maximum 30. Cost: From $460.

Mackenzie River Cruises
P.O. Box 65
Fort Simpson, N.W.T. XOE ONO
403-695-2506   *Canada*

Explore the mighty MacKenzie . . . one of the world's longest rivers . . . on this eight-day cruise between Fort Simpson and Inuvik, well above the Arctic Circle. You'll travel with an experienced guide in a twenty-seven-foot boat especially designed for northern river travel. The beauty of the northern wilderness is breathtaking as you pursue fishing . . . hiking . . . nature study . . . photography or visiting native villages. Cruise highlights include Camsell Bend, with its spectacular scenery; the San Sault rapids; and Fort Good Hope, an historic trapping community. At night, relax in a comfortable tent camp and see the soft glow of the Midnight Sun against the backdrop of the MacKenzie Mountains. Includes: 800-mile, 8-day riverboat tour, full meals, accommodation in tent camps. Sleeping bags and mattresses provided. Dates: June through mid-September. Length of trip: 8 days, 7 nights. Group size: Maximum 5 passengers. Cost: $1,250 per person. Special requirements: Deposit of $250.

Outdoor Alaska
P.O. Box 7814
Ketchikan, AK 99901
907-225-6044 *Alaska*

Outdoor Alaska offers an eight-hour cruise/fly trip into Misty Fjords National Monument from Ketchikan. You'll travel to the monument aboard a fifty-foot diesel-powered excursion vessel and return to Ketchikan in a float-equipped "bush plane." Your cruise takes you into the heartland of this awe-inspiring country. You'll pass beneath towering cliffs thousands of feet high and view New Eddystone Rock, an ancient volcanic plug towering from the depths of Behm Canal. Guides are lifetime residents of the area and the skipper is a marine biologist. Vessels are Coast Guard-inspected and -licensed. Optional overnight hiking and kayaking trips are also available. Includes: Continental breakfast, lunch. Dates: June through August. Length of trip: 8 hours. Group size: 16. Cost: $149.

Pacific Adventures Charter Service
2445 Morena Boulevard, Suite 200P1
San Diego, CA 92110
619-275-4253 *Mexico*

Since Baja's discovery by the Spanish in 1532, a steady stream of adventurers and explorers have found shelter in the many isolated harbors and anchorages along this rugged shoreline. Here, coastal bays, lagoons and wilderness islands contrast with pristine deserts that stretch right to the ocean's shores—providing you with a striking setting for a leisurely voyage of escape, adventure and discovery. There is something to interest everybody: whale watching, seals, dolphin, an incredible variety of birds, superb fishing, excellent photo opportunities, engrossing nature study, easy-going island hiking, fascinating plant life, exciting history, swimming and snorkeling in crystal-clear waters, blue skies and lots of warm sunshine. You'll travel in comfort aboard the brand-new, deluxe long-range vessel, the "Executive," which has been designed along the lines of a custom yacht with safety and comfort in mind. The professional crew and naturalist guide have many years' experience in operating expeditions of this kind in Mexican waters, and the "Executive" is fully U.S. Coast Guard-licensed and -inspected. Includes: All meals, snacks, on-board accommodations, all activities as described, any necessary Mexican licenses and services of professional naturalist guide and crew. Dates: Late December through April. Length of trip: 7 to 10 days. Group size: Up to 38. Cost: Approximately $130 per person per day.

PEREGRINE
EXPEDITIONS

Peregrine Expeditions
Suite 710, 7th Floor
343 Little Collins Street
Melbourne, Vic. 3000 Australia
60 1121 or 60 1122 *India*

This sail-trek expedition is one of the most unique trips offered in the Indian sub-continent. It begins with a train ride from the modern city of Delhi to the timeless holy cities of Hardwar and Rishikesh. Here, five rivers converge to form the mighty Ganges, Hinduism's holiest of rivers. Temples, shrines and bathing ghats house holy men practicing astonishing feats of yoga and penance. It is a fascinating and, at times, unbelievable insight into Hinduism. The trip then returns to Delhi for visits to Agra and the Taj Mahal, on the banks of another sacred river, the Yanuna. At the confluence of the Yanuna and the Ganges, Allahabad, they are joined by a third holy river, the Saraswati, invisible to mortal eyes. Here, the seven-day sailing adventure begins on a traditional Indian barge, fully equipped and under the guidance of an experienced crew. The boat glides past centuries-old villages, ageless shrines and temples, sacred bathing and cremation ghats, and fishermen and farmers working with the same tools as their fathers and grandfathers before them. This tour of the Ganges can really be described as a trip down the very life-line of Indian culture. Includes: Bed and breakfast in Dehli and Varansi, full room and board at all other sites, rail transportation from Delhi to Varansi and return, air transportation from Varansi to Calcutta, all tour fees, experienced leader and local guides. Dates: October through April. Length of trip: 18 days. Group size: 15. Cost: $1,420 Australian dollars. Special requirements: $100 deposit.

South America Reps
P.O. Box 39583
Los Angeles, CA 90039
213-246-4816
800-423-2791 (outside California)
Telex 686167   *Peru*

The 146-foot m/v "Rio Amazonas" sails from Iquitos, Peru every Wednesday for the four-day, three-night voyage to Leticia, Colombia on the Amazon River. Each day, ports of call might include remote Indian villages, a lumber mill, jungle hospitals or towns. You'll have the unique opportunity of seeing Indian dances, trading for handicrafts, spotting strange birdlife, and walking through the jungle dense with a myriad of plants and flowers. Sailings leave Leticia, Colombia every Saturday afternoon, arriving in Iquitos Tuesday morning. Since downriver shore excursions differ from upriver stops, the cruise can be extended to a seven-day journey round-trip from Iquitos. The m/v "Rio Amazonas" boasts sixteen air-conditioned twin cabins with private bath and ten non-air-conditioned cabins with community bath facilities. English speaking guides escort all shore excursions; on-board service also includes multilingual staff. Operated by Paul Wright, former owner of Wright Way Tours. Includes: Airport transfers at embarkation/disembarkation, cabin, all meals, twice daily shore excursions; non-A/C cabins available at $250 pp share double. Dates: Weekly, year-round. Length of trip: 4 days, 3 nights. Group size: Maximum 55 passengers. Cost: $495 per person. Special requirements: $150 deposit to confirm; full payment 60 days prior to sailing. Extensive walking involved.

Viking Yacht Cruises
230 Spruce Street
Southport, CT 06490
213-259-6030
212-221-6788
Telex 4750086 DAYL   *Florida*

Let Captain Bowell show you a stretch of the Florida Keys that will relax you . . . forty-five islands unmatched for warmth and beauty. You'll cruise aboard 112-foot "Viking Explorer," which features air conditioning, heating and private facilities. During the day be amused and enthralled as dolphins and sea lions follow in your wake. Take in Key West, where you can visit Hemingway's home . . . then head for Flamingo, in the heart of the Everglades, a wild-life sanctuary filled with spoonbills, flamingo, herons, pelicans . . . and alligators!! Throughout, you'll dine on typical Keys fare—fresh fish, stone crabs, lobster and Key lime pie. Viking Yacht Cruises is a family-run business with seven years' cruise experience. Includes: Boat passage, meals on board, accommodations and shore-tour bus transportation. Dates: December through April. Length of trip: 3 nights. Cost: $294 per person.

Viking Yacht Cruises
230 Spruce Street
Southport, CT 06490
213-259-6030
212-221-6788
Telex 4750086 DAYL

Greece

Imagine a blissful day spent watching dolphins frolic, swimming in the bluest of waters, or discovering mysterious, legendary islands. When you sail the Aegean you'll visit Santorini, possible site of the lost Atlantis; Delos, sacred since antiquity as the birthplace of Apollo and known for its exquisite ruins; Mykonos, where the action is—from discos to arts and crafts, and Kythnos with its hot springs. Sail into the past and discover the Aegean. Viking Yacht Cruises is a family-run business with seven years' experience operating yacht cruises. Includes: Cruising as per program, bed, breakfast and lunch every day. Dates: April through October. Length of trip: 7 days. Group size: 20–35 people. Cost: From $545. Special requirements: 25% deposit upon confirmation, full payment 35 days prior to sailing.

Culture •
History Expeditions •

Explore distant cultures vastly different from your own—or discover surprising aspects of a people you thought you knew—on behind-the-scenes cultural tours. You'll learn about new and old languages, arts, music, history and celebrations, as well as encountering entirely different ways of life. Above all, cultural and anthropological tours study human diversity. As you travel, you'll discover how, even in the most disparate of cultures, an astonishing number of similar or parallel elements combine to comprise the human unity.

Variety—that's the spice of cultural tours. You have, literally, the whole world from which to choose. See the rituals of the famed Mudmen of New Guinea. Celebrate the summer's harvest with the Ait Hadiddou tribe at Morocco's three-day "Imilchil Betrothal Fair." High in the Himalayan world of Ladakh, a kingdom closed to the outside world until 1974, visit Tibetan monasteries and meet High Lamas. Explore Japan, where ancient and modern cultures exist side-by-side—you can even ride a one hundred mph train by day, and sleep in a Zen Buddhist monastery by night. Visit Pagan, Burma's incredible city of four thousand temples and shrines. Trace English history from the Stone Age to the present on a tour that explores Stonehenge and King's Road. Or learn about our own rich American culture on a study of the Navajo and Hopi Indian homelands.

You'll also find variety in the orientations of the programs. Many tours offer general overviews of the societies they visit, providing background information on all aspects of the culture, and also sightseeing in the surrounding area. Other programs are more sharply focused. Historical tours explore a people through its events; anthropological tours explore a history through its people. Tours geared toward art and architecture reflect the development of values and ideals through aesthetics. You can also choose tours that let you enjoy new food and drinks, or join in the festivities of local celebrations.

Whatever area you're interested in exploring, chances are you can find a travel program that goes there. Key factors to look for in choosing a tour are its strenuousness, the quality of accommodations and meals, and the qualifications of your guides. (These guides will be important on your tour—they'll bridge language and cultural gaps for the group.) Ask the operator what sort of weather conditions to expect, and what clothing is appropriate.

On cultural tours, you can study a society radically different from your own, and at the same time learn a lot about the society in which you live.

SECTIONS OF RELATED INTEREST

Archeology
Art/Architecture
Folklore

Art Explorer's Tours
P.O. Box 26689
San Francisco, CA 94126
415-921-7677

China

This adventure in China includes Beijing, Datong, Xian, Guilin, Shanghai, Suzhou and Wuxi. Among the highlights: the Great Wall; Forbidden City (the Palace Museum); White

Marble Boat; Ming Tombs; Summer Palace; and Xian (where 6,500 clay figures of soldiers and horses of the first emperor are being unearthed). In addition, you'll explore Datong—site of the largest stone cave temples in China. You'll also enjoy a boat ride on the Li River and a performance of the Peking Opera. The trip includes visits to "workshops" where you will see artists carving ivory and jade, hand weaving "oriental rugs," and practicing many other ancient crafts. Hank Baum, B.A., president of Art Explorer's Tours and member of the art faculty at the University of California Berkeley extension, is a noted lecturer and tour leader. Includes: First class hotels, round-trip economy airfare, all transportation, tips and transfers, all meals. Dates: May. Length of trip: 3 weeks. Group size: 10–20. Cost: $3,000 approximately.

Bhutan Travel Service
120 East 56th Street
New York, NY 10022
212-838-6382   *Bhutan*

Explore the previously closed Himalayan kingdom of Bhutan. This unspoiled, ancient region boasts fortress monasteries, temples, and great flowing rivers. Tour members visit Paro, a medieval town set high in the mountains in the midst of a peaceful river valley. Excursions are also made to the ruins of Drukryel Dzong, and by horseback up to the Tiger's Nest Monastery set atop a sheer cliff at ten thousand feet. At Thimphu, the Bhutan capital, you'll see the Tashichhodzong center of government and religion, built in the traditional Bhutanese manner—without using a single nail. Travelers also visit the colorful, outdoor Sunday market and have an opportunity to see a display of archery or a performance of Bhutan's famous mask dances. Bhutan Travel is an agency of Bhutan Department of Tourism. Includes: All land costs, accommodations, all meals, transfers, transportation, guide, sightseeing. Dates: Year-round, every Monday from Bagdogra Airport in India. Length of trip: 7 nights. Group size: No minimum. Cost: $845–$977. Special requirements: One month advance booking.

Black Beauty Tours, Ltd. (ASI/Ghana)
Hotel Continental
P.O. Box 2189
Accra, Ghana, West Africa
76542/76896   *Ghana*

This is a chance to discover Ghanaian culture—the African dances that are so much a part of daily life . . . the local dishes such as fufu with hot groundnut soup, palm soup and Gari foto . . . and the dramatic marriage ceremonies where the natives celebrate for days. You'll stop at Kumasi, "Cultural City" of West Africa, and the villages of Bonwire, Ntoso and Ahwia to see popular Kente weavers, stool carvers and potterers. International Air Transport Association Agent. Member of American Society of Travel Agents, African Travel Association. Includes: Hotel accommodation on MAP (2 meals); ground transportation, entrance fees, arrival/departure transfers, porterage and tips. Dates: Year-round. Length: 7 days, 6 nights. Group size: 15 minimum. Cost: $599. Special requirements: 40% deposit, balance 21 days before arrival.

Cedok
10 East 40th Street
New York, NY 10016
212-689-9720 *Czechoslovakia*

History buffs will jump at this opportunity to participate in a tour of medieval castles and ruins throughout Czechoslovakia. The Czech Travel Bureau (Cedok) leads this expedition to ancient castles and strongholds filled with collections of historical arms and Bohemian artifacts. The castles include those at Cesky, Sternberk, Zlevy and Opocno. The trip also covers some modern-day pleasures such as a tour of Liberec (biannual fashion shows), a sightseeing tour of Prague, a jaunt to Mount Jested, and a visit to Sychrav Castle to view the extensive collection of neo-Gothic arts and crafts. There is also time to visit theater, ballet, opera, famous breweries and night clubs. Includes: Accommodations, meals, ground transportation, guides, sightseeing and entrance fees. Dates: All year. Length: 6 days. Group size: 15–35. Cost: $240–$275.

Canyonland Tours
P.O. Box 460, Dept. STI
Flagstaff, AZ 86002
800-841-7317
602-774-7343 from AZ, AL, HI
Telex 172-029 SPX SRFL *Western United States*

The Navajo and Hopi Indian homelands contain several of the Southwest's foremost scenic areas and natural history sites. Traveling across these lands on this specially-equipped vehicle camping tour, you visit some of the most significant of these places: Canyon de Chelly, which holds one of the largest concentrations of cliff dwellings in the Southwest; Sunset Crater— Wupatki National Monument with its abundant prehistoric pueblos and earth lodges; Monument Valley Navajo Tribal Park, that world-famous, spectacular region of mesas, buttes, and monuments. You see and meet the people who inhabit the areas, and learn about their culture both past and present. Canyonland Tours was established in 1965. Patrick and Susan Conley, owners/operators, each have over twelve years' experience in the outfitting and guiding business in the Southwest. Includes: Direct trip transportation, meals while en route, drive-guide service, Park entry fees, camp equipment, sleeping bag, foam pad, ground cloth, tent (double occupancy). Dates: April through October. Length of trip: 5 days, 4 nights. Group size: 20 guests maximum. Cost: $495 per person. Special requirements: $100 per person deposit necessary to confirm reservation; balance due 45 days prior to departure.

Council on International Educational Exchange
205 East 42nd Street
New York, NY 10017
212-661-1414 *Japan*

Live in a Japanese home and take part in all the family activities . . . share typical Japanese food, visit family friends and relatives and accompany family member to work or school. The Council on International Educational Exchange, in cooperation with the Japan Society, Inc. of New York, offers a summer study/travel program that provides an unusual opportunity to get to know the people and culture of Japan. You'll explore the delights of Tokyo, its Japanese gardens and Kabuki theater . . . sleep in a Zen Buddhist monastery and partake in the discipline of Temple life—its silent meditation and mealtime ritual. Visit Kyoto—imperial capital of Japan for a thousand years . . . totally immersing yourself in the Japanese way of life for what one program participant called "not just a tour, but a cultural, sociological and aesthetic experience." Organization established thirty-five years ago. Includes: Round-trip air fare between New York and Tokyo, hotel expenses, transfer and museum fees, guides and meals during home-stay, temple-stay and visit to Tsumago. Dates: June and July. Length of trip: 24 days. Group size: 35 people. Cost: $2,535. Special requirements: $100 deposit plus membership in Japan Society—$35.

Cross Cultural Adventures
P.O. Box 3285
Arlington, VA 22203
703-243-7194
Telex 440283 ACI UI   *Morocco*

Once a year, a remote valley amid the stark vastness of Morocco's High Atlas Mountains comes alive with color and excitement as thousands gather to attend the "Imilchil Betrothal Fair." In the course of this three-day Berber fair, or *moussem,* as it is called in Arabic, members of the Ait Hadiddou tribe celebrate the summer's harvest, trade goods before the winter snows shut the mountain passes, and hope to assure prosperous futures by finding spouses. Traveling by specially-equipped Land Rovers, you'll spend two days in this land that time seems to have forgotten, allowing you to witness all the activities at the fair. On the way there and back, you will visit spectacular valleys jutting out into the Sahara, giant cedar forests of the Middle Atlas chain, Islam's holy city of Fes, and fabled Marrakech—foremost center of Moroccan handicrafts. The tour leader has spent more than six years living, studying and working in North Africa, including Morocco. Includes: Accommodations in deluxe or first-class hotels, two nights in communal tents at the fair, all meals, transportation by Land Rover, tour leader and local guide. Dates: Late September each year. Length of trip: 2 weeks. Group size: Maximum 12. Cost: $1,500. Special requirements: $300 deposit with reservation, balance six weeks prior to departure.

Cross Cultural Adventures
P.O. Box 3285
Arlington, VA 22203
703-243-7194
Telex 440283 ACI UI   *India*

Tour the wonders of Rajasthan, India's most colorful and culturally rich state—highlighted by a visit to the world's largest camel fair, on the shores of Pushkar's sacred lake. This adventure takes you to fabled capitals of the Maharajahs: Jaipur and the grandiose Amber Palace; the fortress of Jodhpur; Udaipur and its Lake Palace; Bundi, where city gates will close at dusk; Alwar and its school of painting; the walled city of Jaisalmer, where you will mount camels for an excursion into the Thar desert; and the hill resort of Mt. Abu with its great Jain temples. The tour begins in New Delhi and includes the Taj Mahal and the lost city of Fatehpur Sikri. Includes: All accommodations, ranging from Maharajahs' palaces to fully serviced tented camps at the Pushkar fair; all meals, transport by coach, train and air within India, tour leader, guide. Dates: November each year. Length of trip: 3 weeks. Group size: Maximum 15. Cost: $1,650. Special requirements: $300 deposit with reservation, balance six weeks prior to departure.

Express International, Inc.
P.O. Box A, Main Street
Saltillo, PA 17253
814-448-3946
800-458-3606
Telex 845382   *Tibet*

This tour gives you six days in one of the most inaccessible countries in the world—Tibet—surrounded by mountains. Its capital, Lhasa, is one of the few places in the world where airline timetables are determined by the rising and setting of the sun. In Lhasa you'll have the opportunity to see Potala, former home of the Dalai Lamas. Also on the agenda are visits to the street markets and the carpet factories. This tour also includes Peking, Xian and Chendu, Canton and Hong Kong. Members of Association of British Travel Agents. Includes: International air fare, full board (twin-sharing basis) in first class or best available hotel in China and Tibet (room only in London and Hong Kong), all transportation, comprehensive program of visits, visas, airport taxes, tour escort, local guides in each city, portage. Dates: Monthly, April through November. Length of trip: 23 days. Group size: 16. Cost: $6,650. Special requirements: Medical certificate for those over the age of 65, since the tour is physically demanding.

Express International, Inc.
P.O. Box A, Main Street
Saltillo, PA 17253
814-448-3946
800-458-3606
Telex 845382   *China*

The hustle of Shanghai and the stately pace of Peking . . . soaring peaks of Guilin and intimate gardens of Suzhou . . . retrace the great ages of Chinese history on this twenty-five-day excursion. In Xian you'll see the remarkable archeological find of the Terracotta Army—and in Chungking, Shanghai and Wuhan you'll piece together many crucial events of modern Chinese history. You'll also visit Canton and enjoy the excitement of the time-honored cruise along the Yangtse, passing the fabled Gorges. Members of Association of British Travel Agents. Includes: International air fare, full board in first class (twin-sharing basis) or best available hotels, all transportation, comprehensive sightseeing program, visas, airport taxes, tour escort, porterage, transfers. Dates: Weekly, April to October. Length of trip: 25 days. Group size: Up to 30. Cost: $4,560. Special requirements: A medical certificate required by those over the age of 65 years.

Fairway Tours
8D Rosebery Place
Gullane, E. Lothian, Scotland EH312AN
(0620) 842349
Telex 72165G (842349)   *Great Britain*

Take a unique historical journey through the Scottish countryside exploring ancient castles in spectacular settings. Visit Macbeth's castle, and the former home of Sir Walter Scott. Relax and lunch in country inns and pubs dating back to 1300 A.D. Drop in on a famous malt whiskey distillery, and cruise through the Caledonian Canal to Loch Ness, keeping a wary eye out for a glimpse of the legendary Loch Ness monster. This historical tour is planned and frequently escorted by Nigel Tranter, author and leading authority on Scotland's history, heritage and religion. Includes: Accommodations, dinner, bed and full breakfast, luxury coach travel, special banquets, all entry fees, expert guide, ferry charges and VAT. Dates: Spring and autumn. Length: 14 Days. Group size: 40 maximum. Cost: £690 approximately. Special requirements: 10% deposit with reservation.

GEO Expeditions
P.O. Box 27136-STB
Oakland, CA 94602
415-530-4146   *New Guinea*

Papua New Guinea presents startling contrasts among Stone-Age cultures, and between old and new. With Geo Expeditions, you can explore the people of the Trobriand Islands, made famous by anthropological studies of their unique canoe-trading system. You'll travel to the highlands, a highly populated area not explored until 1933. During the drive through the region you'll encounter many fascinating culture groups, including the famous Mudmen of the Asaro Valley, and stop at the Baiyer River Sanctuary to view the exotic bird of paradise. And you'll encounter fabulous carvings at riverside villages as you cruise the jungle-fringed Sepik River. Includes: All accommodations, air within Papua New Guinea, land transportation, most meals, expert leadership. Dates: September. Length of trip: 15 days. Group size: 15 maximum. Cost: $2,175 land. Special requirements: $200 deposit.

GEO Expeditions
P.O. Box 27136-STB
Oakland, CA 94602
415-530-4146   *Indonesia*

Experience the cultural diversity of Indonesia—the Batak and Minangkabau peoples of highland Sumatera, the Toraja of upland southern Sulawesi, the southern Balinese, and the central Javanese. Program includes visits to Jakarta, the national capital; and the famed botanical garden at Bogor; sultan's palace in Islamic central Java; majestic Buddhist monument of Borobudur; and the Hindu temples at Prambanan. Add the many active volcanoes, the coral-girt tropical beaches, and Indonesia is indeed a very different place. First and last nights are in Penang, Malaysia's premier island resort, and in that mini-republic, ultra-modern Singapore. Tour leader is Dr. William L. Thomas, Ph.D. Includes: All hotels, most meals, local transportation, guides. Dates: July and August. Length of trip: 23 days. Group size: 15 maximum. Cost: $2,250 (land) $1,915 (approximate air) from Los Angeles. Special requirements: $200 deposit; full payment 60 days in advance of departure.

Grecian
Holiday

Grecian Holiday
P.O. Box 452
DeKalb, IL 60115
815-758-1911   *Greece*

Philoxeneia. It's the Greek word meaning "friend to the stranger." Come experience Greek hospitality—as well as its rich culture and archeological past—on this informative, aesthetic, romantic adventure. You'll dine at the foot of the Acropolis, watch dazzling Sound and Light performances and sail to the picturesque islands of Aegina, Poror and Hydra—where you can sip some Greek ouzo and relax at the seafront cafes. Let Delphi, or the sanctuaries of Apollo and Athena, or a group of Greek folk dancers beguile you. Delve into the past of Greece and explore Olympia, Pella, Mycenae and much more. Includes: Double occupancy, continental breakfast, lunch or dinner, welcome and farewell parties, three-island cruise, visit to archeological and historic sites, guided tours to national and regional museums. Dates: July and August. Length of trip: 2 weeks. Group size: 25–30 people. Cost: $765 plus airfare. Special requirements: Minimum deposit of $100 per person.

**High Adventure Tours
4000 Massachusetts Avenue N.W.
#1426
Washington, D.C. 20016
202-686-0023**   *Pakistan*

Travel where Marco Polo once traveled along the Old Silk Road and walk the campgrounds of Alexander the Great's army—it's all in spectacular, unspoiled Northern Pakistan. Highlights include Hunza, an idyllic valley of healthy, long-lived people; fascinating archeological sites in Swat; plus the Kyber Pass . . . legendary gateway to India. The scene of conquests for thirty-five centuries, it's still exciting today with its forts and turbaned tribesmen. And, if they're at home, you might also meet the King of Swat and the Queen of Hunza on the journey. Includes: All meals, mountain flights, road travel by mini-bus or open jeeps. Dates: October. Length: 18 days. Group size: 20 maximum. Cost: $3,150 double occupancy from New York.

**High Adventure Tours
4000 Massachusetts Avenue N.W.
#1426
Washington, D.C. 20016
202-686-0023**   *Ladakh*

Journey to the roof of the world . . . to the last Shangri-la. Once part of Tibet and hidden for centuries from the outside word, the unspoiled Himalayan kingdom of Ladakh opened to visitors in 1974. You'll travel to the beautiful Vale of Kashmir, then over a spectacular three-thousand-foot mountain highway into a colorful land of Tibetan monasteries and Lamas . . . of yaks and snowy peaks and warm green valleys. You can meet High Lamas or see the Taj Mahal by moonlight, all in a fascinating, unspoiled part of the world. Includes: Delhi, with sightseeing and a special lecture program, 5 nights on deluxe houseboat in Kashmir, 7 days in Ladakh. Dates: September. Length: 19 days. Group size: 22 maximum. Cost: $3,375 double occupancy from New York.

**High Adventure Tours
4000 Massachusetts Avenue, N.W.
#1426
Washington, D.C. 20016
202-686-0023**   *India*

Live like a Maharajah in the palace hotels of exotic Rajasthan, land of Kings, on High Adventure's deluxe, eight-day journey through exotic India. You'll visit the unspoiled desert city of Jaisalmer, rising like a mirage on the horizon with its golden fortress walls and exquisitely carved houses . . . a perfect town to explore on camel. Discover Jodhpur's splendid fifteenth-century fort with its palatial rooms and courtyards . . . take a boat excursion and watch the sun set over Udaipur . . . fly into the "pink city" of Jaipur and go to the extraordinary seventeenth-century observatory . . . and ride elephants inside the massive fortress of Amber. Includes: Palace hotels in Jaipur, Jodhpur and Udaipur, car trip to Jaisalmer and camel ride through city, all meals, sightseeing tours with local guides. Dates: October. Length: 8 days. Cost: $975.

**Himalayan Rover Trek
P.O. Box 24382
Seattle, WA 98124
206-782-6792
206-454-5022**

or

**Himalayan Rover Trek
P.O. Box 1081
Kathmandu, Nepal**   *Nepal*

Explore the mysteries of the magical kingdom of Nepal, experience breathtaking views of the Himalayas, visit the intriguing city of Kathmandu and wander through native bazaars in Thailand and Hong Kong . . . all especially designed for the curious traveler who is not a trekker. See the Annapurna Range; the ancient capital of Gorkha, only recently accessible by road; and have a jungle adventure in Gaida Wildlife Camp, where elephant safaris and dugout canoes bring you up close to one-horned rhinos and the Royal Bengal tiger. Five days in Thailand will include Bangkok and Chiang Mai with its hill tribes and craft villages. An optional extension to India is also available. Sixteen years' experience in trekking and tour business in Nepal. Includes: Round-trip air fare from Seattle and other West Coast gateways; first-class or deluxe hotels with private bath except best available at Gorkha and Gaida (based on shared twin); American breakfasts; full board at Dhulikel, Gorkha, Gaida and in China; several special meals; special guides and lectures; transfers, sightseeing, tours, wildlife safaris. Dates: October and November. Length of trip: 26 days. Group size: 24 maximum. Cost: $3,675.

**Historic Finland
Tour Designs, Inc.
713 6th Street, S.W.
Washington, D.C. 20024
202-554-5820
Telex 904266**   *Finland*

Formerly ruled by both Swedish kings and Russian czars, Finland has emerged as a country where "East meets West." Explore these intertwined cultures on this tour that highlights the best of Finland, plus Stockholm and Leningrad. You'll explore Helsinki—named Finland's capital by Czar Alexander I and known for its stately nineteenth-century architecture. Visit Turku, Haikko and the medieval trading center of Porvoo. Enjoy a luxurious Silja Line cruise to Stockholm, where you'll tour Town Hall and the Gold Mosaic room where the Nobel Prize is awarded. In Leningrad you'll see the Peter and Paul Fortress, the Winter Palace and Hermitage, plus the Summer Palace at Petrodvorets. Member of American Society of Travel Agents; Intourist-appointed agent. Includes: Round-trip air fare, first class accommodations, most meals, all sightseeing via private motorcoach, 2 theater performances in Leningrad. Dates: June through August. Length of trip: 15 days. Group size: 15. Cost: $2,589. Special requirements: USSR visa processed by Tour Designs.

**KAO International, Inc.
1007 Broxton Avenue
Los Angeles, CA 90024
213-208-6001
Telex 181879 KAO TVL LSA**   *Japan*

The Japan Minshuku tour enables you to see Japan as the Japanese see it. You'll make use of efficient subway and train systems and ride the famous "Bullet Train," which averages well over one hundred miles per hour. Enjoy beautiful man-made parks and wander through the inner gardens of ancient shrines and castles. Visit small towns in the Japanese Alps and picnic on moss-covered rocks that jut out into mountain cascades. But best of all, you'll be staying at Minshuka and Ryokans, Japanese family inns. Upon entering them, you'll exchange your shoes for slippers, enjoy meals that often feature regional specialties, and soak luxuriously in a Japanese bath or "furo"—predecessor of today's "hot tub." And at night, sleep on Japanese-style mattresses laid out on the tatami-matted floors. Four continuous years of operating this type of trip. Includes: Hotel accommodations for 9 nights in twin-bedded rooms, Minshuku and Ryokan (Japanese-style inns) accommodations for 5 days; 17 meals; English-speaking escort; surface transportation, primarily by rail; transfers, porterage, taxes and gratuities. Dates: Year-round on customized basis for individual and groups. Length of trip: From 2 weeks (shorter on request). Group size: Minimum 10 people. Cost: From $900 per person. Special requirements: Being physically able to sit and sleep on Japanese-style, tatami-matted floors, for an extended period of time. Above average amount of walking for sightseeing, in the "back road" cities and towns.

Lindblad Travel, Inc.
P.O. Box 912
Westport, CT 06881
203-226-8531
Telex 221412   *Russia*

Visit ancient Russian cities and towns with historical relics, art and architecture dating back to the ninth and tenth centuries. The program begins in Leningrad, built by Peter the Great and originally named St. Petersburg. It is a treasure-trove of eighteenth-century architecture, and its Hermitage Museum houses one of the world's finest collections of French Impressionists. From here you'll motor to Novgorod and then take an overnight train to Moscow. Highlights include the Kremlin and Red Square, St. Basil's Cathedral, plus cultural events at the Bolshoi or Kremlin Palace. Next you'll continue to Rostov Veliky—its Kremlin is a miracle in stone, wood and metal—then to Zagorsk with its magnificent relics of fourteenth-century Russian culture, before arriving in Yaroslavl on the banks of the Volga. Other tour features include the Botik (Peter the Great Museum) in Pereslavl-Zalessky, Vladimir and Suzdal, with their masterpieces of Russian architecture. Includes: All transportation during the tour except air; hotel accommodations, 3 meals a day, sightseeing, group transfers, visas, escorts, tips, taxes, and service charges. Dates: July through September. Length of trip: 19 days. Group size: 29. Cost: $1,575. Special requirements: $500 deposit at time of booking, balance due 2 months prior to departure.

Lindblad Travel, Inc.
P.O. Box 912
Westport, CT 06881
203-226-8531
Telex 221412   *India, Nepal, Pakistan*

Revisit Shangri-La on this unusual journey through the Indian subcontinent. The program begins in Karachi, Pakistan. You'll visit Gilgit in the heart of the Karakoram range, an old tribal town on the famous "silk route" between China and the Arabian Sea; the Valley of Hunza nestled close to the Chinese border where the people are noted for longevity (the fabled location of Shangri-La); the Kingdom of Swat surrounded by the mighty ranges of the Hindu Kush and the Karakoram (in 327 B.C., Alexander the Great bivouacked his army here). From Lahore you'll cross the border and travel on to the lovely Vale of Kashmir. Then continue to Nepal, visiting classical sites, cities and the Royal Chitwan National Park, the natural habitat of some of Asia's rarest animals. While the program terminates in India's capital city of Delhi, there's an optional extension available to the tiny Himalayan Kingdom of Bhutan. Includes: All transportation during the tour except air, deluxe and best-available accommodations, 3 meals a day, sightseeing, group transfers, visas, escorts, tips, taxes, and service charges. Dates: August through October. Length of trip: 25 days. Group size: 21. Cost: $3,100. Special requirements: $500 deposit at time of booking, balance due 2 months prior to departure.

Lyon Travel Services
1031 Ardmore Avenue
Oakland, CA 94610
415-465-8955   *Great Britain*

Lyon Travel specializes in "back roads—behind the scenes" tours of well-known destinations. Join them this summer for an interesting and leisurely tour of English villages, from the Stone Age through modern times. Each twenty-one-day trip has a different orientation: photography, crafts, manor houses, gardens, etc. Tours are customized to the specifications of each group, which is limited to six participants. Accommodations are in old coaching inns, manor houses and farmhouses. This is the perfect trip for those wishing to enjoy the tranquil and well-ordered charm of the traditional English village. Lyon Travel Services has been in operation since 1975. Includes: All meals, accommodations, ground transportation and admission fees. Dates: July and August. Length: 21 days. Group size: 6. Cost: $2,400. Special requirements: $250 deposit.

Lyon Travel Services
1031 Ardmore Avenue
Oakland, CA 94610
415-465-8955   *Western United States*

Spend twenty-one days on a leisurely but thorough visit to the homeland of the Ansazi, Navajo, Hopi, Zuni and Apache Indian tribes. You'll explore pueblos in Acoma and Taos, historical sites in Santa Fe, Chaco Canyon, Canyon de Chelly, Monument Valley, Second Mesa and Mesa Verde. The Grand Canyon and Rainbow Bridge are also included. You'll come away with greater knowledge and appreciation of the culture and native peoples of the American Southwest. Includes: All meals, motel accommodations, ground transportation and admission fees. Dates: May and June. Length: 21 days. Group size: 6. Cost: On request. Special requirements: $250 deposit.

Napa Valley Heritage Tours
1512 Fourth Street
Napa, CA 94559
707-253-8687   *California*

The history of Napa, California comes alive for you as you learn about its unique heritage . . . a heritage that includes Robert Louis Stevenson and his young bride—a land that contains grand old Victorian homes from the 1800's just waiting for you to wander through. Then step back into the present—take a hot air balloon ride, or a gracefully swooping glider ride, and trek through the Napa Valley wineries—from the large, well-known facilities to the small, exclusive cellars. And end your time of discovery with a picnic, some antique shopping and a hot mud bath. Tour operator is city planning professional specializing in historic preservation. Includes: Custom-planned itinerary, tour guide, air-conditioned van transportation, lunch on all-day tour. Dates: All year. Length: ½ to several days. Group size: 4–9 people. Cost: $20–$60 per person per day. Special requirements: Reservations required, deposits for meals and accommodations.

Serenissima Travel, Ltd.
2 Lower Sloane Street
London, England SWIW 8BJ
(01) 730-7281   *Russia*

Explore the historic cities of Soviet Central Asia conquered by Tamerlane in the fourteenth century. The tour starts out in Moscow, where you'll visit the Kremlin and enjoy an evening of theater. Next fly to Dzhamboul, a major trading center on the ancient silk road. The Mausoleum of Khwaija Ahmad Yasawi, founder of a powerful order of dervishes, awaits you on your tour of Gorod Turkestan. In Bokhara you'll marvel at the tenth-century tomb of the Samanids. At Samarkand, Tamerlane's once-glittering capital, you'll view the conqueror's tomb and at the Shari-i-Sabz you'll see his great ruined palace. All Serenissima tours are accompanied by a noted expert in each field plus a tour manager. Eleventh year of operating world-wide tours. Includes: All-inclusive. Dates: September. Length of trip: 15 days. Group size: Varies. Cost: £1,075.

S.I.T.
2437 Durant Avenue, Suite 208
Berkeley, CA 94704
415-843-8294
EXPLORE **Telex 910-366-7092**   *China, Mongolia*

Learn more about China's fabulous nature and cultures. You'll travel "Kingdom of the Middle"—as well as Mongolia (Inner and Outer)—by bus, bicycle or hike/trek—as circumstances demand. The basic itinerary is modified according to season and interest. Along the way, you'll stay at good class hotels and typical lodges, except for a little splurge now and then (perhaps at the end in Hong Kong). On the "China Walk" program, camping is also featured. If you have the time and the desire you can also visit the Gobi/Altai mountains and the Gobi Desert, including the dinosaur deposits, trek in "China's Tibet," and travel by the Trans Siberian Railroad. You'll also visit such seldom-seen places as the National Parks and Reserves, and attend the unique July NADOM festivities in Mongolia. S.I.T. has been in operation since 1967. Includes: All accommodations, all meals, all land and water transportation, all guiding, taxes, entrance fees. Dates: February through November. Length of trip: 15–32 days. Group size: 15–34 pax. Cost: From $998.

South Seas Gallery Travel, Inc.
353 Bleecker Street
New York, NY 10014
212-741-2777   *New Guinea*

Fascinating adventure in the South Seas awaits you—boats will carry you on an unforgettable voyage on the mighty Sepik River. You'll be captivated by the natives and enchanted by their art—considered among the best primitive art in the world. Following in the footsteps of James Michener, you'll explore the Black Water Lakes and Maprik. Seldom seen by outsiders, Maprik is known for its tall spiritual houses—Haus Tambarans—richly adorned with carvings and paintings. Then visit the famed Mudmen, natives dressed in mud masks and mud-covered bodies who perform ghostly rituals—and watch the Chimbu Players, dressed in feathers and body paints, who re-enact battles and mime village events with startling realism. Includes: All-inclusive from Honolulu and return. Dates: July through November. Length of trip: 15 days. Group size: Varies. Cost: $4,100.

South Seas Gallery Travel, Inc.
353 Bleecker Street
New York, NY 10014
212-741-2777   *Indonesia*

From the crater lake of North Sumatra to the elaborate funerary customs of the Toraja people and the lush tropical ambiance of Bali . . . discover remarkable Indonesia. After a day in Singapore you'll head for North Sumatra's city of Medan and beautiful Lake Toba, a fifty-mile-long crater lake surrounded by mountains, and home of the Batak people. Pass by villages set among rubber, cocoa and tobacco plantations before setting off for intoxicating Jakarta, Sulawesi—often referred to as the "Orchid Island," and beautiful Bali—land of rituals, dances and Hindu Gods whose powers influence every aspect of life, from birth to death. Here you can visit the mysterious Elephant Caves and Sangeh, the holy monkey forest, before setting off for the famed eighth century Buddhist sanctuary in Jogyakarta. Includes: All-inclusive except meals in Singapore. Dates: Monthly. Length of trip: 18 days. Group size: Varies. Cost: $4,577.

South Seas Gallery Travel, Inc.
353 Bleecker Street
New York, NY 10014
212-741-2777   *Burma*

Come to fabled Mandalay. Known as the "Land of Golden Pagodas," Burma has for decades remained in complete isolation from the rest of the world, and preserved an ancient culture and a lifestyle untouched by the lures of the modern West. It is only recently that the gates of this country have opened, and visitors are allowed a glimpse at its unique and fascinating civilization. Highlights of this cultural exploration include: Shwedagon, the most sacred Buddhist temple in Burma; Pagan, an ancient city of four thousand fabulous temples and shrines; Mandalay, the capital of the last monarch; and Inle Lake, peaceful, magical and beautiful. And, of course, there are the Burmese people—warm, gracious and outgoing, and willing to share with visitors the wonders of their country. Includes: All-inclusive from Bangkok. Date: Contact for information. Length of trip: 6 days. Group size: Varies. Cost: $830.

Special Odysseys
P.O. Box 37
Medina, WA 98039
206-455-1960
Telex TWX 910-443-2366   *South Pacific*

This journey takes you to Fiji, Western Samoa, and the Cook Islands. Away from the glitter of tourist palaces, these three distinct island groups offer the chance to experience the true Polynesian lifestyle. The first stop is Fiji, with a strong Melanesian and Indian influence.

Here you'll have time to ease into the tropical tempo before heading to Western Samoa. Deserted lagoons behind coral reefs, people living the traditional way, and an unmatched friendliness greet you. Walk the beaches, snorkel, scuba dive, and enjoy all the coconut milk you can drink. On to Rarotonga in the Cook Islands, a Polynesian gem of wild orchids, frangipani, and glorious singing. You'll visit the remote island of Aitutaki. These trips are both escorted, or with independent itineraries and local hosts. References available on request. Dates: Escorted in May, unescorted year-round. Length of trip: 16 days. Group size: 10 to 15. Cost: $2,130 land cost. Special requirements: $500 deposit, good health and flexible attitude required.

Tunas Indonesia Tours & Travel
29, Jln Majapahit
P.O. Box 457 Jkt
Jakarta, Indonesia
341085
Telex 46542 Tunas Jkt

Indonesia

Step back in time and experience the island paradise of Nias. Learn about their ancient culture, and discover the culture and heritage of the handsome and friendly Dayahs on East Kalimantan. It's a land where you travel by long boats, passing great wooden statues, communal longhouses and lush orchid forests . . . savoring the natural, unspoiled way of life. Includes: Accommodation, full-board meals, transfers and excursions, English-speaking guide, boat charter. The Nias Island tour includes domestic flight Medan—Gunung Sitoli, Nias. Vv. Dates: Nias Island tour—April through August. East Kalimantan tour—year-round. Length: 5 days, 4 nights. Group size: Minimum 2 persons. Cost: Nias Island tour—$1,026 per person. East Kalimantan tour—$791 per person. Special requirements: Full prepayment should reach Tunas one month prior to tour.

Diving, Scuba •
Snorkeling •

Welcome to the rest of the world.

Most of Earth isn't earth—it's water, which covers 75% of the planet's surface. And there's plenty to see below sea level. While fourteen thousand different species of birds and mammals live on land, an astounding twenty-five thousand kinds of fish swarm, swim and undulate through the oceans.

Against the watery turquoise backdrop, snorkelers and scuba divers can swim alongside a dazzling array of brilliantly-hued fish—from the bright yellow angelfish and two-hundred-pound parrotfish of the Philippines to the iridescent, jewel-like queen triggerfish and hamlets of the Caribbean. There are friendly groupers who love to be petted . . . inquisitive schools of yellowtail snapper and graceful eagle rays who glide along the sandy bottom.

Surreal forms and flora shape the underwater landscape. Divers can explore magical "blue holes," circular pits over four hundred feet deep hung with stalactites and stalagmites. And swim through endless forests of elkhorn and staghorn coral . . . past giant sponges and gorgonians. Or see the sheer-walled majesty of drop-offs plunging two thousand feet straight down.

What makes a dive area great? The quantity and quality of marine life—both fish and coral. For example, over eighty varieties of coral thrive in the Caribbean—and about four hundred different kinds grow near Australia's Great Barrier Reef. Aside from that, it depends what you're into—wrecks, chimneys or walls . . . drift diving, night diving or caves.

Here are some favorite destinations that bring a gleam to the eyes of well-traveled divers:

Caribbean

Belize
Bonaire
Cozumel, Mexico
Grand Cayman, Cayman Is.
Roatan, Honduras
San Salvador, Bahamas

Pacific

Hawaii
Heron Island,
Australia

Plus:
Red Sea, Egypt,
Israel
Sri Lanka

Underwater adventure comes in two varieties—scuba diving and snorkeling.

ABOUT SCUBA

Scuba diving is a fairly recent innovation—developed by Jacques Cousteau and Emil Gagnan in the 1940's. Scuba divers carry their own air supply with them—the word itself is an acronym for "self-contained underwater breathing apparatus."

Practically anyone can learn to scuba dive, according to most instructors. You don't even have to know how to swim—the diving schools can teach you that. You just need to be in good general health.

In order to buy or rent scuba equipment or hire a guide—throughout the United States and in most other parts of the world—you must first be a certified diver. For certification, you must take a basic course of instruction which includes both pool and classroom work. To complete the program, you have to take a written exam and be "checked out" during open water dives. After passing the course, you receive a "C-card"—the diver's equivalent of "proof." Depending on which course you take and how fast you learn, the program takes about twenty to forty hours. Costs run about $100–$300.

There are five widely recognized American organizations for scuba diving:

NATIONAL ASSOCIATION OF SCUBA DIVING SCHOOLS (NASDS); 641 West Willow Syreet; Long Beach, CA 90806.
NATIONAL ASSOCIATION OF UNDERWATER INSTRUCTORS (NAUI); P.O. Box 14650; Montclair, CA 91763.
PROFESSIONAL ASSOCIATION OF DIVING INSTRUCTORS (PADI); 1243 East Warner Avenue; Santa Ana, CA 92705.
SCUBA SCHOOLS INTERNATIONAL (SSI); 2619 Canton Court; Fort Collins, CO 80525.
YOUNG MEN'S/WOMEN'S CHRISTIAN ASSOCIATION (YMCA). Contact your local branch.

In general, these groups recognize each other's certifications.

If you're not a diver, but you want to learn diving on your vacation, you have several options:

1. Do the classroom and pool work at home—and arrange to have the open water checkouts during your trip.
2. If you want to see what diving is like, many areas offer a three-hour "resort course"—particularly popular in the Caribbean. You dive with a qualified instructor, who supervises you step-by-step. These short resort courses do not qualify you for certification.
3. Take your complete certification course on vacation. It's a good idea to reserve your place in the course in advance. Some resorts just don't have the staff to handle both experienced divers and learners at the same time—and the experienced divers will get preference.

ABOUT SNORKELING

Giant groupers, iridescent parrotfish, stunning coral formations ... snorkelers can see them just as well as scuba divers. Many of the best diving areas also offer superb snorkeling, with visibility of fifty to two hundred feet.

Snorkelers (the so-called "skin divers") travel lighter than scuba-types. Just don a face mask, snorkel and fins and splash! You're off. For snorkeling, you can stay at the surface—or hold your breath, then dive down twenty or thirty feet or so to explore sea fans or visit with the fish. Many people find snorkeling easier than just plain swimming—the "aids" (mask and fins) enable you to cover more distance with less effort.

Snorkeling is most rewarding along fairly shallow reefs, which support a rich variety of sea life. In particular, areas near reef cuts attract large congregations of colorful fish. Many sites are great for both scuba divers and snorkelers—for example, snorkelers can view spectacular coral and fish by working the edges of drop-offs.

CHOOSING A TOUR OPERATOR

Here are some guidelines to help you evaluate dive tours:

1. Pick your dive destination honestly. Know exactly what you want to do on your vacation. Are you after great diving, pure and simple—or do you want other diversions too, like a posh hotel, gambling casinos and discos?
2. Is the dive shop affiliated with one of the scuba certifying organizations?

These groups also certify instructors and dive masters. Affiliation is another form of quality control, assuring that the operation meets important basic standards.

3. Consistency is all. Water constantly moves and changes—and so does the staff at various dive shops around the world. Check how long the operation has had the same owners/managers. If the dive shop maintains a consistently excellent reputation year after year, it indicates that the people running it know how to hire and train top quality professionals.

4. Do they make it easy for divers to dive? A good operation revolves around the convenience of the diver. Are boats close to the hotel, so you don't have to lug equipment too far? How distant are the most attractive dive sites? Are water tubs available to wash off gear? Is there a secure area for air tanks on the boat? If you're interested in underwater photography, is E-6 developing available? Are there strobes for rent? Is there a knowledgeable photographer around to answer questions?

5. Is the reef protected? A ban against spearfishing and the collecting of live corals preserves the richness and diversity of marine life. At Bonaire—which shows up on everyone's list of favorite diving spots—the reef has been protected for over twenty years. Dive boats even anchor onto fixed buoy markers rather than the reef, helping preserve the ecological balance.

6. Remember—underwater visibility is best during any area's dry season.

7. How many dives a day does the package include?

8. What's the charge for air fills?

9. Are rentals available? If you plan to rent equipment while on vacation, check its availability carefully. Reserve the equipment in advance, send a deposit and get a receipt. Whole vacations have been ruined for divers who arrive at some blissfully out-of-the-way island—only to discover that a key piece of equipment is already rented out.

10. Snorkelers can frequently get reduced dive package rates. Some tour operators give snorkelers a price break, charging them the non-divers rate plus a minimal boat usage fee. It never hurts to ask.

Sections of Related Interest

Cruises
Research Expeditions
Sailing
Yacht Charter

All Florida Adventure Tours
7930 North Kendall Drive
Miami, FL 33156
305-270-0219   *Florida*

Located in Key Largo, John Pennekamp Coral Reef State Park is 120 square miles of underwater paradise, encompassing the only living coral reefs in the continental United States. Surrounded by crystal clear water and populated by a countless variety of colorful sea life, the reefs offer some of the most beautiful underwater scenery in the world. All Florida offers a selection of snorkeling trips to the reef. Scuba diving can be arranged for groups, either at John Pennekamp Park or at Key West. Tour operator is a practicing biochemist with thirty years' management experience. Includes: Varies. Dates: All year. Length of trip: 1 day to 2 weeks. Group size: 15–90 (maximum 35 on some trips). Cost: Varies according to program. Special requirements: Advance deposits; no particular skills, education or training necessary. Tours are customized to level of group.

Aqua Adventures, Inc.
Murray Hill Sta.
P.O. Box 1792
New York, N.Y. 10156
212-725-5330 *Bahamas*

Aqua Adventures offers advanced and novice divers a wide range of specialty dive packages to twenty-seven different resorts in the Bahamas. These tropical islands have the best and most varied diving in the world—from "over the wall to 185 feet" on the world's third largest barrier reef at Andros, to colorful coral gardens at South Ocean Beach, used as locations for the underwater scenes in "Thunderball" and "For Your Eyes Only." Other Aqua Adventures' packages feature San Salvador's famous Riding Rock Inn, known for its underwater photo center, resident photographer and underwater photo classes. Non-divers receive reduced rates and can choose from a wide range of activities, like golf, tennis, horseback riding or casino gambling, depending on the resort. Some areas also offer non-divers a free introductory "resort diving course." Fourteen years' experience. Includes: Hotel accommodations, diving and meals (other features vary by resort). Dates: Year-round. Length of trip: 3–8 days. Group size: 1–30. Cost: $199–$1,199. Special requirements: All divers must have a valid "C" card or take resort course. $100 deposit upon booking with full payment due 30 days prior to departure.

Dive BVI, Ltd.
Virgin Gorda Yacht Harbor
P.O. Box 1040
Virgin Gorda, BVI
(809-49) 55513 *British Virgin Islands*

Scuba dive alongside turtles, manta rays, schools of tarpon, and other exotic sea creatures in the colorful British Virgin Islands. Dive BVI will take you to a variety of dive sites off Virgin Gorda, featuring reefs, caves, wrecks . . . even an underwater chimney. The thirteen sites include "Wreck of the Rhone," film location for the movie "The Deep." Dive BVI also offers introductory afternoon Scuba courses for the non-diving vacationer and a four-day open water certification course consisting of eight open water dives plus lectures. For experienced divers, an advanced open water course to improve navigation and search pattern skills is available along with a Dive Master course for guide and safety officer certifications. Dive BVI boasts a Professional Association of Underwater Instructors international training facility and Professional Association of Underwater Instructors and National Association of Underwater Instructors certified instructors. Diving trips include: Boat transportation to dive sites, refreshments. Dates: Daily, all year. Length of trip: 3–6 hours. Group size: 6–16. Cost: $50 (discounts available for large groups). Scuba Introduction course, $60 per person. Open Water Certification course, $250 per person. Advanced Open Water course, $350 per person. Special requirements: Deposit plus certification card required for equipment rentals.

Dive in Australia
680 Beach Street, Suite 498
San Francisco, CA 94109
415-928-4480
Telex 79072257 *Australia*

It's two thousand kilometers long, traces the Continental Shelf of northeastern Australia from Bundaberg to the tip of faraway Cape York, and is the largest, most complex living coral reef in the world. Dive in Australia invites you to explore the Great Barrier Reef and the Coral Sea with their intensely clear waters, spectacular underwater scenery, giant gorgonians, crinoids, enormous schools of pelagic fish, rays and turtles ... plus delicate shells like volutes, cowries and tritons. Dive in Australia offers a variety of diving packages on six comfortable diving boats ranging in size from fifty to ninety feet, all with complete scuba diving facilities. It you desire to remain shore-based, you can stay at one of four island dive resorts—the tropical and serene Heron Island; the resort islands of South Molle and Hayman, both in the Whitsunday Island group; and the remote luxurious paradise resort, Lizard Island Lodge. Includes: Accommodations, 3 meals a day, weight belt, weights, back pack, tank and air fills. Dates: May through January. Length of trip: 6–12 days. Group size: 1–20. Cost: $1,000–$3,000. Special requirements: Certification card.

Ed-U-Dive
P.O. Box 724
Libby, MT 59923
406-293-6244   *Worldwide*

Excitement and education—that's what Ed-U-Dive offers on its worldwide diving vacations. Worldwide programs include exploration and study in Micronesia, Papua New Guinea, Grand Cayman, the Florida Keys, Bonaire and the Virgin Islands. On these action-packed itineraries, scuba divers have two or more tanks a day—giving plenty of time to observe, explore and photograph colorful coral formations and tropical fish. For snorkelers, the diving locations also have shallow reefs nearby. At informal evening lectures and slide presentations, you can learn to identify fish and invertebrates, study coral reef formations and find out about the local people, culture and ecology. Tour guides are professional educators, researchers, photographers and naturalists, with qualified dive masters for the diving sessions. In many cases, college course credit may be available. Includes: Accommodations, meals, education and dive guide; other facilities vary with location. Dates: Year-round. Length of trip: Varies. Group size: 8–20. Cost: $1,300 and up. Special requirements: Scuba divers must be certified. Deposits from $200 depending on tour.

Evecar Inc. Travel
25 West 43rd Street, Suite 1220
New York, NY 10036
212-354-8303   *Tobago*

Tobago, the legendary island of Robinson Crusoe, is an unspoiled Caribbean paradise filled with overgrown tropical jungles, rugged coves and sun-drenched days. It's also a perfect place to sun and surf—or scuba into its wondrous underwater world. There's something for every diver, from the beauty of coral gardens, colorful fish and huge sponges to the "monsters" of the deep—the sharks, moray eels, sea turtles and barracuda. There are walls to climb, caves to explore, even a shipwreck to satisfy the lust for adventure. Includes: Round-trip transfers, full American breakfast and dinner daily at Mount Irvine Bay Hotel (not at Sandy Point Beach Club, but optional meal plan available), welcome cocktail party; 5 scuba dives include boat, air, guide, tanks, weights. Dates: Year-round. Length: 8 days, 7 nights. Group size: Varies. Cost: $259 EP at Sandy Point Beach Club. $529 MAP at Mount Irvine Bay Hotel. Non-divers deduct $100.

Evecar Inc. Travel
25 West 43rd Street, Suite 1220
New York, NY 10036
212-354-8303   *Barbados*

With perfect weather, cloudless azure skies and white sandy beaches that ramble for miles along the coast, the beauty of Barbados calls out to you for exploration. There's plenty of waterfalls, swimming, shopping and colorful schooners plying the waters. And underwater, there's another world—for divers, complete with a 365-foot sunken freighter whose towering masts, open decks and passageways offer endless chances for snooping. Barbados underwater is a mecca of colorful fish, exciting reefs and exotic sights so fascinating the diving adventurer almost won't want to come out of the waters to sample Barbados at night in all its lavish tropical splendor. Includes: Round-trip transfers, welcome cocktail party, 5-dive package including boat, air, guide, tanks and weights. Dates: Year-round. Length: 8 days, 7 nights. Group size: Varies. Cost: Smugglers Cove: $299 EP. Other hotels: $509 MAP. Non-divers deduct $100.

Fathom Five Professional Divers
P.O. Box 907
Kola, Hawaii 96756
808-742-6991   *Hawaii*

Fathom Five Professional Divers is located on the south shore of Kauai, just moments away from many ideal dive spots. There's Koloa Landing, where you can feed the tame fish, and the Sheraton Caverns (thirty-five to sixty feet) home of many graceful sea turtles. At the "General Store" dive (eighty feet), you could see anything from the remains of a nineteenth-century steamship wreck to hundreds of Lemon butterflies feeding furiously on the plankton-covered reef. Fathom Five specializes in small, personal groups, for both introductory scuba dives (four maximum) and the two-tank boat dives (six maximum) for certified divers. For snorkelers, they offer a relaxing two-hour "Snorkel by Boat" tour (six maximum), a great way to view the island from the water. Certification courses, sales and rentals of snorkel/scuba equipment and airfills are also available. Fathom Five is a National Association of Underwater Instructors Pro Facility. Includes: Boat with captain and guide. Dates: Daily trips. Length of trip: ½ day (3–4 hours). Group size: 6. Cost: $20 (snorkeling) to $55 (two-tank boat dive) per day. Special requirements: None for snorkeling or introductory dives. Basic Scuba certification card for certified divers; 50% deposit.

Fort Bovisand Underwater Centre
Fort Bovisand
Plymouth, Devon PL9 0AB
England
(0752) 42570 or 45641   *Great Britain*

Dive at Fort Bovisand, Britain's largest diving school and center. Vacations and cruises are available for everyone from the complete novice to the advanced diver. Choose from fifty different courses taught by experienced instructors with internationally recognized qualifications (PADI, BSAC, SAA, etc.). Accommodations are within the historic gunrooms of the nineteenth-century Fort Bovisand. Includes: All equipment including diving suit, accommodations, all meals, taxes, instruction. Dates: All year. Length of trip: 1–3 weeks. Group size: Up to 100. Cost: From £109. Special requirements: Ability to swim, minimum age 15, good medical condition, ⅓ deposit plus completed application and medical forms upon booking.

La Mer Diving Seafari, Inc.
823 United Nations Plaza, #810
New York, NY 10017
212-599-0886
Telex 238973 AIIL   *Australia*

One hundred fifty miles behind Australia's Great Barrier Reef lie the famed reefs of the mighty Coral Sea: Marion, Lihou, Flinders, Diamond and more. You'll see and photograph coral in branches and towers, giant clams and tropical fish indigenous only to the Coral Sea. While enjoying unlimited diving all day you'll also see large rays, turtles, seasnakes and sharks—though as everywhere in the world, such predators are no more than curious at the presence of a diver. You will experience fourteen days' cruising and diving on board the fully equipped seventy-nine-foot "Coralita," featuring air-conditioned double cabins and fine meals. Expeditions escorted by specialists and expert photographers and qualified dive instructors. Includes: 2 nights' accommodations in Sydney; touring; all transfers, guide, 14–16 days unlimited diving and equipment, accommodations, meals and color-processing facilities aboard the seventy-nine-foot "Coralita"—or 7 days unlimited diving, services, accommodations, meals aboard the "Takaroa." Dates: July through September. Length of trip: 7–20 days. Group size: 6–12. Cost: $1,400–$4,250. Special requirements: Diving certification and ⅓ of price for deposit.

La Mer Diving Seafari, Inc.
823 United Nations Plaza, #810
New York, NY 10017
212-599-0886
Telex 238973 AIIL   *Mexico*

Boasting one of the world's richest marine faunas, the Sea of Cortez off Baja California, Mexico abounds with spectacular diving opportunities. Summer and fall in the Sea of Cortez are a time of clear water and surface temperatures in the seventies and eighties. Everything is on a massive scale; stunning drop-offs, vast undersea caverns and colorful kaleidoscopes of vibrant marine life. There is also a large marine mammal population, including whales, sea turtles and sea lions. You'll see and photograph rare species, huge schools of pelagics, herds of hammerhead sharks . . . even men riding manta rays. As your diving base you will stay on board the eighty-foot motor cruiser "Don Jose" offering unlimited diving, including some night diving. All tours are escorted by qualified diving guides. Special expeditions are headed by marine biologists and expert underwater photographers. Includes: 1 night accommodation in La Paz, transfers, guide, unlimited diving, diving equipment; accommodations, meals, soft drinks and beer aboard the 80-foot "Don Jose." Dates: June through October. Length of trip: 7–12 days. Group size: 12–16. Cost: $895–$3,250. Special requirements: Diving certification and deposit of ⅓ of trip price.

La Mer Diving Seafari, Inc.
823 United Nations Plaza, #810
New York, NY 10017
212-599-0886
Telex 238973 AIIL   *Ecuador, Galapagos Islands*

While the terrestrial wildlife is well known, few divers are aware that Galapagos' aquatic animals are equally unusual. Both on land and in the sea, one-third of all species you will see and photograph are found only on these remote volcanic islands. La Mer's Galapagos program has you sailing, diving and living aboard a comfortable seventy-foot ketch with double cabins and fine food. You'll sail among the major and remote islands, escorted by a local naturalist guide, exploring colonies of turtles, marine iguanas, seals and more, plus diving two to three times a day in waters full of wonders. Includes: 3 nights' accommodations in Quito; transfers; touring; 14 days of diving, including equipment and services; accommodations and all meals aboard 70-foot ketch; local naturalist guide, private escort and taxes. Dates: March through June. Length of trip: 18 days. Group size: 8. Cost: $3,750. Special requirements: Diving certificate and ⅓ of trip price for deposit.

Diver photographs soft coral formations in the Red Sea. (LA MER DIVING SEAFARI, INC., AMOS NACHOUM)

La Mer Diving Seafari, Inc.
823 United Nations Plaza, #810
New York, NY 10017
212-599-0886
Telex 238973 AIIL   *Egypt, Israel*

Along the coast of the harsh Sinai Desert lies the legendary Red Sea, offering some of the most exciting diving in the world. Breathtaking vertical drop-offs are decorated with stunning coral formations and teem with a kaleidoscope of tropical fish, while occasional eagle and manta rays pass by; sharks cruise and schools of pelagics soar through the crystal-clear blue water. La Mer dives the fabled reefs of the Red Sea; Tiran Straits, Ras Muhamed, Sharem el-Sheikh, and the newly accessible virgin reefs of the Brothers, Shadwan Island and the wreck of the Don Raven. Your group will spend the day diving, not sailing, for you'll live on board the seventy-five-foot motor yacht "Lady Jenny II" or the eighty-five-foot "Red Sea Diver," enjoying air-conditioned double cabins and fine food. All trips escorted by qualified tour guide familiar with the Red Sea. Includes: 2 nights' accommodations in Jerusalem, all transfers, guides, tour of Jerusalem, 10 days' diving and equipment, double occupancy accommodations and all meals on board, 1 night accommodation in Tel Aviv or Cairo. Dates: April through November. Length of trip: 15 days. Group size: 10–11. Cost: $2,850. Special requirements: Diving certification and ⅓ of trip price for deposit.

Ocean Voyages
1709 Bridgeway
Sausalito, CA 94965
415-332-4681
Telex 470-561 SAIL UI   *Costa Rica*

Cocos Island, located in the Pacific three hundred miles off the coast of Costa Rica, is the world's largest uninhabited island. Long ago a favorite hideaway of marauding pirates awaiting Spanish treasure galleons, Cocos is today part of Costa Rica's national park system. It's a lush verdant tropical island, very beautiful with over two hundred waterfalls, many of which plunge directly into the sea. The island holds many treasures for naturalists—unique treeferns and many types of birds, including three unique to the island. But above all Cocos Island has remarkable snorkeling and scuba sites. These are virgin sites, and world class. The fish are abundant (sometimes it's hard to film or photograph underwater because fish cloud the view); and the water is clear, with tremendous visibility even 170 feet down. As your base, you'll live aboard and dive from either the "Victoria" or the "Isla de Ibeza," eighty-two-foot and ninety-six-foot Gaff Schooners, respectively. You'll be guided by expert crew and qualified dive masters, who know the sites of this off-the-beaten-path dive spot. Includes: Dive tanks, air, etc.; divemaster; sailing, etc. All-inclusive for time on the boat, except liquor. Dates: November through May. Length of trip: 15 days. Group size: Up to 15. Cost: $1,325. Special requirements: $200 deposit.

Sobek Expeditions
Angels Camp, CA 95222
209-736-2661
800-344-3284 (except HI, AK, CA)
Telex 172746   *New Guinea*

The Papuan Great Barrier Reef is an underwater menagerie of tropical marine life and brilliantly limned coral. You'll sail, swim, sun and enjoy this living wonder, spending nights camped on a sandy, palm-fringed isle. No diving experience is necessary; the operator is equipped to handle all levels of ability, from novice to expert. Operator has more than ten years' experience. Includes: Everything, except airfare. Dates: May. Length: 14 days. Group size: 5–15. Cost: $1,975.

The Watersports People
508 South Street
Key West, FL 33040
305-296-4546   *Florida*

Learn to dive on the only living barrier reef in the continental United States—with the Watersports People, in tropical Key West, Florida. The Watersports People offer a wide range of diving programs. For novice divers, there's a one-week course leading to Professional Association of Underwater Instructors or Young Men's/Women's Christian Association certification. Vacationing non-divers can "wet" their appetite with an introductory resort course that includes a half-day reef trip. Meanwhile, certified divers can check out the Keys' numerous sunken ship wrecks (according to legend, loaded with pirate treasure) and advanced divers can receive additional training in navigation, rescue, night, deep or drift diving. Includes: Scuba instruction, all scuba equipment, open water dives on the reef, nationally accepted certification upon successful completion. Dates: Bi-monthly, year-round. Length of trip: 1 week. Group size: 2–8. Cost: $225 per person. Special requirements: Fair swimming ability, some snorkeling experience, $50 deposit.

Dog Sledding •

Since earliest times, dog sledding has played an important role in the exploration and settlement of the Far North. Originally used by the native Eskimos and Indians, dog teams were also employed by eighteenth-century fur trappers like John Jacob Astor—and nineteenth-century miners caught up in the fever of the Klondike Gold Rush. Dog sledding has produced its legends—like Jack London's *Call of the Wild*—and its true heroes, such as the valiant relay teams that sped life-saving serum to Nome to prevent a diphtheria epidemic in 1925.

Although snowmobiles have become increasingly popular, dog sledding still provides a reliable means of travel in the icy reaches of North America. Many national parks ban both air drops and snowmobiles, and dog teams help carry supplies and mail to these areas.

The sled dogs themselves—mainly huskies and malamutes—are bred for the task. Their tough feet can withstand the ice, and won't form snowballs between the pads of their paws. Under optimum conditions, teams can pull a several-hundred-pound load for thirty miles or more a day. A racing team can trot along at twelve miles per hour, lope at eighteen miles per hour, although drifting snow, thawing temperatures and overflow water on river ice can slow the pace considerably.

The tours which follow offer prospective mushers a wide-ranging assortment of dogsled adventure from day trips where you can can just ride along admiring the scenery to intensive week-long expeditions in which you learn to feed, harness and drive the dogs. On many of the trips, you'll also be traveling by cross-country ski or snowshoe.

Even at very cold temperatures, life on the trail can be very comfortable if you have the proper clothing. The tour operator will provide you with a complete list of everything you need to bring along; some companies also have some cold weather clothing or sleeping bags available for rent.

Algonquin Canoe Routes
P.O. Box 187
Whitney, Ontario
Canada K0J-2M0
705-637-2699   *Canada*

This winter adventure combines dogsledding, cross country skiing and snowshoeing all on one trip. You'll learn how to drive your own dogsled team in the wilderness area of Algonquin Park, which offers over five hundred kilometers of trails to explore. As you mush along, you'll also be able to observe an incredible variety of wildlife. Over twenty-five years in business. Dates: December through April 15. Length: Daily and weekly. Group size: 40 maximum. Includes: Food, lodging, sauna, instruction, equipment. Cost: $60 (Canadian) per day. Special requirements: 20% deposit.

Denali Dog Tours
P.O. Box 1
McKinley Park, AK 99755
907-683-2321   *Alaska*

Participate in one of the North's most historic, adventurous, and aesthetically pleasing modes of wilderness transportation—dogsledding. Traveling through Denali National Park you'll work right with the musher—driving a large freight team, riding the break or guide pole skis; breaking trail with snowshoes, if necessary; harnessing, feeding and caring for the dogs, and

Traveling by dog team offers a rare opportunity to experience winter in compatibility with one's surroundings. (DENALI DOG TOURS, BILL FORSBERG)

making camp. You'll follow old patrol trails and spend the nights in original ranger patrol cabins or heated tent camps. The Park includes 3,030 square miles of icy, saw-toothed mountains, rolling tundra, and small sheltered valleys—a magnificent wilderness encompassing a complete ecosystem. Alaskan trail meals—bannock, salmon and sourdough—give sustenance for this hearty adventure. Over twenty years' experience. Includes: Food, clothing, cabins, sleds. Dates: November through April. Length: 1–10 days. Group size: 1–5. Cost: $100 per day. Special requirements: Stamina, coordination.

North Country Travelers
P.O. Box 14
Atlin, B.C.
Canada, VOW 1AO
radio/phone through Whitehorse, Yukon, Canada
2M-5017 White Mountain Channel between
8–10 AM and 6–8 PM   *Canada*

Learn how to harness and drive a team of friendly, hardworking huskies. Guests can drive the dogs or cross country ski on this one-hundred-mile, round-trip journey through the Atlin Lake Wilderness. The Atlin area combines an historic Gold Rush atmosphere with some of the most spectacular mountain, glacier and lake scenery in the Yukon. Your destination is an extremely remote log cabin adjacent to the scenic glacier areas of Atlin Lake. Along the way, you can enjoy scenic side trips on snowshoe or skis into secluded areas of Canada's North. Skill level and difficulty of trips can be adjusted to suit the individual. Fifteen years' experience. Includes: Transportation from Whitehorse to Atlin and return, meals and lodging in cabins or tents (bring your own sleeping gear). Dates: December through March. Length: 7 days. Group size: Maximum 6. Cost: $980 per week.

Folklore •

Fairies, leprechauns, trolls, monsters, magicians, brave warriors and beautiful princesses—such is the stuff that folklore and mythology are made of.

Many countries have fascinating sagas that have been handed down from generation to generation—spellbinding stories of ancient traditions, battles and superstitions that are kept alive and told again and again with excitement and colorful detail.

These legends and tales are centuries old—and provide insights into the people and their culture today. Many stories still influence modern-day customs, and are part of the vital, joyous occasions of daily life.

Part of the fun of visiting new countries is steeping yourself in these traditions. The tours that follow can open up ancient worlds to you. And as you stroll through Gastonbury—perhaps the Avalon of Arthurian legend . . . visit Austerlitz, near where Napoleon defeated the Russian and Austrian armies . . . share in a pena (musical circle) in Peru, you may pause to wonder what exactly is myth—and what is history.

SECTIONS OF RELATED INTEREST

Culture/History

Czechoslovak Travel Bureau
10 East 40th Street
New York, NY 10016
212-689-9720
Telex 62467 AUW   *Czechoslovakia*

The annual International Folklore Festival at Straznice takes place during the last weekend of June. This three-day tour includes participation in the Festive Folk Costume Procession of Folklore Groups from Czechoslovakia and abroad; the Main Festival Program with the participation of the best folklore ensembles from the region of Hodonin and Breclav; participation in the program at Straznice (meeting of ensembles from abroad); sightseeing tour of Brno or Gottwaldov; half-day excursion to Kromeriz with its fine arts gallery, State Castle; Buchlovice Castle (eighteenth century, with its exhibition of Baroque interiors and furniture), Buchlov Castle (a thirteenth-century royal castle); Slavkov (Austerlitz) Castle with barrow of peace (seventeenth-century baroque chateau featuring an art gallery and museum with exhibitions on the Napoleonic wars). Includes: Hotel accommodations, all meals, guides, transfers by bus, entrance fees, sightseeing tour of Brno or Gottwaldov, Slavkov (Austerlitz) Castle. Dates: June. Length of trip: 3 days. Group size: 15–35. Cost: From US $136.

Forum Travel International
2437 Durant Avenue, #208
Berkeley, CA 94704
415-843-8294   *Peru*

Forum Travel leads this fascinating tour of Peru to many of the interesting yet little-visited areas of the country. Forum Travel International concentrates on the Peruvian people and

134

their cultural and natural environments as they have developed over thousands of years, highlighting dances, weavings, music, dresses, foods and architecture. You will visit Penas (musical circles), artisans' shops, the private museum Amano, dances and folkloric ensembles, plus the famous ruins of Machu Picchu and Cuzco. Your trip may be extended to include other parts of Peru. In operation since 1965. Includes: Accommodations, meals, ground transportation, guides and local taxes. Dates: Year-round. Length of trip: 14–28 days. Group size: 2–20. Cost: From $1,548.

**International Summer Schools
Warnborough College
Boar's Hill
Oxford OX1 5ED England
(0865) 730901**
Great Britain

The myths and legends of ancient Britain—King Arthur and his knights, the quest for the Holy Grail and Celtic tales—come alive on this two-week study tour. Field trips to historic sites associated with the legends, including Avebury Circle, Stonehenge, Salisbury Cathedral, the Uffington White Horse, Bath and Glastonbury, help make this course unique and memorable. Three hours of college credit may be earned. Includes: Accommodations, breakfast and dinner, lectures, field trips, and course examination and transcript. Dates: June through August. Length of trip: 2 weeks. Group size: Varies. Cost: $895.

Gold Panning •
Treasure Hunting •
Gem Collecting •

"Gold!" In staid Massachusetts settlements, in the foothills of West Virginia and in the great Oklahoma dust bowl, the boisterous cry resounded, and a generation of Americans headed west to seek its fortune.

The year was 1849. Civil strife was brewing, and the industrial revolution, with its standardization of personal lifestyles, lay yet a few decades in the offering. Rampant pioneering zeal drove men and women into new reaches of the untamed frontier. The time was ripe for adventure.

Abandoning their homes, jobs and families, prospectors staked out spartan encampments in the hills of northern California. In hopes of hitting a strike, they panned for gold nuggets with a mixture of rugged pride and desperation. Some hit the Mother Lode; others busted. But all were driven in their quest by a peculiarly American spirit of vigorous self-sufficiency and personal fortitude.

This same spirit breathes excitement into gold panning and treasure hunting adventure packages today. You don't have to forsake house and home for your gold rush, but you can still experience the thrill of rolling up your sleeves and sifting precious gold nuggets from the rough soil.

Like the forty-niners, you'll be moved as much by the quest as by its rewards. You can seek your fortune in a variety of natural treasure chests.

- Relive the excitement of the Alaskan Gold Rush, panning for gold in a mine created by the daring original pioneers.
- Don scuba gear and dive for Spanish treasure in the azure waters of Costa Rica.
- Discover rare and beautiful gems, or reclaim the forty-niners' strikes in the Pacific Northwest.

There's no guarantee you'll hit a lode or uncover untold sums of buried treasure, but the thrill of the hunt sets the blood coursing, and the possibility of striking it rich looms tantalizingly before you. You'll be stepping back into the adventure of an earlier era when the frontiers were open, and people built their fortunes through determination and resiliency. And you'll have a chance to sightsee in the rugged wilderness that inspires awe and respect.

On previous vacations, you've brought home T-shirts, paperweights, and assorted regional handicrafts. This vacation, why not bring back gold?

136

Brazilian Views, Inc.
201 East 66th Street, Suite 21G
New York, NY 10021
212-472-9539   *Brazil*

Ninety percent of the world's semiprecious stones and fifty percent of the world's diamonds come from Brazil. This tour begins in the state of Minas Gerais, where the 752-carat Vargas diamond and a 324,700-carat aquamarine were discovered. Next is Governador Valadares, the biggest Brazilian producer of tourmalines (eighty-seven different colors have been found). Continue to Teofilo Otoni, Minas' mining center for 140 years, known for its wholesale gem dealers. Visit an aquamarine mine and Brazil's largest private collector, whose treasures include an extremely rare group of seventy-two pieces of lepidolite and red tourmalines. Then proceed to Ouro Preto, South America's baroque capital and imperial topaz center, where you'll tour an open pit imperial topaz mine and visit the Museum of the School of Mines, containing one of the world's best mineral collections. Final stop is in Rio de Janeiro, where you can shop for Brazilian amethyst, topaz, tourmaline, emeralds, diamonds and other stones. Includes: Visits as per itinerary, lecture on Brazil's gems and minerals by leading gemologist, introductions to dealers. Dates: May through September. Length of trip: 10 to 14 days. Group size: 15–25. Cost: Under $3,000 (including airfare).

Exploration Holidays and Cruises
1500 Metropolitan Park Building
Seattle, WA 98101
800-426-0600
206-624-8551 in WA & Canada
Telex 32-96-36   *Alaska*

Here is a diversified tour that offers you the opportunity to retrace the history of the Alaskan Gold Rush and learn about the life and culture of the Eskimo. Your tour starts off with a flight to Nome, Gold Rush capital of the Arctic. After seeing the city, you'll stop by a gold mine where you can pan for gold—and leave with a sample. Then jet north to Kotzebue, crossing the Arctic Circle. Here you'll be able to observe Eskimo culture and craftsmanship with native dancing, ivory carving, skin sewing and a blanket-tossing demonstration. Includes: Air transportation to and from Anchorage to Nome and Kotzebue, sightseeing and accommodations. Dates: May through September. Length: 2 days/1 night. Cost: $453.

Municipal Tourist Office
Bahnhofstrabe 13
Idar-Oberstein, West Germany D-6580
06781/27025   *Germany*

Diamonds are a girl's best friend and here's a jewel of a trip for anyone interested in the fascinating world of gem-cutting, gem mines and copper mines. The perfect setting for all this glitter is the robust country of Germany, where you'll explore Frankfurt, attend five gem-cutting seminars, tour the gem mines in the Steinkaulenberg, view the German Precious Stones Museum, go underground sightseeing in the copper mines in Fischbach and the slate quarry in Bundenbach, and top it all off with a wine-tasting excursion through the Wine Museum in Bernkastel. Includes: Bus transfer from and to Frankfurt, hotels with breakfast buffet, welcome dinner, gem-cutting seminar (5 lessons—3 hours each) plus certificate of participation, excursions according to program, entrance fees, wine-tasting, English-speaking tour guide. Dates: Year-round. Length: 7 days. Group size: 6–20 people. Cost: DM 1,090 per person. Special requirements: Prepayment of DM 100 per person.

**Northwest Adventures
North 8884 Government Way
Hayden Lake, ID 83835
203-772-7531
800-635-1379**   *Pacific Northwest*

Roll up your sleeves and pan for gold, just like the men and women of yesteryear. Or discover a rare and beautiful five-star garnet. This company offers a variety of goldpanning and gem-collecting adventures in the Pacific Northwest. Riches can be found . . . and if you fail to find your retirement fund, you will have enjoyed fun-filled days in search of treasure amid some beautiful scenery. Includes: Varies according to trip. Dates: May through November. Length: 1–10 days. Group size: 5–65. Cost: Varies. Special requirements: 25% or $100 deposit.

**The Treasure Hunter, Inc.
P.O. Box 558
Manvel, TX 77578
713-489-9156**   *Costa*
Telex 792333 via Tlx Hou Treasure Hunter   *Rica*

Look for gold nuggets, Spanish piece-of-eight coins and pre-Colombian artifacts while staying at a comfortable, isolated retreat on Costa Rica's Sierpe River. This is a real adventure in one of the last remote, almost unexplored regions of the world, where the traveler can be surrounded by beautiful scenery while doing real treasure searching and exploration along with professionals. Scuba divers as well as treasure hunters find many superb sites to explore in this natural wonderland known for its flora and fauna. You can also visit San Jose's fine museums, known for their display of gold artifacts. Operator has over ten years' experience in treasure hunting. Includes: Food, lodging, boats, guides, ground transportation and airfare from Houston. Dates: December through June. Length: 8 days. Group size: 12 people. Cost: $995. Special requirements: 50% deposit.

Hiking •
Trekking •
Walking •

Hiking, trekking and walking differ from backpacking in that, as you trek through the wilderness, you don't have to carry the weight of the world (or even your own supplies) on your shoulders. You have a beast of burden—van, horse, camel, llama, mule, or porter—to tote your gear. Or you can hike hut to hut—or lodge to lodge—where you'll take your meals and spend the nights. All you have to carry is your clothing.

Hiking without heavy packs removes some of the restrictions on mobility. You can cover more miles, over more varied terrain. Or you can take it easy along gentle paths, studying the local architecture as well as the flora and fauna.

Whether you embark upon a vigorous trek or leisurely ramble, hiking tours give you a feeling of independence. You venture into the wilderness under your own impetus. On foot, you become aware of all of the smells and sounds of the forest. There's no vehicle to insulate you from the scenery, or whisk you away at a speed that blurs all of the details. You can see, touch, explore, photograph, and rustle about in whatever countryside presents itself.

The only limitation on hiking tours is that the areas must be navigable by foot, which allows almost the entire solid earth. Variety is the spice of hiking adventures.

- Hike at the foot of stately Mt. Fuji along ancient samurai trails, spending barefoot evenings in traditional Japanese Ryokan, and relaxing with mineral baths and shiatsu massages.
- Wander along the enchanting country of the Swiss Alps as your guide points out the highlights and history of the region.
- Climb Mt. Apo in the Philippines, hiking beneath towering mahogany trees, past steaming sulfur chimneys, hot springs, geysers, and carnivorous pitcher plants.
- Venture into the volcanic wilderness of Alaska, an unspoiled region of grizzly bears and massive ice sculptures.

In the listings which follow, you'll find a tremendous diversity of ambulatory adventures—both gentle strolls and rigorous expeditions—everything from walking tours of Count Dracula's Transylvanian Alps to classic assaults of the great peaks of the Himalayas. The tour operators can let you know how strenuous the trips are, and what special skills, if any, are required.

In their brochures, you'll find that many outfitters grade their programs as to their degree of difficulty and strenuousness. For example, one operator classifies expeditions as follows:

Trips are ranked by both a letter and a numerical grade. The numerical grade (1, 2 or 3) takes into account "subjective" factors (length of daily walks, physical exertion, trail conditions, or extremes of temperature).

1: Easy   2: Moderate   3: Strenuous

The letter grade (A,B,C,D,E) denotes "objective" distinctions, such as the altitude reached on the trip or any special experience required.

GRADE A: These non-hiking trips can be undertaken by almost anyone who is in good health and enjoys a moderately active life.

GRADE B: Hiking, below fifteen thousand feet. Average six to ten miles per day. These trips are for people who enjoy excellent health and who, in the normal course of their lives, spend most of their weekends hiking, running, skiing or in other active outdoor sports.

GRADE C: Hiking and altitudes above fifteen thousand feet. These trips are for people truly in top condition.

GRADE D: In addition to assuming that you are in excellent condition, this rating requires that you have practical experience in basic use of climbing equipment (ropes, ice axe, crampons) and some general mountain knowledge.

GRADE E: These trips require at least three years of solid experience in the skills appropriate to the expedition.

Each operator should explain its own grading system; some may be less stringent than others. Check descriptions or contact the operator before you finalize your tour plans.

Organized hiking trips offer two big advantages: the tour operator organizes portage details and offers expertise in the areas visited. You won't have to worry about leading your mule over a craggy mountain pass—just get your unencumbered self across it, and your gear will follow. Most tour operators specialize in specific areas, so the guides are experts at meeting the challenges of the region. They'll know the best trails to take, what equipment to bring, and how to judge the weather. They'll also be able to provide background information on the plant and animal life, and point out off-the-trail lookout points that offer spectacular views.

Whether you hike around Cape Cod or the Cape of Good Hope, you'll want comfortable, supportive footgear. Mountain climbing on almost any level calls for sturdy hiking boots. Light hiking boots or somewhat rugged walking shoes will be fine on less intense hikes. Break in any footgear well in advance of your trip—get the blisters at home, if get them you must.

Your tour operator should recommend appropriate shoes or boots, along with a list of clothing and other equipment you'll need to bring. Your clothing should be mostly cotton and wool—natural fibers breathe best and keep the moisture off your skin. Other essential gear might include a sleeping bag, rain poncho and knapsack for lunchtime snacks, camera, etc.

When evaluating different tours, pay particular attention to pacing: how many miles do you cover each day and over what kind of terrain? If a tour encompasses high elevations, the itinerary should allow you time to adjust to the altitude. Check whether there are any layover days, when you can just rest up or explore an area in depth. Many tours leave ample time for photography, in-depth nature study and other wilderness pursuits. On some programs you spend the nights in inns or huts, which may offer additional activities. If you're interested in observing wildlife, check the migration patterns of the regions you consider. Migrations generally coincide with the changeover of the seasons or rainy periods—as does the flowering of plants.

Hiking is a tremendously varied and inexpensive way to learn about the world around you. Whether you're scaling rock faces or sauntering along country lanes, camping out or soaking up local color in small inns, you'll discover that some of the most fascinating places in the world are the ones you can get to on foot.

Above the Clouds Trekking
P.O. Box 398
Worcester, MA 01602
617-799-4499　　　　　　　　　　　　　　　　*Romania*

Try trekking in the land of Count Dracula—the Transylvanian Alps. After a day of relaxed sightseeing in Bucharest, you'll drive to Busteni, where a cable car ride will bring you to the trailhead. From here, it's a two-day trek via Mt. Omu (8,200 feet) to reach Count Dracula's famous Bran Castle. Then for the next week you'll follow the crest trail of the Fagaras Mountains, Romania's highest. After a leisurely day strolling through the ancient walled city of Sibiu, take to the trail again for a three-day trek in the Retezat Mountains. Drive to Durau, via Sighisoara, Dracula's birthplace. The last short trek, in the Ceahlau Mountains, provides stunning views of Lake Izvoru Muntelui and caps off your adventure in this "undiscovered" trekkers' paradise. Accommodations in the mountains are in huts. Curative mineral baths are available in many places. Includes: All meals and accommodations (hotels in the cities, inns in the mountains), all meals, internal ground and air transport. Dates: June and October. Length of trip: 21 days. Group size: Maximum 15. Cost: Land $1,345. Special requirements: Physically fit and active. $200 deposit.

Above the Clouds Trekking
P.O. Box 398
Worcester, MA 01602
617-799-4499   *Spain*

If you are looking for the less-traveled path, the Spanish side of the Pyrenees has much to offer. From Barcelona, you'll drive to Viellas, in the shadow of Pico de Aneto—at 11,233 feet, it's the highest peak in the Pyrenees. From here, you'll cross the flanks of El Posets and Monte Perdido, two other eleven-thousand-foot peaks. The valleys, villages, and shepherds along the way provide a strong feeling for an earlier Europe. Accommodations are in "refugios," mountain inns. Upon completion of the trek you will drive to Pamplona to witness the running of the bulls. Includes: All meals and accommodations (hotels in cities, refugios in mountains), internal transport. Dates: June/July. Length of trip: 21 days. Group size: Maximum 15. Cost: Land $1,385. Special requirements: Physically fit and active, $200 deposit.

Above the Clouds Trekking
P.O. Box 398
Worcester, MA 01602
617-799-4499   *Nepal*

In Nepal, "land of festivals," the ten-day-long Dashain is "the festival of festivals." Offices and shops close, exotic feasts are prepared, towering bamboo swings are erected for children to frolic on, and excitement fills the air! Your trek begins in Dhulikhel, a short bus ride east of Kathmandu. After a visit to Namo Buddha, a Tibetan Buddhist monastery, you'll descend to the Rosi River. Where it flows into the great Sun Kosi River, you'll board a river raft and continue to the market town of Okhaldhunga and its fabulous weekly bazaar. The height of the festival is spent in Rumjatar, garden spot of Nepal. You'll join the Nepali Hindus for ceremonies at the temple, and the subsequent feast. On the final day of Dashain, you join them in receiving the "tika," the vermilion powder dabbed on the forehead as a blessing by a priest or family elder. Steve Conlon, director, has lived over five years in Nepal. Includes: 4 nights' hotel in Kathmandu (before and after trek) with breakfast, all meals and accommodations (tents) on trek, services of guide, cook, and porters. Dates: October. Length of trip: 21 days. Group size: Maximum 12. Cost: Land $1,350. Special requirements: Physically fit, $200 deposit.

Above the Clouds Trekking
P.O. Box 398
Worcester, MA 01602
617-799-4499   *Nepal*

Of the ten thousand trekkers who visit the Everest region yearly, fewer than one hundred use the route traced by Tilman in 1950 on the original Everest trek. Here's your opportunity to follow in the footsteps of the men who conquered Everest. After flying into Tumlingtar, east of the Khumbu, you'll trek over Salpa Pass, affording views of Kanchenjunga, Mahalu, and Everest along the way. The villagers we meet have seldom seen foreigners. After climbing Kala Pattar, for the classic close-up view of Everest, you leave the base camp area heading south with the rivers, the traditional exit route of the Sherpas. Steve Conlon, director of Above the Clouds, has lived over five years in Nepal. Includes: 4 nights' hotel in Kathmandu with breakfast, all meals and accommodations on trek, services of guide, cook, and porters. Dates: September/October and March. Length of trip: 30 days. Group size: Maximum 15. Cost: Land $1,695. Special requirements: Physically fit, active daily life, $200 deposit.

Above the Clouds Trekking
P.O. Box 398
Worcester, MA 01602
617-799-4499   *Japan*

This Northern (Kita) Alps expedition is longer and more difficult than the standard treks. Beginning at Keiyakidaira, you'll trek for two weeks through some of the most rugged terrain Japan has to offer. En route there are climbs of Tsurugi, Yakushi and Yari, non-technical but demanding. Alpine meadows, deep gorges and breathtaking vistas punctuate the trails between the yamagoya, your mountain hut accommodations. The meals are Japanese, as are the other trekkers you'll meet along the route. Post-trek, you take the train to Kyoto for a personalized, intimate tour of some select temples and shrines. Return to Tokyo is by the famous Bullet Train. Smoke Blanchard, trip leader, has more than twenty years' experience in Japan. Includes: All accommodations (hotel in Tokyo and Kyoto, inns along the trail), all meals, guided tours in the cities, all internal transport—including the Bullet Train. Dates: August. Length of trip: 23 days. Group size: Maximum 15. Cost: Land $2,100. Special requirements: Physically fit, $200 deposit.

Annapurna Travel & Tours (P), Ltd.
Durbar Marg, P.O. Box 1414
Kathmandu, Nepal
(977) 12339, 13940, 13530   *Nepal*

This is the land of isolated Sherpa villages scattered high in the misty mountains . . . where strangers bid you "Namaste" ("I salute you") as you pass high amid the rocky cliffs . . . of breathtaking views, snow-capped peaks, icy streams and field after field of fragrant wildflowers bursting with intoxicating smells. On your nine-day trek to Helambu through the Himalyas, with stops at exotic locations such as Gulbhangjyang, Gothkharka and Tarkeyghyang, the dazzling sights will ease you into a delicious tranquility. Licensed by H.M.G. Nepal; member of American Society of Travel Agents and Pacific Area Travel Association. Includes: Hotel accommodation with breakfast in Kathmandu and all equipment and food during trek. Dates: September through May. Length of trip: 9 days. Group size: 4 to any number. Cost: Varies. Special requirements: Trekking permit, from H.M.G. Nepal, which can be arranged by operator.

Annapurna Travel & Tours (P), Ltd.
Durbar Marg. P.O. Box 1414
Kathmandu, Nepal
(977) 12339, 13940, 13530   *Nepal*

This trek through Nepal begins in Kathmandu, home of "The Living Goddess" whose spiritual power commands the homage of the King himself. Then it's on to Pokhara, one of the loveliest spots in the Himalayas, where the foaming waterfalls of the Seti Gorge play out their water musicals, and the entire mountain range welcomes you. Continue to Naudanda for a panoramic overview, with the majestic peaks of Annapurna and Machhapuchhare in the distance. Then before you know it, you're at a large unspoiled Gurung village and headed toward Dhampus, passing forests blanketed with wild orchids and beautiful rhododendrons. Licensed by H.M.G. Nepal; member of American Society of Travel Agents and Pacific Area Travel Association. Includes: Hotel accommodation at Kathmandu with breakfast and all equipment and food, etc. during trek. Dates: September through May. Length of trip: 7 nights, 8 days. Group size: 4 to any number. Cost: Varies.

Bark Eater Lodge
Allstead Mill Road
Keene, NY 12942
518-576-2221   *New York*

Located in a one-hundred-fifty-year-old farmhouse in the high peaks region of the Adirondacks, Bark Eater Lodge is only minutes away from Lake Placid. The Bark Eater offers self-guided hiking and climbing trips in the Adirondack wilderness area. The beginner and intermediate expedition consists of six days of unlimited hiking and climbing with free time to relax, explore and enjoy the breathtaking scenery. An experienced guide accompanies you for four days of the trip. There are also tennis and swimming facilities available for your pleasure. Bark Eater also offers a three-day trip for those with a little more experience. This tour covers scenic evergreen and hardwood forests filled with wildlife and lovely spring-fed brooks. In winter, the Bark Eater maintains several miles of cross-country trails, suitable for skiers of all levels. Twenty years' experience. Includes: Accommodations, meals, pick-up and drop-off at trail head, guides, maps, taxes and tips. Dates: May through October. Length of trip: 3 or 6 days. Group size: 2–10. Cost: $95 for 3-day trip, $280 for 6 days.

Basque Country Tours
3641 Dimond Avenue
Oakland, CA 94602
415-530-0244   *Spain*

Become intimately acquainted with an untouristed corner of Europe—the wildly beautiful mountains, Cantabrican coast, and pastoral countryside of the mysterious Basques. On these two-week walking tours through the Pyrenees and the Basque Country, you'll travel through ancient green valleys, alpine meadows, glacier lakes, and criss-cross the border between France and Spain over beautiful mountain passes. You will sleep in comfortable mountain chalets, and descend into picturesque provincial villages to savor the exquisite cuisine and fine hotels of the Basque people. During the summer you can enjoy sea bathing in the Bay of Biscay, as well as the music, dancing, and running of the bulls during the traditional local festivals. In winter, cross-country skiers can follow many of the same routes. Cultural, photographic, climbing, and downhill ski trips are also available. Includes: Land costs except restaurant meals; equipment; hotels, refugio accommodations and meals; guides; use of Land Rover or micro-bus. Dates: Throughout year; more in summer. Length of trip: 2 weeks. Group size: 6–15. Cost: $950. Special requirements: Ability to walk 5–6 hours per day over easy terrain carrying 15 lb. pack.

Bhutan Travel Service
120 East 56th Street
New York, NY 10022
212-838-6382
Telex 220896 BTS UR   *Bhutan*

Of the many treks possible in Bhutan, this is the longest, wildest and most exciting. It crosses many high passes in the previously inaccessible Laya and Lunana areas of northern Bhutan, and traces through untouched mountain wilderness very close to the Tibetan border. Here you'll come up close to the great snow ranges of the Inner Himalaya, and see some of the most remote and interesting settlements in the kingdom. You'll climb above the yak herders through meadows full of alpine flowers, and have the chance to see rare Himalayan wildlife. This is true wilderness trekking and a challenging adventure. Agency of the Royal Government of Bhutan, Department of Tourism. Includes: Accommodations, all meals; guide; trekking staff; tents; all equipment except sleeping bags; pack ponies; transfers and transportation. Dates: June through September. Length of trip: 28 days. Group size: Minimum 6, Maximum 15. Cost: $2,430. Special requirements: Two months advance booking. No technical mountaineering skills required, although two peaks are available for technical climbing, if desired, on the trek.

Bivouacs Du Bout Du Monde
Scientrier
47800 Roche-Sur-Foron
France (50) 25-52-29
Telex 290 301 Paris   *West Africa*

Trek high into the mountains of West Africa through wonderful canyons and oueds. This is the land of the famous mountains of Hoggar, all accessible by easy-to-strenuous routes through regions with exotic names—Thezoulaigs, Garet el Djenoun and In Acoulmou. Discover the plateaus and sandstone aiguilles of Hombori's mountains, in which many areas lie unexplored. Climb up 750-meter Mount Taga for an incredible view of high peaks. See the Dogons' villages in the cliffs and the nomadic Peulhs who live on the desert plain. Travel to the mountains of Air, north of Agadez in the middle of the Sahara, where the Touregs dwell in the valley of this beautiful range. Wander through many neolithic sites for a sense of the antiquity of this region. Ten years' experience. Includes: Food, camping and climbing equipment, transport by 4-wheel-drive truck. Dates: November through March. Length: 3–12 weeks. Group size: 10–12. Cost: $800–$3,000.

China Passage, Inc.
302 Fifth Avenue
New York, NY 10001
212-564-4099
800-223-7196
Telex 668916 *China*

On this program, you'll do extensive walking and camping in the Chinese countryside. You'll have the rare opportunity to visit Hainan, a large tropical island thirty miles off Guangdong province, as well as the isolated Daoist retreats and nature reserves of northern and western Guangdong. Once called the "Rose Jeweled Kingdom" because of its extensive rose quartz deposits, Hainan is characterized by a diversity of natural resources, scenery and ethnic groups. Its inland mountain region, covered by dense ebony and rosewood forests, is the home of a large tribal population. Tobacco, sugar cane, coffee and cotton grow in the fertile plains. You'll also visit the coastal areas, noted for their commercial and cultural activities as well as their unspoiled white sand beaches. Founded 1980. President, Fredric M. Kaplan is Chairman of US-China Peoples Friendship Association. Includes: All transportation, accommodations and meals in China. Dates: Monthly, June through April. Length: 21 or 23 days. Group size: 10–20. Cost: $1,115–$1,410 land.

Churchill House Inn
R.D. #3
Brandon, VT 05733
802-247-3300 *Vermont*

Hike from inn to inn along Vermont's famed Long Trail in the Green Mountains. Eight country inns on an eighty-mile section of this wilderness trail offer the hiker friendly atmosphere and fine food at the end of the day. The trips are self-guided with a choice of trails enabling vacationers to plan according to their hiking ability and to allow for other activities such as sightseeing, shopping, bicycling and canoeing along the way. Inns include Long Run Inn, a former lumberjack's hotel dating back to the 1800's; and Tucker Hill Lodge, known for outstanding American and French cuisine. Includes: Lodging and meals at 8 inns, car shuttle, maps and hiking tips. Dates: Memorial Day through late October. Length of trip: Variable. Group size: Up to 12. Cost: Variable, $446 for all eight inns. Special requirements: Advance reservations and deposit.

Country Walking Tours
6195 Santa Clara Place
Rohnert Park, CA 94928
707-584-0411 *Great Britain*

Walk through the gentle countryside of England, Scotland or Wales staying in comfortable village inns, stone cottages and farmhouses. Amble at a leisurely pace past farm landscapes, rugged coastal scenery, wild heather and bracken-covered mountains. Hike along five thousand-year-old footpaths, roads built by the Roman Legion and nineteenth-century canal towpaths. Enjoy some of the rural institutions such as the village pub and tea room. The routes are selected to combine scenic beauty and interest with walking comfort, usually covering five to seven miles a day. Examples of the regions visited include the Cotswold Hills,

Cornwall, Snowdonia, the Lake District and the Scottish Highlands. Your guides will be residents of the area and leaders in such organizations as the local Naturalist's Trust, Ramblers Association, field clubs and historical society. Established 1979. Includes: Accommodations, breakfast, coach. Dates: June through September. Length: 4–18 days. Group size: 25 maximum. Cost: $350–$1,600. Special requirements: $100 deposit.

Dial Europe
6595 NW 36th Street
Miami, FL 33166
800-327-7241   *Switzerland*

To see the real world of the Alps, you must go on foot. Dr. George Hudson leads this walking tour from Montreux to Muerren—along mountain footpaths, up through high pastures, past herds of prize cattle and roughhewn timber chalets, and through fields of wildflowers. Once above the tree line, the tour enters a world of mountain torrents and massive glaciers. Accommodations range from fine resort hotels in Gstaad and Lenk to stone huts for mountain climbers or the fragrant straw of a farmer's barn. The ascents are steep and the hiking is strenuous but there is no technical climbing or ropework. No equipment is needed except good boots and a strong will. This is a program for those who have always wanted to climb a mountain, but who would prefer not to do it alone. Organized in connection with the Tourist Authorities of Lenk, Bernese Oberland, Switzerland. Includes: Round-trip airfare via Lufthansa German Airlines, first-class hotels and 3 nights in Alpine hut dormitories, 3 meals a day, American and Swiss guides. Dates: Late summer. Length of trip: 2 weeks. Group size: 10–25. Cost: $2,000 per person. Special requirements: Good physical condition.

Directions Unlimited
344 Main Street
Mt. Kisco, NY 10549
914-241-1700 (Collect)   *Switzerland*

Imagine the wonder of walking throughout the Valais Alps—the roof of Europe. You are your own transportation. Your guide will point out the wonders of these mountains and introduce you to the mountain people you will meet on your way. Directions Unlimited has been in operation for fourteen years. Includes: Daily transportation of luggage, hotel, all meals, tips, taxes, transfers, escort. Dates: April through October. Length: 1 week. Group size: 20. Cost: $395–$495. Special requirements: Excellent physical condition.

Discovery Tours Sabah SDN BHD
P.O. Box 1355
Kota Kinabalu, Sabah
East Malaysia
(088) 57735
Telex MA80730   *Malaysia*

The Kadazan people call it "Akin Nabalu"—"home of the spirits of the departed." Malaysia's Mount Kinabalu, with its distinctive "toothy" profile, offers trekkers a variety of terrain on the climb—from jungles dense with moss and orchids, to stunted trees and stark granite slopes at the treeline and the awesome views from the summit, 13,455 feet up. Although the climb is not technical, it'll give you the feeling of being at the top of the world. Includes: Mountain guide, porter, sleeping bags, land transportation, accommodations. Dates: On request. Length of trip: 3 days. Group size: Varies. Cost: On request. Special requirements: Physically fit, no heart problems.

Forum Travel International
2437 Durant Avenue, #208
Berkeley, CA 94704
415-843-8294   *South America*

Join Forum Travel on any of a variety of trekking expeditions in Peru, Ecuador and Bolivia. One such tour is a Pan-Andean adventure, combining three of the Andes' most striking regions into a remarkable montage of towering summits, remote pastoral scenes, Inca roads and ruins, and dense jungle foliage of the river valleys and below Machu Picchu. Another unique trip follows the Inca Trail across the jungle to Machu Picchu. A variation on the basic trail, this trek is not yet overrun with tourists. Forum Travel International offers several other variations on the Inca Trail route, plus treks through the Palcay Valley. In operation since 1965. Includes: Accommodations, meals, guides, group equipment and local taxes. Dates: Weekly, April through October. Length of trip: 1–3 weeks. Group size: 2–20. Cost: From $336. Special requirements: Good health.

Garrett-Lipp and Associates, Inc.
P.O. Box 3236
Lacey, WA 98503
206-491-6836   *Switzerland*

Pull on your hiking boots and discover the beauty of Switzerland from its remote valleys ringed by majestic Alpine peaks and huge glaciers to its elegant cities. Take a steamer on Lake Zurich and enjoy the sophistication of Switzerland's largest city before traveling to Pontresina, base for hikes into the surrounding mountains and cable-car rides affording breathtaking views of the countryside. Then it's just a train ride away to undiscovered, sunny Poschiavo and hikes through picturesque mountaintop villages before traveling towards Brunnen and Lucerne in the heart of William Tell country. You'll cross over a covered frescoed bridge dating from 1333 as you amble through these ancient towns on your way to a hearty Swiss dinner. All hikes are day hikes—no camping, no backpacking. Mountain climbing can be arranged for an additional cost. Includes: Hotel without private bath, double occupancy; all breakfasts and dinners (except 1st night), most lunches; Swiss holiday pass for transportation on trains, cable cars, lake steamers, cog railways, postal buses; transfers; personal guide throughout. Dates: End of June, early July and mid-August. Length of trip: 15 days. Group size: 20 maximum. Cost: $1,090. Special requirements: Swiss Hike is geared to average active persons. There are "Easy Hike Options." Hiking boots required for high trail hiking; clothing list supplied upon registration and payment of $150 deposit.

<table>
<tr><td>

Guides
for
All
Seasons

</td><td>

Guides for All Seasons
P.O. Box 97
Carnelian Bay, CA 95711
916-583-8475 Call collect from USA

</td><td>

Austria,
Switzerland

</td></tr>
</table>

Summer hiking in Austria and Switzerland is a delightful experience, and one available to mountain enthusiasts of all ages. Each day you'll hike from hut to hut, with additional hiking available for the more energetic. Only small packs need be carried, since bedding and food will be provided at each hut along the way. For even greater variety in these mountains with their thousands of trails, spend time hiking in the Austrian Alps, then travel by train to the Swiss Alps. Here, explore the Bernese Oberland and a final visit to the majestic Matterhorn with time for the adventurous to climb its lofty heights. Good food, spectacular views and international camaraderie will help make this trip a memorable experience. Includes: Most meals, land transportation, lodging, guide. Dates: Summer. Length: 16 days. Group size: 20 maximum. Cost: $1,150.

<table>
<tr><td>

Guides
for
All
Seasons

</td><td>

Guides for All Seasons
P.O. Box 97
Carnelian Bay, CA 95711
916-583-8475 Call collect from USA

</td><td>

Nepal

</td></tr>
</table>

Only on foot can the traveler to Nepal realize and experience the full range of exotic sights in this remote country. You'll pass through native villages seldom visited by outsiders—camp out in open fields carpeted with wildflowers—and follow the route of your Sherpa scout through high mountain passes. You'll arrive by raft or Land Rover at Royal Chitwan National Park, where you'll ride elephants, paddle in canoes in search of wild boar and crocodiles, scamper after colorful birds and trail the near-extinct Indian one-horned white rhino. Includes: All lodging, ground transportation, Sherpa staff, tents, all food while trekking, mountain guide, porters, trekking permits. Dates: September through May. Length: 21–35 days. Group size: 16 maximum. Cost: $950–$2,240. Special requirements: Moderate to excellent level of fitness.

<table>
<tr><td>

Guides
for
All
Seasons

</td><td>

Guides for All Seasons
P.O. Box 97
Carnelian Bay, CA 95711
916-583-8475 Call collect from USA

</td><td>

Japan

</td></tr>
</table>

Combine the best of two worlds! On this trek, you'll not only hike and climb (optional) in the North Alps of Japan, but you will also have a chance to experience the Japanese way of life. You spend six days hiking in the mountains, resting each night in a local inn. Small packs for carrying clothing are all that you'll need, since excellent food and lodging will be prepared by an attentive local staff in each lodge. You sleep on futons in tatami-matted rooms with thick layers of warm quilts. The traditional *ofuro* (hot bath) is almost always available—even in the mountains. A few days to visit Mt. Fuji and the Hakone Lakes National Park are also planned. Weather cooperating, you may try for the summit of this inspiring peak. Time in Kyoto and Tokyo will balance out your visit to Japan. Includes: All lodging, group transportation, breakfasts and dinners except 2 while in cities, mountain guide. Dates: May/June and September/October. Length of trip: 16 days. Group size: Maximum 20. Cost: $1,260. Special requirements: Moderate level of fitness—no mountain climbing ability is required. No steep cliffs or narrow, precipitous trails are involved.

Himalaya, Inc.
1802 Cedar Street
Berkeley, CA 94703
415-540-8031   *Nepal*

Nepal's subtropical climate makes winter an ideal time to explore its Himalayan foothills. This trip provides an excellent introduction to trekking in Nepal, since you'll be at altitudes less than ten thousand feet. Your route takes you away from the common trekking destinations and traverses some of Nepal's most scenic countryside. From the hilltops, you confront sweeping panoramas of the Himalayan crest beginning with Dhaulagiri in the west, past the Annapurna summits Lamjung Hima (22,912 feet), Manaslu (26,760 feet) and Himalchuli (25,895 feet). In addition to the numerous hamlets along the way, you'll visit three large hill towns of the colorful Gurung clan. Leaving the road near Trisuli Bazaar, you climb up from the river valley to Gorkha. Then descend to the valley of the Marsyandi Lhola (river) below the impressive ramparts of Manaslu and Peak 29. Continuing west, you visit Ghanpokhara, the prosperous former Gurung capital, and skirt the slopes of Lamjung Himal to Siklis, the largest and liveliest of the Gurung villages. You'll emerge from the hills at Pokhara where you relax by the lovely Phewa Tal (lake) before returning to Kathmandu. Founded 1977. Includes: Hotels and meals in cities, all camping gear while on trek, all meals while on trek, porters, all transportation required for trekking itinerary. Dates: December through March. Length of trip: 22 days. Group size: Up to 15. Cost: $1,275. Special requirements: Introduction to trekking in Nepal—altitudes not above 10,000 feet.

Himalaya, Inc.
1802 Cedar Street
Berkeley, CA 94703
415-540-8031   *Japan*

This three-week trip is highlighted by a nine-day traverse of the Kita Alps in northern Japan and four days in the ancient capital of Kyoto. The Kita Alps rise to more than ten thousand feet from a base near sea level. Your route leads steeply through forests at the lower elevations, and often along narrow rocky trails on the peaks. The walking is strenuous, and the nights are spent Japanese-style in fully staffed, comfortable mountain huts rather than camping out. You'll eat rice, fish, sushi and pickled vegetables, sleep on tatami mats and bathe in communal hot springs, and become acquainted with some of the Japanese mountain enthusiasts following the same route. After the trek, there is time to visit Tokyo and to explore the many temples and shrines of Kyoto, a living museum of Japanese art. Founded 1977. Includes: Breakfasts are provided with hotel accommodations in cities. Two meals and lodging are provided on mountain walks. Dates: September. Length of trip: 3 weeks. Group size: Up to 15. Cost: $1875. Special requirements: Excellent physical condition—we require a medical form signed by a physician.

Himalaya, Inc.
1802 Cedar Street
Berkeley, CA 94703
415-540-8031 *China*

On this trip to Sichuan Province you'll explore the remote region where the vast Tibetan plateau rises from the plains of the Yangtze River Basin. After visiting Beijing, you'll fly to Chengdu in the heart of China's lush rice-growing region. Then strike out by road for Tibetan plateau, overnighting at guesthouses en route to the Wolong Reserve. This area protects not only the Giant Panda, but also gives you a chance to glimpse monkeys, bharal and exotic birds. From the road end at the Red Flag Commune, you will trek for seven days to the base of Mount Siguniang ("Four Maidens Mountain"), a sheer granite, 21,600-foot peak above forested valleys. This area was first visited by Westerners in 1980 and is one of the least-explored wildernesses in China. The return to Beijing is by way of Xian with its magnificent archeological digs at the tomb of Chin Shi Huang, China's first emperor. Founded 1977. Includes: All transportation within China, hotels in cities, all meals, camping equipment except for sleeping bags and pad. Dates: September and October. Length of trip: One month. Group size: Up to 15. Cost: $4,150. Special requirements: Good physical condition.

Himalayan Rover Trek
P.O. Box 24382
Seattle, WA 98124
206-454-5022
206-782-6792 *Nepal*

As your route follows the steps of Tenzing and Hillary as far as the Everest base camp, your trek passes through the famous Sherpa trading center and capital, Namche Bazaar, and Thyangboche, site of the great monastery. Pine forests give way to twisted alpine dwarf-trees as you gain altitude; the villages where you stay are home to the friendly Sherpa people for whom hospitality is a point of honor. And for a fitting closing to your journey, you will have a farewell dinner in the home of your Nepalese hosts in Kathmandu. Includes: Complete trekking arrangements including English-speaking Sherpa guides, cook and camp staff; porters; all camping equipment; all meals on trek; deluxe hotel with breakfasts in Kathmandu; transfers; trekking permit; sightseeing; necessary air transportation within Nepal. Dates: November and April. Length: 26 days. Group size: Maximum 12 people. Cost: $1,285. Special requirements: Good physical condition and accustomed to regular strenuous exercise. Maximum elevation on trek: 18,000 feet.

Himalayan Travel, Inc.
P.O. Box 481
Greenwich, CT 06836
800-243-5330 *Nepal*

Your adventure begins with a breathtaking flight from Kathmandu to Biratnagar, on the Indian border. The trekking starts in the subtropical Terai of Nepal. Your first sight of the Himalayas comes while crossing the Mahabarat Range. The trek then drops to the Arun River to focus on the various peoples living and working along the trail. Most numerous are the Limbus and Rais, earliest-known settlers of Nepal. Climbing away from the Arun, the trek continues through the Honqu and Inukhu valleys, home to the Sherpas. Then, on to the Dudh Kosi Valley and Namche Bazaar. From here on the program is flexible. Possibilities include a climb of Kala Patar (18,298 feet) and exploration of the Thami and Gokyo Valleys. Six years' experience outfitting trekking and rafting trips in Nepal. Includes: Hotels in cities, most meals and equipment, guide, cooks, porters and land transportation. Dates: December. Length of trip: 35 days. Group size: 15. Cost: $1,595. Special requirements: Hiking and camping experience is required.

Himalayan Travel, Inc.
P.O. Box 481
Greenwich, CT 06836
800-243-5330   *Nepal*

Himalayan Travel, Inc. invites you on an "Instant Everest" trek through the Solu Khumba region of Nepal. You are met at the airport by your Sherpa guides and porters to prepare for the trek to Namche Bazaar. There will be plenty of time to explore the market where Sherpa and Tibetans from the higher and more remote villages mix with Rais and Tamangs from the lower, warmer hills. The highlight of the journey is the Thyangboche Monastery, completely surrounded by the world's highest peaks: Everest (29,028 feet), Lhotse (27,923), Nuptse (25,850), Kantega (22,235) and Ama Dablam (22,494). Six years' experience outfitting trekking and rafting trips in Nepal. Includes: Hotel accommodations in Kathmandu, flights within Nepal, equipment and meals on trek, and complete staff of Sherpa guides, cooks and porters. Dates: October through May. Length of trip: 12 days. Group size: 15. Cost: $695. Special requirements: Hiking and camping experience preferred.

Himalayan Travel, Inc.
P.O. Box 481
Greenwich, CT 06836
800-243-5330   *Sri Lanka*

Sri Lanka has been blessed with a great variety of flora and fauna. Your trek will be a series of short journeys, allowing ample time for exploration and discovery. You'll be able to visit ancient cities, temples, fishing hamlets and rural villages, crossing habitats ranging from coastal river swamps and dense lowland jungles, to high mountain forests and open fields. The first stop is Ratnapura, "City of Gems," where according to legend King Solomon had his fabled mine. Two days are spent in Wirawilla Bird Sanctuary and Ruhuna National Park, where sloth bear, elephant, wild boar, buffalo, leopard, deer and other jungle wildlife abound. You will also have the opportunity to explore the vast inland lagoon area of the Gal Oya National Park, Peak Wilderness region, tea estates, and the city of Kandy where every evening is marked with a ceremony displaying the sacred tooth relic of Buddha. Six years' experience. Includes: Hotels in cities, most meals, trekking and rafting equipment, guides, cooks and porters. Dates: September, December and March. Length of trip: 23 days. Group size: 15. Cost: $1,645. Special requirements: Hiking and camping experience preferred.

Himalayan Travel, Inc.
P.O. Box 481
Greenwich, CT 06836
800-243-5330   *Bhutan*

Himalayan Travel, Inc. has obtained permission from Bhutan authorities to lead treks to the fabulous peak of Chomolhari (22,676 feet), Bhutan's most revered mountain. For the pioneer trekker, this offers a tough, but exciting and rewarding route through the Himalayas. The trek commences in the lovely Paro Valley with a stop at Taksang Monastery ("Tigers Nest"), which clings to a sheer cliff. It takes five days and two (15,118-foot) passes to reach the glaciers at the foot of Chomolhari. Here, you'll camp at the ruins of the ancient fortress and watchtower of Drukgygel, "Victorious Druks." In constant view of the great peaks, you'll continue to the deserted Lingshi Dzong to explore the tremendous glaciers. There is a very good chance of seeing the elusive blue sheep and musk deer native to the region. Six years' experience. Includes: Hotels in cities, camping equipment, meals, guides, cooks, porters and ground transportation. Dates: May and September. Length of trip: 20 days, 13 trekking. Group size: 15. Cost: $2,390. Special requirements: Hiking and camping experience preferred.

Hugh Glass Backpacking Company
P.O. Box 110796
Anchorage, AK 99511
907-243-1922   *Alaska*

North of the Arctic Circle lies a wilderness so remote that it remained unexplored until the 1920's—the Central Brooks Range. Here, Hugh Glass Backpacking's expedition travels alongside the great Koyukuk River, between the peaks known as the Gates of the Arctic. This is the land of wolf and moose, of sheep and grizzly bear, where the lighting is ethereal

Trekkers in the tiny kingdom of Bhutan can see masked dancers at the Wandiphrodang Festival. (HIMALAYAN TRAVEL, INC., BOB ASHFORD)

and sunsets linger for hours. Hugh Glass Backpacking's Wrangell Mountains trek gives a different picture of Alaska, a geologic history of the past millenniums. The trail roams past volcanoes shrouded in an eon of snow, high walls of blue ice, stones marked with the ochre and rust of passing time. This is mountain wilderness at its best, home of the grizzly, wolf, Dall sheep, caribou and moose. With Hugh Glass Backpacking, you can also trek back into the Ice Age in the St. Elias Range, the highest coastal mountain range in the world. Here you'll experience a vast mosaic of fractured ice, glaciers, pools of blue meltwater, valleys cloaked with wildflowers, warped and tilted rock. Over ten years' experience; member Alaska Wilderness Guides Association. Includes: Round-trip transportation from Anchorage, tents, group gear, meals and guides. Dates: June through September. Length of trip: 5–14 days. Group size: 6. Cost: $375–$1,500. Special requirements: 20% deposit.

InnerAsia
2627 Lombard Street
San Francisco, CA 94123
415-922-0448
Telex 278716 TIGER   *China*

InnerAsia's China programs include trips to remote Tibet, crossing the Tibetan Plateau by jeep to the base of Mount Everest. You'll also visit Inner Sichuan Province, still relatively unknown to foreigners and home to many Tibetans; and Kashgar in Far Western China, one of the most important caravan stops along the Ancient Silk Road. Of particular interest is a trek via Kashgar to the base camp of K2, the world's second highest mountain. This trip will include a five-day camel safari from the roadhead south to the base of the mountain. InnerAsia founder Jo Sanders organized the first American mountaineering expedition to China since the 1930's and led the first American group ever to cross the Tibetan Plateau from China to the base of Mount Everest. Includes: All transportation, food, and lodging within China; sightseeing in cities visited; interpreter, liaison officer and cooks; all camping gear except sleeping bags. Dates: May through October. Length of trip: 23 to 30 days. Group size: 6 to 15 maximum. Cost: $4,000–$8,000.

Intimate Glimpses

Intimate Glimpses
P.O. Box 6091
San Diego, CA 92106
619-222-2224   *Switzerland*

"The Four Cultures of Switzerland" program offers twenty-one days of unhurried travel with four to six days at various romantic inns—allowing you to experience behind-the-scenes' Switzerland. You'll travel by train, postal bus, lake steamer, cable—even by chair-lifts—and enjoy daily walks passing historic sights and scenic delights. Highlights include medieval Grisons, aglow with flowery meadows; the river Rhine; Ticino, land of botanical isles, serene valleys, castles and cafes; Zermatt with its majestic Matterhorn; Lake Geneva, with a French accent on vineyards, romantic chateaus and culinary delights; and Bernese Oberland, known for its folkcrafts, waterfalls and dramatic views. Includes: Accommodations, dining, transportation. Dates: Summer and fall and on request. Length: 21 days. Group size: 14 maximum. Cost: $2,095. Special requirements: $200 deposit.

Intimate Glimpses

Intimate Glimpses
P.O. Box 6091
San Diego, CA 92106
619-222-2224   *Japan*

Unhurried, behind-the-scenes travel offering complete immersion in Japanese culture, customs and comforts is the focus of this program. Twenty days of "walks with elegance" reveal remote fishing villages, ancient samurai trails and Imperial palaces. Rural rambles go past unspoiled lakes with reflections of Mt. Fuji, along alpine pathways sprinkled with waterfalls, into private gardens and heralded shrines, and into the studios of folk artists. Accommodations are in traditional Japanese *ryokan,* idyllic inns where shoes are out; and include relaxing mineral water baths and revitalizing shiatsu massage. Transportation is also by railway, including the fast and famous Bullet Train. Includes: Accommodation, meals, land travel. Dates: Spring and fall, and on request. Length: 20 days. Group size: 14 maximum. Cost: $2,395. Special requirements: $200 deposit.

Intimate Glimpses

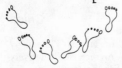

Intimate Glimpses
P.O. Box 6091
San Diego, CA 92106
619-222-2224   *Massachusetts*

Discover the cobblestoned paths, cranberried trails and colonial village greens of Cape Cod and the Islands in the golden glow of autumn. On these walking tours, you'll have time to pause and savor the natural wonders, historical sights, architectural gems, celebrated local foods and warm hospitality of this region. The Cape offers ambles among lighthouses and windmills, through cozy villages, coastal preserves, and into whaling captains' mansions. Along the way, you'll meet pioneering islanders and learn about the seafarer's art of scrimshaw. Transportation by minibus, ferry and private plane augments walking in these New England seascape communities. At night, romantic eighteenth- and nineteenth-century country inns provide a cozy welcome. Includes: Accommodations, dining, transport. Dates: Fall and on request. Length: 14 days. Group size: 12 maximum. Cost: $1,495. Special requirements: $200 deposit.

Jamaica Camping and Hiking Association
P.O. Box 216
Kingston 7, Jamaica
809-927-5409   *Jamaica*

Jamaica offers something for everyone—from reggae to rum, calypso and coral. Start off with a stay at Negril, with its unsurpassed six-mile white sand beach, fabulous sunsets and turquoise waters just right for snorkeling. Then head inland to Jamaica's only wildlife sanctuary at Marshall's Pen Great House and hike the birding trails. After a day of river canoeing on the scenic Black River and Morass, continue to the wild and deserted south coast of Treasure Beach and Gut River. A visit to the Castleton Botanical Gardens and famed Dunns River Falls are memorable. Accommodations include luxury cabanas, Great Houses and camping in this natural wonderland. Top off your stay with a reggae session in Kingston. The tour operator also offers a hiking and coffee tour of the 7,500-foot Blue Mountains, which produce some of the world's best coffee. Includes: Land transportation, accommodations, food, guide. Dates: All year. Length: 1 week. Size of group: 2–20. Cost: $235–$445. Special requirements: 50% deposit.

Journeys International
P.O. Box 7545-ST
Ann Arbor, MI 48107
313-665-4407   *Peru*

Peru offers tremendous cultural and natural diversity. This adventure begins with a stay in a remote and rustic jungle lodge in the Amazon rainforest, where moonlight canoe excursions and visits to the Yagua Indian village will give you a true feel for the jungle. Then sense the grandeur of the ancient Incan Empire in the Urubamba Valley, in Cuzco—the seat of their vast culture, and the lost city of Machu Picchu. After visiting the Archeological and Gold Museums in Spanish colonial Lima, the odyssey includes a trip to the mystifying, ancient Nazca lines on the desert coast. Another highlight is an overnight stay in the homes of local people on Taquili Island in Lake Titicaca—offering spectacular views of the Andes. Exceptional handicrafts, especially weaving and knittings in soft llama and alpaca wool are available. All the hiking is easy, and there's no camping involved. Established 1978. Includes: Meals, lodging, ground and air transport in Peru, rafting equipment. Dates: August. Length: 20 days. Group size: Maximum 15. Cost: $1,725 with 10% tax-deductible contribution for conservation and community development project.

Journeys International
P.O. Box 7545-ST
Ann Arbor, MI 48107
313-665-4407   *Peru*

This exciting trip begins with a five-day Amazon River camping safari exploring remote tributaries by riverboat. You travel up rivers dense with tropical undergrowth, searching out jungle wildlife and remote villages. The trekking portion of the trip leads you through the remote region of Vilcabamba, where lush tropical lowlands contrast with towering, snow-capped Andean peaks. Here, the Inca left behind entire cities, fortresses, aqueducts and an elaborate road system, still used by local inhabitants. You tread the very same routes used by the Indians as they crossed the jungle to Machu Picchu. Since the terrain is steep and rugged, prior packing and hiking experience is recommended. Includes: Lodging, meals, air and ground transportation within Peru, guides, pack animals, group camping gear, rafting equipment, and a tax-deductible contribution to aid conservation efforts in Peru. Dates: July. Length of trip: 20 days. Group size: 12. Cost: $1,285. Special requirements: Good physical health, camping and hiking experience, $300 deposit.

Journeys International
P.O. Box 7545-ST
Ann Arbor, MI 48107
313-665-4407   *Nepal*

Join Journeys International for an extended Himalayan discovery adventure in Nepal, including trekking, whitewater rafting and jungle exploration. You will be accompanied by expert guides and instructors, and a full staff of cooks, porters and assistants. The trekking portion of this trip is not covered in most guide books; as a result, the cultures and environments you encounter en route are little influenced by previous travelers. The rafting portion

Take time out from your trek—with an elephant safari in search of rhinos, tigers and other big game in the Royal Chitwan National Park, Nepal. (JOURNEYS, WILL WEBER)

includes three and a half days on some of the most challenging whitewater in Nepal. Then it's on to Royal Chitwan National Park for elephant safaris in search of rhino, tiger and other large mammals. There is also time for independent exploration of the ancient city of Kathmandu. The cost of the trip includes a tax-deductible contribution to the Earth Preservation Fund for projects aiding conservation in remote areas of Nepal. Established 1978. Includes: Lodging, meals, group camping gear, ground transportation, guides, porters, permits and contribution to Earth Preservation Fund. Dates: November through April. Length of trip: From 16 days. Group size: 12. Cost: $1,325. Special requirements: $300 deposit.

Journeys International
P.O. Box 7545-ST
Ann Arbor, MI 48107
313-665-4407 *Nepal*

Nepal's great peaks, hills, rivers, jungles and villages offer unlimited possibilities for trekkers. Journeys International has developed an extremely varied Himalayan exploration program. Tour leaders include Sherpa and other Nepalese staff, as well as American experts. Many trips include homestays with the families of guides. One of Journeys' most popular treks crosses the Arun Valley, deepest in the world. This is a perfect trek for anyone seeking Himalayan wilderness and a look at remote cultures little influenced by Westerners. Views of the east face of Everest, Makalu and the entire Kanchenjunga Range are spectacular. The richest rhododendrons in the world cover the hills of this area and are in full bloom beween January and June. More species of birds are found here than anywhere else in Nepal. There is also swimming, elephant-back exploration, and observation safaris in the junglelands. Established 1978. Includes: Lodging, meals, group camping gear, guides, porters, trekking permits, local transportation and a tax-deductible contribution to conservation and community development projects in Nepal. Dates: December. Length of trip: 23 days. Group size: 12. Cost: $1,325. Special requirements: Good physical health, hiking experience, $300 deposit.

Kashmir Himalayan Expeditions
Boulevard Shopping Complex
P.O. Box 168
Srinagar, Kashmir, India 190001
78698
73913 *India*

Kashmir Himalayan Expeditions offers a great variety of tours in the Indian states of Jammu and Kashmir. They can arrange cross-country and downhill skiing, bicycle tours, raft expeditions, houseboating, bird watching, and walking and trekking tours throughout the region. Trekking is their specialty and they have arranged some of the most exciting adventures on the Indian subcontinent, including a vale of Kashmir trek featuring gentle walks and sightseeing through pine forests, sheep-herding villages, ancient monasteries and the fabled Kashmir lakes; a Kashmir alpine expedition traveling through colorful spring meadows and penetrating deep into the Himalayas to Lake Gangabal; a Himalayan pilgrimage to Amarnath Cave, last resting place of Lord Shiva, the triple peaks of Vishnu, Brahma and Shiva; and Buddhist Ladakh (The Indian Little Tibet); plus many, many other exciting trips. Kashmir Himalayan Expeditions has been in operation since 1970. Includes: Accommodations, meals, guides, domestic air and ground transportation and sightseeing. Dates: Year-round. Length of trip: 14 days and up. Group size: Variable. Cost: From $420 to $990.

Lute Jerstad Adventures
P.O. Box 19537
Portland, OR 97219
503-244-6075
Telex 360484 *India, Nepal*

In India and Nepal, altitudes range from sea level to over twenty-nine thousand feet with climatic conditions varying from arctic to subtropical. The wildlife is as diverse as the geography. The king of all beasts, the Royal Bengal Tiger, lives protected in national parks and wildlife sanctuaries. Other wildlife includes leopard, the gaur (the world's largest wild ox), Asian buffalo, freshwater dolphin, garial and mugger crocodiles, two thousand species of birds, deer, bear, wild ass, ibex, Great Indian One-horned Rhinoceros and the Bactrian camel. Lute Jerstad Adventures offers a wide range of trekking and climbing opportunities year-round—from northwestern India with its Buddhist monasteries carved out of sheer rock cliffs . . . to the deserts of Rajahstan . . . to Everest Base Camp. Lute Jerstad, one of the company founders, was part of the first American team to climb Mount Everest (1963); the firm has fifteen years' experience outfitting treks. Includes: Tents; sherpas; food on trek; permits; porters/ponies; foam pads; sleeping bags (in Nepal); hotels; transfers; sightseeing. Dates: Year-round. Length of trip: 7–25 days. Group size: 6–20. Cost: $1,000–$2,500. Special requirements: Good physical condition; $200 deposit.

**Mountain Travel
1398 Solano Avenue
Albany, CA 94706
415-527-8100
Telex 335-429**   *Russia*

The Caucasus Mountains stretch from the Black to the Caspian Sea. This itinerary focuses on the Central Caucasus in the Baksan Valley, with its deep forests of poplar and beech, high thickets of stunted birch and rhododendron and alpine meadows carpeted with wildflowers. Mount Elbrus (18,841 feet), the highest peak in Europe, is located here. Climbers in the group will have a chance to climb this lofty mountain, which offers a highly challenging but not technically difficult high altitude ascent. Then trek across a major pass of the Caucasus into Svanetia, a Georgian mountain region with a thousand years of history dating back to the Crusades. Stay in Mestia, a small Georgian village with stone streets, ancient town squares and traditional Svanetian homes with high watchtowers. Sixteenth year of operation. Includes: Accommodations, ground and air transport in USSR, camp meals. Dates: September. Length: 24 days. Group size: 6–15. Cost: $1,890.

**Mountain Travel
1398 Solano Avenue
Albany, CA 94706
415-527-8100
Telex 335-429**   *Peru*

Trek to Machu Picchu through the Cordillera Vilcabamba, a range which juts out of the lowlands and has glaciers feeding the Amazon. You'll cross a spectacular fifteen-thousand-foot pass in the shadow of magnificent Mt. Salcantay (20,574 feet) and Mt. Palcay (18,645 feet), eventually linking with the Inca Trail that leads to Machu Picchu. Hike on to the Cordillera Vilcanota, a range of ice peaks that rise from the Altiplano. The route circles Mt. Ausangate (20,945 feet) where you'll camp in splendid meadows at fourteen thousand feet, with Indian shepherds and herds of llama and alpaca for colorful company. From your camp's edge, watch the spectacle of a calving glacier as Ausangate's glaciers drop house-size blocks of ice into Lake Pucacocha. In between treks, relax at comfortable country inns and visit superb archeological sites from the days of the Incan Empire. Sixteenth year of operation. Includes: Camping gear, porters, pack animals, ground transport, camp meals, accommodations. Dates: April through August. Length: 22 days. Group size: 6–15. Cost: $2,850.

Mountain Travel
1398 Solano Avenue
Albany, CA 94706
415-527-8100
Telex 335-429   *China*

No part of China is more remote and isolated than the extreme western corner of Sinkiang Province. The landscape presents a wide-open setting of high windswept plains dotted with the yurt dwellings of nomadic Kazakh shepherds, dominated by the brooding peaks of Mt. Kongur (25,320 feet) and Mt. Muztagata (24,757 feet). Little has changed since the days of the "Silk Road," when camel caravans passed through on a trade route between China and the Mediterranean. This journey undertakes short treks to the bases of both mountains, with local herdsmen as guides and using camels as pack animals. You'll also visit the fascinating oasis town of Kashgar, tour the vast archeological legacy of Xian and enter the Forbidden City in Beijing. Sixteenth year of operation. Includes: Meals, accommodations, camping gear, airfare in China, camels. Dates: July through August. Length: 29 days. Group size: 8–15. Cost: $4,500.

Nantahala Outdoor Center
U.S. 19 West, Box 41
Bryson City, NC 28713
704-488-9221   *Nepal*

The small kingdom of Nepal is a land of contrasts. From the windswept heights of the Himalayas, it is only a short distance to the tropical jungles of Chitwan National Park. A land of serene Buddhist culture, terraced villages, shadowed forests and open meadows, exotic wildlife, towering mountains and tumultuous rapids for thrilling whitewater adventure. Nantahala Outdoor Center offers a wide variety of trips combining treks around Mt. Everest, Annapurna and Gorkha with whitewater rafting on the Sun Kosi and Trisuli rivers. Ten years' experience; many on staff are championship paddlers. Includes: Meals, lodging, equipment, guides. Dates: October through March. Length of trip: 22 to 38 days. Group size: 15–20 people. Cost: $1,390–$2,100. Special requirements: Good physical condition; experience in whitewater only if one kayaks instead of rafts.

Pacific Exploration Company
P.O. Box 3042
Santa Barbara, CA 93105
805-687-7282   *New Zealand*

This New Zealand walkabout features a variety of hiking excursions in the scenic national parks, highlighted by the incomparable Milford Track in the majestic Southern Alps on the South Island. Starting from Auckland, you'll head south to Urewara National Park for a three-day, twenty-mile hiking expedition along the Whakatane River. With Maori guides, you'll observe the Park's unusual flora and fauna—including the kiwi whose calls can be heard at night. On your trip, you'll also explore underground glowworm caves by boat; hike past Rotorua's boiling lakes, bubbling mud and spouting geysers; climb an active volcano; and enjoy exciting river rafting on Tongariro National Park. Includes: Accommodations, local transport, most meals, camping arrangements. Dates: October through March. Length: 23 days. Group size: 17 maximum. Cost: $1,890. Special requirements: $250 deposit.

Pacific Exploration Company
P.O. Box 3042
Santa Barbara, CA 93105
805-687-7282 *Australia*

This "Australia Walkabout" features a series of field trips and hiking excursions in the Outback for travelers who enjoy moderate hiking and close contact with nature. Overnight field trips include four days' hiking in the eucalyptus and blue gum forests of Blue Mountains National Park, site of the weirdly beautiful limestone Jenolan Caves. Four days are also spent on a Desert Outback Safari between Ayers Rock and Alice Springs led by guides of Aboriginal descent who share their secrets of the desert. Kangaroos, dingos, emus and wild camels are part of this wild scenery. Other excursions include the tropical Cape York Peninsula to view Aboriginal rock art sites, plus animal life such as parrots and crocodiles. A camping trip to an island on the Great Barrier Reef for boating, snorkeling and reef walks on the coral-fringed reef completes this trip. The itinerary includes stopovers in Sydney, Alice Springs and Cairns. Includes: Accommodations and camping arrangements, local transportation, most meals. Dates: May through September. Length: 23 days. Group size: 17 maximum. Cost: $2,190. Special requirements: $250 deposit.

PEREGRINE EXPEDITIONS

Peregrine Expeditions
Suite 710, 7th Floor
343 Little Collins Street
Melbourne, VIC. 3000 Australia
60 1121
60 1122 *Bhutan*

Few visitors have been privileged to trek into the unexplored regions of Bhutan. This trek covers the route to the base camp of Chomolhari (7,315 kilometers), only recently opened to trekkers. The trip begins with a warmup trek in the valley of Paro to the gravity-defying monastery of Takstang, or "Tigers Nest," clinging to the side of a one-thousand-meter cliff face. From Paro, the trek continues through forests of oak and birch, rhododendron and juniper, and high up into the yak pastures. Sights en route include beautiful alpine lakes, tumbling ice falls, ruined dzongs, rugged yak herders with their flocks and the world's rarest mountain sheep, the bharal. There is also time to explore the weekly markets and surrounding villages. Includes: Full board, sleeping bags, experienced and local guides. Dates: October and May. Length of trip: 18 days. Group size: 15. Cost: $2,833 Australian. Special requirements: Physical fitness; $100 deposit and balance due 90 days prior to trip.

Philippine Travel Bureau, Inc.
G/F Builders' Centre
170 Salcedo Street
Legaspi Village
Makati, M. Manila
Philippines
(818) 9384
(818) 9784 *Philippines*

Climb Mount Apo in the exotic Philippines. No mountaineering or special skills are needed for this magnificent journey through lush, tropical rainforests. You'll walk beneath giant mahogany trees ... see steaming sulfur chimneys, hot springs, and geysers ... pass dainty orchids and carnivorous pitcher plants growing wild alongside waterfalls and cascades. Along the way, you'll view exotic wildlife—colorful butterflies and rare birds such as the Mt. Apo mynah and the island thrush, found only in high elevations. Includes: Guide, tents, round-trip air fare from Manila to Davao, land transportation, sightseeing, meals. Dates: April and May. Length of trip: 4 days. Cost: On request. Special requirements: Good physical condition; all camping equipment except tents.

Rio Bravo, Inc.
P.O. Box 6004
McLean, VA 22101   *Peru*

Original Indian paving, exciting lost cities, panoramic vistas, and rich flora have made the Inca Trail to Machu Picchu one of South America's most famous treks. Lost for four hundred years, this twenty-eight-mile route to the past starts at Chilca. For five days, you'll hike past ferns and orchids in cloud forests; across passes reaching 13,650 feet, within sight of hanging glaciers; down to ruins, through Indian tunnels and bridges to arrive at mysterious Machu Picchu as did the Inca—through the Gateway of the Sun. Porters carry all equipment; cooks prepare omelets, salads, steaks; the route provides the scenery; guides entertain with Inca history and legends; and you can just soak it all in—pisco and wine included. (After the trek, you can also soak your body in the hot waters of Aguas Calientes.) Includes: Leader; porters; all transportation; meals; lodging (on economy treks clients provide their own tents); admission and guide to Machu Picchu. Dates: All year. Length of trip: 7 days. Group size: 1–15. Cost: $365–$500.

Routeburn Guided Walk
P.O. Box 271
Queenstown, New Zealand
Phone: 100   *New Zealand*

Does hiking through ancient forest, past crystal-clear lakes and snow-capped alps sound appealing? Then try the Routeburn Guided Walk through two of New Zealand's most spectacular national parks—Mount Aspiring and Fiordland. Enjoy outstanding views of mountain torrents and waterfalls and a large variety of luxurious alpine flora. Small parties are escorted by two skilled guides who point out interesting sights along the way and bring hikers safely to their destination. Accommodations and meals are provided in Routeburn's privately-owned, well-stocked cabins, consisting of two bunk rooms with six bunks each, hot showers, and a communal living area. The pace is slow and steady to allow maximum enjoyment of the outstanding views. Fourteen years' experience operating this tour. Includes: All transportation, accommodations and meals. Dates: Mid-November through April: Spring, summer and fall in New Zealand. Length of trip: 4 days. Group size: 14 plus 2 guides. Cost: NZ$240. Special requirements: Good health.

S.I.T. (Special Interest Tours)
2437 Durant Avenue, Suite 208
Berkeley, CA 94704
415-843-8294
Telex 910-366-7092 ADVENCEN   *Europe*

Europe—with its great variety, traditions and long history—can best be discovered and understood step-by-step, on foot. Experience the joy in slowly having this continent open itself to the inquisitive but respectful traveler. Explore Italy, Austria, France, England, Wales, Germany, Greece, Turkey, Rumania, Iceland, and Scandinavia by walking/hiking tours. Stay overnight in romantic inns, country lodges, mountain huts, and even with friendly locals. Auxiliary transportation is often close-by for those who may tire early. In operation since 1967. Includes: Accommodations, meals, guides. Dates: March through October. Length: 5–29 days. Group size: 2–20. Cost: from $234.

Serenissima Travel, Ltd.
2 Lower Sloane Street
London, England SWIW 8BJ
(01) 730-7281   *France*

Discover the Loire Valley on this relaxed walking tour. Stroll through the deer-filled park surrounding Chambord, the famous chateau built by Francois I. Examine the fine collection of historical portraits at the Chateau of Beauregard. In the lush Touraine, walk along the river Indre to Pont de Ruan, full of literary associations with Balzac. After walking through the low hills along the Vienne, visit the tombs of the Plantagenet kings. A motorcoach will transport travelers to and from each morning and afternoon walk (about five miles each). All Serenissima tours are accompanied by a noted expert in each field and a tour manager. Eleventh year operating world-wide tours. Includes: All-inclusive. Dates: May. Length: 8 days. Cost: £595.

Sobek Expeditions
Angels Camp, CA 95222
209-736-2661 in CA, HI and AK
800-344-3284   *Ethiopia*

The "Great Unknown" only remains in a handful of remote areas around the world; Ethiopia is one of those places. In parts of Ethiopia, discovery may still happen with every footstep. There are untrod paths and rock-hewn churches hidden in the mountain valleys of this history-drenched country. Join Sobek's highland trek to Ethiopia's highest peak, Ras Dashan (15,160 feet); to the Tisissat (Blue Nile) falls; a float trip on the Awash River; past desert nomads, camel caravans, hot springs, and oases. In addition, Sobek visits the principal churches and castles of the old empires and absorbs some of the fascinating history of Abyssinia. Includes: Everything except air fare. Dates: November. Length of trip: 30 days. Group size: 5–12. Cost: $2,675. Special requirements: Top physical condition essential since trek is of advanced difficulty; ages 18–65; $300 deposit.

Sunrise Adventures
P.O. Box 1790
Glenwood Springs, CO 81601
303-945-1366   *Utah*

After a short visit in Natural Bridges National Monument, you'll camp the first night on the rim of the Dark Canyon Plateau, an excellent vantage point for photographing this vast and colorful desert panorama at sunset. The following five days will be spent on the floor of four-thousand-foot-deep Dark Canyon, exploring tributaries along the way, and camping beside lush oases. You'll be hiking under huge sandstone walls, beside clear streams and pools, surrounded by abundant wildlife. Color photography enthusiasts will have an opportunity to capture on film the rare beauty of the desert in bloom in this remote and undisturbed area. Includes: Transportation (from Durango), food, group equipment. Dates: April, May, October. Length of trip: 7 days. Cost: $475. Special requirements: Reasonably good physical condition; deposit $225.

**Surf Tours
1314 South King Street, Suite 1060
Honolulu, Hawaii 96814
808-538-6768
ITT 734-1918 ZUBHI**   *Hawaii*

Hawaii's unique topography offers you a great variety of hiking trails to choose from—from living tidal pools to majestic mountain peaks. With Surf Tours, novices as well as experienced hikers can climb Diamond Head for panoramic views of Leeward Oahu. From Kaena's coastal pools to Mauna Loa's sub-arctic summit, your qualified guide will lead you safely through your hike while informing you about Hawaii's flora and fauna, historical points of interest and native folklore. Special hikes on all islands can be arranged for individuals, groups, organizations and the handicapped upon request. Established and licensed in 1977. Includes: Ground transportation, meals, guides, equipment, permits. Dates: Year-round. Length of trip: 2–8 hours. Group size: 3–10. Cost: $47–$142 per person. Special requirements: 20% deposit to confirm reservation; full prepayment 48 hours prior to hike.

**The African Experience
7 Cherry Street
Lexington, MA 02173
617-862-2165**   *Namibia*

Camp and trek in Gemsbok National Park, Namib Desert, and Etosha National Park, all known for their amazing assortment of wild animals. This safari explores all of the known attractions of these areas, and also gets away from the well-used routes to explore areas not usually visited by tourists. Camp out at organized, comfortable sites in the bush and desert for a real sense of the heart of Africa. Nine years in business. Includes: Meals, local transport, equipment, hotel in Johannesburg, guide. Dates: Monthly except January and April. Length: 21 days. Cost: $1,266. Special requirements: Good physical condition, must share all camping duties.

**The Earth Preservation Fund
P.O. Box 7545-ST
Ann Arbor, MI 48107
313-665-4407**   *India*

The Earth Preservation Fund is a non-profit corporation established to promote programs for environmental conservation and community improvement worldwide. Earth Preservation Fund is sponsoring this cultural trek into the Indian regions of Kashmir and Ladakh. The trip begins in Srinagar, capital of Kashmir. There are magnificent views of the western Himalayas, including the massive Naga Parbt. The more remote Ladakh was opened to the outside world only in 1975 and is relatively unexplored. Known as "Little Tibet," Ladakh is home to the largest living remnant of the great Tibetan civilization and Buddhist tradition. Trekkers travel through this high altitude desert under spectacular snow-capped peaks and a deep blue sky, crossing ever-changing, colorful landscapes. The trek visits remote villages and passes through high mountains, exploring cultures and environments unchanged since the days of Alexander the Great. Seven years' experience. Includes: Accommodations, meals, American guide, Ladakhi guides and porters, group camping gear, ground transportation and a tax-deductible contribution to an EPF-funded local solar energy project. Dates: July through September. Length of trip: 23 days. Group size: 15. Cost: $1,620. Special requirements: Good physical health; hiking experiences; $300 deposit.

The Earth Preservation Fund
P.O. Box 7545-ST
Ann Arbor, MI 48107
313-665-4407   *Nepal*

Earth Preservation Fund is offering an Everest Sherpa country trek deep in the Mt. Everest National Park. Native Sherpas, your guides in the region, will welcome you with warm hospitality into the homes of family and friends. The approach to Everest brings you through communities dominated by Brahmins, Chetris, Sunnars, Newars and other cultural groups characteristic of this predominately Hindu kingdom. You will pass rice-farming communities, markets, schools, tea shops and villages. The local people are quite friendly; they are as interested in you as you are in them. As the climbing begins, you'll cross and recross the rushing glacial waters of the Dudh Kosi, or "Milky River." At last you arrive in Namche Bazaar, a natural amphitheater protected from weather and blessed with a major natural spring. Many of the staff are from this area and usually the group stays with a Sherpa family. The trip continues with day treks and short walks before your return flight to Kathmandu. Although this is a demanding trek, no technical climbing skills or equipment is required. Six years' experience. Includes: Accommodations, meals, bilingual guides, transportation, group camping gear, and a tax-deductible contribution to EPF-funded solar energy projects in the Himalayas. Dates: October through May. Length of trip: 23 days. Group size: 8. Cost: $1,340. Special requirements: Good physical condition, hiking and camping experience, $300 deposit.

Ultimate Escapes, Ltd.
2506 W. Colorado Avenue
Colorado Springs, CO 80904
303-578-8383
Telex 499 2665   *Mexico*

La Barranca del Cobre, or Copper Canyon, a vertical world almost as deep and more remote than the Grand Canyon, is the home of the Tarahumara Indians. The world's most remarkable runners, these Indians often run two hundred miles nonstop. Following a day and a night in El Paso, Texas, you'll go by rail to Divisadero, where your trekking trip into the Barranca del Cobre starts high in the Sierra Madre Occidental. With pack animals and Tarahumara guides, you'll trek down into tropical canyons to enjoy warm springs and sand beaches. Along the way, you'll visit Indian villages and prehistoric cliff dwellings. All trips are led by outdoor professionals. Includes: Transportation from El Paso, Texas; lodging in superior hotels; all meals except in Chihuahua; group equipment; guide; pack burros. Dates: October through April. Length: 11 days. Cost: $595. Special requirements: Good health and physical condition.

Western Frontiers
P.O. Box 6145
Salt Lake City, UT 84106   *Colorado,*
801-484-4421   *Montana,*
Telex 453030 FMWSLC   *Wyoming*

Hike, river raft and ride the range on this comprehensive trip through the Rocky Mountains. You'll begin amidst fourteen-thousand-foot peaks in Rocky Mountain National Park, where the first portion of the trip emphasizes hiking in Rocky Mountain National Park, Teton National Park and Yellowstone. In between these scenic wonders, visits to hot springs and dinosaur quarries add a change of pace. Following Yellowstone, the Old West comes into focus as you journey to Cody, Wyoming for a rodeo and visit to the Buffalo Bill Historic Center, which houses the Buffalo Bill Memorabilia, Winchester Gun Collection, and superb Plains Indian Exhibit. Next, you'll embark on a three-day cattle drive on a twenty-thousand-acre spread in Wyoming and Montana. Round out your trip with hikes through Glacier National Park and a two-day river trip on the Flathead River near Glacier. In operation since 1979; all guides have minimum five years' experience on rivers and overland trips, member Western River Guides Association, Utah Guides and Outfitters, Travel Industry Association of America. All guides certified in first aid and CPR. Includes: All camping equipment, meals, guides and transportation. Dates: June through August. Length of trip: 18 days, 17 nights. Group size: 10 maximum, 5 minimum. Cost: $1,285. Special requirements: No prior experience needed, good health required. Deposit of $250 required at time of booking.

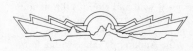

Western Frontiers
P.O. Box 6145
Salt Lake City, UT 84106
801-484-4421   *Western*
Telex 453030 FMWSLC   *United States*

This nineteen-day journey through the heart of the West offers not only the best of the national parks between San Francisco and Denver, but also includes a two-day, two-night rafting trip on the Colorado River, two days of powerboating and fishing on Lake Powell, and a jeep trip through the Navajo Indian Reservation in Monument Valley. The trip emphasizes hiking through Yosemite and the high country of the Sierras, Zion, Bryce, Grand Canyon, and Arches National Parks, paying particular attention to the flora and fauna, national and human histories of the areas visited. In operation since 1979, all guides have minimum of five years' experience, certified CPR and advanced first aid. Fully licensed by Interstate Commerce Commission, Member Western River Guides Association, Utah Guides and Outfitters, Travel Industry Association of America. Includes: All camping equipment (tents, sleeping bags, sleeping pads, canteens, daypacks), all meals unless otherwise indicated in itinerary. Dates: July, August. Length of trip: 19 days, 18 nights. Group size: 10 maximum, 4 minimum. Cost: $1,390. Special requirements: Moderate hiking involved. Clients should be in good health; no heart problems please, as trip covers elevations from sea level to 11,000 feet as well as having possible temperature changes from 25° F to 100+° F.

Western Frontiers
P.O. Box 6145
Salt Lake City, UT 84106
801-484-4421
Telex 453030 FMWSLC   *Arizona, Utah*

On this twelve-day, in-depth exploration of Utah and Arizona's canyon areas, you'll hike through the National Parks of Zion, Bryce, Capitol Reef, Arches, and the Grand Canyon. The expeditions focus on the history of the Fremont and Anasazi Indian cultures, as well as the geology of these unique areas. Included in the trip is a jet boat and jeep exploration of

Canyonlands National Park, a jeep trip through the Navajo Indian Reservation in Monument Valley, and an air flight through the Grand Canyon. In operation since 1979; all guides have minimum five years' experience as river and overland guides, are well versed in natural and human history of area, licensed by Interstate Commerce Commission; member Western River Guides Association, Utah Guides and Outfitters, Travel Industry Association of America. Includes: All camping equipment, meals, guides, and transportation. Dates: June through September. Length of trip: 12 days, 11 nights. Group size: 10 maximum, 5 minimum. Cost: $910. Special requirements: Moderate hiking skills; good health, no heart or blood pressure problems. Deposit of $250 required at time of booking. Travelers should note that the temperature of these areas can be quite extreme during the summer months and should be well prepared for desert hiking.

Wilderness Expeditions
P.O. Box 755 Cooma
NSW 2630 Australia
(0648) 21 587   *India*

With Wilderness Expeditions, you can choose from a large number of treks into the remote and awe-inspiring areas of India and Nepal. One highlight is a two-week trek into the area known as the valley of the flowers. Here in the ancient state of Garhwal, rhododendrons, irises, primulas, poppies and other prized garden flowers grow wild and glorious throughout late spring and summer. Also within the borders of Garhwal are some of the Himalaya's highest peaks and the headquarters of the Ganges, the holiest river in India. Another Wilderness Expeditions trek combines a two-week traverse of the Annapurna range with a four-day, wild whitewater river ride back out. Yet another trip combines trekking with two weeks of traditional hatha yoga in the foothills of the Himalayas. On all trips, you'll be accompanied by experienced Australian and local guides. And, since porters will transport all camping gear and food, you need to carry only a day pack. Founded 1977. Includes: Everything, including airfare (usually from Sydney). Dates: Year-round. Length of trip: 16–36 days. Group size: 4–15. Cost: Approximately $25 per day.

Wilderness Expeditions
P.O. Box 755 Cooma
NSW 2630 Australia
(0648) 21 587
Telex AA 27330 Baroff   *Tasmania*

Wilderness Expeditions' wide range of programs allows you to explore Australia with ease—you carry only your personal gear and they do all the rest. So come explore Kosciusco National Park, where you'll hike high up weather-beaten ridges to alpine meadows filled with a colorful display of wildflowers, rushing streams and waterfalls. For a different side of Tasmania go on a wilderness beachcombing trek to the deserted coastal area of southern New South Wales. Stride over heathland and secluded sands, past wave-swept rock platforms and sheer cliff faces. Off shore, dolphins and seals can often be seen frolicking in the water. Study the varied bird life including penguins, osprey and sea eagles. Go body surfing, fish off the rocks or just relax and sunbathe. Licensed and insured. Includes: Camping equipment, food, transport, guide. Dates: September through May. Length: 2–9 days. Group size: 3–9. Cost: $55 per day.

Wilderness Travel
1760-HB Solano Avenue
Berkeley, CA 94707
415-524-5111
Telex 677 022   *Peru*

Southeastern Peru not only possesses some of the most spectacular mountains in South America, but was also the seat of power of the extraordinary Inca Empire. This adventure takes you on treks through two mountain ranges near the Incan capital of Cuzco. The first trek goes through the Cordillera Vilcabamba, where you'll spend five days in the vicinity of the impressive Salcantay (20,574-feet) and Humantay (19,239-feet) peaks. After crossing a fifteen-thousand-foot pass between the two mountains, you'll descend to a subtropical zone of coffee and banana plantations. Then a short train ride takes you to Machu Picchu, fabulous Lost City of the Incas, for an overnight and following full day exploring the ruins. You'll spend an additional day visiting Inca fortresses in the Urubamba valley before setting off on the second trek, a six-day circuit of Mt. Ausangate (20,644 feet). The Indians in this area adhere closely to elaborate traditional dress and Quechua, their native tongue. Along the route you'll also see herds of llamas and alpacas, camp beside hot springs and view spectacular peaks and glaciers. Participants carry only day packs; horses transport baggage and camping equipment. Includes: All accommodations, all land transportation, all meals but five (in cities), camp helpers, pack animals, all camping equipment except sleeping bags. Dates: June through August. Length of trip: 21 days. Group size: 5–15. Cost: $1,690. Special requirements: General good health, fitness; 1st deposit $200, 2nd deposit $400 4 months prior.

Wilderness Travel
1760-HB Solano Avenue
Berkeley, CA 94707
415-524-5111
Telex 677 022   *New Guinea*

This introduction to Papua New Guinea's remarkable diversity takes you through lush tropical forests, atop the nation's highest peak, into tribal villages, along black sand beaches and swimming through coral reefs. Your adventure begins with a flight from the capital, Port Moresby, to the highland trading town of Kundiawa. From here, you'll travel by bus through spectacular Gembogl Gorge on the way to the trailhead at Kegasugal. On a three-day trek to the top of Mt. Wilhelm (fifteen thousand feet) you'll meet friendly Chimbu highlanders in their traditional dress of possum skins and beaten bark, with elaborate headdress of cockatoo feathers. Continuing through changing forest zones, you may spot the elusive bird of paradise (42 species) as you ascend to the Pindaunde Lakes and the summit of Mt. Wilhelm. Returning via Goroka, you'll fly to the coastal town of Madang with its beautiful island-studded harbor—"The archipelago of contented men"—for snorkeling among brilliant coral reefs. Then it's on to the volcanic island of Manam just off the coast to explore black sand beaches, villages and the slopes of a perfectly shaped volcano. Extensions to the Ramu River, a week-long dugout canoe trip to spirit houses in the jungle, and a Solomon Seas Islands outrigger canoe trip are also available. Expert guide in Papua New Guinea previously conducted the government census, knows highland tribes thoroughly. Includes: All accommodations, all land and water transportation in Papua New Guinea, all meals but one, guides and camp helpers/porters, all camping equipment except sleeping bags. Dates: June 10 and July 8. Length of trip: 15 days. Group size: 5 minimum; 15 maximum. Cost: $1,190. Special requirements: 1st deposit $200, 2nd deposit $400 4 months prior.

Wilderness Travel
1760-HB Solano Avenue
Berkeley, CA 94707
415-524-5111
Telex 677 022   *Italy*

The Leaning Tower of Pisa ... Etruscan ruins ... Roman baths ... neat farms and oak woods—see them all on this hiking excursion through Italy. You'll visit the perfectly preserved twelfth- and thirteenth-century walled town of San Gimignano, with its lavish frescos and churches. Walk amid hillsides of vineyards and oak groves to Colle Val d'Elsa, stopping at the charming converted lodgings of a farmhouse in Strove. For the last stretch, hike along farm tracks and mule paths to Siena, "Antechamber of Paradise," with its many major works of art, noted architecture and beautiful central piazza. Along your route, you'll stay in small, often family-run hotels, enjoying excellent local cuisine. An escort vehicle transports the luggage between overnight stops, so you'll only need to carry a day pack. Excursions to Florence or other towns may be included. Includes: Accommodations, meals, transportation. Dates: May and September. Length: 12 days. Group size: 5–15. Cost: $1,190. Special requirements: 1st deposit $200, 2nd deposit of $400 4 months prior to departure.

Wind Over Mountain
410 Highland
Boulder, CO 80302
303-444-8028   *Nepal*

Wind Over Mountain is offering a two-week fitness trip to the Annapurna Sanctuary in Nepal led by fitness expert Donna Hinton. Your goal is not to "conquer" a mountain but rather to complete your Himalayan walk feeling comfortable, happy and accomplished. Donna will give daily instruction in cardiovascular endurance, muscle strengthening and flexibility. The Nepali staff will carry everything but daypacks, and will set up camp and prepare simple, wholesome and delicious meals. The sanctuary is one of the most awe-inspiring places in the world, affording spectacular views. An optional extension to the Maldives is available for those who wish to relax in the tropics after the trek. Founded 1974. Includes: Hotel in Delhi and Kathmandu, meals on trail, porters, bilingual Nepali guide, daily fitness instruction and services of a health professional. Dates: October and November. Length of trip: 14 days. Group size: 10–12. Cost: $1,595.

World Wide Trekking, Inc.
1440 Broadway, Room 1372
New York, NY 10018
212-840-4343
800-223-7552   *Corsica*

Rugged Corsica is more a mountain than anything else. Monte Cinto, rising 8,890 feet out of the azure Mediterranean, caps the birthplace of Napoleon. The Grande Randonne 20 (great walk) winds its way through the rugged and exposed slopes of the Corsican highland. The complete walk would take about three weeks to complete, but your group starts in the isolated town of Bastellica, just east of the capital, Ajaccio. The route takes in the peaks of Monte D'oro (7,800 feet), Monte Renoso (7,900 feet), Monte Tozzo (6,900 feet) and Monte Cinto. Nights are spent bivouacking out, or in mountain hostels, like Haut Asco, at the foot of Monte Cinto. The trekking is rugged and allows those who want a challenging two-week vacation a chance to test themselves. At the end of the trek three nights are spent at the beach resort of Calvi, located in the north. Twelve years' experience. Includes: Food, equipment, leader, support vehicle, hotels. Dates: July through October. Length of trip: 2 weeks. Cost: $600 land only.

World Wide Trekking, Inc.
1440 Broadway, Room 1372
New York, NY 10018
212-840-4343
800-223-7552   *Ethiopia*

For centuries it remained secluded from the world by natural barriers. For the past seven years, it has endured problems from within and without. Today the barriers are down and Ethiopia—the roof of Africa—is open. Trekking through the Great Rift Valley, surrounded by the Gelada Baboon (the "Yeti of Africa") and great birds, such as the lammergeyer and falcon, you'll see why this country is so special. Places of interest include the Palaces of Gondar, Tississat Falls and the rock-hewn churches of Lalibeli. The trek will also spend a number of days in the Semien and Bale Mountains; rugged terrain but worth the effort. Twelve years' experience. Includes: Food, guides, equipment, leader, hotels. Dates: December through February; May through October. Length of trip: 2–3½ weeks. Group size: 6–15. Cost: $2,000 land only.

World Wide Trekking, Inc.
1440 Broadway, Room 1372
New York, NY 10018
212-840-4343
800-223-7552   *Greece*

Just twenty-five miles from the Albanian border, the Pindos Range boasts Greece's second highest summit: Mount Smolikas (8,610 feet). Staying at local tavernas and homes in the villages you trek through, you'll experience the traditional culture of the area. The Greeks are one of the most hospitable people on the globe and they prove it with unbridled enthusiasm for the trekkers that pass through their homes. On some nights, you'll also bivouac by cool mountain streams. Three different itineraries are offered for varying abilities of fitness. Included on some programs are the cliff-top monasteries of Meteora. Twelve years' experience. Includes: Most food, hotels, leader, support vehicle, some equipment. Dates: June through October. Length of trip: 2 weeks. Group size: 6–15. Cost: $600 land only.

World Wide Trekking, Inc.
1440 Broadway, Room 1372
New York, NY 10018
212-840-4343
800-223-7552
Peru

World Wide Trekking invites you to adventure in Peru, home of the condor and a multitude of other no less exotic breeds. These trips combine rafting, trekking and cultural explorations. You'll learn about the Inca civilization, which could divert rivers, fill rooms full of gold, and mold three-hundred-ton bricks of granite into earthquake-proof palaces—and distrusted mass communication. Here, literacy never existed by law and vital messages of state were transmitted as knots in a piece of string. Feel the legends come alive as you travel down the ancient Inca Trail. Twelve years' experience. Includes: Equipment, hotels, leaders, guides, food. Dates: June through October. Length of trip: 2–4 weeks. Group size: 6–15. Cost: $1,500 land only.

World Wide Trekking, Inc.
1440 Broadway, Room 1372
New York, NY 10018
212-840-4343
800-223-7552
Nepal

Nepal, home of eight of the world's fourteen highest peaks (all over eight thousand meters), presents outdoor enthusiasts with a wide range of vacation possibilities. World Wide Trekking offers over fifteen different treks, combined with raft trips and game park exploration. Choices range from the leisurely stroll on an eight-day Annapurna foothills trek, to the strenuous eighteen-day Island Peak ascent (20,300 feet). For the person who wants to take the same road that Tilman took thirty years ago, they also follow the Tilman Approach into the Solu Khumbu, running up the Arun River Valley. All treks are led by people who know Nepal, and very often are well-known personalities in a particular outdoor field. Twelve years' experience. Includes: Guides, equipment, food, hotel, office staff, leader. Dates: October through May. Length of trip: 2–4 weeks. Group size: 6–15. Cost: $1,300 approximately.

Horse Riding •
Packing •
Carriage Tours •
Events •

Planning a vacation on horseback? Well, you can choose from—

- Horse packing through the magnificent Grand Tetons of Wyoming
- Riding to the hounds in Ireland
- Galloping across Kenya's Great Rift Valley on an amazing riding safari
- Learning to drive a four-in-hand stagecoach along the cobblestone streets of a Bavarian village

In fact, you can do nearly as many things with horses as there are breeds of horses . . . and there were over sixty of those at last count. Novices can learn the basics . . . experts can improve their calf-roping or equitation . . . and everyone can savor incredibly scenic surroundings while being very much a part of nature themselves.

There are horse trips available for riders of all levels—from pack trips aboard docile trail horses to cross-country gallops on full-throttle thoroughbreds. If you have your own horse, you can take him/her along on some of these vacations as well. Meanwhile, for the vicarious equestrian, there are trips where you don't have to climb into the saddle at all, but can ride elegantly in horse-drawn carriages, or travel comfortably on a wagon train.

For outdoor enthusiasts of all persuasions—backpackers, trekkers, birdwatchers or photographers—horseback riding enables you to see the country . . . on someone else's hoofs. Some of the world's most spectacular landscapes are found in mountainous regions like the Rockies, Andes or Pyrenees. When you travel by horse, you don't have to be in terrific shape, you don't need to worry as much about altitude, and you can watch the view—instead of watching your footing. In addition, you can cover more distance, more comfortably, on horseback. To spend ten days in the wilderness, you need a sixty-pound pack. You can carry it yourself—or get a horse.

For those of you heading out on the trail, here are some pointers that can help you plan your trip:

1. Check skill requirements carefully with the operator. In general, pack trips can accommodate riders of all levels, while foxhunting, dressage or calf-roping demand experienced riders.

2. What kinds of horses will you be riding? If you're a novice, you'll proba-bly want a quiet horse on the trail. Meanwhile, advanced riders will want a high-performance mount for sports like jumping or cross-country.

3. What type of saddle? A Western saddle, with its horn and built-up seat, offers more security for beginners. The flatter "English-type" saddle, used for jumping, hunting, dressage or polo, requires more fine-tuned riding balance. Appropriately enough, Western saddles are common in the Western part of the United States, as well as portions of Spain and Latin America (the Western saddle descends from the Moorish saddle used by the Spanish conquistadors). Expect to find English saddles in most of Eu-rope.

4. Horse packing vs. horse trekking—there is a difference. On a pack trip, you'll be camping out under the stars—either in your own sleeping bag or in an outfitter-supplied tent. On a trek, you'll ride every day to a different destination—a country inn, mountain lodge or ranch—where you'll spend the night, enjoying a hot shower, home-cooked food and a comfortable bed. The following morning, you saddle up and ride to your next stop-over. Horse trekking is much more common in Europe than in the United States, although the idea is starting to catch on over here.

5. How much riding will you do each day? What kind? For example, you'll spend about four to six hours a day in the saddle on a pack trip or trek, covering fifteen to eighteen miles, depending on terrain. For advanced in-struction in jumping, reining or dressage, you'll generally have one to two hours of instruction a day, with perhaps some time for riding on your own.

6. Will you care for your mount yourself—or will a groom, wrangler or guide handle the feeding, cleaning, tacking and other chores?

7. Are the outfitters and guides licensed and/or bonded? As you look through the listings of horse packers in the United States, you'll fre-quently see "licensed and bonded" included among their qualifications. This means that they meet the knowledge, skill, safety and financial re-quirements established by their respective states. Contact the state's Out-fitters Board or Fish and Game Commission for more information about licensing or references on an individual operator. For information about a foreign tour operator, contact that country's national tourist office. See page 361 for a complete list of names and addresses.

8. About fishing. In the Western United States, many pack trips and treks also offer a chance to indulge in some superb fishing. If you're planning on catching your own breakfast, ask in advance whether you're going to need a fishing license for that area.

9. Of horses and charleyhorses. If you haven't ridden in a while, invest in a riding lesson or two before you canter off into the sunset. By getting those muscles stretched into shape, you can avoid saddlesores and charleyhorses on your vacation.

10. Know what to expect. On a pack trip, the horses walk most of the time—so don't anticipate galloping across the canyons. The pack stock must travel slowly because of their loads, while high altitude and rugged terrain are additional factors. Meanwhile, fox hunts have long-standing rules for dress and etiquette. Guests should not pass a hunt member in the field; only male hunt members of the hunt can wear the traditional scarlet coat ("pinks"). Read up before you go.

SECTIONS OF RELATED INTEREST

Llama/Mule/Camel Expeditions
Covered Wagons

Action Tours
3857 Sunset Street
Burnaby, B.C. V5G 1T4 Canada
604-430-2124 *Spain*

Get to know Spain from the saddle. The route covers the southern region of Atlantic Cadiz (Andalusia), traveling along ancient sheep trails, cattle tracks, wagon and bridle paths. Each group is accompanied by a guide and a Land Rover to carry luggage ahead. Riders can visit small hill towns and gallop along quiet sandy beaches, with the coast of Africa on the horizon. Lodging is at the El Santiscal Ranch and at comfortable hotels en route. Riding tours in the Castile region also available. Licensed by Registrar of Travel, British Columbia. Includes: Accommodations (double occupancy), all meals and picnics with wine, horses and tack, guides and use of the Land Rover. Dates: All year. Length of trip: 9 days. Group size: 8–16. Cost: $668 per person. Special requirements: Basic knowledge of riding. Not suitable for beginning riders.

Action Tours
3857 Sunset Street
Burnaby, B.C. V5G 1T4 Canada
604-430-2124 *Great Britain*

Ride to the hounds on this "English Moors" riding and fox-hunting holiday. Stay at an old country inn on the Devon-Cornwall border. The package includes four days of riding with a guide on both Dartmoor in Devon and Bodmin Moor in Cornwall. There are thirteen hunts within a fifty-mile radius of the hotel. Participation can be arranged, rental of hunter horses is extra. Riders not wishing to join the hunt can attend the start of the meet, enjoying a stirrup cup with the huntsmen. Licensed by Registrar of Travel, British Columbia. Includes: Double-occupancy accommodations with private bath; hacking horse, tack, and guides; two or three meals daily; return rail ticket to London/Exeter; and a rental car with unlimited mileage. Renting a "hunter" is extra. Dates: October through April. Length of trip: 7 days, 6 nights. Group size: 15. Cost: $600 per person.

American Wilderness Experience
P.O. Box 1486
Boulder, CO 80306
303-444-2632 *Wyoming*

This true cowboy experience starts with a barbeque—giving you a chance to meet new friends, croon tunes around the campfire, and enjoy honest Western hospitality. After a restful night's lodging, you'll ride high into the Gros Ventre Range. It's the Indian word for "Fat Belly Mountains," and the abundant wildlife, thick forests, plump trout, and mountainsides of wild berries give proof to the name. Two very comfortable backcountry hunting camps serve as wilderness outposts offering such luxuries as a heated mess tent, walled sleeping tents, corrals, and a full-sized kitchen. The fishing is the best Wyoming has to offer and it is not unusual to be visited in camp by moose and elk. On layover days side rides are offered to various high lakes and ridge tops. From atop Sleeping Indian Mountain you get a 360° view of seven major mountain ranges including the Tetons, Wind Rivers, Hoback, Absaroka, and Yellowstone regions. Paul Crittenden has over fifteen years' experience guiding and outfitting wilderness trips. Includes: Pre-trip lodging, hayride and barbeque, all gear, base camp lodging on the hill, all meals, horses, saddles, guide, wranglers, cook, trailhead transportation, riding instruction. Dates: Summer, fall. Length of trip: 5 days, 5 nights. Group size: 6 to 15 guests (crew of 4). Cost: $495. Special requirements: No experience required. $100 deposit at time of booking.

American Wilderness Experience
P.O. Box 1486
Boulder, CO 80306
303-444-2632   *New Mexico*

A chartered plane will take you on a spectacular flight from Albuquerque to the trailhead on the edge of the Gila Wilderness. You'll spend the next six days exploring the awesome Gila on horseback. America's first Wilderness Area, the Gila is full of history, color and legend. The thick forests of pine, aspen, and oak served as the last refuge for Geronimo and his band of renegade Apaches. Terrain is both alpine and desert, with Indian ruins dotting the backcountry. Mountain lion, wild turkey, bear, elk, eagle and deer populate the area. The riding is somewhat challenging due to the primitive condition of many of the trails. Three camps are established—all along fresh mountain streams. Many wilderness hot springs can be found in the region and can be reached on side rides. Outfitter Harley Paul has over five years of experience guiding and outfitting wilderness pack trips. He is a national champion rodeo calf roper and has a lifetime of experience handling horses. Includes: Chartered flight to the trailhead from Albuquerque and back, all gear, all meals, guide, wranglers, cook, horses, saddles, riding instruction. Dates: Spring, summer, fall. Length of trip: 6 days, 5 nights. Group size: 4 to 12 guests (crew of 4). Cost: $710 from Albuquerque, $510 from Glenwood, N.M. Special requirements: No experience is required. $100 deposit at time of booking.

American Wilderness Experience
P.O. Box 1486
Boulder, CO 80306
303-444-2632   *Colorado*

Encompassing the San Juan Mountains of southwestern Colorado, the Weminuche Wilderness contains more fourteen-thousand-foot peaks than any other range in the Rockies. You'll spend six days riding its remote backcountry through scenic glacial valleys, across rushing rivers, and along the Continental Divide. Three camps are established and side rides are planned to glacial lakes abundant in trout. Elk, bear, deer and eagle populate the region and reward a quick eye. Besides opportunities for excellent fishing and photography, you'll be hiking, swimming, rafting, and receiving instruction on riding and saddling your horse. Meals are hearty, with fresh trout offered daily. Outfitter Dobbin Shupe has over thirty years of experience outfitting and guiding wilderness pack trips. Licensed, bonded and insured. Includes: Orientation breakfast, all gear, all meals, transportation to the trailhead, guide, wranglers, cook, horses, saddles, riding instruction. Dates: Summer, fall. Length of trip: 6 days, 5 nights. Group size: 6 to 15 guests (crew of 4). Cost: $495. Special requirements: No experience required. $100 deposit due at time of booking.

American Wilderness Experience
P.O. Box 1486
Boulder, CO 80306
303-444-2632   *Arizona*

The historic Superstitions are a remote region of desert, mountain and canyon terrain characterized by rugged scenery, towering saguaro cactus, abundant wildlife and desert wildflowers. You'll spend five days exploring the back country on horseback, visiting thirteenth-century Salado Indian cliff dwellings, ancient pictographs, luxurious springs, and high mountain passes. Listen to the tale of the Lost Dutchman's Mine and visit prospecting sites where people searched in vain for a hidden fortune in gold. Three camps will be established with side rides planned for layover days. Gourmet campfire dinners will be served each evening, topped off by a cup of cowboy coffee and endless tall stories of Apache Indians, Spanish explorers, and bloodthirsty prospectors. The outing takes place in the spring, the only time of year that this wilderness is comfortable for travel. Outfitter Jim Brink has over fifteen years' experience outfitting and guiding wilderness pack trips. He packs for the Sierra Club and American Forestry Association. Includes: Horseback exploration, all gear, all meals, trailhead transportation, naturalist guide, crew of wranglers and cooks, horses, saddles. Dates: March, April, May. Length of trip: 5 days, 4 nights. Group size: 4 to 12 guests (crew of 3). Cost: $385. Special requirements: No experience required. $100 non-refundable deposit due at time of booking.

Black Otter Guide Service
P.O. Box 68 STI
Pray, MT 59065
406-333-4362   *Montana*

Horsepack in comfort through Montana's untouched Absaroka-Beartooth wilderness. The friendly and experienced family of Duane and Ruth Neal provide everything from home-cooked meals to wilderness knowledge. Gentle horses are available for all ages and abilities during the spectacular sixteen-mile ride over majestic Wallace Pass to the semi-permanent Grizzly Creek tent camp. Ride, hike, fish for abundant trout, or photograph the beautiful wildflowers and wildlife. Sixteen years' experience, member Montana Outfitters and Guides Association. Includes: Horses, guides, meals and fully-equipped tent camp. Dates: Mid-July through August. Length of trip: 6 days. Group size: 12 maximum. Cost: $375 per person. Special requirements: Reservations with $125 deposit. Bring your own sleeping bag, fishing gear and personal items.

Burnt Ranch Stables
P.O. Box 122
Burnt Ranch, CA 95527
916-629-2005   *California*

Burnt Ranch Stables designs its pack trips into spectacular Salmon/Trinity Alps Primitive Area for small groups of adventurers who appreciate a well-stocked camp with fresh foods and roomy tents. Located in the Shasta/Trinity National Forest in northwest California, this untouched region is superb for photography, birdwatching, hiking, riding, or just working on a suntan. Excellent fishing is found in the many sparkling streams and alpine lakes. Previous riding experience is helpful but not essential since the stable's relaxed, well-fed, and healthy horses are generally well-mannered. Owner-guided operation, licensed. Includes: All equipment except sleeping bag and fishing gear, all meals, transportation from the stable to the trailhead, guides. Dates: July through September 5. Length of trip: 5 days. Group size: 6. Cost: $425 per person. Special requirements: $50 reservation deposit.

Canyonland Tours
P.O. Box 460, Dept STI
Flagstaff, AZ 86002
800-841-7317
602-774-7343 from AZ, AK, HI
Telex 172-029 SPX SRFL   *Arizona*

Probably the most enduring symbol of the West is the cowboy on horseback. Join this tradition of wide open spaces, fire-lit evenings, and memorable adventure as you ride with modern-day wranglers through the Kaibab National Forest and along the North Rim of the Grand Canyon. From places such as Big Saddle, Timpanagos Point, Parisswampitts Springs and Fence Point, you'll enjoy a variety of spectacular vistas of Grand Canyon. Camp in the forest or on the canyon rim, relaxing with friends around the campfire. Families and novices through experienced riders are welcome. Patrick and Susan Conley, owners of Canyonland Tours, have each worked in the guiding and outfitting business in the Southwest for over twelve years. Includes: Direct trip transportation; meals on trip; guide service; riding horse; bedroll; camp equipment. Dates: May through September. Length of trip: 3 days, 2 nights. Group size: 20 guests maximum. Cost: $295 per person. Special requirements: A $100 per person deposit.

Castle Leslie Equestrian Centre
Glaslough, County Monaghan
Ireland
Monaghan (047) 81700   *Ireland*

A private estate in the heart of Ireland's Lakeland, Castle Leslie covers one thousand acres of forest, open parkland, a wildlife sanctuary and three lakes. Suitable for all levels of riders, the Centre provides novices with quiet, steady horses and ponies, while quality Irish hunters are available for more experienced equestrians. Riders may also bring their own horses. Up to four hours of riding every day, including lessons, cross-country riding, "Horn Hunts," picnics, and leisurely hacking through beautiful Irish woods and countryside. In addition, Castle Leslie has twenty-five miles of varied cross-country courses, with over two hundred prepared and natural obstacles. Other activities include good pike and trout fishing, swimming, tennis, visits to historic sites and homes, golfing, rowing and sailing. Visitors are quartered at the baronial-style hunting lodge, complete with hunting prints and Victorian furnishings. Winner of the United Dominions Trust Award for Tourism, 1979. Includes: All riding, tuition, picnics, accommodations and meals. Travel to the Centre from Dublin and Aldergrove Airports

Riders enjoy a cross-country gallop on Irish hunters. (CASTLE LESLIE EQUESTRIAN CENTRE)

can be arranged. Dates: All year. Length of trip: 1 week. Group size: 1–10. Cost: £320–£350 per person.

**Cedok
10 East 40th Street
New York, NY 10016
212-689-9720**   *Czechoslovakia*

Cedok is the official Travel Bureau of Czechoslovakia and the sponsor of this six-day riding program at Marianska Lazne Spa, near Prague. Instructional facilities and horses are available for both beginner and advanced riders. The trip also includes spa visits and tours of museums, historical monuments and churches in Marianska Lazne, Karlovy Vary and Prague. You may also wish to visit the Grandhotel Moskva, Hajovna Tavern, Prague Castle and the Colannade of Czechoslovak–Soviet Friendship. An optional night program includes night clubs, brasseries, opera, ballet and theater. Includes: Accommodations, full board, guides, ground transportation, sightseeing, spa visits and fees. Dates: Spring, summer and fall. Length: 6 days. Group size: 15–35. Cost: $215–$243. $11 per hour of riding instruction.

**Clearwater Outfitters
P.O. Box 163-F
Pierce, ID 83546
208-476-5971**   *Idaho*

Vacation on horseback through the beautiful wilderness of Idaho's Mallard-Larkins Pioneer area. You'll have the chance to see elk, deer, bear and mountain goat plus the many small critters that inhabit the area. In addition, sparkling rivers and high mountain lakes supply excellent trout fishing. Clearwater Outfitters offer horsepack trips to suit the needs of the individual. You can choose to stay at one campsite for several days to relax, fish, and explore—or move on to a new camp daily. The amount of horseback riding can be adjusted to suit the rider. No previous riding experience is necessary. Clearwater's horses are gentle, sure-footed and very experienced on mountain trails. Twenty years' experience. Includes: Horses, crew, meals, camps, supplies, (except sleeping bags). Dates: Mid-July through Mid-

September. Length of trip: 5 days minimum. Group size: 4–8. Cost: $85 per day per person (group discounts available). Special requirements: Minimum age for singles is 16 years; 10 years with family group. Deposit required.

Diamond H Bar L Outfitters
P.O. Box 1
Ovando, MT 59854
406-793-5618   *Montana*

This summer, see for yourself why they call Montana "Big Sky Country." Horsepack through the Bob Marshall Wilderness which, combined with the Scapegoat to the south and the Great Bear to the north, encompasses over 1.5 million acres of wilderness land. In summer, wildflowers and shrubs transform the landscape into an emerald green, while elk and deer wander down from lofty slopes to bask in the sunshine. Bring a camera and photograph the Chinese Wall, Sugarloaf and Scapegoat mountains. Out of the saddle, you'll have plenty of time to explore ice caves, hunt for geodes and observe the remnants of Indian battles fought in the area. Eleven years' experience; member Montana Outfitters and Guide Association. Includes: Guide, meals, horses, all equipment (except personal gear, fishing licenses, and sleeping bags). Dates: June through September. Length of trip: 5 and 12 days. Group size: 12 maximum. Cost: Approximately $90 per person per day. Special requirements: Children must be 10 years or older for mixed groups, 6 years or older for custom-family trips.

FITS Equestrian
2011 Alamo Pintado
Solvang, CA 93463
805-688-9494   *Africa, Europe*

FITS Equestrian offers a wide range of rides throughout Europe, Africa and other countries from galloping across the endless Puszta of Hungary . . . to trotting through quaint Swiss villages, and ambling from castle to castle in France. Accompanied by a knowledgeable local guide ("randonneur"), you can savor the hospitality and friendliness of Ireland . . . discover the soul of Andalusia, land of flamenco, bullfights and castagnettes . . . unlock the mystery of Morocco, a world of fairy tales, nomads, endless mountains and shimmering beaches . . . or view the amazing wildlife of Kenya—all on horseback. These trips are not for beginners, but are geared to riders, western or English style, who can handle their horses in various terrain and sit in the saddle up to six hours at a stretch. You'll learn about the horses of each country, since you'll be mounted on regional breeds well-suited to the local climate and conditions. Since your luggage will be transported by car, you need only carry a camera with you. At night, you'll stay in small, comfortable inns. Includes: Horses, saddles, guide, accommodations, meals. Dates: Year-round. Length of trip: Varies. Group size: 6–12. Cost: Approximately $100 per day. Special requirements: For experienced riders. $200 deposit.

On horseback, travelers can appreciate the stunning beauty of Wyoming's Gros Ventre Range. (GAME HILL RANCH)

Game Hill Ranch
P.O. Box 1022
Bondurant, WY 82922
307-733-4120 *Wyoming*

Come where cold mountain streams flow down the mountainside . . . a gangly calf moose wades across a bog . . . hawks soar above sage-covered ridges. Wyoming's Gros Ventre and Wyoming Ranges are wild, unspoiled, and traveled by few. The family-operated, working Game Hill Ranch guides expeditions into the adjoining wilderness. Trustworthy horses and qualified guides lead campers up mountainsides past spectacular waterfalls, and through pine forests. This lush region encourages an abundance of wildlife, including unusual plants and birds, and animals with their young. Tours are small and personalized, and travel to favorite lakes and meadows on a moving camp basis with well-planned campsites and excellent food. Special photography safaris can be arranged. In operation since 1973; licensed. Includes: Meals, tents, sleeping bags, guides, horses, all camping equipment except personal gear. Dates: June through September. Length of trip: 3, 5, 7, or 10 days. Group size: 6 maximum. Cost: $600/7-day trip. Special requirements: 25% deposit to confirm reservation.

Glacier Raft Company
P.O. Box 264
West Glacier, MT 59936
406-888-5541 *Montana*

Combine the beauty of horsepacking with the thrill of whitewater rafting on a Glacier Raft tour. Centered around the Great Bear Wilderness and Glacier National Park in Montana, the tour starts with a scenic flight to the Shafer Meadow Ranger Station. From there, adventurers set out for three days of horseback riding through the wilderness, stopping to fish in high mountain lakes and camping in the back country of Montana. Two days of whitewater rafting and fishing along the southern border of Glacier National Park rounds out this beautiful wilderness adventure. Seven years' experience; licensed; member Montana Outfitters and Guides Association. Includes: Flight from West Glacier to Shafer Meadow, horses, guides, tents, equipment, all meals, rafting equipment and oarsman/guide. Dates: July. Length of trip: 5 days. Group size: 4–15. Cost: $475 per person. Special requirements: Fairly good physical condition, sleeping bag, fishing gear if desired, $100 deposit.

L. D. Frome, Outfitter
RFD
Afton, WY 83110
307-886-5240 *Wyoming*

Saddle up and ride into scenic areas of the Teton Wilderness. Here the smell of leather, sagebrush and woodsmoke will be your companions . . . the starry skies will watch over you at night . . . and sourdough hotcakes glistening with syrup, steaks seared over an open fire and fresh-brewed coffee will keep you fit for your outdoor adventures. The days will be spent exploring—as you catch sight of moose and coyote or take time out to fish, you'll feel like part of the Old West. The outfitter offers both horse packing and horse trekking—so you can spend the nights either camping outdoors under a moonlit sky, or bedding down at a dude ranch or lodge. Operator has eighteen years' experience as Wyoming Wilderness outfitter. Includes: Horse, guide, food, accommodations in dude ranch or lodge, or all camp gear. Dates: June through September. Length of trip: 4–10 days. Group size: 20 maximum. Cost: $90 per day. Special requirements: $50 deposit per person.

McGee Creek Pack Station
Rt. 1, Box 162
Mammoth Lakes, CA 93546
619-935-4324   *California*

Imagine yourself on a horse headed up the trail taking in the beauty of quaking aspen, a monk's hood flower by the waterfall, a few deer peeking at you through willows, a rugged peak dropping to a velvet green meadow—all can be yours to see and photograph in California's Eastern High Sierra. McGee Creek Pack Station breeds, raises and trains its own registered Morgan horses which are fun and comfortable to ride. McGee Canyon is colorful and uncrowded, with mountain streams and lakes containing abundant golden rainbow and eastern brook trout. Dunnage and burro pack trips are also available. Fourteen years' experience. Includes: Can include camping gear, food, horses, transportation, animals, depending on trip. Length of trip: Mid-June through Mid-October. Length of trip: Any desired. Group size: 25 maximum. Cost: All-expense pack trip: Approximately $90 per person per day. Special requirements: 20% deposit to confirm reservation.

McKenzie's Trails West
P.O. Box 971
Rocky Mountain House, Alberta TOM 1TO
Canada
403-845-6708   *Canada*

Travel above the timberline and cross cloud-rimmed passes on this unforgettable horseback excursion through the Canadian Rockies. The family-run "McKenzie's Trails West" offers pack trips through remote regions of the High Country. Base camp is located ninety miles west of Rocky Mountain House near Abraham Lake. From there, tours set out for the magnificent wilderness where eagles glide and the grizzly bear and bighorn sheep make their home. You'll stay in roomy, waterproof tents and enjoy good home cooking. At night, watch the sun set behind the mountains as you enjoy a friendly evening around the campfire. Thirty years' experience, licensed and bonded. Includes: Transportation from and to Calgary International Airport to point of departure, all meals, horses, tents, and equipment (except sleeping bags). Dates: July and August. Length of trip: 3, 6, and 12 days. Group size: 12 maximum. Cost: $325 and up. Special requirements: $100 deposit. Participants should be in reasonably good physical condition. No children under 10 years of age.

Mystic Saddle Ranch
P.O. Box 165
Mt. Home, ID 83647
208-587-5937   *Idaho*

Explore the Sawtooth wilderness of central Idaho—a spectacular region of glacial valleys, snow-fed streams and alpine meadows about an hour's drive from Sun Valley. Mystic Saddle Ranch runs five-day horsepack trips, with gentle horses that make even young children or novice riders feel comfortable. Experienced guides show you the way to seldom-visited mountain peaks, hidden meadows and glistening streams jumping with trout. On the trail, western meals are prepared family-style from flapjacks, bacon and eggs in the morning to fresh vegetables, fruit and meat for dinner. In addition, Mystic runs spot pack trips (where horses and guides take you to the lake of your choice, then return at a pre-arranged time and place to lead you back out of the wilderness). Hiking trips with pack stock also available. Fifteen years' experience, licensed and bonded. Five-Day Horsepack Trip Includes: First and last nights' lodging in motel, meals while on pack trip, camping equipment, wranglers, packer, cook, riding and pack horses. Dates: Mid-July through September. Length of trip: 5 days. Group size: 4–16. Cost: $475 per person.

RANGE TOURS

Range Tours
1540 South Holly Street
Denver, CO 80222
303-759-1988
800-525-8509   *Colorado*

Join Range Tours for a horseback trip in the West Elk wilderness area of Colorado's Gunnison National Park. West Elk offers two hundred thousand acres of untouched wilderness in which to ride, camp and observe deer, elk, beaver and bighorn sheep. It is a rugged, majestic mountain area, yet safe to travel and enjoy from horseback. "City dudes" who have never ridden a horse (or who have forgotten how!) are welcome to ride some of the gentlest, best-trained trail horses in Colorado. More experienced riders will find mounts to match their abilities. Provisions are packed in by mules, to allow riders to fully enjoy this western adventure. Includes: Round-trip transportation from Montrose, CO to base camp, all meals, group gear, horses, guides, taxes and service charges. Dates: June through September. Length of trip: 4, 6 and 7 nights. Group size: 8–10. Cost: $320–$525. Special requirements: Good physical condition.

Rutas A Caballo S.A.
Agustina de Aragon, 14, 1 C
Madrid 6, Spain
4027009 or 4029500   *Spain*

Rutas A Caballo offers horseback tours of Spain designed to show riders scenery that the average tourist might miss. Explore beautiful medieval villages and castles . . . picnic on a mountain slope . . . dine at a typical Segovian restaurant. Riders follow bridle paths, cattle tracks and the ancient trails of the Mesta—etched by flocks of merino sheep generations ago. Tours extend through the beautiful Castile and Andalusia regions and are led by a bilingual hostess. Riders stay in comfortable hotels and always have a Land Rover or Microbus at their disposal. Registered organization supported by the Spanish Ministry of Tourism. Includes: Accommodations, full board, wine with meals and picnics, hostess, fully-equipped horses, transfers to and from hotels and airport, transportation of luggage. Dates: Year-round. Length of trip: 9–14 days. Group size: 8–16. Cost: $510–$954. Special requirements: Some riding experience (though one need not be an expert), 20% deposit.

Saddle Treks
P.O. Box 114
Main Creek Road
Dungog, NSW 2420
Australia
(049) 921713   *Australia*

Ride horseback through Australia's remote and beautiful Barrington Tops National Park—a high, mountainous region just north of Hunter Valley. Saddle Treks is a family business run by Sandy and Rosie Logie. Sandy personally leads all the treks while Rosie plans the "tucker" (food). Tours begin at the Main Creek base camp, a 3½-hour drive from Sydney. From there, you'll set out for the park, enjoying sub-alpine scenery. Wild brumbies (horses), wallabies, and kangaroos abound, and travelers with a quiet approach and sharp eye will observe koalas, echidnas, and platypus. Because of the remoteness of the area, this trek is for those with some previous riding experience. Plenty of time is provided to explore the campsite areas or have a swim before enjoying a fine, freshly-cooked meal which includes wine with dinner. Includes: Camping equipment, tents, meals, horses, tack, leader. Dates: March through June; October through December. Length of trip: 6 days, 7 nights. Group size: 12. Cost: $495 per person. Special requirements: Some riding experience.

Surf Tours
1314 South King Street, Suite 1060
Honolulu, HI 96814
808-538-6768
Telex 734-1918 ZUBHI   *Hawaii*

Ride with friendly Paniolas (Hawaiian cowboys) across the uncrowded countryside of the islands brilliant with flowers. Take a trip to Maui's Haleakala Crater, where molten lava erupted hundreds of feet in the air leaving a sixty-square-mile bowl of cinders. Enjoy a scenic descent starting from two thousand feet, down to sea level on the famed Kalaupapa switchback trail. Here you will discover the old but unspoiled Hawaii and listen as knowledgeable paniolas share native legends and folklore with you. Whether you are an experienced equestrian or a novice, your ride will become a breathtaking experience and could be the highlight of your island visit. Horseback riding is available on Kauai, Oahu, Lanai and the Big Island (Hawaii); ranging from a few hours to several days in length. Established and licensed in 1977. Includes: Ground transportation, meals. Dates: Year-round. Length of trip: 2 hours to 2 days. Group size: 3–10. Cost: $35–$225 per person. Special requirements: 20% deposit to confirm reservation, full prepayment 48 hours prior to excursion.

Teton Expeditions, Inc.
P.O. Box 218
Rigby, ID 83442
208-745-6476   *Wyoming*

Ride about fifty miles of the Crest Trail of the magnificent Teton Range. Much of the trip actually lies within the boundaries of Teton National Park. Some of the country is above tree line, with snowbanks, mountain lakes and trails rising to elevations of nearly twelve thousand feet. Licensed and bonded; in business for over twenty years. Includes: Horses, guides, meals, two-person tents and other miscellaneous items. Transportation from Driggs, Idaho to trip's start and finish also included. You furnish personal clothing, a sleeping bag, flashlight and camera. Dates: Every Tuesday in August and September. Length of trip: 5 days, 4 nights. Group size: 10 maximum. Cost: $555 per person. Special requirements: $150 reservation, some riding skill desirable but not necessary.

Ultimate Escapes, Ltd.
2506 W. Colo. Avenue
Colorado Springs, CO 80904
303-578-8383   *Colorado*

Ultimate Escapes' five-day "Surf and Turf" excursion combines wild water rafting on the Arkansas River and horsepacking into the Sangre de Cristo range. Ride horseback through this alpine region, climbing switchbacks, crossing mountain meadows and camping by natural lakes. From there, it's two days' rafting down some of the best whitewater in Colorado. Horsepack-only trips are also offered for those who want to spend more time riding the range. Dependable, trailwise Appaloosas (home-breds all) take travelers across high passes and up craggy mountain ridges where riders can gaze at alpine flowers, blue skies and distant peaks. Tenth year of operation. Includes: Round-trip transportation to Colorado Springs, meals, tents, rafts, horses, all necessary equipment, guides, accommodations. Dates: June through October. Length of trip: 5 days, 4 nights. Group size: 4–12. Cost: "Surf and Turf" $449; "Ride Only" $195 for 3 days, $290 for 5 days. Special requirements: Good health and moderately good physical condition.

Von Thielmann Tours
P.O. Box 87764
San Diego, CA 92138
619-462-3419
619-291-7057   *Austria,*
Telex 910-335-1607 MESA-SERV SD6   *Bavaria*

You are cordially invited to take a fabulous journey in horsedrawn carriages through beautiful Bavaria and Austria. Admire the wonders of baroque and rococo architecture as you visit Bavaria's most colorful royal castles, fortresses, churches and cloisters. Away from the busy roads and motorways, you will travel with four or five other guests in a comfortable Landau or in a spacious four-in-hand stagecoach. The English coach, built around 1875, is still in the same condition as it was when it rolled along English country roads one hundred years ago. The route takes you through meadows, fens, woods, mountainous countryside, past numerous ponds and lakes, through prettily-decorated villages, deserted farms and hidden-away hamlets. You may halt to swim in one of the many smaller lakes or stop in a clearing of the woods for a bite to eat, or lunch in one of the quaint old inns along the way. The coach will be driven by an experienced groom, but if you like, you can learn to operate the horse carriage yourself. Twenty-five years of international special interest and sports tours. Includes: Air fare if desired, tour in comfortable horse carriage, hotels, meals, beverages, entertainment. Dates: From April through September. Length of trip: 3 days to 2 weeks. Group size: 8 to 30. Cost: Varies.

William J. O'Conner Riding Stables
Ballyard
Tralee, County Kerry
Ireland
(066) 21840   *Ireland*

Hark to the bleat of lambs . . . the ripple of a stream . . . the tread of your mount's hoofs on this horseback exploration of Ireland's magnificent Dingle Peninsula. Tours run by O'Conner Stables use beaches, bridle paths and mountain trails to explore areas otherwise inaccessible. Located in County Kerry (southwest Ireland), the Dingle Peninsula offers spectacular scenery including mountains, valleys, lakes, forests and beaches, all dotted with cottages and picturesque villages. You'll trek through rugged mountains, ride along quiet country roads lined with fuchsia hedges, and gallop on golden beaches surrounded by rolling dunes. Accommodations are in first class guest houses approved by the Irish Tourist Board. Sixteen years' experience. Includes: Accommodations, full board, horse, guide. Dates: May through October. Length of trip: 5 or 8 days. Group size: 10. Cost: £220–£395. Special requirements: Ability to canter figure eight with control and gallop in the open required. $100 deposit.

House •
Villa •
Condo Rental/
Exchanges •

They say home is where the heart is. And whatever your heart yearns for—be it an apartment in a Renaissance palazzo in Florence, a castle in Spain or a condo in Maui—chances are you can rent it for your next vacation.

Rentals offer you several advantages over hotel/motel stays. You have true privacy and convenience—move right in, unpack your bags, browse through the library or the record collection, and stroll into the kitchen for a lunchtime snack. No lobbies to traverse, no bell captains to tip . . . just your temporary home, sweet home.

Importantly, rentals enable you to immerse yourself in a neighborhood—not a tourist complex. When in Rome, you can do as the Romans do—sip your morning capuccino in that lively cafe right downstairs, pluck an orange from a tree in your own backyard, or cheer on the local soccer team at the weekly game.

Another factor to consider is cost. Rentals can cost less than stays in many hotels or motels. Besides, you'll have the benefit of a kitchen for your own use. By preparing your own breakfast and an occasional lunch, you'll be able to save up for a dinnertime splurge at the best restaurant in town.

Or if you like, take the advice of Gerald and Sara Murphy: living well is the best revenge. Some of the best-appointed residences come with antique furniture, in-ground swimming pools, club memberships . . . even the family butler, chauffeur and other retainers.

ABOUT HOME EXCHANGES

You can also vacation rent-free by swapping your own home for someone else's. Home exchange is exactly what the name implies: you trade a stay in your apartment or house for somebody's London flat, Loire chateau or Caribbean bungalow. With home exchange, frequently your only vacation expense will be transportation to and from your holiday home. You'll have no hotel bills, no caretaker expenses for home or garden, no boarding fees for pets, no car rental fees if automobiles are also exchanged. Many people also swap country club privileges, boats and household help—all while enjoying the comforts of a real home.

Another important element is the refreshment of breaking routine. As one satisfied home exchanger described it: "There's a tingly feeling of adventure, walking into another family's world. It's wonderful to discover new people, as evidenced in their home."

Whether you're renting or exchanging, here are some tips for planning your holiday.

1. First, decide on what kind of place you're seeking. Do you want to be in the center of town or a secluded retreat? Is the home located near what you want to do on your vacation—whether it's sightseeing or sunning?
2. Getting around: Is there convenient public transportation? Will you have

to rent a car? How do you get there from the airport—can the rental service arrange transfers?

3. If you plan to spend most of your time at the home, its layout, furnishings and amenities become important. But if you're using it as a base for excursions, central location should have priority.

4. How many does it sleep? In what kind of rooms—real, private bedrooms or a walk-through living room with convertible couch? Will the people you're traveling with be happy with those arrangements?

5. What recreational opportunities are nearby? Does your rental/exchange cover use of tennis, swimming, golf and other facilities? If not, how much will you have to pay?

6. What amenities are included? Are linens provided? How about appliances—is there a dishwasher . . . washer/dryer? If you're a gourmet cook, ask what equipment and gadgets come with the kitchen.

7. About food: Check what comes with the house. Is there a working supply of coffee, sugar, spices—or do you have to start from scratch? (In some rental places, it is customary to replace whatever you use up—find out if that applies.) If you plan on eating in a lot, is shopping nearby? Ask whether the rental service will provision the residence for you.

8. Be honest with the rental service about your likes and dislikes. Are you a fanatic for cleanliness? Do you tremble at having responsibility for two-hundred-year-old antiques for the week?

9. Has the referral agency or broker personally inspected the properties they list? If so, they can give you a better description and feeling for the residence, neighborhood and conveniences.

10. Even rentals and exchanges have check-in and check-out times. Coordinate these with your flight times. If you foresee any difficulties, discuss them with the service—way in advance.

11. Find out whether children or pets are permitted.

12. Doublecheck what rental fees include. Although most will cover utilities, such as gas and electric, some may charge extra for these. Long-distance telephone charges are almost always billed separately.

13. For rentals, reservation deposits are generally required, with full payment due one to two months prior to arrival. Find out what the cancellation penalty is if you need to call off your vacation.

14. Security deposits may also be required, and the agency may ask you for personal references. (After all, you're being entrusted with several hundred thousand dollars worth of property.)

Vacation Exchange Club, Inc.
12006 111th Avenue, Unit 12
Youngtown, AZ 85363
602-972-2186   *Worldwide*

How about a holiday in rent-free splendor? You can cut your vacation costs without cutting your fun with home exchange. Vacation Exchange Club publishes a directory in February and April that lists names, addresses and description of homes offered for exchange by club members. You'll make new friends and feel like a native when you choose to vacation this way. A feeling of adventure starts the moment you decide to swap your residence for someone else's . . . whether it is a ski chalet in New Hampshire . . . a brownstone in New York . . . or a penthouse in Rome. Directory published since 1960. Includes: Each directory lists approximately 6,000 homes in 40 countries available for holiday exchange. Dates: Year-round. Cost: $22.70. Your home is listed in either the February or the April Exchange **Book**, and you receive both editions. $15.00: You receive both books, but your home is not listed in either of them.

Villas International
213 East 38th Street
New York, NY 10016
212-685-4340
800-221-2260
Telex 422469   *Caribbean, Europe, Mexico*

Villas International offers over twenty thousand fully-equipped, inspected vacation properties throughout Europe—including apartments in London, Paris, Madrid, Rome, Florence; English and Scottish country cottages; Riviera villas, Loire chateaux, cottages in Provence/Dordogne in France; Tuscany, Venice, Sicily in Italy; the Greek islands of Corfu, Crete, Mykonos; Spain's Costa del Sol, Costa Brava and Mallorca; chalets in the Swiss and Austrian Alps; plus Germany and Yugoslavia. Properties rent weekly or monthly and range from a modest $200 per week to $20,000 per month for something very special! Six years in business. Includes: Varies according to property—can include maid, cook, etc. at some locations. Dates: Year-round. Length of trip: 1 week and up. Group size: Any. Cost: $200–$5,000 per week. Special requirements: Prepayment 8 weeks before rental.

Language Study •

Are the days when you spoke a second language not as close as they once were? Maybe an occasional phrase pops into your thoughts, leaving you yearning for the days when you could piece together the fragments into cogent thought. Maybe your second tongue is passable, but could use some sharpening up. Or perhaps you've always wanted to learn a new language, but never got around to it.

Chances are what's put you off language studies is the unappetizing thought of having to parse regular and irregular verbs in all tenses and moods, year after year after year. You want to learn the language, not be drilled in rules.

Special language programs offer an alternative to these stiff academics.

In a few accelerated weeks, you'll immerse yourself in the full richness of the language. You'll learn the rules, but more important, you'll learn how to apply them. In these programs, your new tongue becomes part of your life—not an artificial routine.

Language study programs are as diverse as they are innovative. You can:

- Study the language and culture of Spain at the University of Madrid, combining classroom lectures with outings to bull fights, the theater, and Spain's historical sights . . .
- Brush up your Japanese in six weeks in Tokyo, studying in small groups and exploring the cultural highlights of the city . . .
- Learn German and explore the German countryside—the Rhine Valley, the Black Forest—during a four-week program at the University of Heidelberg . . .
- *Parlez vous* like a native, and enjoy Parisian society at an accelerated program at the University of Paris-Sorbonne . . .

Picking your language—and your holiday destination—is the easy part. Next you have to choose the program that gives you the most of what you want out of a language studies program. Here are some points to keep in mind:

1. Levels. If you're a fresh beginner, you don't want to be thrown into a classroom with a group of students who could pass for natives. Similarly, an advanced student could yawn the weeks away if stuck with beginners. Most programs offer several levels of instruction. Evaluate your skills honestly—or take an aptitude test—before you enroll.
2. Thrust. If you want to learn to read German, find a program that concentrates on reading skills. If you want to engage in a *tête-à-tête* with the Parisians look for a conversation-oriented course. Teaching methods also vary, from lectures and reading sessions to language labs and supervised conversation. Many programs give you a feel for the culture behind the language through a variety of field trips. These trips also remind you that you're on vacation.
3. Shelter and sustenance. Even though you're there to learn, you're still on vacation. So accommodations and meals are important. Some programs house you in dorms, others in private homes or hotels. Similarly, some include meals, others leave you to apply your newly-acquired skills reading from the local menus.
4. The fine print. A lot of small considerations weigh heavily in the quality of your trip. Like the qualifications of your professors. Many programs are taught by skilled college professors with the experience and enthusiasm to bring language studies to life. If you wish, you might be able to receive college credit for your course. Finally, check whether the program is tax-deductible as an educational expense.

Centro De Idiomas, S.A.
Leandro Valle 22 Pts. No. 6
Mazatlan, Sinaloa, Mexico
2-20-53

Mexico

Want to brush up on your Spanish while cooling off on a white sandy beach within sight of the Sierra Madre Mountain range? You can at the Centro De Idiomas, a language center located in Mazatlan, a fast-growing resort area noted for surf fishing, scuba diving, parasailing and the delicate sea shells that are scattered along the beaches. United States professionals find it a perfect setting for learning Spanish. Small classes are taught at all levels, and with a variety of teaching methods to help the student learn that much faster, including records, newspaper articles and a "chatting tour" where students meet the local people and chat in Spanish. With emphasis on oral skills, you'll be talking and thinking in Spanish before you can say *hasta lavista*. Includes: 2-week session, 4 hours daily conversational Spanish in groups of 5, qualified teachers, shared room homestay with Mexican family, special weekly activities. Dates: Year-round, every two weeks. Length of trip: 2-week minimum stay. Group size: Maximum 5. Cost: $380. Special requirements: Age 16 and over.

European Studies Association
121 Topaz Way
San Francisco, CA 94131
415-641-5502

Spain

Learn or improve your Spanish at the Instituto de Cooperacion Iberamericana, located on the campus of the University of Madrid. Madrid has museums, libraries and cultural activities available, and provides an ideal base for travel in Spain. Classes are offered at all levels from elementary to advanced. The four-week program broadens your knowledge of Spanish culture through activities such as lectures, museum tours, theater, bull fights, concerts and excursions to areas of importance in Spanish history, such as Toledo, Avila, Aranjuez and Segovia. Intermediate and advanced students may attend lectures on Spanish civilization, including history, politics, economics, literature, and dance. College credits available. Program director is a professor from San Francisco State and a native of Madrid. Includes: Language study, lodging, all meals, transit allowance, culture and civilization lectures and visits plus excursions to Toledo, El Escorial, Avila, Aranjuez, Segovia, etc. Dates: July. Length of trip: 4 weeks. Group size: 20. Cost: $1,475.

European Studies Association
121 Topaz Way
San Francisco, CA 94131
415-641-5502

Germany

Study German for four weeks at one of Germany's oldest and most famous universities, the University of Heidelberg in the center of the city. You can learn or improve your knowledge of German language and civilization through classes at all levels from beginning to advanced. During the program, you'll attend lectures on Heidelberg's history, tour historic landmarks and museums, and enjoy a river cruise, dances, films and concerts. Weekend activities include trips to the Rhine Valley, Rothenburg, Black Forest and Nuremburg. College credits available. Program director is professor of German at San Francisco State University. Includes: Language classes at University, lodgings, all meals, German culture and civilization activities with visits to Rothenburg, the Rhine Valley, Nuremburg, the Black Forest, etc. Dates: Mid-July to Mid-August. Length of trip: 4 weeks. Group size: 20. Cost: $1,515.

European Studies Association
121 Topaz Way
San Francisco, CA 94131
415-641-5502   *France*

French classes at the University of Paris-Sorbonne are offered for students of all levels, from beginning to advanced, with four- and six-week programs available. In addition to language study, you'll attend lectures, demonstrations and excursions to improve your knowledge of French culture: museum, industry and architectural tours; theater and ballet performances; lectures on French politics, cinema and art. Weekend excursions to sites such as Versailles, Chartres, Giverny and the Loire Valley are also included as part of the program. College credits available. Experienced foreign study operator; program in conjunction with San Francisco State University and Los Angeles Community College District. Includes: Language classes at the Sorbonne, lodging, breakfast, some meals, extensive culture and civilization activities with visits to Mont St. Michel, Chartres, Versailles, Loire Valley, etc. Dates: July or July to Mid-August. Length of trip: 4 or 6 weeks. Group size: 50. Cost: $1,385.

European Studies Association
121 Topaz Way
San Francisco, CA 94131
415-641-5502   *Italy*

Four- and six-week travel/study programs offer you a variety of courses in Italian, from beginning to advanced, at the University for Foreign Students in Perugia, Italy. Situated midway between Florence and Rome, Perugia is an ideal location for summer studies, as well as a cosmopolitan center for students to gain knowledge of Italian culture and history. You'll stay with selected Italian families to gain insight into the Italian way of life and learn Italian more rapidly. As part of your studies, you'll attend lectures, theater and tours of local industries, churches, and vineyards. Scheduled weekend trips include visits to Florence, Assisi, Siena and Rome. Program director is Professor of Italian at San Francisco State University. Includes: Language classes at University, lodging with families, all meals (with families), culture and civilization lectures and excursions to Florence, Siena, Rome, Assisi, Spoleto, etc. Dates: July or July and August. Length of trip: 4 to 6 weeks. Group size: 20. Cost: $1,140.

European Studies Association
121 Topaz Way
San Francisco, CA 94131
415-641-5502   *Japan*

Improve your Japanese with intensive, small classes at the International Christian University in Tokyo. Classes are offered at all levels from beginning to advanced with a maximum of ten students per section and four hours of class per day, Monday through Friday. In addition, lectures, demonstrations and excursions will help give you added insight into Japanese culture and life: tea ceremonies, theater performances, lectures on Japanese politics, film, and folk crafts. On weekend excursions, you'll visit Kyoto, Nikko, Hakone, Shinjuku, Kamakura and many other areas of Japan. American university credit available. Program director is professor of Japanese in San Francisco with native knowledge of Japan. Includes: Language classes in small groups at University, lodging, all meals, transit allowance, culture and civilization activities with trips to Kyoto, Nikko, Hakone, Kamakura, Shinjuku, etc. Dates: July and first half of August. Length of trip: 6 weeks. Group size: 15. Cost: $2,010.

La Sonrisa Institute
2629 Sixth Street
Santa Monica, CA 90405
213-396-9541   *Mexico*

A new adventure in intercultural living, La Sonrisa Institute offers you an opportunity to study Spanish and experience Mexico from the inside. Year-round programs feature intensive and conversational Spanish instruction, workshops, tours, fiestas and social/intercultural events. Language classes are taught by native teachers, fully accredited, with no more than five students to a class. Workshop/course topics cover the full spectrum of Mexican life and culture from "Prehispanic Civilizations" to "The Changing Mexican Family." University and professional credits are available. In Cuernavaca and Guadalajara, you'll live with carefully-screened Mexican families, allowing full cultural and linguistic immersion. In Acapulco, you will stay at the lovely Ritz or Auto Ritz Hotels and study Spanish with specially-trained teachers, with plenty of free time to enjoy the beaches, or fish, scuba and snorkel in the Pacific Ocean. Four years in operation; specially-trained native language teachers. Program coordinators are licensed educators and specialists in travel and intercultural dynamics. Includes: Lodging (double occupancy) and 3 meals a day, Spanish classes, workshops/courses, ground transfers; University credits optional. Single rates available on request. Dates: Year-round. Length of trip: 1–2 weeks; may add more weeks. Group size: 1–30. Cost: $325–$875. Special requirements: $150 deposit.

Llama/Mule/Camel
Expeditions •

Looking for a new twist on a hiking trip? Want to find out why T. E. Lawrence called camels "rich mounts of the Arabian princes?" How about venturing into the world of Heidi ... as you ride sure-footed mules through the Alps?

In this section, we've gathered together an assortment of hiking expeditions, all enhanced by four-footed companionship. Hiking with packstock—whether it's llama, mule, burro or camel—proves that six feet are better than two. On your hike, you carry only a daypack, while the quadruped in question totes your personal belongings, camping gear and provisions. And with camels and mules, they'll carry you along too.

On a practical level, using packstock offers definite benefits to hikers. Because the animal carries all supplies, you can enjoy more amenities—tents instead of just sleeping bags, fresh foods instead of freeze-dried. And since you won't be lugging a 30–40 pound load on your back, you can take on more rugged terrain at higher altitude without tiring. The carefree, "carry-free" nature of packstock hikes makes them great for families with small children.

Sharing your adventure with a llama, mule, burro or camel has another advantage—they're fun to be with. Animal companionship adds something to a wilderness journey, helping link you with the vastness and spontaneity of nature. En route, you'll have plenty of time to savor your surroundings, since packstock travels slowly because of their loads.

Each animal adds a different point of view to your trek: llamas ... gentle, intelligent and inquisitive; no, downright nosy ... camels, "ships of the desert," who are a lot jollier than their press notices would indicate ... and patient, hard-working mules, more sure-footed in the mountains than any horse.

With whichever four-footed friend you hit the trail, here are some points to consider:

1. Will the animals carry all the gear, or will you have to tote some yourself? Is there any weight limit to what you can bring? Llamas, for example, can handle loads of seventy to eighty pounds. (If overloaded, they sit down and refuse to budge.)
2. How strenuous a trip is it? How many miles a day will you cover—over what types of terrain? Is altitude or climate a factor? Will you have free time to explore, fish, read?
3. Will you be camping out or staying at hotels/motels/inns? If camping, do you trek to a new site each day or stay at a base camp and make day hikes? (Base camps give you the option of staying put in camp to relax if you don't feel like hiking.)
4. Are transfers included to and from the trailhead?
5. Is it your responsibility to care for, load up and feed the animal yourself, or does the guide do it?
6. The tour operator will provide you with a complete list of what to bring. Most outfitters supply all camping gear except sleeping bags. If you don't have your own, check whether these can be rented.

Colorado Adventure Network
194 South Franklin Street
Denver, CO 80209
303-722-6482 *Colorado*

See the spectacular Rockies, fish in rarely-visited streams, photograph elk, deer, bear and bighorn sheep ... all on this llama expedition into the back-country of Colorado. You'll spend your days exploring and hiking and your nights eating delicious, soul-satisfying meals cooked over an open fire. Pack horse trips also available. Tour operator registered with the Colorado Guide and Outfitter Association; fifteen years' experience. Includes: Experienced guides, pack animals, all cooking and eating utensils, tents, sleeping bags and pads/cots. Dates: June through September. Length: 7 days. Group size: 6 to 10 people. Cost: $60 to $125 per day. Special requirements: Reasonably good health. Deposit 50% prior to the trip, balance due 30 days before departure date.

Directions Unlimited
344 Main Street
Mt. Kisco, NY 10549
914-241-1700 (Collect) *Switzerland*

Travel the breathtakingly beautiful Valais Alps on Swiss Alpine mules, an almost forgotten way to see the magnificent sights of these mountains. The slow, easy pace of the mules allows time to enjoy the beauty and tranquility of nature surrounding you. Direction Unlimited has been in operation for fourteen years. Includes: Transportation of luggage, hotel, all meals, tips, taxes, transfers, escort. Dates: April through October. Length: 1 week. Group size: 20. Cost: $395–$495. Special requirements: Excellent physical condition.

Lost Coast Llama Caravans
77321 Usal Road
Whitehorn, CA 95489 *California*

Have you ever hugged a llama? You can when you take a llama pack trip along the "Lost Coast" of California—an eighty-mile stretch of rugged coastline where you can still find traces of native Indian culture dating back four thousand years. This is a land of contrasts: majestic fir forests and moist fern glens, grassy meadows, clear mountain streams and the Pacific's pounding surf. Here's a chance to share tasks at the campsite, to learn low-impact camping skills and to eat fresh-cooked fireside meals while you experience outdoor living with your knowledgeable guides and the gentle llamas. California guide license, insured and bonded, with four years' experience; EMT trained. Includes: Meals, pack llama to carry gear. Dates: July through September. Length of trip: 4–7 days. Group size: 8–10 people. Cost: $50 per person per day. Children 12 and under receive a 15% discount.

Mountain Travel, Inc.
1398 Solano Avenue
Albany, CA 94706
415-527-8100
Telex 335-429

Algeria

The Sahara, the largest desert in the world, offers an infinite variety of rock-ribbed plateaus; sandstone canyons, volcanic mountains; beach-like gold washes filled with oleander, tamarisk and thorn trees; and date palms, acacia trees and many wildflowers. On this expedition, you'll travel a mountainous region of the Sahara—the Hoggar Mountains—by camel and by foot, experiencing the way of life of the nomadic Touareg guides—the blue-robed "nobles of the desert." There are rock carvings, paintings, awesome volcanic spires and shifting sands to enthrall the eye, as you camp under the stars surrounded by neolithic engravings of cattle and hunters, basalt gorges or erosion-carved river beds. Tour operator has sixteen years' experience. Includes: Camping equipment and meals, pack animals, guides, accommodations, ground transportation, sightseeing. Dates: January and October. Length of trip: 18 days. Group size: 6–15 people. Cost: $2,100. Special requirements: Previous hiking experience helpful. No previous camel-riding experience is necessary.

Gentle, intelligent and very inquisitive, llamas are easy on the terrain because of their soft-padded feet. (SIERRA LLAMAS)

Sierra Llamas
P.O. Box 509
Loomis, CA 95650
916-652-0702   *California*

Lead a llama through California's breathtaking Tahoe Sierra Mountains or along the beautiful Point Reyes National Seashore. Enjoy trekking through these wonderlands while well-trained, woolly llamas with names like Spanky, Alfalfa and Buckwheat carry packs, equipment and fresh food. You'll start the day with fluffy buttermilk pancakes, and finish the evening with a glass of wine, hearty main course, salad and dessert. Sierra's trips are a leisurely-paced five or six miles a day with frequent stops for looks at the flora and fauna of the region, photography, fishing, and just enjoying the spectacular scenery. Arrangements for pre- and post-trip river rafting or accommodations in quaint bed and breakfast inns can be made through Sierra. Licensed and bonded. Includes: Experienced naturalist guide, llamas, all meals and all equipment except personal gear and sleeping bags. Dates: May through October. Length of trip: 3 days. Group size: 8. Cost: $180 per adult, $135 per child under 13. Special requirements: Good health, one day deposit, balance due 3 weeks before departure.

Sun Valley Trekking Company
P.O. Box 2200
Sun Valley, ID 83353
208-726-9595   *Alaska, Idaho*

The best way to experience the beauty of Sun Valley, especially at dusk as the sun sets over the mountains leaving a reddish-orange glow in the sky . . . or feel the awesome might of Yellowstone National Park as the dawn brings into view all the magnificence of one of our greatest parks . . . the best way to really travel this land is by foot. On your trek, you'll have the services of expert guides—plus llamas to carry your gear. Sun Valley Trekking also offers a glacier backpack/raft trip through the wilds of Alaska. All personnel licensed by the Idaho Outfitters and Guides Board. Includes: Varies according to trip planned, everything from guide services and instruction only; to the deluxe trip with food, all equipment, llamas and a French chef. Dates: June through October. Length of trip: 1–15 days. Group size: 5–14 people. Cost: $40–$2,000. Special requirements: $150 non-refundable deposit, balance 30 days in advance of trip.

The African Experience
7 Cherry Street
Lexington, MA 02173
617-862-2165
Telex 823-348   *Ethiopia*

Ethiopia is not on the typical tour routes but offers enormous geographical variety. The mule trekking adventure combines a bit of the history and cultural flavor of the country with the magnificent Simien Mountains. To get the most from the area, you traverse the Simien Mountains with overnight stops at mule stations or camping areas from Sankabar to Geech and Chenek. You have a vivid picture of the countryside and even the possibility of some game-viewing along the way. Nine years in business. Includes: All hotels/camps, all meals except while in Addis, all sightseeings and equipment, services of local guides. Dates: Year-round from Addis Ababa. Length of trip: 14 days. Group size: Minimum 4 persons. Cost: $1,200. Special requirements: Need to bring your own sleeping bag.

Mountaineering •
Rock/Ice Climbing •

Huge, awe-inspiring, rude projections of earth and rock, mountains pose a call to adventure . . . a challenge with a seemingly invincible adversary. The mountains dare you to throw aside your comforts and advantages, and test your true mettle on an unbiased proving ground.

There's nothing practical about climbing a mountain. In fact, after most climbs, you're right back where you started from. On level ground, admiring the towering peak. Nor is mountain climbing particularly "fun," in a strict sense. It's not like dancing or going for a dip in the ocean.

Why, then, does one climb a mountain? Mallory's wistful response reveals the spirit behind mountaineering: "Because it is there." Its very presence—irrefutable and antithetical to anything human civilization has tried to achieve—demands attention.

Mountaineering, at advanced levels, can involve sophisticated equipment. But it isn't about equipment. It's about a simple confrontation: the climber vs. the mountain. On any level, the basic challenge exists. And on any level, the rewards are reaped through personal fortitude.

The rewards? At the tree line, the dense trees and foliage through which you have hiked give way to an open rock face. Digging fingers and toes into tenuous holds, you lift yourself onto a level shelf. You breathe deeply the clean mountain air. The sun is brilliant, the sky an almost surreal blue. The water from your canteen, fresh from a mountain stream, cools your throat and sprinkles refreshingly across your face. You look out. As far as the eye can see, soft green mountains ripple playfully under the sun. You are, literally and figuratively, standing on top of the world.

This thrill is essentially the same at one thousand feet as it is at ten thousand feet. Beginners can attain it; experts continue to discover it anew. If the thrill is the same, why climb the higher peaks? Again, we'll defer to Mallory.

Climbs come in all sizes and degrees of difficulty. You may need no equipment beyond a lithe step and a persevering spirit. Nor is experience always necessary. Many programs offer instruction that allows people to attempt more adventurous climbs than they could otherwise.

Rock climbing requires ropes and special techniques (such as belaying and rappelling) to surmount near-vertical rock faces. Ice climbing similarly involves sophisticated methods used to mount the great snow-capped peaks or other steep ice formations. In addition to teaching climbing skills, many programs offer instruction in first aid, camping, and map reading.

Pick a level that best suits your experience, health, and goals. If you want to hike up mountains and gaze out over broad vistas, you'll get great satisfaction from basic programs that put you onto the mountains in a hurry. If you're after something more adventurous—like rappelling down sheer rock faces, or chimneying between vertical ice columns—take a rock- or ice-climbing course taught by certified professionals. Look for a course with the best ratio of teachers to students. For the unregenerate expert climber, the summit of Everest, or other towering peaks, beckons.

Whatever level you choose, you'll probably need at least some gear. Good boots that give you sure traction and strong ankle support are a must. Cotton and wool clothing keeps you most comfortable under both hot and cold conditions. Thick layers—so you can add or subtract as the temperature changes. The tour operator will tell you the details about what you have to bring. It's best to bring only what's necessary. Choose your essentials carefully—good equipment that's suited to the terrain makes your job a whole lot easier.

The tour operator will also suggest age and health guidelines, based on the strenuousness of the climb and how much weight you will have to carry. They might recommend a little pre-climbing exercise, so you'll be able to go farther with less difficulty on the slopes.

With proper instruction, you can go as far as you like. And there's nothing like the thrill of making it to the top.

Colorado Mountain School
P.O. Box 2106 T
Estes Park, CO 80517
303-586-5758 *Colorado*

There is an old Japanese saying, "The body roams the mountains and the spirit is set free." Colorado Mountain School gives people the opportunity to experience this feeling, whether they be hikers and backpackers, beginning rock climbers, or serious alpinists. Featured courses include basic rock climbing; aid climbing (using stirrups, leading and seconding, hanging belays and rappelling); Big Wall climbing (with pendulums, tension traverses, hauling, and hanging bivouacs); and Alpine snow climbing (ice axe, self-arrest, belaying and anchoring, front pointing and glissading). Colorado Mountain School is the only guide school approved to operate within Rocky Mountain National Park. Director Mike Donahue has over thirty years' mountaineering experience. Includes: Group and technical gear, meals on extended trips. Rentals available for personal gear. Dates: All year. Length of trip: 1 day to 1 month. Group size: Varies with activity. Cost: $35 and up. Special requirements: 25% deposit.

Himalayan Travel, Inc.
P.O. Box 481
Greenwich, CT 06836
800-243-5330
Telex 4750032 *Nepal*

An in-depth exploration of Nepal's high Solu Khumbu region adjacent to Mt. Everest, this twenty-three-day trek and mountaineering seminar climaxes with a climb up a 20,235-foot Himalayan peak. Beginning with a flight to the Lukla Airstrip (9,200 feet), you proceed up the Dudh Kosi Valley to the central Sherpa village of Namche Bazaar (11,300 feet) and the spectacularly situated Buddhist monastery at Thangboche (12,600 feet). You'll spend several days here acclimatizing and exploring. The next leg of the trip takes you slowly higher to the yak herders' settlement of Lobuche (16,175 feet). From here a day trip is planned to Kala Patar (18,500 feet) with panoramic views of Mt. Everest. Retracing your steps for a day, you then proceed up the Imja Valley to the east of Everest. At the valley head, surrounded by the highest mountains on earth, is the final destination—20,235-foot Island Peak. After basecamp is established, you can attend seminars on basic mountaineering technique. Fit and well-acclimatized members may then attempt the summit, a moderately technical but physically demanding climb. Successful summiters are rewarded by views that are nothing short of incredible! Six years' experience outfitting trekking, mountaineering and adventure travel trips on the Indian sub-continent. Includes: Experienced American trip leader, complete staff of Sherpa guides, cooks and porters, all community camping equipment, all meals on trek, transfers, hotel accommodation in Kathmandu. Dates: March to April. Length of trip: 32 days. Group size: Maximum 15. Cost: $1,425. Special requirements: Camping and hiking experience required.

Interlocken
RD 2, Box 165-B
Hillsboro, NH 03244
603-478-3202 *Alaska*

Explore Alaska's wilderness, from her Pacific islands to her majestic snow-capped mountain peaks. Interlocken concentrates on a study of Alaska's abundant wildlife and the role it plays in the ecosystem. This expedition begins with a five-day sea-kayak journey to explore islands off the Kenia Peninsula. Traveling beneath the midnight sun, you'll glide past harbor seals and whales, observe puffins and bald eagles, and feast on native salmon, trout, clams and mussels. The expedition returns to land for the next stage of the adventure, two weeks of mountaineering in Alaska's interior. Switching to heavy packs, the expedition continues with a trek across the tundra observing and photographing caribou, moose and mountain sheep along the way. Ascending the summer snows of the Alaska Range, hikers will learn snow- and ice-climbing techniques, ice-axe use, belays and anchors, traveling in rope teams, and crevasse rescue. The final adventure is a climb of the nine-thousand-foot, seldom-climbed Ice Fall Peak. Interlocken has been offering travel programs since 1967 and wilderness programs since 1970. Includes: All transportation in Alaska, meals, lodging, climbing and group equipment. Dates: Summer. Length of trip: 4 weeks. Group size: 10. Cost: $1,375. Special requirements: Minimum age 16.

International Alpine School
P.O. Box 333
Eldorado Springs, CO 80025
303-494-4904 *Colorado*

The goal of the International Alpine School is to teach classical and modern techniques by integrating instruction with actual climbing experience. Courses are individually oriented and emphasize mental and physical conditioning, as well as ecological awareness. Instruction and guide services are offered for the novice, intermediate and advanced climber. Rock climbing is offered year-round. Each climber is encouraged to advance as far as time and ability permit. Safe, modern techniques are stressed with added emphasis on achieving a high level of free-climbing ability through on-the-rock practice. Ice climbing has been revolutionized in the last ten years and International Alpine School prides itself on teaching the latest techniques. Climbers can look forward to climbing incredibly steep, beautifully intricate floes of winter ice, experiencing the elation of chimneying between translucent pillars of green ice. The only sound heard is the tinkling of ice as points gain purchase. Each day ends with a relaxing soak in a natural outdoor hot spring. Instructors are certified through International Alpine School. Includes: All technical gear, lunch on course, 4 nights' lodging with ice climbing. Dates: All year for rock climbing; winter only for ice. Length of trip: 5 days. Group size: No more than 3 climbers to each guide. Cost: $325 for rock climbing, $365 for ice. Special requirements: $100 deposit, basic rock experience is necessary for ice climbing.

International Alpine School
P.O. Box 333
Eldorado Springs, CO 80025
303-494-4904 *Nepal*

Realize a dream—experience the grandeur of Mt. Everest and the Himalayas first-hand. The trip begins with three days of acclimatization and sightseeing in exotic Kathmandu, then off to Lamosangu for a ten-day trek through spectacular scenery. The approach to Everest is through tropical rice valleys, banana groves and terraced hillsides. The trek follows the Dudh Kosi River past rhododendron and pine forests to the Sherpa "capital" of Namche Bazaar (11,400 feet). The trail winds its way past Ama Dablam (22,494 feet), Thanserku (22,208 feet), and Kantega (22,340 feet). The climbing begins up the Khumba Glacier to Everest base camp and ascends Kala Patar (18,400 feet) for unparalleled views of three of the four highest peaks on Earth: Everest, Lhotse, and Makalu. Qualified climbers may arrange to ascend Island Peak (20,238 feet). The trek is retraced to Lukla for the flight over the Himalayas back to Kathmandu. The tour is led by Carl Harrison, co-director of International Alpine School and is accompanied by Sherpa cooks and porters. Includes: Hotel in Kathmandu, tents on peaks, all transportation in Nepal, all meals except in Kathmandu, guide and porter fees.

Dates: December through March. Length of trip: 28 days. Group size: 8. Cost: $2,100. Special requirements: $200 deposit, balance due 30 days before departure.

International Alpine School
P.O. Box 333
Eldorado Springs, CO 80025
303-494-4904   *British Isles*

Experience classic climbs and magnificent hiking in the birthplace of rock climbing, the British Isles. Journey along the rugged Welsh coastline and scale the spectacular seacliffs of Gogarth. Climb the Dream of White Horses with the ocean pounding below; ascend Mt. Snowden, highest point in Wales; hike across moorlands to the gritstone outcrops of Derbyshire; scale the crags of Scafell Pike in the Lake District of England; and experience Scotland's Glencoe and the notorious Ben Nevis. The trip provides a unique blend of rocks and culture, from sea cliffs to pubs. Carl Harrison, a well-known rock climber and mountaineer, raised on Derbyshire gritstone and Welsh granite, will lead all tours. Carl is co-director of International Alpine School and has been climbing for twenty-one of his twenty-nine years. Includes: All accommodations, bed and breakfast at climbers' huts and historic inns, all transportation in Britain, technical gear, and guide fees. Dates: June through September. Length: 15 days. Group size: 6 with 2 guides. Cost: $1,590. Special requirements: $200 deposit, balance due 30 days before departure.

International Alpine School
P.O. Box 333
Eldorado Springs, CO 80025
303-494-4904   *Alaska*

With International Alpine School, you can discover the little-known "Little Switzerland" of the awesome Alaska Range. The area offers dozens of unclimbed peaks and hundreds of potential routes of all difficulties on rock, ice and mixed ground. Situated between the Kahiltina and Kanikula Glaciers, this is true exploratory mountaineering in a wilderness setting. The trip starts in Talkeetna, Alaska, three hours north of Anchorage on the scenic Alaska Railroad, then flies via ski plane back into the Ice Age. Day climbs, overnight, and multi-day forays will be made from base camp in the Pika Glacier. There will also be an opportunity to trek back out to civilization at the end of the expedition. The trip is designed around the tastes and abilities of the climbers. Guides are certified through International Alpine School. Includes: Tents, group gear, meals on course, all technical gear, air support and guide fees. Dates: July. Length: 21 days. Group size: No more than 3 climbers to each guide. Cost: $1,900. Special requirements: $200 deposit, balance due 30 days before departure.

International School of Mountaineering
Club Vagabond
CH1854 Leysin, Switzerland
025-341321   *Switzerland*

International School of Mountaineering is situated near the principal climbing areas of Chamonix, Zermatt and the Oberland. The School's curriculum covers all aspects of mountaineering from basic theory to the most advanced developments in rock and ice climbing. Their three programs—Alpine Introductory, Intermediate, and Rock—are flexible to adjust to weather, mountain conditions and climbers' potential. The staff/student ratio is usually 1:2 to assure a first-rate, action-packed climbing holiday. Courses blend Alpine rock, snow and ice techniques, plus a varied climbing program starting with rock climbing in Leysin and then moving to the Mount Blanc Range or the Swiss Valaisan Alps. A crevasse rescue session is also scheduled during the week-long course. All instructors are fully qualified British and Swiss mountain guides, skilled in navigation, first-aid, mountain rescue. Includes: Bed, breakfast and dinner, technical gear, 6 days of instruction plus transportation during those 6 days. Dates: June through September. Length of trip: 6 days. Group size: 2 students per instructor. Cost: $375.

Mountain Travel
1298 Solano Avenue
Albany, CA 94706
415-527-8100   *Alaska*

Mountain Travel offers a climbing seminar in the heart of Alaska's Denali (McKinley) National Park. The setting is breathtaking, surrounded by the snow-covered peaks of the Alaska Range, including McKinley (20,320 feet), Foraker (17,402 feet) and Hunter (14,573 feet). The expedition begins with a spectacular charter flight to Kahiltna Glacier at the base of Mt. McKinley, where camp will be set up. From here, the adventure continues by ski or snowshoe to Peak 8,760 for instruction and practice in rope handling, belaying, glissading, snowclimbing techniques and use of the ice axe. The next step is an alpine climb of Peak 10,200 with additional training and honing of newly-acquired skills. The final climb of the Kahiltna Dome (12,225 feet) puts climbers to the test. A Mt. McKinley expedition, following the West Buttress route, will be arranged for experienced climbers only. Mountain Travel offers tours in more than fifty countries on all five continents and is now in its sixteenth year of operation. Includes: Tents, climbing gear and camp meals. Dates: June. Length of trip: 14 days. Group size: 5–12. Cost: $1,090 plus charter flight $275. Special requirements: Previous backpacking experience is helpful, climbers must be in excellent shape (capable of heavy load carrying).

The
Mountaineering
School at Vail, Inc.

Mountaineering School at Vail, Inc.
P.O. Box 3034
Vail, CO 81658
303-476-4123   *Colorado*

The Mountaineering School at Vail offers both beginner and advanced rock climbers an excellent opportunity to test their skills. With base camp at 11,200 feet in the Gore region of Colorado, this area provides some of the most breathtaking scenery in the world. A six-day beginner class will teach basic skills such as rope handling, rappelling and glissading. Advanced climbers will learn leadership techniques plus the mechanics of direct aid, nut placement and anchoring. Whatever your level of ability, this program provides the finest instructors and a great chance to take that first step toward Everest. Founded in 1970; operated under a United States Forest Service permit since 1970. Includes: Food, climbing gear, camping equipment. Dates: June through September. Length of trip: 6 to 10 days. Group size: 8. Cost: $285–$385. Special requirements: No experience necessary, except for 10-day advanced course.

Sierra Wilderness Seminars
P.O. Box 707
Arcata, CA 95521
707-822-8066   *California*

Sierra Wilderness Seminars' programs range from introductory courses in backpacking, rock climbing, and cross-country skiing to more advanced and technical seminars in ski mountaineering, peak climbing, summer mountaineering and survival. Practical training includes the basics—packing a backpack, walking comfortably, energy conservation, and campsite selection—plus ice axe and crampon use, snow cave construction, avalanche detection and peak climbing in more advanced classes. Environmental awareness, mountain safety and conservation are stressed on all seminars. Winter courses take place in Crater Lake and Lassen National Parks; summer courses in the Sierra Nevada. Four years' experience teaching mountaineering. Includes: Transportation to and from trailheads; from Lone Pine office; all food, instruction, permits, cooking and mountaineering equipment. Dates: June through September. Length of trip: 3–12 days. Group size: 10 participants. Cost: $180–$400.

Southwest Wilderness Center
Dept. T
P.O. Box 2840
Santa Fe, NM 87501
505-982-3126   *New Mexico*

Backpack and rock climb the spectacular Pecos Wilderness area—home of beautiful meadows with exploding color, swift mountain streams and majestic thirteen-thousand-foot peaks. Come face to face with deer, elk and mountain sheep as they roam the forests and ridges . . . or spot hawks and golden eagles as they soar above you. This glorious setting is the perfect place for learning about rock climbing, geology, flora, and fauna. Third year of running wilderness courses. Includes: Transportation from Santa Fe, food, all gear (except personal clothing), backpacking, camping, and mountaineering instruction. Dates: Late April through September. Length: 9 or 14 days. Group size: 5–10 people. Cost: $395 for 9 days. $575 for 14 days.

Sunrise Adventures
P.O. Box 1790
Glenwood Springs, CO 81601
303-945-1366   *Mexico*

Enjoy the full diversity of sunny Mexico, beginning with its highest mountains and finishing in the crystal-clear waters of the Caribbean coral reefs. Four days are spent traveling by mini-bus through the mountains and Indian villages of Central Mexico, culminating with an ascent of North America's third tallest summit, El Pico de Orizaba (18,851 feet). A train ride through the scenic Yucatán is capped off with eight days of snorkeling and diving around Isla Majeres, Isla Contoy, Kelha, Cozumel and Tulum. Sunrise Adventures has led mountaineering expeditions for 14 years. Includes: All transportation and lodging from Mexico City, meals in the field, group equipment and first aid. Dates: December through March. Length of trip: 14 days. Group size: 8. Cost: $750. Special requirements: Good physical condition, one-half of trip cost is required as deposit.

Sunrise Adventures
P.O. Box 1790
Glenwood Springs, CO 81601
303-945-1366   *Alaska*

Sunrise Adventures leads mountaineering expeditions in the Western United States, primarily in Utah, Colorado and Alaska. You'll travel in small groups to fascinating and remote areas, usually on foot, enjoying a high standard of comfort in camp. Exploration of North America's tallest mountain, 20,320-foot Denali (Mt. McKinley) begins with a bush flight and drop-off on the seven-thousand-foot level of Kahiltna Glacier. Ascension of the West Buttress affords views of some of the most spectacular mountain scenery on earth. This very demanding expedition ends with a trek back out to civilization. Custom trips into the area can be arranged. Ten years' experience organizing and leading mountain expeditions. Includes: Transportation from Anchorage, meals, group equipment and first aid. Dates: May, July. Length of trip: Approximately 25 days. Group size: Varies. Cost: $1,800. Special requirements: Top physical condition; 3 years' mountaineering experience; some glacier and high altitude experience is preferred; $900 deposit.

Nature Expeditions •

Nature trips are designed to widen our exposure and fortify our appreciation of the incredible living creatures of the earth. Programs take eager adventurers to exotic wildernesses, in search of rare and beautiful flora and fauna. The trips are almost as varied as nature herself. You can discover remarkable wildlife close to home, or travel to distant quarters for a glimpse of plants, birds, or animals that exist nowhere else in the world.

- Explore the Amazon, which comprises half of the world's tropical rain forest area. Penetrate the dense jungle by the Amazon River—second in length only to the Nile. Observe the jungle's forty thousand plant species, and keep your eyes peeled for animals: jaguars darting through the foliage, spider monkeys swinging by their tails, anteaters waving their snoots. Overhead, the trees are teeming with over 530 species of birds, including an abundance of toucans, parrots, and macaws.
- Or head to Nepal for a wildlife safari, Indian-style—on the back of an elephant. Scour the jungle for the great one-horned rhinoceros, deer, wild boar, sloth bear, and a variety of monkeys. In Royal Chitwan National Park, you can observe over four hundred varieties of birds, as well as buffalos and fresh water dolphins.
- Travel to the "islands that time forgot"—the Galapagos—home of animal species that exist nowhere else in the world. From his observations on these islands, Charles Darwin developed his theory of evolution. Although the Galapagos are known for their giant tortoises, they also play host to a number of rare creatures. You can snorkel among dolphins, see flamingoes strut on the sand, and try your hand at identifying millions of sea birds.
- Here in North America, you can get an eyeful of natural splendor. Bring your camera for a photo safari through the Southern Appalachians . . . see the stately flight of a red-tailed hawk in New York's Adirondacks . . . look out for elk or bighorn on a dawn trek into the Colorado Rockies . . . scan the prairies by air on a flightseeing expedition in the "Four Corners" area . . . or learn the secrets of edible plants at a workshop in Wisconsin's Northwoods.

Still want more? Wildlife adventures await in Costa Rica, Nova Scotia, Greenland, British Columbia, and on the Australian outback.

Once you choose an area you'd like to explore, the next step is to pick a program that matches your interests. If you're a weekend bird watcher, or you like looking at unusual plants and animals, pick a trip that concentrates on sightseeing and photography. If your interests run to the scientific, satisfy them on a research expedition. You'll attend lectures and study the flora and fauna of a region in depth.

Take the seasons and animal migration patterns into consideration when planning your trip. Animals and plants gear their life-cycles around temperature and rainfall. Showers facilitate germination, and bring forth young plants. During the dry season, animals find that their preferred watering holes have dried up. They roam the area in search of new sources of water. In cold areas, the winter freeze locks up ponds and lakes. Birds fly to warmer climates; many animals hibernate.

Ask the tour operator, or read up to find out the migratory patterns of the region. Variations may be a small matter—sometimes you just have to go to a different quarter of a reserve. If you have to fix the date of your vacation in advance, pick the area that's at its most interesting during that period.

The expertise of your guides can make a reserve come alive for you. Many guides are university professors, or research botanists or zoologists. They'll make the difference between studying an environment and looking at plants and animals. A top guide in the Amazon can identify a good portion of the 530 bird species.

Another major consideration is accommodations. In more developed regions, you can explore the wilderness by day, and enjoy the comfort of a modern hotel by night. For other areas, communion with nature includes camping out. (Check with the tour operator whether you need to bring a sleeping bag.)

Nature trips as a rule do not require too much rigorous physical labor. Given the variety of programs available, the hardest task is choosing the one. Whichever you choose, you'll learn something new about your fellow creatures on earth.

SECTIONS OF RELATED INTEREST

> *Birdwatching*
> *Botany*
> *Research Expeditions*
> *Whalewatch*
> *Wildlife Safaris*

Afognak Wilderness Lodge
Seal Bay, AK 99697
907-486-3276

Alaska

Enjoy the adventure of a wilderness retreat on Afognak Island, located in the Gulf of Alaska only twenty minutes by float plane from Kodiak. Kodiak brown bear, elk, deer and fox roam the island's mountains and forests, while offshore sights include the world's largest concentration of sea otters, plus seal, sea lions, whales and porpoises. Bald eagles, hawks and falcons also inhabit the island. Activities include wildlife photography, hiking, beachcombing, and even sunbathing, although many guests come just for the spectacular sport-fishing the island offers. Salmon, trout, halibut, bass and more populate the rivers and sea surrounding the Lodge. The log cabins were built by hand by Roy and Shannon Randall, owners and operators of the Lodge, and feature indoor plumbing, carpeting, and other amenities. Twenty-one years' experience. Includes: Accommodations, all meals (if you like, you can catch, pick, or collect your own), and daily guided boat travel. Dates: All year, primarily spring through fall. Length of trip: Any length, but 6 days is recommended. Group size: 1–12. Cost: $175 per day. Special requirements: 50% deposit.

Aitken Spence Travels, Ltd.
P.O. Box 5
Colombo, Sri Lanka
(01) 36735/36755
Telex 21142
AIKEN CE
21598

Sri Lanka

Discover the wildlife of Sri Lanka on this expedition into its national parks. Observe monkeys, water buffalo and elephants in the 488-square-mile Rohunu National Park. In Kumana Bird Sanctuary, you'll have a chance to see a wide variety of rare aquatic birds nesting in the mangrove swamps. Rare flowers and vegetation abound in Hakgala Botanical Gardens. Don't miss the herd of elephants in Gal Cya National Park, or the sleek leopards of Wilpattu National Park. Includes: Visiting all sites of wildlife and flora. Dates: Year-round. Length of trip: 8 days. Group size: Maximum 15. Cost: From $300.

Amazon Safari Club, Inc.
P.O. Box 252A
Elverson, PA 19520
215-286-5911

Peru

Experience the beautiful and exotic Amazon jungle, one of the least explored regions left on earth. From Iquitos, Peru, tour members travel by boat fifty miles down the Amazon River to a comfortable lodge—where they spend five nights deep in the jungle. Daily journeys by motorboat, canoe, or foot include visits to lakes for piranha fishing and to the primitive village of the Yagua Indians. Tapirs, anteaters, jaguars and over two thousand other mammals live in the jungle, which is also a bird-watcher's paradise. And with its average temperature of 80° and high rainfall, the Amazon region acts like a mammoth hothouse for exotic plants like ferns, bromeliads and orchids. Extensions to Lima, Cuzco, and Machu Picchu available along with a special once-a-year, thirteen-day expedition by boat up the Napo River to the most remote jungle area accessible. Operating trips to the Amazon exclusively since 1973. Includes: Airfare from Miami, accommodations in jungle, most meals, sightseeing. Dates: July (departs every Saturday). Length of trip: 7–12 days. Group size: 1–10. Cost: From $999 per person. Special requirements: $200 deposit 45 days before departure, good health.

Australian Wildlife Tours
P.O. Box 575
Canberra, A.C.T. Australia 2601
(062) 81-2112

Australia

See the Australian Outback by plane! Australia is so large that the most practical way to see it is by light aircraft. Your pilot-guide will identify points of interest, and land in remote areas so you can study the wildlife, natural wealth, and Aboriginal peoples that make up Australia's heritage. Trips center around wildlife watching and photography; fishing; opal mining; exploring historic sites and early pioneer settlements; and meeting Aborigines and learning of their culture. Sites and activities include visits to sheep stations and vineyards; trips to the paddle-steamers on the Murray River and Kinchega National Park; tours of Sturt National Park at Tibooburra with its gold and opal mining relics; and the waterfowl areas of the Macquarie Marshes Nature Reserve. Lodging is at bush hotels and country inns, or camping if preferred. Includes: 3 meals plus afternoon tea. All accommodations are in addition to the tour cost. Dates: April through November. Length of trip: 1–5 days. Group size: 2–5. Cost: $600 per person.

Bathurst Inlet Lodge
P.O. Box 820
Yellowknife, NWT
Canada X1A 2N6
403-873-2595
Telex 034-4-5564

Canada

Explore Canada's Arctic from Bathurst Inlet Lodge, located in a small Inuit community north of the Arctic Circle. Each day, you can select from a wide variety of trips by land or water. Musk oxen, caribou, wolves and grizzly bear are among the animals raising their young in this area. Birding highlights include peregrine and gyrfalcon eyries, golden eagle, loons, eiders and a wealth of high Arctic shorebirds. Eskimo culture is especially rich here, and you can view ancient Eskimo tent rings, burial grounds and inukshuks (stone men). There's also terrific fishing for Arctic char, lake trout and grayling. Fourteen years in operation. Includes: All-inclusive from Yellowknife. Dates: Mid-June through August. Length of trip: 1–2 weeks. Group size: Maximum 20. Cost: From $1,950.

Camp Denali
P.O. Box 67
Denali National Park
AK 99755
907-683-2302 (Winter)
907-683-2290 (Summer)   *Alaska*

Deep in the heart of Alaska's Denali National Park is thirty-two-year-old Camp Denali, a Shangri-La for the naturalist, adventurer and photographer. More than thirty-five species of wildlife roam the tundra of this subarctic alpine world. Spend time hiking, backpacking, canoeing, rafting or leisurely observing the Park's animals, birds, wildflowers and geological features. The panoramic views of snow-capped Mt. McKinley (highest mountain in North America at 20,320 feet) are superb. Stay in comfortable log cabins that have wood stoves for heat and sleep two to six people. Meals are served family-style at the lodge; in the evening there are evening slide presentations by staff naturalists. Thirty-second year of operation. Includes: Lodging, meals, equipment, land transportation, guiding, lectures and workshops. Dates: June through September. Length: 4–7 days. Group size: 32 maximum. Cost: $120 per day. Special requirements: $200 deposit.

Stunning views of 20,320-foot Mt. McKinley and the Alaska Range reward the hiker.
(CAMP DENALI)

Colonel Sam Hogan, Safaris
Casilla A-122
Quito, Ecuador
450242   *Ecuador*

Journey deep into the jungles of Ecuador with Colonel Sam Hogan. Explore the upper Amazon River Basin on the borders of Colombia and Peru, traveling on wild lakes and rivers, and fishing for tucunare (peacock bass) arawana and giant catfish. You'll see exotic wildlife, butterflies, birds and flora, and jungle Indians. Previous clients ranged from ten to eighty-six years old. Retired Colonel Sam Hogan has sixteen years' experience in the Amazon. Includes: Sleeping accommodations, land and water transportation, guides, meals and fees. Dates: All year. Length of trip: 7 days, 6 nights. Group size: 1–6. Cost: $1,350 for one. $565 per person for 4 or more. Special requirements: 25% deposit.

Dillman's Sand Lodge, Inc.
P.O. Box 98
Lac du Flambeau, WI 54538
715-588-3143   *Wisconsin*

Located in Wisconsin's Northwoods, Dillman's is a comfortable, family-oriented resort offering "Nature Study Workshops." For spring, a program on trees, shrubs, spring birds and wildflowers features daily field trips—plus a special night owl hunt. Or check out Mother Nature's larder with an early summer course about edible wild plants. You'll learn all the ins and outs of food foraging—from picking to preparing. In September, novice and intermediate mycologists (mushroom hunters) can study how to identify, prepare and preserve the savory wild mushrooms that flourish in the Great Lakes Region. All workshop instructors are professionals in their fields. For non-naturalists, Dillman's also offers golf, swimming, horseback riding, and tennis along with good food and comfortable accommodations. Includes: Accommodations, breakfast, dinner, tuition, instructor's fee, all resort recreational facilities. Dates: May through October. Length of trip: 3–6 days. Group size: 10–25. Cost: $185–$375.

Everglades Canoe Outfitters, Inc.
39801 Ingraham Highway
Homestead, FL 33034
305-246-1530   *Florida*

Visit Everglades National Park plus the Dry Tortugas, whose warm Gulf of Mexico waters favored creation of fascinating coral reefs. This extremely diverse trip includes snorkeling, boating, canoeing, and walking. You'll paddle through the mangrove forest, by tropical hardwood hammocks, and see the native orchids, rare Wurdemann's heron, great blue heron, and possibly, the American crocodile. Visit the Miccosukee Indians and take an airboat ride in search of the endangered Everglades kite. Visit the National Audubon Society's Corkscrew Swamp Sanctuary, one of the largest stands of mature bald cypress trees in the nation. Stroll through a natural cathedral—a great place to find nesting wood storks. In the afternoon, wade knee-deep through the Fakahatchee Strand, a cypress swamp, to find orchids and tree ferns. Everglades Canoe Outfitters operates under a contract with Everglades National Park. Includes: Double-occupancy in first-class hotels, motorcoach transportation, most meals, group admissions, services of naturalist-facilitator and guides for canoe trips. Dates: November through May. Length of trip: 8 days. Group size: Varies. Cost: $695. Special requirements: Participants should be in good physical condition. Some activities may be considered strenuous. Deposit: $100 per registrant.

Exploration Holidays
1500 Metropolitan Park Building
Seattle, WA 98101
800-426-0600
206-624-8551 (In WA & Canada)
Telex 32-96-36   *Alaska*

Spend the day cruising Glacier Bay, known for its active tidewater glaciers. Along the coast, glaciers, deep fjords and lofty snow-capped mountains combine with lush forests and abundant wildlife—eagles, whales and seals—to create a landscape of stark splendor. At night stay at the deluxe yet rustic Glacier Bay Lodge, nestled in a moss-covered primeval forest setting. Exploration Holidays also offers a four-day trip to Alaska's Pribilof Islands, famous for their bird and seal rookeries. Accompanied by an experienced guide, you'll watch the wildlife from special viewing blinds, allowing up-close observation and photography. You'll also learn about the proud heritage of the four hundred Aleuts who inhabit the community. Includes: All transportation from point of departure, accommodations and sightseeing. Dates: Late May through September. Length: 1–4 days. Cost: $236–$689 per person.

Forum Travel International
2437 Durant Avenue #208
Berkeley, CA 94704
415-843-8294
Telex 910-366-7092 ADVENCEN   *South America*

This adventure takes you to some of the most famous natural and cultural sites in South America. Cruise the enchanted Galapagos Islands, "suspended in time" with their unique wildlife. Travel via outboard canoe up the untamed Tambopata River to the Explorer's Inn, located deep in the heart of Peru's Amazon jungle. From this three-star lodge, you'll be able to observe a dazzling variety of tropical birds and plants, as well as crocodile and piranha. In Ecuador, you'll journey through the "Avenue of the Volcanos" past Cotopaxi, the world's highest active volcano. Roam the ruins of Machu Picchu, mighty citadel of the Incas. Aboard the High Andes Railroad, cross Peru's legendary altiplano, passing flocks of llamas, towering peaks and Indian villages. Visit the Uros' reed islands on Lake Titicaca, highest navigable lake in the world. Drive into Bolivia and wander thru the hustle and bustle of the local Indian markets. In operation since 1965. Includes: All land and water transportation, all accommodations, sightseeing and entrance fees, guides, most meals. Dates: Year-round. Length: 12–22 days. Group size: 2–20. Cost: From $1,334 per person.

GEO Expeditions
P.O. Box 27136-STB
Oakland, CA 94602
415-530-4146   *Australia*

Come to Australia's exciting north, a living museum of unique species of marsupials and spectacular, brilliantly colored birds. Highlights include a fourteen-day wilderness safari into the largely unexplored Kimberly Plateau, during which you'll travel via air-conditioned, all-terrain vehicles and bushcamp in tents. You'll also cross the central desert including Alice

Springs and Ayers Rock, and explore the Great Barrier Reef. Throughout the trip, the emphasis is on informality, sunshine and comfort. Tour leader is Dr. William L. Thomas, Professor of Geography, California State University (Hayward), and vice president of GEO Expeditions. Length: 29 days. Group size: 15 maximum. Cost: $2,250 (land). Special requirements: $200 deposit, willingness to bushcamp in tents and sleeping bags.

Great Expeditions, Inc.
2956 West 4th Avenue
Vancouver, B.C., Canada V6K 1R4
604-734-4948   *Canada*

This cruise takes you to the homeland of the Haida and Kwakiutl people, whose cedar canoes plied the crystal waters from California to Alaska over a century ago. It's a land of intricately carved totem poles . . . luxurious hot springs . . . and green rain forests. Starting near Queen Charlotte City, you'll sail down the coast of the proposed South Moresby Wilderness Area, stopping each day to go ashore, wander intertidal zones, spend time at bird colonies and even hike in alpine country. Back on ship you'll be dazzled by the waterlife—from colorful starfish to mighty ocra whales—and overhead the rare peregrine falcon might swoop by. The sailing vessel is equipped with aquariums, microscope, diving gear, kayak, shore launch and research library. Member of Pacific Area Travel Association; established in 1977. Includes: Sailboat, meals, guide. Dates: Summer. Length of trip: 10 days. Group size: 15 people maximum. Cost: $1,030. Special requirements: $300 deposit.

Great Expeditions, Inc.
2956 West 4th Avenue
Vancouver, B.C., Canada V6K 1R4
604-734-4948   *Galapagos Islands*

Come face to face with the giant Galapagos turtle in the land where Charles Darwin formed his theory of evolution. The Galapagos—where flamingoes gracefully move through quiet lagoons . . . playful dolphins frolic as you snorkel . . . home of the only equatorial penguins in the world. The small size of your boat party enables visits to islands that are off-limits to large cruise ships—and with a naturalist guide on board you'll see fabulous vistas, dramatic volcanic formations, and sea turtles coming to the beaches to lay their eggs. Member of Pacific Area Travel Association; established in 1977. Includes: Sailboat, accommodation, all meals aboard the boats, sightseeing tour in Quito. Dates: Monthly from January to September. Length of trip: 14 days on islands, 3 days in Ecuador. Group size: 15 maximum. Cost: $1,590. Special requirements: $300 deposit.

Innerasia
2627 Lombard Street
San Francisco, CA 94123
415-922-0448
Telex 278716 TIGER   *Nepal*

On this wildlife safari, you'll stay at the Tiger Tops Jungle Lodge, Tented Camp, or Tharu Village, which lie deep in the heart of the 360-square-mile Royal Chitwan National Park,

Meet the giant tortoises for which the Galapagos Islands are named. (GREAT EXPEDITIONS)

seventy-five miles southwest of Kathmandu. From the backs of elephants, you'll explore the surrounding jungle searching the tall grass for the great one-horned rhinoceros, deer, wild boar, sloth bear, and monkeys. Accompanied by naturalists from Tiger Tops, enjoy jungle walks to view some of more than four hundred species of birds and the colorful flora of the park. You'll also get glimpses of wild buffalos, fresh water dolphin and mugger crocodile. Includes: Elephant ride from Meghauly airport to lodge; services of experienced naturalists; nature walks, elephant wildlife safari, Land Rover drives, boat trips. Optional overnight excursions to Tharu village and Tented Camp. Dates: October through May. Length of trip: 2 days or more. Group size: Varies. Cost: Varies with duration. Special requirements: Good health and a spirit of adventure.

Koksetna Camp
P.O. Box 69
Iliamna, AK 99606
907-345-1160 (ask for WHJ-67-Chulitna)   *Alaska*

Sara and Charles Hornberger invite you to experience the solitude, quiet and tranquility of their Koksetna Camp, located in Lake Clark National Park and Preserve. You can boat and hike along the Chulitna River, Lake Clark, and their shores to observe a multitude of birds, wildflowers and wildlife—including moose, caribou, otter, beaver, muskrat, fox, lynx . . . sometimes brown and black bears. In May, Turner Bay at Koksetna Camp is host to thousands of swans, ducks, geese, shorebirds, hawks, eagles, owls. From July 20, red/sockeye salmon can be observed spawning in the many beautiful rivers that flow into Lake Clark. If you like, fish for grayling, dolly varden, lake trout and pike for your dinner. Accommodations are large comfortable log cabins. Sara Hornberger cooks up hearty, family-style meals featuring home-baked breads and desserts, garden fresh vegetables and Alaskan seafoods. The Hornbergers have operated the wilderness lodge and guide service for thirteen years. Includes: Meals, lodging, guide service, transportation by boat while on trip. Dates: Year-round. Length: As desired. Group size: Maximum 10. Cost: $200 per day. Special requirements: 30% deposit to confirm reservation.

Las Ventanas de Osa
P.O. Box 820
Yellowknife, NWT
Canada X1A 2N6
403-873-2595
Telex 034-4-5564   *Costa Rica*

Carved out of the virgin jungle five hundred feet above the Pacific, Las Ventanas de Osa is a private lodge on the verdant southwest coast of Costa Rica. Here, you can be as relaxed or as active as you desire. Hike jungle trails with knowledgeable local guides and visit rural cocoa and banana plantations. Experience wild places . . . observe wild things. Giant tree ferns and towering trees form a dense canopy over one of the world's last virgin stands of tropical forest. Costa Rica is "bird rich"—with toucans, parrots, tanagers, frigate birds and humming-birds, the jewels of the jungle. See white-faced howler monkeys, coatimundi and agooti. After a day's exploration, enjoy the sun-bathed beaches, swim in fresh water pools and savor the beautiful surroundings of the lodge. Includes: All inclusive from San Jose, including transfers, meals and sightseeing. Dates: All year except October. Length: 4–12 days. Group size: 19 maximum. Cost: $570–$1,500 per person.

Logos Enterprises, Inc.
P.O. Box 704
New York, NY 10013
212-278-1405
212-938-7824   *Colombia*

Destination: The Amazon—for a thrilling tour that ranges from the cosmopolitan to the primitive. Your journey to adventure begins in Bogota, home of Simon Bolivar, the Liberator, and a city of dazzling beauty. Here you'll view the glittering treasures of El Dorado at the Museum of Gold. Then it's on to the Amazon—also known as "Green Hell"—and a boat ride up this magical river. You'll stop off at an island whose thirty-two thousand inhabitants delight you—all of them monkeys. You'll also explore the primitive villages of the Yagua and Ticuna Indians. Then it's back to civilization and Cartagena for nightclubs, discos and gambling. Includes: Transfers, accommodations, first-class hotels, sightseeing (includes 1-day trip along the Amazon River), hotel tax. Dates: Year-round. Length of trip: 10 days. Group size: 25 maximum. Cost: $624 plus air fare. Special requirements: $100 deposit. Full payment due 30 days prior to departure.

National Wildlife Federation
1412 Sixteenth Street N.W.
Washington, DC 20036
703-790-4363   *Canada*

Conducted by the National Wildlife Foundation, Conservation Summits emphasize nature study, outdoor recreation, conservation issues and folk culture. On this program you'll explore the varied coastal habitats and ecosystems of Nova Scotia. Field trips may take you through the rolling verdant hills of Nova Scotia to investigate osprey nesting sites or to explore the mysteries of Atlantic salmon migration. Or, you might head for the fertile estuaries where shorebirds, waterfowl and possibly a bald eagle or two can be seen. Naturally, the beaches will provide excellent study sites for dune ecology, oceanography, beachcombing as well as offering recreational opportunities for swimming and oceanside cookouts. The National Wildlife Federation has been operating Conservation Summits for fourteen years. Includes: Activities focusing on nature study, outdoor recreation skills, conservation issues, and folk culture with programs for adults, teens and children. Accommodations not included. Dates: Summer. Length of trip: 6 days. Group size: 400. Cost: $130 for adult, $70 for teen, accommodations extra. Special requirements: Membership in NWF (membership costs begin at $7).

National Wildlife Federation
1412 Sixteenth Street N.W.
Washington, DC 20036
703-790-4363   *North Carolina*

Get a taste of real mountain life on the National Wildlife Foundation's Conservation Summits. On this program, you'll tap your feet to ballads, old-time clog dancing and the sound of the guitar and banjo played against the background of the Blue Ridge Mountains. Visitors here are still greeted with warm Southern hospitality. Spend your days investigating the wildflowers and mushrooms, butterflies and birds of the Southern Appalachians, or try your hand at sketching, reading a map and compass and much more. Field trips along the scenic Blue Ridge parkway, folk arts programs, night walks and mountain sing-alongs round out your six days of discovery. The National Wildlife Federation has been operating Conservation Summits for fourteen years. Includes: Activities focusing on nature study, outdoor recreation skills, conservation issues, and folk culture with programs for adults, teens and children. Accommodations not included. Dates: Summer. Length of trip: 6 days. Group size: 400. Cost: $130 for adult, $70 for teen, accommodations extra. Special requirements: Membership in NWF (membership costs begin at $7).

National Wildlife Federation
1412 Sixteenth Street N.W.
Washington, DC 20036
703-790-4363   *New York*

Conducted by the National Wildlife Foundation, Conservation Summits emphasize nature study, outdoor recreation skills, conservation issues and folk culture. On this program you'll travel north to the wild back-country of the Adirondack Mountains and Lake George, deep in the most expansive wilderness tract in the United States. Watch a beaver making its way along the shore, or a red-tailed hawk soaring overhead. You can explore the homes and habitats of the wildlife native to these picturesque mountains. There's time for woodcarving and flycasting, sailing and swimming too. End the day with an owl walk or a quiet moment by the lake. The National Wildlife Federation has been operating Conservation Summits for fourteen years. Includes: Activities focusing on nature study, outdoor recreation skills, conservation issues, and folk culture with programs for adults, teens and children. Accommodations not included. Dates: Summer. Length of trip: 6 days. Group size: 400. Cost: $130 for adult, $70 for teen, accommodations extra. Special requirements: Membership in NWF (membership costs begin at $7).

National Wildlife Federation
1412 Sixteenth Street N.W.
Washington, DC 20036
703-790-4363   *Colorado*

Conducted by the National Wildlife Foundation, Conservation Summits are outdoor discovery vacations emphasizing nature study, outdoor recreation skills, conservation issues and folk culture. At their Rocky Mountain Summit, you can explore the breathtaking wilderness of the high country. Imagine the excitement of a dawn trip into the Rockies, with the prospect of mule deer, elk or bighorn around any turn. Arrange your day to include fascinating programs on wildlife and outdoor living, and still have plenty of free time for the many recreational activities available. Join friends for an early morning photography trip or an evening of star gazing. From demonstrations on how to bake wholesome breads to forums on endangered species, the Rocky Mountain Summit is filled with discovery. The National Wildlife Federation has been operating Conservation Summits for fourteen years. Includes: Activities focusing on nature study, outdoor recreation skills, conservation issues, and folk culture with programs for adults, teens and children. Accommodations not included. Dates: Summer. Length of trip: 6 days. Group size: 400. Cost: $130 for adult, $70 for teen, accommodations extra. Special requirements: Membership in NWF (membership costs begin at $7).

Nature Expeditions International
474 Williamette Avenue
P.O. Box 11496
Eugene, OR 97440
503-484-6529   *Galapagos Islands*

This twenty-day expedition studies the natural history of the Galapagos Islands, one of the earth's greatest natural laboratories. In a stark, volcanic landscape, millions of sea birds, land and marine iguanas, fur seals and sea lions, and the endangered Galapagos tortoise make their home, largely unaffected by and unafraid of man. Spend time hiking, snorkeling and photographing wildlife while traveling among the islands on the comfortable motor-sailing yacht *Encantada*. Because of the small group size, you'll be able to visit sites closed to larger groups. Each expedition is accompanied by a Nature Expeditions International biologist and a local naturalist guide. Special nature photography trips also available. Over ten years in business. Includes: All meals except in Quito, accommodations in hotel and yacht. Dates: January, April, June, July, August. Length: 20 days. Group size: 10–20 maximum. Cost: $2,390. Special requirements: Ability to travel on small boat.

Nature Expeditions International
474 Williamette Avenue
P.O. Box 11496
Eugene, OR 97440
503-484-6529   *Mexico*

The Sea of Cortez, situated between mainland Mexico and the Baja California peninsula, encompasses unique desert island wilderness and inland sea that shelters a kaleidoscopic array of rare desert plants, tropical birds, fish-eating bats, land iguanas, and bountiful marine life. Separated from the continental mainland for millions of years, these islands have evolved distinct personalities that provide a fascinating natural history laboratory for the naturalist and photographer alike. Blue-footed boobies, giant barrel cactus, California sea lions, garden eels, and a resident population of finback whales are a few of the fascinating life forms found in this region. Join Nature Expeditions International aboard the comfortable motor-yacht Baja Explorador to explore, study, photograph, hike, snorkel, and relax among one of the finest wildlife islands in the Gulf of California. In business for over ten years, Nature Expeditions International specializes in wildlife and cultural expeditions worldwide. Includes: All meals (except San Diego and LaPaz), accommodations, land and ship transportation, leadership and instruction. Dates: April. Length of trip: 9 days. Group size: 18. Cost: $1,290.

Nature Expeditions International
474 Williamette Avenue
P.O. Box 11496
Eugene, OR 97440
503-484-6529   *Australia*

Nature Expeditions International offers a 24-day expedition to study Australia, the earth's largest island and smallest continent. You'll visit wilderness reserves, desert and island habitats, sheep stations and small towns. Highlights include a tenting adventure in the magnificent Outback and Arnhemland; staying with an Australian family, and exploring the Great Barrier Reef and Heron Island. Along the way, you'll see kangaroo, koala, wallaby, wombats and crocodile; observe spectacular wildflowers and birdlife; and examine the aboriginal cave paintings of the Northern Territory. Nature Expeditions International has been in business over ten years. Includes: Land transportation, tips, accommodations, meals except in Sydney, Brisbane and Darwin. Dates: July and October. Length: 24 days. Group size: Maximum 16. Cost: $2,490. Special requirements: Good health.

Nature Expeditions International
474 Williamette Avenue
P.O. Box 11496
Eugene, OR 97440
503-484-6529   *Alaska*

Voyage through a land of lofty mountains, mammoth glaciers, millions of salmon and enormous bears—it's difficult to describe Alaska in anything less than superlatives. This wildlife expedition is specially designed for first-time visitors who wish to experience the variety of wildlife and magnificent scenery that Alaska has to offer. You'll enjoy a three-day exploration of Glacier Bay aboard the M.V. Chaik, a comfortable fifty-foot motor-yacht. Glacier Bay abounds with humpback and killer whales and porpoises. You'll also see harbor seals enjoying the chilly waters of this sixty-five-mile long bay with its sixteen active tidewater glaciers. Then visit Katmai National Monument, where you can observe nearby volcanoes that puff and rumble or watch an Alaskan brown bear scoop up shimmering salmon with its paw. Beneath the icy gaze of 20,230 foot Mt. McKinley in Denali National Park, you'll explore the winding stream valleys and glacial terrain populated by caribou, grizzly bear and eagles. Evening lectures complement the numerous opportunities for hiking, wildlife photography and nature study. In business for over ten years, faculty of thirty college teachers as trip leaders. Includes: All meals except in Juneau, Anchorage, and Fairbanks; all accommodations, land transport and transfers; ship charter; tips. Dates: June through August. Length: 17 days. Group size: Maximum 16. Cost: $2,490.

North Country Travelers
P.O. Box 14
Atlin, British Columbia
Canada V0W 1A0   *Canada*

Bruce and Jeaneil Johnson and their two daughters will personalize your trip into the British Columbia Atlin Lake Wilderness Area. Thirty miles south of Atlin proper, their homestead features a sauna, vegetable garden, chickens, goats and two dozen prize-winning sled dogs. Their territory is the Atlin and Tagish Lake system—headwaters of the legendary Yukon River. You can travel by freight canoe (a twenty-two-foot Indian-made canoe) to the remote end of Atlin Lake, and by individual canoe to Llewellyn Glacier, abandoned gold mines and nearby mountains. The area is an unspoiled paradise populated by black bear, moose, eagle, beaver and mountain goat—a photographer's dream. Bruce breeds, trains and runs the best huskies in the North and they are available for winter sledding excursions. Other activities include snowshoeing and cross-country skiing, panning for gold, day hikes and treks, and fly casting for Arctic grayling, right in the Atlin River—the Johnson's front yard. Includes: Travel from Whitehorse to Atlin and return, lodging in cabins and tents, fishing gear, home-cooked meals featuring fresh eggs, baked goods and your own fresh-caught fish. Guests should bring a sleeping bag and small backpack. Dates: June through September. Length of trip: 7 days or more. Group size: 2–8. Cost: $850 per week Canadian. Special requirements: Good health.

Pacific Sea Fari Tours
530 Broadway, Suite 1224
San Diego, CA 92101
619-226-8224   *California*

Strung along the California coast like a natural necklace, the Channel Islands are a living marine sanctuary. Explore colorful, free-form grottos, ancient Indian sites and the weather-knarled shores of this wonderful world. Discover the many forms of land and marine creatures which roam, crawl, fly, swim and splash throughout these enchanted isles. Special attractions include the California sea-lions, brown pelicans, gray whales and island foxes. Fifteen years' experience. Includes: All meals, accommodations, naturalist leaders. Dates: May, June, September through November. Length of trip: 6 days. Group size: 20. Cost: $840.

S.I.T.
2437 Durant Avenue, Suite 208
Berkeley, CA 94704
415-843-8294
EXPLORE   Telex 910-366-7092 ADVENCEN   *Peru*

Situated in the heart of the upper Amazon basin rain forest, the Explorer's Inn provides bird watchers and nature enthusiasts with easy access to undisturbed jungle. The virgin forest surrounding the Inn has been declared a wildlife reserve, and ornithologists have recorded over 530 species, including parrots, toucans, macaws, kingfishers, hummingbirds and harpy eagles. Monkeys, anteaters, coati, deer, otter, ocelot, sloths, jaguar, peccary and other mammals often can be viewed within close proximity to the lodge. Another bonus for nature lovers is the abundance of butterflies and unusual insects that thrive in this strange, lush habitat. Resident biologists serve as guides and also give evening lectures on jungle ecology. S.I.T. has been in operation since 1967. Includes: Accommodations, meals, guides, land and water transportation, airport pick-up. Length: 7–28 days. Group size: Varies. Dates: Year-round. Cost: $55 per day. Special requirements: Good health.

S.I.T.
2437 Durant Avenue, Suite 208
Berkeley, CA 94704
415-843-8294
EXPLORE   Telex 910-366-7092 ADVENCEN   *Costa Rica*

Monkeys and manatees . . . wild orchids, ocelots and an active volcano—see them all on this expedition to the finest of Costa Rica's national parks. Your trip starts off with Poas volcano, where you can actually stand on the edge and look a thousand feet down into the bubbling cauldron. Then visit Monteverde Cloud Forest, perhaps the last place in the world to see the resplendent green and gold quetzal, sacred bird of the Aztec Indians. At Fortuguero National Park, you'll glide through the tropical rain forest searching for manatees and turtles, while howler and spider monkeys perform acrobatics overhead. Your journey culminates with two days at Corcovado, last remaining virgin tropical rain forest in Central America. Here huge trees—some more than two hundred feet high—tower over a rich profusion of vegetation. Unusual animals include peccaries (wild pigs) and coatimundis, long-tailed relatives of the raccoon. Includes: All lodging, camping equipment, and all water transportation within Costa Rica, most meals, guide services. Dates: All year. Length: 8–15 days. Group size: 2–20. Cost: From $756. Special requirements: Good health.

South America Reps
P.O. Box 39583
Los Angeles, CA 90039
213-246-4816
800-423-2791 outside California
Telex 686167　　　　　　　　　　　*Peru*

Known as "The River Gold," the Amazon flows from headwaters in the Peruvian Andes for 3,900 miles to the Atlantic—making it the second-longest river in the world. On this adventure, you share the cost of chartering a boat for a one-hundred-mile voyage down the Amazon to the Napo River campsite. First night is spent at the Amazon Camp near Iquitos, Peru for introduction into jungle living with a preliminary jungle hike. Leave the camp early the second morning on a thatch-roofed "colectivo"—a fifty-five foot long, ten foot wide native craft—with two boatmen, a cook and an English speaking guide/naturalist for the three night stay at the Napo campsite. The floor of the thatched-roofed building at Napo is raised off the ground; mosquito netting and a floor sleeping pad complete the sleeping facilities. (Bring your own sleeping bag.) From the campsite, you'll enjoy excursions to the large Yaguas Indian village as well as frequent jungle walks, boat and dugout canoe expeditions. Includes: Round trip airport transfers, 1 night with all meals at Amazon Camp, plus jungle walk; 3 nights at Amazon-Napo Camp; all meals, English speaking guide/naturalist. Dates: Year-round; scheduled departures. Length of trip: 5 days, 4 nights. Group size: Maximum 8 passengers. Cost: $350. Special requirements: Extensive walking involved; must be experienced in camping and hiking—very primitive campsite at Napo area.

Southwest Safaris
P.O. Box 945
Sante Fe, NM 87501
505-988-4246　　　　　　　*Western United States*

Southwest Safaris will take you to the most remote and exciting corners of the Great American Southwest—the "Four Corners" area of New Mexico, Colorado, Utah and Arizona. The trip emphasizes the value of air travel. Flightseeing not only eliminates days of traveling time, it also provides perspectives on time, landscapes and human activities on a broader scale than can be comprehended from the ground alone. After travelers land at the respective locations of interest, whether the Grand Canyon, a remote trading post, Canyonlands National Park, or the Goosenecks of the San Juan River, they are met by four-wheel drive vehicles or rafts, as appropriate to the area under study, for a closer examination of the natural and cultural aspects of this relatively untouched frontier. All tours emphasize the study of geology, archeology, ecology and American history. Ten years in business. Includes: Bushflying, jeeping, and rafting; guides, all meals, lodging and transportation in the field. Tents provided on camping trips; sleeping bags may be rented. Dates: Year-round. Length of trip: 4 days and 5 days. Group size: 5 persons. Cost: 4-day $995, 5-day $1,295. Special requirements: No special skills required. $100 deposit per person when making reservations.

Special Odysseys
P.O. Box 37
Medina, WA 98039
206-455-1960
Telex TWX 901-433-2366　　　*Canada, Greenland*

Travel to the very top of the world with Special Odysseys. The company runs a variety of programs to the High Arctic and Greenland. You can fly to the North Pole and join the select few adventurers who have stood on both the Geographic and Magnetic Poles. On North Ellsmere Island, fish for Arctic Char and view the fascinating wildlife of the north, including the Arctic wolf and the musk ox. In Greenland, cruise aboard a coastal ship through the immense icebergs of Disco Bay. Greenland presents an unusual blend of Danish and Inuit culture, and you'll be able to observe reindeer, green meadows and ancient ruins from the period of Eric the Red. Or travel by helicopter, snowmobile, ship and twin engine plane to the High Arctic of Canada's Northwest Territories. Hike, fish and learn about the rich culture of the Eskimos. Includes: All inclusive from point of departure. Dates: April and August. Length: Varies with trip selection. Group size: 14–16. Cost: $2,995–$6,600. Special requirements: Good health.

The Earth Preservation Fund
P.O. Box 7545-ST
Ann Arbor, MI 48107
313-665-4407   *Costa Rica*

These trips take in the abundant natural diversity of this small, peaceful country, especially its many national parks. You'll hike and explore the Pacific and Caribbean shores, among lush jungles, mountain cloud forests, and active volcanos. The trips are timed to coincide with some of the best events of each season, including bird migrations, turtle nesting, wildlife observation and cultural celebrations. During the July visit, for example, you'll be able to observe giant three-hundred-pound green sea turtles clambering out of the sea at midnight to lay their eggs. Many other opportunities abound for seeing and photographing exotic tropical birds, flowers and wildlife. In addition, you'll spend three exciting days of whitewater rafting on remote tropical rivers, under the supervision of professional river guides. Six years' experience. Includes: Lodging, camping and rafting equipment, meals, transportation, American and Costa Rican naturalist guides. Dates: February and July. Length: 15 days. Group size: 15. Cost: $1,365 per person. Includes 10% tax deductible contribution to support sea turtle conservation and protect national parks in Costa Rica.

The Earth Preservation Fund
P.O. Box 7545-ST
Ann Arbor, MI 48107
313-665-4407   *Caribbean*

Explore the undiscovered Caribbean and experience the natural beauty and easy-going lifestyles of Guadaloupe and Dominica. You'll explore lush rainforests and active volcanos . . . swim in hot waterfalls and mineral pools . . . visit historic forts, observe Caribe Indian lifestyle and handicrafts, and participate in the Carnival celebration. You'll also have plenty of time to snorkel among beautiful staghorn coral reefs teeming with diverse marine life. The trip is hosted by the Eastern Caribbean Natural Area Management Program, and Dominica Conservation Association, who will discuss their efforts to conserve the natural and cultural resources of these unspoiled tropical islands. Six years' experience leading trips. Includes: Sail charter and ground transportation, lodging, guides, meals. Dates: February. Length: 15 days. Group size: 15. Cost: $1,595 (land rate). Includes 10% tax deductible contribution to protect national parks and support environmental education in local schools. Special requirements: $300 deposit.

Tunas Indonesia Tours & Travel
29 Jln. Majapahit.
P.O. Box 457 JKT
Jakarta, Indonesia
341085
Telex 46542 TUNAS JKT   *Indonesia*

Explore off-the-beaten-path in Indonesia. Visit Irian Java, one of the last frontiers on earth. See thick, impenetrable jungles, snow-capped mountains, Baliem Valley (inaccessible by land or sea), the Lost Civilization of the Lanis and the Asmat wood-carvings and war canoes. Discover the tiny, barren island of Komodo, home of the enormous Komodo lizard, believed to be the real-life counterpart to the mythological, fire-breathing dragon. Travel to Krakatoa, the still-active volcano that in 1883 produced the greatest explosion in recent history. At the western end of Java, tour the Ujung Kulon game reserve, famous for its panthers, peacocks and rare population of one-horned Java rhino. Another must for wildlife enthusiasts is the Bohorak Nature Reserve and its Orangutan Rehabilitation Center—where domesticated orangutans are taught to live free in the wild. Includes: Meals and accommodations, guides, domestic flights, boat charter and land transportation, taxes. Dates: All year. Group size: Minimum 2 people. Cost: $600–$1,460. Special requirements: Full payment one month prior to departure.

Weber-Alyeska Wilderness Guides
P.O. Box 10-1663
Anchorage, AK 99511
907-345-2081   *Alaska*

Enjoy a relaxing wilderness retreat on the shores of Alaska's Kroto Lake. A variety of outdoor activities are available nearby, and you'll have daily guided excursions into the near and far surroundings. Fish in streams chock-full of fat trout. Study the thriving wetland ecology . . . perhaps maybe spy on a moose or brown bear. Kayak, canoe or raft on the sparkling clear rivers. Hike through the Dutch Hills, picking mushrooms and berries for your dinner. At day's end, unwind in a hot tub while gazing up at the magnificent Mt. McKinley. Your cabin is accessible only by foot, so you're sure to have plenty of peace and quiet. Enjoy good conversation over the home-cooked, family-style meals. Over thirty years' experience in adventure travel; twenty-two years in Alaskan adventure travel. Includes: Transportation, meals, lodging, excursions. Dates: June through September. Length of trip: 2 days or more. Group size: Up to 16. Cost: $75 and up.

Wilderness Alaska/Mexico
Bissel Rd. STB
Hunters, WA 99137
509-722-3263   *Alaska*

Each year 130,000 caribou from the Porcupine Caribou herd migrate north to their calving grounds in the Arctic National Wildlife Refuge in Alaska. Observe caribou during the post-calving migration back to Canada, as you experience the arctic tundra ecosystem during its most intense season—spring. With twenty-four hours of daylight warming the tundra, many plants and wildflowers are bursting forth—including pussy willows, shooting stars, buttercups and dryas. You might also see barren ground grizzly, wolves, moose and other arctic wildlife. The base camp setting provides the option of exploring on your own or with the guide on daily tundra walks. Six years' experience. Includes: Tents, food and cooking gear, guide, aircharter from Barter Island. Dates: June and July. Length: 8 days. Group size: 8–12 people. Cost: $859. Special requirements: Camping experience, $200 deposit.

Wilderness Experiences
P.O. Box 440474
Miami, FL 33144
813-695-3143   *Florida*

For the first time ever, the Central Plains of the Everglades National Park is open for public access. Tour operator Jan Jacobson has designed his own "swamp machine" to penetrate this untouched heart of the 'Glades. The machine meets (and exceeds) environmental standards, and travels with quiet luxury through the flora and fauna of the Plains. You'll ride twelve feet up, enjoying a panoramic view of the tropical trees set in the vast sea of sawgrass. Be sure to bring a camera to capture the rare beauty of orchid-covered swamp trees, airplants, ibis, egret, heron, deer, 'possum and 'gators. Biologists and botanists share their knowledge and love of this unique wilderness area and an on-site research lab is open to clients. Custom trips for educational, photography, birding, and other interests can be arranged. Licensed by the United States Department of the Interior. Includes: Transportation to and from Miami, all meals and gear. Handicapped groups can be accommodated. Dates: All year. Length of trip: 1–3 days, with camping right on the swamp machine. Group size: 4–24. Cost: $65–$235.

Wilderness Travel
1760-HB Solano Avenue
Berkeley, CA 94707
415-524-5111
Telex 677 022   *Ecuador*

On this expedition, you'll penetrate into remote areas of the Amazon rainforest. Your adventure begins in Quito, Ecuador, where you'll spend four days exploring the Andean highlands around the city, visiting Indian markets including the excellent weaving and handcrafts market of Otavalo. Then cross the Continental Divide and descend the Amazonian flank of the Andes, stopping at Coca Falls and other places for birding and observing changing ecological zones. In the Cofan Indian village of Dureno, meet your expert guide, Randy Borman. The son of missionaries, Randy has lived nearly all his life among these Indians and now administers a local agricultural community. For a week you travel through the Amazon jungle in dugout canoes (with outboard motor) along the lakes and rivers, staying in stilted thatched huts and taking day-hikes under the rain forest canopy. Birds range from macaws and toucans to kites and eagles; wildlife includes monkeys, tapir, crocodiles and capybara. You'll learn a great deal about Indian customs and beliefs, hunting and fishing practices, uses of native plants, and jungle wilderness survival. Includes: All accommodations, all land and water transportation, all meals in jungle, all but 5 meals in cities, all camping equipment except sleeping bags. Dates: February through November. Length of trip: 17 days. Group size: 5 minimum, 15 maximum. Cost: $1,390. Special requirements: 1st deposit $200; 2nd deposit $400 4 months prior.

Wonder Bird Tours
500 Fifth Avenue
New York, NY 10036
212-840-5961   *Trinidad, West Indies*

In June, an annual two-week Tropical Ecology seminar is held at the ASA Wright Nature Center in Trinidad. With leaders Dr. John Moyle and Ms. Jo Anne Sharpe (a Ph.D. candidate), students examine the diversity, behavior and inter-relationships of plant and animal life in the wet tropics. On your explorations, you will encounter rare tree ferns, and numerous epiphytes including the colorful bromeliads (one species which collects water at its base provides a home to algae, mosquito larvae, and tiny crabs); insectivorous, parasitic, and resurrection plants; insects which mimic lichens, bark twigs, and each other; army and leaf-cutting ant columns; manakin dancing grounds, toucans and bellbirds; and vividly-colored Morpho and Caligo butterflies. There will be a trip to Tobago to explore tide-pool organisms, the coral gardens and multi-hued fish of Buccoo Reef. Throughout the course, the leaders will emphasize the fragility of the tropical ecosystem and the need for habitat conservation of endangered species. Includes: Private bath, three meals daily, transfers, field trips with transportation (including two days in Tobago), boat trips, gratuities to household help, personal feedback from seminar leaders. Dates: July. Length of trip: 15-day seminar, 14 nights. Group size: 20 participants. Cost: $725. Special requirements: Suitable for amateur and professional students of tropical ecology. Deposit of $50.

Wonder Bird Tours
500 Fifth Avenue
New York, NY 10036
212-840-5961   *Trinidad, West Indies*

The annual, two-week seminar for The Study and Photography of Insects held at the ASA Wright Nature Center in Trinidad, takes place in mid-June. Leaders Raymond Mendez and Dr. Betty Faber teach life history of insects; the social behavior of colony insects—army ants, bees, wasps, termites; the preservation and mounting of insects for a study collection; methods of identification; close-up photography of insects using a diopter or macro lens; how to recognize insect habitats; and live insect care. Night walks around the Center's trails will reveal the nocturnal activities of arthropods. Special butterfly-collecting trips to Valencia Gate and St. Andrew's Trace produce an enormous variety—there are 622 species in Trinidad and Tobago. An outing to Caroni Swamp has a breathtaking finale when thousands of Scarlet Ibis and egrets flock into the mangroves to roost for the night. A two-day visit to Tobago highlights trap door spiders, and snorkeling around the Buccoo Reef. Includes: Private bath, three meals daily, transfers, field trips with transportation (including two days in Tobago), boat trips, gratuities to household help, personal feedback from seminar leaders. Dates: Mid-June. Length of trip: 15-day seminar, 14 nights. Group size: 20 participants. Cost: $725. Special requirements: Suitable for amateur and professional students of tropical ecology. Deposit of $50.

Opera •

A night at the opera takes on a special elegance when the performance is by internationally acclaimed stars at one of the world's top opera houses. And it's even more enchanting when you enjoy the best seats in the house, and thoughtful VIP flourishes like a private limousine and a feast of gourmet dining.

Opera tours provide these touches in programs designed for the opera lover's refined palate. The operators are generally aficionados themselves, so they know how to take care of you. They buy blocks of tickets at the start of the season, so they get the best seats for the best performances—operas for which you often couldn't even buy standing room on your own.

Besides taking you to legendary performances and festivals, many programs also include cultural tours of the areas visited. As you attend performances in Italy's renowned opera houses, building up to an evening at La Scala, you can tour the famous museums and churches of Rome, Florence, Venice, Turin and Naples. Or tour the galleries of the Santa Fe and Taos art centers before attending an evening of opera under the stars at the Santa Fe Opera.

Many operators provide deluxe accommodations and gourmet meals—a grand style tour from the curtain call to the encore. Tours are available in various lengths, from overnight trips to longer programs for festivals. But long or short, you can expect great performances, an itinerary tailored to your tastes, and fellow travelers with whom you share a love for the highest art. Bravo!

Dailey-Thorp Travel, Inc.
Park Towers South
315 West 57th Street
New York, N.Y. 10019
212-307-1555
                                                                                    Italy

This program will include the best selection of operatic schedules in Italy during either February or March. Traditionally this is the height of the winter season in Italy and a performance is planned for every night of this ten-day tour. Rome, Florence, Venice, Turin and Naples are possible destinations on this tour which of course will end at La Scala, temple of Italian bel canto. Italy can be especially appealing during the winter when the tourist season is not at its peak. Special emphasis will be placed on the meals on this tour, since the quality of Northern Italian cuisine is second to none. In addition to providing the best available tickets to performances at the famous opera houses the trips feature deluxe accommodations, arts-oriented sightseeing and special events. Dailey-Thorp, Inc., specialists in opera and music festival tours for over ten years, also runs programs in other European countries and throughout North America. Includes: Best available seats at opera performances, hotels, breakfast, some meals. Dates: February and March. Length of trip: 11 days. Group size: 20. Cost: $1,900 (land).

Maupintour Opera Tours
P.O. Box 807
Lawrence, KS 66044
800-255-4266   *Southwest United States*

Enjoy great works under the stars at the outdoor Santa Fe Opera. 1984 marks the twenty-eighth season of this distinguished opera company. Maupintour members attend four performances which might include works by Strauss, Donizetti, and others. During the day, visitors explore many points of interest including the exclusive galleries of the Santa Fe and Taos art centers. Free time is included for travelers to pursue their own special interest. Travel by motor-coach takes tour members through some of the most scenic areas of the Southwest where nature mixes with Indian, Mexican and Spanish influences to create a delightful spectacle of old and new. Over thirty-two years' experience. Includes: Accommodations, most meals, tour manager, tips, taxes, luggage handling, entrance fees, opera tickets, entertainment, and special events. Dates: August. Length of trip: 9 days. Group size: 40. Cost: $1,165. Special requirements: Air fare is additional, $150 reservation deposit.

TOURACO INTERNATIONAL

Touraco International
331 Madison Avenue
New York, NY 10017
212-682-4362
Telex 236294
                                    New York

Grand opera, performed in the grandest style. On-stage at the Metropolitan Opera, great stars such as Dame Joan Sutherland . . . Luciano Pavarotti . . . Mirella Freni . . . Placido Domingo . . . Marilyn Horne . . . Sherrill Milnes . . . Dame Kiri Te Kanawa . . . Jon Vickers . . . Leontyne Price . . . Jose Carreras . . . make history set to the music of the masters. Like the rarest gem, an experience deserving the finest setting. Touraco International offers exclusive programs with guaranteed Orchestra seating for the Metropolitan Opera, choice of first-class or deluxe hotels and—depending on the program—an array of VIP inclusions such as private limousine and gourmet dining. You can choose from convenient one- and two-night weekend programs with customized itineraries, and weekday performance schedules as well. So envelope yourself in the glorious sound . . . thundering emotions . . . sumptuous theater . . . that is operatic art at its most spectacular. Includes: Hotel and local taxes, Lincoln Center tour, one Orchestra opera ticket. Limousine and pre-opera dinner are also options. Dates: Weekends, September through April. Length of trip: 1–2 nights (2 days). Group size: Individuals & groups up to 80. Cost: On request.

Outdoor Skills •
Wilderness Survival •

Outdoor skills courses don't just teach wilderness techniques. They teach the magic of human potential. While you're learning the fine points of rock climbing or wilderness survival, you'll also learn about yourself. You'll find you can do things that you never dreamed possible. You'll draw upon reserves you never thought you had. As you meet challenges without trepidation, you'll discover new fortitude and new confidence. And once you find them, they'll be yours for life.

Where do you find them? You find them in challenge. You find them in a methodical mastery over an indomitable power. You find them by going head to head with the untamed forces of nature. But mostly, you find them in yourself.

Outdoor skills courses teach techniques that allow you to push yourself safely to your limits. They don't advocate rash shows of bravado. You're in control. That's where true self-awareness and strength lie.

Aside from the basic reward, which remains fairly constant, wilderness programs run the gamut. You can build igloos in the Colorado Rockies . . . load a pack mule for mountain expeditions in Idaho . . . master water craft skills and become a professional river guide . . . or confront the wilderness alone and empty-handed on a three-day survival mission.

For most courses, you do not need any previous experience. You're there to learn, not to show off what you know. All you need is a willing spirit and good enough physical health to meet the challenges of the course. The tour operator should suggest any health requirements or recommendations.

Training generally starts from ground zero. You'll learn all the basics—the right way. Most disciplines involve several related skills. If you're into rock climbing, you can expect a healthy dose of backpacking, camping, and rope handling training. Between runs on the white water rapids, river adventurers learn the secrets of boat repair, life saving, and "reading" a river.

The tour operator will supply virtually all of the equipment you'll need. The courses are run under strict control conditions, so the instructors make sure that all participants have quality gear well suited to its task. You may need a sleeping bag, and you'll definitely want sturdy outdoor clothing and boots. The operator will tell you what's appropriate.

Because of the risks involved in any rigorous outdoor activity, tour operators are scrupulous in keeping group sizes small enough to allow complete supervision. Check the instructor-to-student ratio and the qualifications of the instructors.

From there, you're ready to go. If you're interested, there are even special programs geared for professionals, women, and teachers. In any outdoor skills course, the work is hard. But it is worth the effort to discover just how much you can achieve.

SECTIONS OF RELATED INTEREST

See also chapters for specific activity; i.e. backpacking, camping, hiking, river rafting.

All-Outdoors Adventure Trips
2151 San Miguel Drive
Walnut Creek, CA 94596 *California*

All-Outdoors River Guide School is invaluable for people who want to become professional river guides. Participants learn about river characteristics, equipment and safety considerations. Oar raft, paddle raft and kayaking skills are covered. Off-river time is spent in related learning activities such as raft repair, boat rigging, rescue and safety procedures. Additional practice time during the season is available to those completing the River Guide School. A portion of the school fee is subsidized by All-Outdoors for those who become competent to qualify as an All-Outdoor guide. Operated under United States Government permits. Includes: All rafting equipment, food, local transportation and instruction. Dates: April and August. Length: 6 days. Group size: 10–18. Cost: $360. Special requirements: Wet suit for the spring season (rental available), sleeping bag (rental available), $60 deposit. CPR and first-aid training is recommended.

Clearwater Outfitters
P.O. Box 163-F
Pierce, ID 83546
208-476-5971 *Idaho*

Clearwater Outfitter's Guide and Packer Training Program is designed for the serious individual who wants to gain professional level experience in back-country guiding and packing. Courses are individualized to allow hands-on experience in practical skills such as wrapping and loading of cargo on pack mules, livestock management, guide skills, woodsmanship and camp craft. There is a four student maximum to further assure each participant's proficiency by the end of the program. The course starts at Clearwater Outfitter's Idaho ranch and moves to field work and study in remote mountain camps and on pack trips. The work is hard and challenging, but there is also time for relaxation, riding, fishing and exploring. Successful completion of the program qualifies participants to become licensed guides. Clearwater Outfitters offers job placement assistance. Leo Crane, operator of Clearwater Outfitters, has twenty years of professional experience. Includes: Room and board, all supplies and equipment except personal gear and sleeping bags. Dates: July through September. Length of trip: 8 weeks. Group size: 4 maximum. Cost: $2,000. Special requirements: Minimum age of 18. Previous hunting and livestock experience is helpful.

Colorado Outward Bound School
945 Pennsylvania
Denver, CO 80203
303-837-0880 *Colorado, Utah*

Experience personal growth through adventure. Outward Bound offers the unique opportunity to push your limits while learning and enjoying back-country activities like mountaineering, backpacking, ski-mountaineering, and whitewater rafting. Learn to live and travel safely in the wilderness, gain experience in everything from packing a backpack to decision-making. Summer mountaineering courses are held in some of Colorado's most beautiful ranges, surrounded by rugged peaks, alpine tundra, subalpine meadows, clear lakes, forests and streams. Spring and fall backpacking and rock climbing are taught in the canyonlands of Utah and feature route finding, back-country first aid, geology, anthropology, and environmental awareness. Winter in the Rockies is the setting for the most physically demanding course of back-country skiing, camping, igloo building, avalanche training and rock and ice climbing. Whitewater rafting trips through remote Western canyons and fast-moving rivers combine camping, hiking, leadership and teamwork with the excitement of river running. Instructors are highly skilled and technically experienced. Special programs are also available for business people, teachers and women. Includes: Technical gear, meals, and instructions. Dates: All year. Length of trip: 5–23 days. Group size: Variable. Cost: $250–$975. Special requirements: Minimum age is 16½; physical exam is necessary.

East/West Wilderness Expeditions
P.O. Box 611C
Bethel, ME 04217
207-875-5255   *Maine*

East/West's expeditions teach wilderness skills and environmental awareness, emphasizing low impact, "no-trace" camping. Physical and philosophical growth is achieved through the day-to-day sharing of decisions, responsibilities and good times. Backpacking expeditions take place in the mountains of western Maine, in or near the White Mountain National Forest. The woods are lush green from spring through fall and full of moose, deer, bear and beaver. Picturesque waterfalls and crystal-clear lakes invite swimmers for refreshing dips. Canoe trips run through the Allagash Wilderness Waterway in Maine's North Woods, with special attention paid to wildlife. No previous experience is necessary for either expedition. Special programs are offered for senior citizens, women or men only, families' with younger children and for businesspeople. Bob Elliot, leader of East/West, holds degrees in Ecology, Geology and Education, is a Registered Maine Guide, and has instructor certification with the National Outdoor Leadership School (NOLS). Includes: Food, group equipment, and canoes. Dates: All year. Length of trip: 8–14 days. Group size: 8–10. Cost: $380–$650. Special requirements: Personal clothing and gear, $100 deposit with application.

Outward Bound
384 Field Point Road
Greenwich, CT 06830
203-661-0797
800-243-8520   *United States*

Outward Bound is the oldest and largest adventure education organization in the United States. The courses cover backpacking, rafting, mountaineering, sailing, skiing, cycling and more! Each experience is physically and spiritually challenging, but no special skills are required; Outward Bound teaches everything from knot tying to rappelling. Emphasis is on personal growth, self-reliance, and team work as well as basic outdoor skills. There are five schools—in Colorado, Minnesota, North Carolina, Hurricane Island, Maine and the Pacific Northwest—offering classes in over a dozen states. Separate courses are offered for juniors (14–16 years), women over 30, executives and other special interest groups. Academic credit and financial aid are available. Twenty-first year in the United States. Includes: All equipment and supplies (except footwear and personal clothing) and transportation to and from course sites. Dates: All year. Length of trip: 5–26 days. Group size: 8–12. Cost: $625–$1,000. Special requirements: $25 application fee.

Wilderness Odyssey
P.O. Box 2051
Traverse City, MI 49685
606-275-6424

Michigan

Wilderness Odyssey offers survival and backpacking courses closely patterned on the training received by United States Air Force flight personnel. This includes the skills and knowledge essential to back-country backpacking, survival and rescue for several geographic locations and climatic conditions: arctic, sub-arctic, temperate, shore, desert, tropic, and ocean. The primary goal is to build confidence through knowledge. High quality education is condensed into a six-day course which teaches, demonstrates and evaluates survival skills. The Odyssey begins at Ranch Rudolf, a rustic resort ten miles south of Traverse City, Michigan. The field phase of training is received while hiking and camping in adjoining Fife Lake Forest. All Wilderness Odyssey instructors are former U.S.A.F. survival instructors. Includes: Food, group equipment, and shelter materials. Dates: All year. Length: 6 days. Group size: 12. Cost: $250. Special requirements: Personal gear, $50 deposit.

Photography •

Some people take photographs on vacation. Others go on vacation to take photographs.

Looking through the viewfinder, do you feel genuine excitement when a schooner sails into frame, spinnaker billowing gracefully into the rosy sunset? As you wander the streets of a distant city, do you reach for your camera upon encountering a colorful farmers' market or folk dancers or a lively cafe?

Many of the adventures featured in this book offer superb photographic opportunities—from wildlife safaris to hot air balloon expeditions and visits to stately homes. But the programs which follow are specially geared to camera buffs, not only placing photographers in beautiful surroundings, but also teaching them how to take better pictures.

Among the ways that these programs are designed for photographers:

—Guide/Instructor: On these trips, you will usually be accompanied by an experienced photographer who will provide helpful pointers—such as the best *f*-stop for shooting a sunrise or horse race . . . techniques for photographing a bear fishing for salmon, a Balinese dancer, or Navajo child in Monument Valley.

—Unusual itineraries: You'll not only see the tourist sights, but journey off-the-beaten path to quaint villages and remote regions that embody the essence of an area . . . and make for great photographs.

—Time of day/time of season: The tour operators generally schedule departure dates to coincide with the most stunning season displays—from fall foliage to folk festivals. In addition, they'll plan sightseeing stops to take advantage of various lighting conditions—the sun breaking through wispy morning mists, the lengthening shadows and golden colors of late afternoon.

—Pacing: The amount of time spent at various places is geared to the needs of photographers, to allow plenty of time to compose shots and experiment with different angles.

—Special photo sessions: Many of the tour operators listed here also arrange special shoots for their tour members. Some also retain models in native costume to pose at various famous sites.

Whatever type of vacation you're planning, here are some useful tips for traveling photographers:

1. If you'll be using a new camera on your trip, shoot about two to four rolls of film at home and have them developed before you go. This will help you get used to how this particular camera/light meter/lens works.

2. Be sure to buy plenty of film in advance. It's almost always cheaper and easier to purchase it at home. Also bring along extra camera batteries on your trip. In certain areas it could be difficult to find the brand you need.

3. About x-rays: X-rays used at airport security checkpoints *can* damage film, according to a study conducted by Kodak. And the effects of x-rays on photographic films are culumative: if you're traveling through several airports, your luggage will be screened each time, and the effects on film worsen. Color film is especially sensitive, and the new high-speed ASA 1,000 films are extremely susceptible to damage.

Photographers can request that airport security personnel hand-inspect their camera and film; although the staff will usually comply, they are not required to do so. You can also buy a lead-lined pouch to protect film against the x-rays.

Avoid packing film in luggage you will check in. The x-rays or fluoroscope used to probe this luggage can fog both unexposed and unprocessed film, making it useless. A lead pouch does not safeguard film effectively against these devices.

4. Consider purchasing an inexpensive filter to protect your camera lens. Ultraviolet or skylight filters are good choices, not only helping safeguard the lens, but also enhancing photos without changing them drastically.

5. Prepare in advance for the conditions under which you'll be shooting. If you could get pretty wet (like on a rafting or canoeing trip), you might want to carry your camera and film in a watertight case. For travel in humid areas like the tropics, perhaps keep a small packet of desiccant in the case. In a very dusty or sandy area (on an African safari, for example), it's a good idea to keep your camera in plastic bag when not in use.

6. Bring along a soft brush for dusting off your lens, and use lens cleaning liquid and special paper to remove dirt and smudges from lens and filters.

7. If you're traveling abroad, register your camera with United States Customs at the airport to avoid hassles when you re-enter the country. Be sure to allow plenty of time: airports have a habit of tucking away Customs in the furthest corner from your flight's departure gate.

Alaska Wildlife Photography
P.O. Box 1557
Homer, AK 99603   *Alaska*

Come photograph the magnificent sights of Alaska's Kachemak region ... from the huge glaciers to the active volcanos ... the schools of killer whales or the McNeil River Brown Bear Sanctuary—world-renowned for its large concentration of the huge Alaskan brown bear. Here, it's not uncommon to view twenty bears at a time, fishing for salmon, sunbathing and frolicking in the icy waters. Your hosts Kevin and Lucinda Sidlinger offer a variety of Alaskan experiences—hiking, non-technical mountain climbing, photography, fishing, or plain old-fashioned relaxing. Bird-watchers can focus on the many birds flying over-head ... the fox sparrow, black-legged kittiwake, horned puffin and the cormorant. You can also see and savor Alaska on a llama trek. Includes: Tents, sleeping bags and pads, meals, guide service, llamas, canoes. May through September. Length: Minimum of 3 days. Group size: 8 people. Cost: $125 per day per person. Special requirements: Reasonable good health; 50% deposit of total price to confirm reservation; balance due 60 days in advance.

Canyonland Tours
P.O. Box 460, Dept. STI
Flagstaff, AZ 86002
602-774-7343
800-841-7317
Telex 172-029 SPX SRFL   *Western United States*

Travel in specially-equipped vans with a professional photographer through remote regions of the Southwest. These photo workshops take you into the heart of this wild, spectacular land of canyons, arches, Indian ruins, slickrock and high mountain meadows. One itinerary travels through the Hopi and Navajo Indian Reservations. You photograph in such world-famous sites as Canyon de Chelly and Monument Valley. Another workshop tours the magnificent wonderlands of Arches and Canyonlands National Parks. The workshops will emphasize use of the 35-mm camera, and will concentrate on landscape and close-up nature work. Instructors will offer individual help to all, whether beginner or advanced student. Depending on the needs of each group, a variety of basics will be covered. Patrick and Susan Conley, owners-operators, each have over twelve years' experience in the outfitting and guiding business in the Southwest. Their company, Canyonland Tours, was established in 1965. Includes: Direct trip transportation; meals while en route; professional photographic instruction; driver-guide service; Park entry fees; camp equipment; sleeping bag, foam pad, ground cloth, tent (double occupancy). Dates: April through October. Length of trip: 7 days, 6 nights. Group size: 20 guests maximum. Cost: $695 per person. Special requirements: $100 per person deposit.

Corporate Travel and Tours
21335 Mary Lynn Drive
Waukesha, WI 53186
414-784-8430   *India, Nepal*

Tigers, leopards, rhinos and exotic birds—photograph them all in the former hunting grounds of the Maharajahs. Corporate Travel features photo safaris to the lush wildlife sanctuaries of India and Nepal. Capture the splendid Bengal tiger on film—from elephant back, riding a well-trained pachyderm who will slowly amble through the jungle, cleaning foliage out of the way. Tours also include visits to traditional Indian cultural and historic sites—old and new Delhi, Agra's famed Taj Mahal, and breathtaking Tiger Tops in Kathmandu, Nepal. Various safaris also visit the Keoladeo Ghana Bird Sanctuary in Bhartapur, the Kanha and Bandogarh big game sanctuaries, the "Pink City" of Jaipur, and the erotic Khajuraho Temples in Madhya Pradesh. Accommodations in the cities are in luxurious 5-star hotels; in the game reserves, at the ex-hunting lodges of former maharajahs. Includes: Round-trip air fare from New York, all in-country flights and land transportation, guides, accommodations, all meals, baggage handling, and tips. Dates: November through February. Length of trip: 18 days (post-tour options available). Group size: Maximum 20. Cost: $3,870. Special requirements: Deposits.

Exploration Holidays and Cruises
1500 Metropolitan Park Building
Seattle, WA 98101
800-426-0600
206-624-8551 in WA & Canada
Telex 32 96 36   *Alaska*

"The Great Photo Safari" shows photographers and wildlife enthusiasts the full spectrum of Alaska's Aleut, Eskimo and Indian cultures plus its varied wildlife and dramatic geographic features. Destinations include the bird and fur seal rookeries of the Pribilofs; Anchorage and its magnificent surroundings; the Eskimo Village of Kotzebue across the Arctic Circle; the "Land of Katmai," one of Alaska's most spectacular wilderness areas; Denali National Park to view massive Mt. McKinley; Fairbanks for a sternwheel riverboat cruise and a visit to the Trans-Alaska Pipeline; Juneau with a visit to the Mendenhall Glacier; and Glacier Bay National Park. Includes: Round-trip Seattle air fare, airport transfers at tour destinations, sightseeing and hotel accommodations. Meals not included. Dates: June through August. Length of trip: 16 days, 15 nights. Group size: Contact for information. Cost: $3,249.

International Photographic Tours
2230 North University Parkway, Building 7B
Provo, UT 84604
801-373-8747
800-453-1476   *Eastern United States,*
Telex 388 378 RMH PRVO   *Canada*

A picturesque exploration of Nova Scotia's rugged Atlantic coastline, quaint maritime seaports, and spectacular scenic countryside is combined with a glorious experience in the colorful autumn forests of New Hampshire, where little white chapels and covered bridges dot the gentle New England landscape. Then journey through the pages of colonial American history to Boston. Trip leaders/photography instructors consist of internationally recognized photographers and university photo-instructors. The company has ten years' worldwide tour operation experience. Includes: Land and sea transportation, accommodations in first or superior tourist class hotels, some meals, sightseeing excursions, tour director and guide services, photographic consultation and instruction. Dates: September and October (fall foliage). Length of trip: 13 days. Group size: 10–15. Cost: $875.

International Photographic Tours
2230 North University Parkway, Building 7B
Provo, UT 84604
801-373-8747
800-453-1476
Telex 388 378 RMH PRVO   *Australia*

Experience the undersea wonderland of the Great Barrier Reef; the blazing sunrise colors of Ayer's Rock, the world's largest monolith; Queensland's sun-drenched gold coast; Canberra, Australia's graceful capital; the magnificent museums and gardens of Melbourne; Victoria's spectacular off-shore rock formations; the unsurpassed scenic beauty of Tasmania's lakes and mountains; and the sculpted beaches, magnificent harbor and world-famous opera house of Sydney. Trip leaders/photograph instructors consist of internationally recognized photographers and university photo-instructors. The company has ten years' worldwide tour operation experience. Includes: Land and sea transportation, accommodations in first or superior tourist class hotels, some meals, sightseeing excursions, tour director and guide services, photographic consultation and instruction. Dates: October through December. Length of trip: 18 days. Group size: 10–15. Cost: $1,290 each.

International Photographic Tours
2230 North University Parkway, Building 7B
Provo, UT 84604
801-373-8747
800-453-1476
Telex 388 378 RMH PRVO   *Greece*

A four-day luxury cruise of the legendary Greek Islands and Turkey is combined with Athens and a four-day tour of the highlights of classical Greece. Explore and photograph the ancient ruins of Athens' Golden Age, quaint villages and countryside, and temples of the ancient Greeks' mythical gods. At sea in the Aegean, your ports of call include: Santorini, the "Black pearl of the Aegean"; Crete, center of the five-thousand-year-old Minoan civilization; Rhodes, with its walled harbor and amazing Temple of Athena; Biblical Patmos and Ephesus; and Mykonos, a wealthy resort island of white-washed villages and sun-drenched beaches. Trip leaders/photography instructors consist of internationally recognized photographers and university photo-instructors. The company has ten years' worldwide tour operation experience. Includes: Land and sea transportation, accommodations in first or superior tourist class hotels, some meals, sightseeing excursions, tour director and guide services, photographic consultation and instruction. Dates: September. Length of trip: 14 days. Group size: 10–15. Cost: $890.

International Photographic Tours
2230 North University Parkway, Building 7B
Provo, UT 84604
801-373-8747
800-453-1476
Telex 388 378 RMH PRVO   *New Zealand*

New Zealand is a land of incomparable scenic beauty, an island country of contrasts and spectacular scenery. From Auckland, the tour highlights include: Northland's picturesque

Bay of Islands, the amazing glow worm caves of Waitomo, Rotorura's thermal wonders, the active volcanoes Ruapehu and Ngauruhoe, and historic Wellington. Then experience the beautiful South Island, with its sparkling lakes, sheep-covered lush green countryside, dramatic glaciers, breathtaking fjords, and the majestic Southern Alps. Trip leaders/photograph instructors consist of internationally recognized photographers and university photo-instructors. The company has ten years' worldwide tour operation experience. Includes: Land and sea transportation, accommodations in first or superior tourist class hotels, some meals, sightseeing excursions, tour director and guide services, photographic consultation and instruction. Dates: October through December. Length of trip: 18 days. Group size: 10–15. Cost: $1,290.

International Photographic Tours
2230 North University Parkway, Building 7B
Provo, UT 84604
801-373-8747
800-453-1476
Telex 388 378 RMH PRVO   *Alaska*

Experience America's last frontier. From Vancouver you'll enjoy a seven-day luxury cruise through the famed Inside Passage. Then explore Alaska's heartland at your own pace in a private motorhome. Highlights include: McKinley/Denali National Park, Kenai peninsula, Homer, Fairbanks, Anchorage, Ketchikan, Juneau, Skagway, Columbia Glacier, and the fjords, glaciers and wildlife of the Inside Passage. Trip leaders/photography instructurs consist of internationally recognized photographers and university photo-instructors. The company has ten years' worldwide tour operation experience. Includes: Land and sea transportation, accommodations in first or superior tourist class hotels, some meals, sightseeing excursions, tour director and guide services, photographic consultation and instruction. Dates: July. Length of trip: 15 days. Group size: 10–15. Cost: $1,890.

Lyon Travel Service
1031 Ardmore Avenue
Oakland, CA 94610
415-465-8955   *Eastern United States*

Lyon Travel's three week tour of Maine, New Hampshire and Vermont is planned around the special needs of photographers. You will travel along the Maine Coast to Acadia National Park, then swing west and south, with stops at photographic sites like Motif #1 and the Jenne Farm. You'll also cover old mills, church steeples, and tidy farms—all enhanced by the reds and yellows of the autumn foliage season. You'll stop and go as you please to places such as Salem, Waterbury, Stowe, Plymouth and other historical and architectural centers. Lyon Travel Service has been leading photography tours since 1975. Includes: All meals, accommodation in inns and motels, ground transportation and admission fees. Dates: October. Length of trip: 21 days. Group size: 6. Cost: $2,200. Special requirements: $250 deposit.

Thru the Lens Tours, Inc.
5855 Green Valley Circle
Culver City, CA 90230
213-645-8480
800-521-LENS toll free
Telex 910 340 7063 LENSTOUR LSA   *Peru*

Take your photographic equipment to the Land of the Incas, where many natives still adhere to ancient folkways and dress, all set against a majestic mountain backdrop. From novice to advanced, all photographers will find a special thrill and challenge in capturing the sights of the "Indian countries" of South America . . . from the picturesque city of Quito, Ecuador to the thatch-roofed villages and snow-capped volcanoes encountered along the route to Ibarra . . . from Cuzco, a Peruvian city of cobblestoned streets nestled in the Andes, to Machu Pic-chu, the fabulous "Lost City" of the Incas. Small groups and excellent photographic leadership provide an informal and congenial atmosphere for gaining an insight into the culture and history of the region. Over thirty years' experience operating photographic tours. Includes: Hotels, most meals, land transportation, sightseeing, baggage handling, tour manager, photographic instruction. Dates: May. Length: 3 weeks. Group size: 20 people maximum. Cost: $3,295 (land). Special requirements: $250 deposit.

Thru the Lens Tours, Inc.
5855 Green Valley Circle
Culver City, CA 90230
213-645-8480
800-521-LENS toll free
Telex 910 340 7063 LENSTOUR LSA   *Pakistan*

Capture on film the spectacular scenic beauty of the Himalayas and many other spectacular shots—Chitral, an isolated mountain valley with hot springs and an unparalleled view of Tirich Mir; the remote mountain station of Skardu, base for all major climbing expeditions in the area including K-2, the second highest mountain in the world; and the beautiful valley of Shigar, with its picturesque people, lush orchards and mighty snow-capped mountains. Both beginners and advanced photographers are welcome; instruction is designed to enhance the enjoyment of all skill levels. Over thirty years' experience operating photographic tours. Includes: Hotels, all meals, land transportation, sightseeing, tour manager, photographic instruction. Dates: September. Length: 3 weeks. Group size: 17 maximum. Cost: $3,645 (land). Special requirements: $250 deposit.

Thru the Lens Tours, Inc.
5855 Green Valley Circle
Culver City, CA 90230
213-645-8480
800-521-LENS toll free
Telex 910 340 7063 LENSTOUR LSA   *Japan*

The backroads of Japan offer unlimited photographic opportunities—the colorful lantern parade of the Oeshiki Festival; the indigo waters of Lake Towada; spectacular volcanic highlands of Hachimantai, famed for its many boiling mud-pots; grottoed cliffs and fjordlike bays with dazzling white quartz beaches; old-fashioned fishing villages; and bigger-than-life religious shrines. Both beginners and advanced photographers are welcome; instruction is designed to enhance the enjoyment of all skill levels. Over thirty years' experience operating photographic tours. Includes: Hotels, all meals throughout tour, surface transportation, sightseeing, tour manager, photographic instruction. Dates: October. Length: 4 weeks. Group size: 17 maximum. Cost: $5,495.

Thru the Lens Tours, Inc.
5855 Green Valley Circle
Culver City, CA 90230
213-645-8480
800-521-LENS toll free
Telex 910 340 7063 LENSTOUR LSA   *The Orient*

From the boisterous profusion of Singapore's open-air markets to the subtle symbolism of an ancient Balinese dance . . . from the sophistication of gentle Bangkok to the Burmese hill country where fishermen row their dugouts with their legs . . . your Bali-to-Burma adventure will be a never-ending cascade of picture-taking delight. The exciting capital cities of Indonesia, Burma and Thailand are balanced by restful excursions into cool green mountains and idyllic island villages where skilled artists and craftsmen such as Thailand's deft laquerware painters, Burma's nimble-fingered cigar rollers, and Java's patient batik workers live. Both beginners and advanced photographers are welcome; instruction is designed to enhance the enjoyment of all skill levels. Over thirty years' experience operating photographic tours. Includes: Hotels, most meals, land transportation, sightseeing, baggage handling, tips and taxes, tour manager, photographic instruction. Dates: November. Length: 4 weeks. Group size: 20 people maximum. Cost: $4,595. Special requirements: $250 deposit.

Thru the Lens Tours, Inc.
5855 Green Valley Circle
Culver City, CA 90230
213-645-8480
800-521-LENS toll free   *Western*
Telex 910 340 7063 LENSTOUR LSA   *United States*

Some people bring back memories from a vacation—you can bring the whole vacation home with your magnificent photographs of all the wondrous sights you've seen. Capture forever the vistas of Canyonlands National Park . . . unique sandstone formations in Arches National Park . . . Monument Valley with its gigantic buttes and spires, gnarled desert vegetation and colorful Navajo population . . . the prehistoric cliff dwellings at Betatakin . . . prehistoric ruins of Navajo life . . . a mining town where fortunes were made and lost overnight . . . and the awesome Black Canyon of the Gunnison. Both beginners and advanced photographers are welcome; instruction is designed to enhance the enjoyment of all skill levels. Over thirty years' experience operating photographic tours. Includes: Hotels, some meals, surface transportation, sightseeing, tour manager and photographic instruction. Dates: September. Length: 2 weeks. Group size: 20 people maximum. Cost: $,1975 (land). Special requirements: $250 deposit.

Wonder Bird Tours
500 Fifth Avenue
New York, NY 10036
212-840-5961   *Trinidad, West Indies*

Each August, Asa Wright Nature Center in Trinidad holds a two-week Nature Photography seminar. Leaders Herman Kitchen and Paul Jeheber will instruct you on getting wildlife to cooperate; developing picture stories; editing slide shows and motion picture films; and making prize-winning photographs. Besides working around the Nature Center, which is richly populated with wildlife—brilliantly colored flowers, insects, butterflies, and birds—you are taken on exciting field trips. At the Caroni Swamp see thousands of Scarlet Ibis on their evening flight to roost in the mangroves. An overnight trip to Tobago provides the chance to go snorkeling and photographing around the Buccoo Reef. At the Grafton Estate, dozens of blue-crowned motmots and rufous-vented chachalacas are easy camera targets as they feed and preen close by. Includes: Private bath, three mails daily, transfers, field trips with transportation (including two days in Tobago), boat trips, gratuities to household help, personal feedback from seminar leaders. Dates: August. Length of trip: 15-day seminar, 14 nights. Group size: 20 participants. Cost: $725. Special requirements: Suitable for amateur and professional students of tropical ecology. Deposit of $50.

Railway Trips •

Legends of dusky-eyed ladies swathed in furs aboard the *Orient Express* . . . of spies and crown princes fleeing incognito across Manchuria . . . border crossings . . . whistle stops . . . the tinkling of crystal in the dining car.

Going places? If you want to reach your destination as quickly as possible when you travel, by all means hop a plane. But if you believe that getting there is part of the adventure, if words like Pullman or *wagon-lits* set your imagination racing until you can almost feel the side-swaying rhythm of the cars, hear the plaintive whistle slicing through the velvet night . . . then a vacation by rail is for you.

As Paul Theroux wrote in *The Great Railway Bazaar*, trains are about travel, not just transportation. And whether you want to experience the romance and intrigue of the great trains—or simply see where you're going between stops—you have a wide variety of train vacations from which to choose.

Relive the style and splendor of the *Orient Express* as you steam across Europe aboard the original sleeper and dining carriages—all painstakingly restored to their former elegance. Or travel through Russia and Siberia with the *Trans-Siberian Express*, meeting the local people and sampling local cuisine along the way. Right here at home, you can even travel in luxury from coast to coast in your own private sleeping car. Other railway jaunts can feature mountain scenery in Mexico or stately homes in England. Along the way, most railway trips schedule stops featuring sightseeing excursions, cultural events, sightseeing, local cuisine . . . maybe even a visit to the Great Wall of China. So all aboard!

Continental Rail Tours
P. O. Box CR
Saltillo, PA 17253
814-448-3946
Telex 845382 EITC SLTL   *United States*

Travel in luxury from coast to coast in your own private sleeping car. Relive the days of gracious travel, when the trip across the American continent was an adventure to be savored. Trips include overnight stops en route at selected hotels in New Orleans, Chicago, Denver, Reno (dependent on route used), transfers to and from hotels by limousine, and all meals. Bands and pianist provide entertainment aboard the trains. Each day fresh local food is transformed into regional gourmet specialties for personal service to passengers in the elegant surroundings of the diner. These cars are also available for private charter within the United States. Members of American Society of Travel Agents. Includes: All meals, train travel, sleepers, transfers, hotels, limos, entertainment en route. Dates: Approximately every two weeks from New York to Los Angeles. Length of trip: 9 days, 8 nights. Group size: 20–50 (maximum). Cost: $3,075–$3,735. Special requirements: Deposit $600 per person payable on reservation. For reservations call 800-458-3606.

**EXPRESS
international
incorporated**

Express International Inc.
P.O. Box A, Main Street
Saltillo, PA 17253
814-448-3946
800-458-3606
Telex 845382   *Worldwide*

The Central Kingdom Express is a 9,331 mile train journey from London to Hong Kong, the result of four years of planning. In the 1920's and '30's the overland route was the main link between London and Hong Kong. Today travelers can recapture this spirit of travel and sense of adventure as they cross the continents of Europe and Asia by train, passing through ten different countries. The tour stops over in Paris, Berlin, Warsaw, Moscow, Irkutsk, Ulan Bator (Outer Mongolia), Datong, Peking, Xian, Luoyang, Nanking, Shanghai, Canton and Hong Kong. On this journey, you'll encounter many contrasts . . . sometimes the unexpected. Tour is also available in an East to West direction "land only" (Hong Kong to London). Tour in operation since 1979. Includes: International airfare; full board (twin sharing basis) in first class or best available hotels; all transportation; comprehensive sightseeing program in each city visited; visas; airport taxes; tour escort throughout and local guides in each city. Dates: Weekly, April through October. Length of trip: 45 days. Group size: 24–28. Cost: $6,100. Special requirements: Passengers over the age of 65 years are required to send a medical certificate with their reservation as the tour is physically demanding.

Express International, Inc.
P.O. Box A
Saltillo, PA 17253
814-448-3946
Telex 845382   *Europe*

The "Nostalgic Orient Express" is composed of cars from the 1920's—the finest era in rail travel. These cars were among the most luxurious and had the largest compartments of any built, and featured interiors by Lalique and Prou. Many of the cars were put into service originally on trains which are world famous, such as "Train Bleu," "Rheingold," and "Orient Express." The cars are now available privately through Express International, Inc., and they are making several public trips in the coming year. There will be a Zurich to Istanbul and return trip lasting eight days, and several other trips of differing durations. On the overnight trips the passengers will enjoy the comforts of the luxurious sleeper cars, and will dine in splendor in the "Sud Express" dining car. A bar car will supply you with an aperitif before meals, and a nightcap before retiring. Includes: All train, meals, sightseeing, sleeping berths. Dates: Various. Length of trip: 4–18 days. Group size: 50–100. Cost: $2,500 and up. Special requirements: Deposit $250. Formal dress for dinners en route.

ITG International Travel Groups, Inc.
175 Fifth Avenue
New York, NY 10010
212-475-7773
Telex 238763   *Worldwide*

ITG offers a variety of programs journeying overland from London to Hong Kong. The twenty-three-day, "Red Arrow Express" makes stopovers in Moscow, Irkutsk, Ulan Bator (Mongolia), Peking and Canton, with guided sightseeing. For people who want to capture the excitement of traveling overland from London to Hong Kong, but only have a limited amount of time, the twenty-three-day "Tian an Men Express" uses a combination of air and rail travel. Then there's the ultimate rail trip—the forty-five-day "Central Kingdom

Express"—making its way exclusively by train from London to Hong Kong. Includes: All meals, all transportation, all air, visas, etc. Dates: Year-round. Length of trip: 23–45 days. Group size: 15–25. Cost: $3,900–$6,650.

Russian Travel Bureau, Inc.
20 East 46th Street
New York, NY 10017
800-847-1800   *Russia*

Cross Russia aboard the Trans-Siberian Express. Completed in 1916, the railroad follows the old trading roads to Asia for silk, cotton, spices and teas. You'll spend four and a half days traveling the portion from Moscow to Irkutsk, passing through wheatlands, steppes and the Siberian tundra. Major stops include Kirov, Sverdlovsk, Omsk and Novosibirsk. The program also tours Moscow and the Kremlin; Tashkent; Samarkand and Leningrad, including the Hermitage Museum and Petrodvorets summer palace. Established in 1959. Includes: All meals, Russian-speaking American tour director, sightseeing, three theater events, farewell champagne dinner, boat excursion to Lake Baikal, flight bag and Russian primer book. Dates: Monthly, April through October. Length of trip: 18 days. Group size: 20. Cost: $1,950. Special requirements: $200 deposit per person.

Sanborn Tours, Inc.
P.O. Box 2081
Austin, TX 78768
512-476-7424   *Mexico*

Awesome mountains towering above valleys full of mangos, bamboo and orchids . . . trackless wilderness where mountain lions hunt deer . . .cool winds whispering through pine forests—this is Mexico's majestic Copper Canyon, a system of gorges deeper and longer than the Grand Canyon. Starting in Chihuahua, the Chihuahua Pacific Railway winds its way through the Sierra Madres to Los Mochis, passing jungle rivers, deep gorges, white waterfalls and vivid blossoms. Travelers are accompanied by an experienced professional escort who relates local history and folklore and also handles all travel details. Accommodations range from air-conditioned hotels in the cities to rugged, rustic lodges in the Canyon. Tour itinerary can combine Copper Canyon with Mazatlan or Baja California. Over thirty years' experience; over twenty years' experience operating Copper Canyon tours. Includes: Tour escort, hotel accommodations, six meals, transfers and transportation, sightseeing, hotel, and meal taxes, gratuities, luggage handling. Dates: Year-round Sunday departures. Length of trip: 5 or 8 days. Group size: Up to 34. Cost: $245–$397. Special requirements: $50 deposit upon booking; all booking is made through travel agents. Trip is rugged, not for mobility impaired or for anyone with severe heart or respiratory conditions.

Venice Simplon Orient-Express, Inc.
1 World Trade Center, Suite 2847
New York, NY 10048
212-661-4540 (in N.Y.)
800-223-1588 (nationwide)   *Europe*

All aboard! Take a ride on the train of kings—The Orient Express, an opulent train whose former passengers included Leopold II of Belgium; Charles, Emperor of Austria-Hungary;

and Edward, Prince of Wales (later King VIII) and his lady love Mrs. Simpson. Surround yourself in the luxury of Lalique crystal and mahogany as the 1920's meet the 1980's for a most elegant journey. Go from London to Venice or return, savoring the lights and sounds of Paris, Milan and the beautiful European countryside while you are traveling on the ultimate train of elegance and romance. You can join the Orient Express for all or part of her journey. Includes: Rail and ferry travel, as specified on the train ticket; plus the services of a company representative or local office in London, Paris, Milan, and Venice. Meals included vary according to which portion of trip you take. Dates: Year-round. Length: 24 hours (complete trip). Cost: $85–$595 one way. Special requirements: $50 deposit to secure reservation. Certain baggage allowances apply.

Venice Simplon Orient-Express, Inc.
1 World Trade Center, Suite 2847
New York, NY 10048
212-661-4540 (in N.Y.)
800-223-1588 (nationwide)   *Great Britain*

Embark on a very special travel experience . . .take a train that returns you to the age of style and luxury while it takes you to some of the most exciting historical places in England. Relax aboard original Pullman carriages paneled in rosewood and mahogany, enjoying lunch or tea. Let the train take you to tiny, moated thirteenth-century Hever Castle, childhood home of ill-fated Anne Boleyn, second wife of Henry VIII. Or visit Leeds Castle, England's foremost medieval castle, where you can see rare black swans and a fine private art collection with works by Toulouse-Lautrec and Degas. Or travel on the train to Beaulieu, a magnificent thirteenth-century abbey. Also at Beaulieu is the National Motor Museum, where over two hundred vintage motor cars can be found. Includes: Inclusive train and executive coach travel, lunch, tea and guided tour. Dates: April through November. Length of trip: 5 hours. Cost: Leeds Castle, $125, Hever Castle, $125, Beaulieu, $165. Special requirements: Full payment required within 7 days of departure.

Voyages Jules Verne, Inc.
516 Fifth Avenue
New York, NY 10036
212-719-4780
800-223-5336
Telex 225976   *Worldwide*

Peter the Great's Leningrad . . . the Central Asian kingdom of Tamberlaine . . . Genghis Khan's domains . . . and the Peking of the Ming emperors . . . see them all on this sweeping journey from London to Hong Kong. Along this "Golden Road to Far Cathay," you'll learn about the distinctive Russian, Mongolian and Chinese cultures of Central Asia. Besides traveling by air, you'll go by rail through the vast Siberian taiga, Gobi desert of Mongolia and plains of Northern China. Then cruise by riverboat down the swirling Yangtse River. In operation for four years; associate member of American Society of Travel Agents; use Association of British Travel Agents tours operators. Includes: Air transportation (based on around the world fare), meals, sightseeing, guides, etc. Dates: April through October. Length of trip: 45 days. Group size: 24. Cost: $6,100. Special requirements: $700 deposit required.

Religion •

Religious pilgrimages certainly have their precedent. Since the Exodus, they have constituted major historical events.

On a less-grand scale, religious tours today give travelers the chance to see the historic landmarks of their faith, or to observe the ways of others. Like the pilgrims of the past, you'll travel in groups of people with whom you share a common bond—either of faith or historical interest. And like the pilgrims, you'll gain a greater understanding of religion over the course of your travels.

The paths of religious tours are varied. Some take an historical approach—others are deep spiritual quests. You can pay homage at the House of the Virgin Mary or Grave of St. John in Turkey ... trek to the Himalayan outposts of Buddhism ... view Passion Plays, festivals and holy relics.

Or you can absorb the spiritual values of the wilderness itself. As English author Malcolm Muggeridge proposed, the most sublime state a human being can aspire to is "being in the wilderness alone with God."

More than anything else, religious orientation gives focus to your vacation. You don't need to be a zealot to enjoy the sightseeing. In the places you'll visit, holy sites are often central to the history of the land and the character of the people. These programs function superbly as historical and artistic tours as well. You'll see some of the pillars of ancient architecture—centuries-old temples, basilicas, and cathedrals—filled with extensive collections of paintings, sculptures, and other ornaments. In addition, you'll see the ancient vestments of the faith, intricately and richly decorated articles of devotion.

Religion has been at or near the center of human history and philosophy since the beginnings of civilization. Religious tours offer you a look at ancient and modern cultures through their beliefs, and lend a new perspective to your own life.

**Bhutan Travel Service
120 East 56th Street
New York, NY 10022
212-838-6382
Telex 220896 BTS UR** *Bhutan*

Visit newly opened Central Bhutan, where much of the Kingdom's religious and cultural history is centered. Highlights of the program include Tongsa Dzong, largest fortified monastery in Bhutan; Jakar Dzon, "The Castle of the White Bird"; sacred Jambey Ihakhang and Kurjey Monastery, which holds the imprint of Guru Padmasambhava against a rock wall. Both these temples are among the oldest in Bhutan, built in the eighth century. Other visits are made to the sacred lake of Membertso, and to the many other temples and monasteries in this legendary valley, where the Lamaistic Red-Hat sect of Mahayana Buddhism has flourished undisturbed for centuries. Agency of the Royal Government of Bhutan, Department of Tourism, first branch opened outside Bhutan. Includes: All land costs including accommodations, all meals, transfers, transportation, guide, sightseeing, etc. Dates: March through June; September through November. Length of trip: 15 days. Group size: Minimum 6. Cost: $1,330. Special requirements: One month advance booking.

Cross Cultural Adventures
P.O. Box 3285
Arlington, VA 22203
703-243-7194
Telex 440283 ACI UI   *India*

On this varied journey, learn more of traditional Tibetan Buddhist culture and experience the natural majesty of the regions where it survives. You begin with a study program in Upper Dharmsala, India's largest Tibetan community and headquarters for the Dalai Lama's government in exile. Here you will participate in the activities of the various traditional study centers. (An extended program at the medical center can be arranged for people interested in traditional Tibetan medicine.) From there, jeeps, ponies, and trekking take you to the fascinating former Himalayan kingdoms of Ladakh and Zanskar. Hidden amid twenty-thousand-foot peaks, the spectacular monasteries of these high valleys are living museums of ancient Tibetan Buddhism. At trip's end, you'll relax in houseboats in the Vale of Kashmir and visit Delhi and the Taj Mahal. Tour leader for this venture is an American scholar of Tibetan Buddhism and experienced trekker; trek led by Indian mountaineering staff; study portion in Dharmsala under the auspices of the Tibetan Government in Exile. Includes: All transportation within India; all meals—restaurants in cities, camp meals prepared during trekking portion; accommodations in first-class hotels/houseboats in cities; tents and camping equipment supplied (except sleeping bags); porters and pack animals; camp staff (except American tour leader). Dates: Late August and early September. Length of trip: 3 weeks. Group size: Maximum 10. Cost: Approximately $2,800. Special requirements: Excellent health, some mountain trekking experience. Deposit $400 due with reservation; full payment six weeks prior to departure.

Pekin Tours, Limited
Sehit Nevres Boulevard 15/B
P.O. Box 505
Izmir, Turkey
9-51-214507   *Turkey*

Now you can relive the glory and the beauty of a bygone era when you travel through the fascinating land of Turkey, stopping to reflect at many Biblical sites, shrines and holy places. You'll explore the Cappadocia area with its underground cities and rock-carved churches; travel to the ruins and extraordinary excavations of Ephesus; visit the Basilica and Grave of St. John and the House of the Virgin Mary; cross the mighty Dardanelles by boat and tour the countryside en route to mysterious Istanbul. Includes: Hotels, meals, coach, guide, entrance fees, service charges, taxes, usual tipping. Dates: April through October. Length: 17 days. Group size: 20 plus 1 tour escort. Cost: $488. If air fare from and to New York is requested add $678.

The Knobs
535 Jackson Street
Campbellville, KY 42718
502-789-3189   *Worldwide*

The exotic, wild Serengeti Plain in Tanzania or the valleys of Central Malaysia call out to you, the magnificent vistas high in Nepal or the Andes of Peru are waiting to be discovered.

Now you can explore all these wondrous places in the company of kindred spirits—Christians seeking adventure with a desire to maintain a certain level of fellowship and conduct. Experience local customs and cultures all over the world with people you're going to feel right at home with. Includes: Land costs, trip leader, porters, meals (in the field). Dates: Year-round. Length: 14–24 days. Group size: 10–20 people. Cost: $1,400–$2,600. Special requirements: Trips rated A, B, C, by level of strenuous activity. No special skills.

THE WORLD OF
TRADE WIND TOURS

Trade Wind Tours
11 Grace Avenue
Great Neck, NY 11022
800-645-2000   *Europe*

In 1634, the villagers of Oberammergau made an oath that if they were spared from the Black Plague, they would present a play portraying the life and passion of Jesus Christ every ten years. The people were spared—and true to their word, they have continued their performances through today. 1984 marks the 350th-year anniversary of this important religious event. The Play is enacted on an open-air stage set against a magnificent mountain background. The cast is composed of hundreds of actors, all of whom must be native Oberammergauers. Depicting the New Testament story of Jesus from the Entry into Jerusalem until the Resurrection, the performance runs seven hours and is accompanied by a full orchestra and choir. This tour features first-class seats at the Passion Play, and the best private homes for stays in Oberammergau. In addition to the Passion Play, the tour visits Lucerne, Geneva, Paris, Amsterdam, Nice, Venice, Florence and Rome. Fifty-three years' experience. Includes: First class hotel accommodations, some meals, transfers, porterage; all local half-day sightseeing tours include an English speaking guide and admissions; full day excursions are fully escorted; all tours are fully escorted/hosted. For the Oberammergau stay portion, stays are included in the best private homes, tickets to the famous Oberammergau Passion Play, and deluxe motorcoach transportation. Dates: May through September 1984. Length of trip: 15 days, 13 nights. Group size: 15–40. Cost: From $877.

Travel Plus—India
P.O. Box 300
New Lebanon, NY 12125
805-656-1932   *India*

Travel Plus will open the door to India for you—the Ashrams, spiritual centers, monasteries, temples, and the gurus. You plan the trip of your dreams, and Travel Plus will make it a reality—whether you want to sightsee or mix culture and religion . . . go first class or economical all the way. Your every step can be planned ahead or you can decide what to do on the spur of the moment, traveling in everything from private car to public bus. This is a unique travel approach, individualized to your needs—a way of experiencing total enjoyment in exotic India. Includes: Varies. Tour operator will attempt to find partners for single travelers. Dates: Year-round. Length: 14–60 days. Group size: 1–32 people. Cost: $500 and up. Special requirements: $6.00 plus $.50 postage is required for purchasing "India Notebook" a guide to India. Price is deducted from your tour.

Western World Tours
735 State Street, Suite 208
Santa Barbara, CA 93101-9990
805-963-7832
800-241-7663 In California
Cable: WWTOUR   *Israel*

This comprehensive, first-class motorcoach tour of historic and modern Israel visits the many centers of Christian heritage. In Jerusalem, you'll visit the Old City, Western Wall, the Temple Mount, Dome of the Rock, the Via Dolorosa with the Stations of the Cross, the Church of the Holy Sepulchre, and more. Sites in the New City include the Knesset, the Yad Vashem Holocaust Memorial and the museum housing the Dead Sea Scrolls. Day trips outside of Jerusalem and cross-country touring will include Jericho, the Dead Sea, Masada, Nazareth, Cana of Galilee, Tiberias, Sea of Galilee, Tabgha, Capernaum, the Mt. of Beatitudes, Safed Area, Haifa, Druze Village, and Caesarea. Founded and owned by involved Christians, Western World Tours has twenty-five years of experience in handling customized ground tours for Christian leaders and organizations. Includes: Airport transfers, 7 nights accommodations in 4-star hotels, buffet breakfast and dinner daily, sightseeing with English-speaking guide/escort in modern air-conditioned coaches, entrance fees, porterage and cable car on Masada. Dates: Year-round—every Saturday. Length of trip: 8 days. Group size: Varies. Cost: $549. Special requirements: $100 deposit per person at time of booking.

Research
Expeditions •

- Excavating ancient Indian cliff dwellings in the American Southwest
- Mapping the fantastically beautiful coral formations of the Caribbean
- Tracking the migration patterns of whales off the Alaskan coast

Here's your chance to join a journey of discovery—to participate in scientific inquiry into the very essence of our planet and its inhabitants.

Scientific research isn't something you can only watch in T.V. documentaries or read about in glossy magazines. You yourself can be there, taking an active part. Various research organizations need more than donations of money—they need interested and enthusiastic volunteers to give their time and energies to ongoing projects.

For the most part, no previous experience is necessary. The research teams will teach you all the skills you need, and will make use of the abilities you already have—from photography to scuba diving. You'll learn by doing, under the supervision of top experts in their respective fields—gathering samples, analyzing data, observing animals.

Because many research projects are run by non-profit organizations, your program fees and travel expenses may be tax-deductible; ask the organization and your accountant for details. In addition, the educational nature of the projects means that students might be able to earn academic credit; check with your school or university.

On a research expedition, you'll experience more than a vacation. You'll do your own part in continuing the great scientific tradition of experimentation and observation. The past, present and future are awaiting your discovery.

Alaska Discovery
P.O. Box 26
Gustavus, AK 99826
907-697-3431   *Alaska*

Study the glaciation, plant and animal life of Alaska as you embark on a two-week kayak trip through the interior of Glacier Bay National Park. Learn the ABC's of the area's wildlife—the fun-loving seals, gentle whales and exotic birds, and gather data for independent study projects. The University of Alaska-Juneau and Alaska Discovery, Inc. have joined together to offer you this unique opportunity of learning in the field. Head instructor for the course is Greg Streveler, a former Glacier Bay ranger with a masters degree in ecology from the University of Wisconsin. He served as the park's chief research biologist from 1972 until 1979. Includes: Meals, kayaks, equipment, instructors, chartered air flights and all transportation within the park. Dates: June and July. Length: 2 weeks. Group size: Contact for information. Cost: $450. Additional tuition fees, payable to UAJ for enrollment and credit issuance, are $75 for Alaska students and $195 for out-of-state residents.

Center for American Archeology at
Northwestern University/Crow Canyon Campus
1911 Ridge Avenue
Evanston, IL 60201
312-492-5300 *Colorado*

The Southwest is a land filled with history in a setting of rugged mountains and mesas, red rock canyons, fertile river valleys and barren deserts. It's a land that once belonged to the prehistoric Anasazi ... the nomadic bands of Utes and Navajos ... Spanish explorers ... hardrock miners ... notorious outlaws and brave pioneers ... and now the land belongs to you. The programs offered at the Crow Canyon campus allow people of all ages to enjoy the widest possible range of archeological experience. As an Associate, a special friend of archeology, you can participate directly in various research programs. Includes: Room, board, transportation during the program, instructional materials. Dates: Summer and fall. Length of trip: Usually 5 days, 6 nights. Group size: 40 people. Cost: $300 (tax-deductible). Special requirements: $25 deposit.

Earthwatch
10 Juniper Road
P.O. Box 127 H
Belmont, MA 02178
617-489-3030
Telex 951404 *Worldwide*

Earthwatch is a non-profit organization which offers people the opportunity to join any of more than eighty field research expeditions in over thirty countries around the globe. Their worldwide range of projects currently includes archeology (archeoastronomy, marine archeology, paleoarcheology and more); animal behavior (of whales and dolphins, fish, large mammals, insects, sea turtles and birds); marine sciences (oceanography, corral reef studies, cetacean research); and tropical forest ecology. Over the past decade, Earthwatch has matched the interests of over five thousand volunteers with the scientific objectives of some of the world's top researchers. Includes: Accommodations, meals and daily travel from arrival at staging area until the end of the project. Dates: Year-round. Length of trip: 2-3 weeks. Group size: 4-14. Cost: $500-$2,000. Program expenses as well as transportation costs to and from the staging area are tax-deductible, since the participant is performing a volunteer service. Special requirements: Applicants are selected purely on the basis of the enthusiasm and interest they can bring to the research at hand, with the exception of dive projects, which require scuba certification.

Great Expeditions, Inc.
2956 West 4th Avenue
Vancouver, B.C., Canada V6K 1R4
604-734-4948 *Caribbean*

Thar she blows! Join a team of scientists as they sail the Caribbean carrying out whale surveys and reef studies. As the wind fills the sails of the eighty-foot schooner, you'll sail across crystal blue waters from St. Lucia to St. Vincent and the Grenadines. This is a chance to participate in exciting marine projects as they are happening. You'll learn about oceanography, West Indian history, marine botany, underwater photography and seamanship as you sail through quiet secluded bays and unspoiled reef areas on this working vacation. Established in 1977, the agency is fully registered and insured under Travel Act. Member of Pacific Area Travel Agency. Includes: Sailboat, guide, meals. Dates: Christmas and spring. Length: 14 days. Group size: Maximum 16 people. Cost: $1,590. Special requirements: $300 deposit.

Marine Environmental Research, Inc.
P.O. Box 1167
Monterey, CA 93942
408-646-8511 *Worldwide*

Marine Environmental Research is a non-profit research and educational organization whose purpose is to provide participants with the opportunity to experience remote parts of the world while making a meaningful contribution to the pool of scientific knowledge. You'll join whale researchers in southeast Alaska, California or the South Seas while experiencing life at sea aboard the legendary brigantine "Varua." With over three hundred thousand miles of Pacific voyaging, this ninety-three-foot research vessel has been described as the most beautiful sailing vessel of her size ever built. You'll assist whale researchers in their studies of the population dynamics of humpback and gray whales while learning hands-on deep water sailing and navigation. Founded in 1976. Includes: All meals (continental and seafood cuisine), single or double berths. Dates: Summer/Alaska, Winter/California, 1985 South Seas expedition planned. Length of trip: 1 to 6 weeks. Group size: Maximum 10. Cost: $700 per week. Special requirements: All ages accepted, no experience in sailing or research necessary; $200 non-refundable deposit.

The Cousteau Society, Inc.
930 West 21st Street
Norfolk, VA 23517
804-627-1144 *Worldwide*

Explore remote areas rarely intruded upon by man with Project Ocean Search—a series of intensive field-study programs conducted by The Cousteau Society. Each summer, the project explores a different area. There are plenty of opportunities for scuba diving and snorkeling as you study the sea life, the reefs and fantastically beautiful coral formations and perhaps do some underwater photography. Projects are designed to accommodate divers and nondivers alike. Expedition includes marine scientists, logistics staff and divemaster. Conducted by The Cousteau Society in association with the University of Southern California College of Continuing Education. Includes: Varies with program. Contact for details. Dates: Summer. Length of trip: Usually 2–3 weeks. Group size: Approximately 35 people. Special requirements: Must be 16 years of age or older; medical examination by physician required.

Tour Plan Pacific
P.O. Box 4188
Christchurch, New Zealand
Telex NZ4346 *New Zealand*

See the total solar eclipse off the New Zealand coast in November 1984. Tour Plan Pacific, in close collaboration with the Carter Observatory, New Zealand and the Royal New Zealand Astronomical Society, have planned an expedition onboard a chartered ship to chase the total solar eclipse off New Zealand's coast in November 1984. The expedition is ideally suited to astronomers, scientists and eclipse aficionados. The program includes lectures and discussions with leading astronomers. Includes: Ship's berth, meals, sightseeing, hotels, transportation, lectures and discussion groups with leading astronomers. Dates: November 1984. Length of trip: 17 days plus options. Group size: Up to 60—limited. Cost: On request.

**University of California
Research Expeditions Program
2223 Fulton Street Desk STI
Berkeley, CA 94720
415-642-6586**   *Worldwide*

The University Research Expeditions Program can provide you with an opportunity to share the work and excitement of scientific discovery as a member of small research expeditions in the United States and abroad. You can usually join the expeditions for two to four weeks, providing vital field assistance as you learn to excavate, map, conduct oral history interviews, observe animal behavior and share in a full range of other field activities. Among the projects have been the mapping of the Valley of the Kings in Egypt, botanical surveys in Chile and Tanzania and diving expeditions in Australia and French Polynesia. Brochures describing current expeditions are available upon request. No previous experience is necessary for most projects—just a desire to learn and a willingness to share the research work and expenses. Project leaders are University of California scientists and researchers engaged in on-going field research. Includes: Food, accommodations, all equipment, instruction. Dates: Year-round. Length: 2–4 weeks. Group size: 6–10. Cost: $500–$1,500. Special requirements: Scuba certification necessary for diving projects.

River Rafting •

Thinking about a river rafting trip? Here's what some recent vacationers have said about their river rafting trips:

"I never had so much fun! The scenery was beautiful, I loved the rapids and the guides were the greatest—they made it look easy. The memories will stay for a long time."

"It was super. I'm so enthusiastic about the trip, now all my friends want to go!"

"It wasn't just a vacation . . . it changed my life."

Or as Mark Twain wrote in *Huckleberry Finn*, "You feel mighty free and easy and comfortable on a raft." Whether it's the limpid waters of Alaska's Noatak, the mighty Colorado roaring through the Grand Canyon or Nepal's tumultuous Trisuli, river rafting offers a sublime opportunity to flow in harmony with nature.

While river rafting, you'll experience water in all its varied moods—furious, stampeding, exploding . . . playful, drifting, lazing. You'll discover sparkling waterfalls in secret canyons . . . hidden turquoise grottoes dense with rhododendron and ferns . . . awesome whitewater and thrilling chutes. You'll also feel the joy of seeing eagles soar on thermals overhead . . . watching columbine burst into bloom in meadows . . . exploring Indian caves and abandoned mining camps that link you to dreams of men and women who lived centuries ago.

The tour operators and outfitters in this section have the knowledge, equipment and experience to give everyone a superb river adventure—from confirmed beachcombers to advanced whitewater enthusiasts. If you've never gone river rafting before, they'll teach you the basics—from setting up camp to how to read a river. Or if you're a seasoned river runner, you can join exploratory expeditions on previously uncharted waters.

Although river rafting is exciting, it's not dangerous, when undertaken with the supervision of an expert guide. Almost anyone in good physical health can enjoy a rafting trip. Safety records in river rafting are excellent, and accidents are very, very rare. Many outfitters have operated twenty or thirty years without mishap, and they're quick to point out that rafting is safer than highway driving.

Another point—it is not necessary to know how to swim. All rafters—swimmers and nonswimmers alike—are required to wear United States Coast Guard-approved life jackets at all times while on the water in National Parks like the Grand Canyon; life jackets are also required by law on all federal and most state-controlled rivers.

River-running crafts are rugged and functional, and come in all shapes and sizes—from thirteen-foot inflatable rafts to thirty-five-foot pontoons . . . even hardy wooden dories. The rafts have large buoyancy tubes, upturned bows and sterns to help keep out splash and spray and are made of thick nylon neoprene or nylon-hypalon. If punctured, they can stay afloat because of their multiple air chambers. What kind of raft is best? Most outfitters follow a basic rule of thumb: "Big raft—big river; small raft—small river."

OAR VS. PADDLE RAFTS

Perhaps your biggest decision in choosing a river vacation is whether you want an oar-powered or paddle raft.

In an oar-powered raft, your guide uses large (ten to fifteen-foot) oars to maneuver the craft down the river. If you like, you can help out by paddling along. Oar rafting gives you the opportunity to experience more challenging whitewater than you could handle on your own. On Class V runs—among the toughest—most tour operators use oar boats exclusively or else require extensive rafting experience for paddlers.

In a paddle raft, it's you and your raftmates who, under a guide's direction, propel your boat through the rapids. Paddling is easy and fun. No experience is necessary and you get a feeling of accomplishment from steering your raft through tricky passages. You'll also build up an incredible camaraderie with your raft team.

If you want the best of both worlds, many rafting outfitters run both oar boats and paddle boats on the same trip—and travelers can take turns paddling to see what it's like.

Which should you choose—oar or paddle? Whichever you think you will enjoy most—the goal is to have a great vacation.

OAR/PADDLE RAFTS VS. MOTORIZED RAFTS

There's also the question of oar/paddle rafts versus motorized rafts. Both are equally maneuverable and safe. Motor rafts can hold more people and enable you to cover more distance in the same amount of time. On some rivers, motor rafts are not permitted (starting in fall of 1983, they're not allowed through the Grand Canyon from September through December). Oar and paddle rafts offer a more direct, personal involvement with both the power and the tranquility of the river. Once again, which you choose is a matter of preference.

ABOUT RAPIDS

Rapids put the "wild" into whitewater. They can vary from short drops to half-mile-long chutes . . . wide boulder fields to narrow channels . . . run straight or corkscrewed. Whatever their idiosyncrasies, they're guaranteed to give you a whole new perspective on life.

Rapids don't move all that fast—rarely above ten miles per hour. But when you're catapulting through white frothing fury, you'll feel like you're on the roller coaster ride of a lifetime.

What determines the difficulty of a rapid? Several factors, including:

Slope (or gradient): Slope of a river is generally expressed in number of feet dropped per mile. A slope of less than ten feet per mile means that a river is slow, while a gradient of more than twenty miles makes a river fast and challenging. Some classic rapids, like Lava Falls in the Grand Canyon or Forks of the Kern in California, plummet at an astonishing sixty feet per mile. (Sixty feet per mile doesn't sound like much. It is. You just have to be there.)

Roughness: How smooth is the stream bed? Boulders, gravel and ledges along the streambed create turbulence.

Constriction: Water accelerates if it has to flow through a constriction or bottleneck (a narrow canyon gorge, for example).

Flow/volume: The flow of a river is generally measured in *cfs* (cubic feet per second). Rafting rivers generally range from eight hundred cfs (small) to ten thousand (huge). The volume of a river can fluctuate greatly with rainfall, seasonality and other factors. Although most rivers are tougher to run at high water, some are easier.

All these elements combine to form the various tricks and treats of river running: huge haystacks, souse holes, curlers and boulder gardens.

HOW RIVERS ARE RATED

Rivers worldwide are classified according to difficulty—from easiest to toughest. The International River Classification System (commonly called the International Scale) is used throughout North America, Europe and elsewhere. There's also the "Western Scale," used on many rivers in the western United States. Here's what the scales mean:

DIFFICULTY RATING SCALE

International	Description	Western
–	Flat water.	0
I	Very easy. Small waves, wide channels with no serious obstacles.	1, 2
II	Medium. Regular waves not over two feet in height. Moderate rapids with clear passages.	3, 4
III	Difficult. Waves are numerous, up to three feet in height and irregular, with rocks and eddies; rapids with clear but narrow passages; need expertise to maneuver around obstacles.	5, 6
IV	Very difficult. Long rapids, powerful waves, dangerous rocks, boiling eddies; strong maneuvering required; should be run by experts only.	7, 8
V	Extremely difficult—many dangers. Long and violent rapids one after the other, riverbed obstructed, big drops, strong current, very steep gradient; large volume of water. All possible precautions must be taken.	9, 10
VI	Unrunnable or at the absolute limit of runnability. For daredevil experts only.	U

A river's difficulty rating is usually based on the ratings of its most difficult rapids. If an individual rapid is much tougher than the rest of the river as a whole, you might see a rating of, for example, II^5—meaning that although the river has medium difficulty, stretches have extremely difficult Class V rapids.

If this is going to be your first run, you might prefer starting out on an easier, Class III river before taking on the bucking bronco fury of Class IV. For Class V rivers, previous experience is generally mandatory. However, many rafting outfitters plan their expedition routes so you can get your feet wet (literally) on easier sections during the first few days of a run before tackling more challenging whitewater downstream.

River ratings are only approximate. High water, cold water and the kind of equipment used can affect the difficulty of a run.

WHAT A RIVER TRIP IS LIKE

If you're planning your first river trip, you might be wondering what it's going to be like. Although there's no such thing as a "typical" rafting expedition, here's an approximate idea of what you can expect.

Awaken just as the rosy glow of dawn chases the last stars from the clear skies above. Already there's the hearty aroma of fresh coffee brewing and bacon grilling, as your guides show that they know as much about good cooking as river running. After breakfast, board your unsinkable, heavy rubber raft—make sure that you keep gear you'll want during the day—like your camera and suntan oil—handy. As you head down river, your guide will point out things of interest—a bear ambling along the forest edge, deserted homesteads and Indian caves.

You'll hear the rapids before you see them—a tremendous roar as the surging waters charge through the canyon. Near the rapids, the noise becomes deafening. As your pulse quickens, you doublecheck your lifejacket, brace your feet against the heavy gear box in front of you and tighten your hold on the cross ropes. You are about to surrender yourself to the unstoppable power of the river.

The raft accelerates as the current grabs hold, hurtling it on its headlong plunge between boulders and waves. The spray drenches you in sheets. Now the raft skirts the churning edge of a whirlpool, then ferries right to avoid the huge hole lurking behind a submerged rock.

As suddenly as it began, the maelstrom is over. Once again, the river eases into sapphire tranquility. Along the shore, a doe and fawn come down to drink. As you wipe the spray from your eyes, you look at your raftmates with a wide, wide grin.

In general, you'll spend about four to eight hours a day on the river, covering ten to twenty miles. The rest of the time, you'll be ashore—hiking through side canyons to hidden pools, hot springs and waterfalls, exploring archeological sites and Indian caves or doing some serious hanging out.

In late afternoon, you'll arrive at camp—which might be a white sandy beach, grassy meadow or dense grove of fir and pine. Part of the fun is selecting the spot for your own personal campsite, with cozy tent and sleeping bag. (In answer to that question, "Where's the 'bathroom?' ": The Forest Service thoughtfully provides permanent sanitary facilities along many popular rafting rivers, like the Salmon. Otherwise, the outfitter will usually set up a portable toilet in a tent for complete privacy.)

While you settle in, your guides are busily preparing dinner—tonight it's chicken teriyaki plus salad, fresh fruit and chocolate fudge brownies. After dinner, you sit around the campfire, someone strums the guitar and you swap tales of the day's run.

A river journey is a wonderful way to participate in the vast beauty of nature—and share a unique adventure in the warm companionship of new-found friends.

Ready to go? Then check out the selection of river outfitters which begins on page 254.

WHAT TO BRING

The tour operator will supply you with a *very* complete list of what to bring. A sample packing checklist might include:

- 2 pairs of shorts
- 2 swimsuits
- 1 pair long pants
- 2 shirts (at least 1 long-sleeved for protection against the sun)
- 2–3 pairs socks (they get wet fast)
- underwear (remember you'll usually be wearing a bathing suit under shorts during the day)
- 2 pairs tennis or nylon jogging shoes (to protect your feet in the raft and while walking on shore; hiking boots weigh too much and are unnecessary)
- light jacket or windbreaker
- rain poncho or 2-piece rain suit
- sun hat (one that ties on)
- plus personal items (suntan lotion, lip protection, bio-degradable soap, etc.)

Depending where you're going, certain other items will turn up on the operator's list—wet suits for early spring, wool shirts, down windbreakers etc.

The outfitter will also give you complete instructions about what personal camping gear you need to bring—sleeping bags, ground cloths, etc. Many outfitters will be able to rent you camping equipment—everything from sleeping bags and tents to waterproof duffels for your gear and watertight ammo cases for cameras.

As a guideline, most outfitters ask you to limit gear to about thirty pounds per person, including clothing, personal items and camping equipment.

AGE LIMITS

For the most part, age is no barrier to river rafting, as long as the participant is in good physical health. Most of the tour operators listed in this book have had several spry seventy- and eighty-year-olds join them on their trips. On the young side of the scale, parents should use their discretion about how wild and woolly a journey their child can handle. Some tour operators do not encourage children younger than twelve on expeditions on Class IV whitewater, and may require participants on Class V trips to be at least sixteen years old. In our listings, we include any age limitations under the section "Special requirements."

WHEN TO GO

The "best" time to go varies from river to river. Tour operators schedule their tours to take advantage of optimal weather and water conditions on each river—some are runnable only during spring high water; others (usually dam-controlled) provide superb rafting all year. Each session presents its own charms: late spring highwater, early wildflowers, summer swimming.

The outfitter can furnish you with details about weather—temperature, rainfall, etc.

FOR PHOTOGRAPHY

A river rafting journey can provide you with once-in-a-lifetime photo opportunities. It also presents some unique challenges, since as a rule, cameras and water do not mix well. With forethought, however, you can take shots that are picture-perfect.

1. If you just bought a new camera, shoot and develop about two to four rolls before you go away, for practice—to get used to the light meter, loading and unloading features and make sure that everything is in working order.

2. To keep your camera and film dry, use an Army surplus ammunition case, which is absolutely watertight. They come in two sizes: 3½ x 7 x 10 inches and 7 x 7 x 10 inches. You can line the case with stiff foam for extra protection. In very humid areas such as the tropics, you might want to keep a small packet of desiccant in the case to absorb moisture. Many river outfitters either furnish ammo cases as part of your standard gear or rent them for a nominal fee.

3. Another alternative for keeping photography equipment dry are heavy-duty flotation bags. As their name implies, they do float, and come in bright yellow for easy spotting should they plunk overboard.

4. Bring more film than you think you're going to need. Take along films of various speeds: ASA 64 is excellent for bright daylight shots; also bring some ultra-fast ASA 1000 films for nighttime pictures around the campfire.

5. Except in calm waters, it's tough to take good photos while on the raft. To capture the heart-stopping thrill of shooting the rapids on film, shoot them from shore. Most raft outfitters give you the opportunity to go ashore and take pictures of your companions as they run an exciting stretch of whitewater—friends will later take pictures of you and you can swap photos later on.

6. If you do spend a lot of time in and around the water, consider purchasing an underwater camera. A top-of-the-line 35mm camera like the Nikonos sells for about $280; you can

also buy an inexpensive, water-resistant 110-format camera like the Minolta for about $65–$80.

HOW TO CHOOSE A RIVER RAFTING TRIP

Here's a checklist of things to consider in choosing a river rafting outfitter:

1. Oar vs. paddle trip: Does the guide use oars to propel and maneuver the boat, or do you and your raftmates paddle the raft under the direction of the guide? ·

2. Oar/paddle trip vs. motorized raft: A motorized raft can cover more distance in less time than an oar or paddle boat. It's also noisier and doesn't foster the feeling of "one-ness" with the river.

3. What is the pace of the trip? How many hours a day do you spend on the river? Is there free time to hike, fish, swim and relax?

4. Do you need to bring your own camping gear (tents, sleeping bags, etc.) or does the outfitter supply it? Is equipment available for rent? Are you expected to help set up camp or do the guides do all that?

5. Does the operator supply waterproof duffels for your personal gear or do you need to bring/rent your own? (A supply of heavy duty garbage bags can improvise nicely.) How about watertight ammo cases for camera and film?

6. About food: Raft trips generally include all meals from start to finish. Along with the growing enthusiasm for river rafting, outfitters pay increasing attention to the quality of their food. Riverside dining is truly a movable feast—fare ranges from chuck wagon hearty to continental gourmet ... and even vegetarians can find happiness with fresh salads and fruits.

Menus might include omelettes or pancakes for breakfast, thick sandwiches for lunch, and barbequed steak, baked potatoes or corn on the cob for dinner. Savvy Dutch oven cooks take pride in turning out everything from quiche to stuffed chicken breasts ... plus strawberry yogurt cheesecake and walnut brownies for dessert. By reading through the outfitter's brochures or contacting them directly, you can get an idea about what to expect.

7. About beverages: Depending on the outfitter, refreshments might include soft drinks, lemonade or fruit punch. Alcoholic beverages are often not included—and some outfitters don't provide sodas either. Check with the operator for details. Usually you can B.Y.O.B. (bring your own booze), which you must transfer into unbreakable containers. Beer, soda, and wine are generally over and above your thirty-pound gear allowance. If you plan on stocking up on beer or alcoholic beverages for your journey, ask the outfitter about local liquor laws. Many states, such as Arizona, do not permit purchases of beer or liquor before noon on Sunday (a frequent starting day for rafting trips).

8. Is transportation included to and from the put-in and take-out points? Because of airline schedules and connections, will you need to overnight in a hotel before and after your trip? How convenient is the airport—will you need a rental car? Might the outfitter pick you up?

9. It's a good idea to reserve early. On some rivers, the number of rafters is strictly limited; other rivers can only be rafted a few weeks a year—and reservations go fast.

In this section, we have rafting expeditions for all ages, interests and levels of experience—everything from one-day trips to extended river adventures. Since many outfitters run the same stretches of river, we've arranged the river rafting listings differently from the other sections of the book.

First you'll find a detailed profile of each major river—its classification, scenery, wildlife and other characteristics; followed by a brief description of the various operators who run each river.

A final word about river rafting. It's addictive. As one participant put it, "First you ask when's the next rapid. After that, it's 'Where's the next river?' "!

SECTIONS OF RELATED INTEREST

Canoeing/kayaking

Alaska

CHICKALOON RIVER

NOVA Riverrunners
P.O. Box 444
Parkgate Building, 2nd Floor
Eagle River, AK 99577
907-694-3750
Telex 090-26659 *AK/Chickaloon*

This heli-rafting adventure begins at King Mountain Lodge, seventy-six miles northeast of Anchorage. Here you'll board the helicopter for a shuttle flight up the Chickaloon—your view of the river and valley is unsurpassed as you cruise at tree-top level to the headwaters. That evening, you'll pitch camp at the foot of Castle Mountain, where you can relax and experience the timelessness of Alaska's backcountry. Morning breaks with a hearty breakfast and an unforgettable river run. NOVA has been operating river raft trips for over nine years; member of Alaska Association of Mountain and Wilderness Guides; most guides are EMT trained. Includes: River raft trip, helicopter flight, all meals, rainsuit, rubber boots, life jacket, waterproof bag. Dates: June through September. Length of trip: 2 days, one night. Group size: Minimum 6; maximum 12. Cost: $235 per person midweek, $265 per person weekends. Special requirements: Good health, no skill necessary for guided trips.

CHILIKADROTNA RIVER Class II and III (Moderate)

The Chilikadrotna River ("Chili") rises in Lake Clark National Park of South Central Alaska, surrounded by the magnificent Alaska Range. The headwaters of the Chilikadrotna flow past glacier-carved valleys and rigid peaks, with active glaciers and a profusion of wildlife, including moose, caribou, black and grizzly bear. Before it joins with the Mulchatna River, the Chili plays through a series of rapids, each spilling into crystal pools that brim with silver salmon, rainbow trout, pike and grayling.

Far Flung Adventures
P.O. Box 31
Terlingua, TX 79852
915-371-2489 *AK/Chilikadrotna*

With Far Flung Adventures, you can run the Chili from the headwaters of Twin Lakes (Lake Clark National Park) to New Stuyahok, covering over three hundred miles. National Park Service and Bureau of Land Management licensed, seven years of service. Includes: Guides, gear, safety equipment, waterproofing, tentage, food and preparation of food, ground and air transportation. Dates: July through September. Length of trip: 10 to 14 days. Group size: 9 to 12. Cost: $1,200. Special requirements: Deposit of $200 per person, personal health information and liability waiver, foul weather gear (listed in brochure), sleeping bag, eating kit.

COPPER RIVER

The Copper River of South Central Alaska is a cross section of all the qualities that make Alaska a special land. Along its route, wild tributaries like the Chitina each add to the speed and volume of the master river. The Childs and Miles Glaciers border the river for several miles, putting on a magnificent show as they chip off icebergs. Abercrombie rapids and numerous others along the Upper Copper yield whitewater thrills, while birders, wildlife observers, photographers and anglers will delight in the variety of the Copper River countryside. This is also gold rush country, where abandoned mining towns immortalize Alaska's frontier history.

Alaska Travel Adventures
200 North Franklin Street
Juneau, AK 99801
907-586-6245
800-227-8480
Telex 090-45380   *AK/Copper*

Alaska Travel Adventures offers a variety of programs on the Copper River. The Upper Rivers trip takes you from the Kennecott Mine (abandoned in 1938) to the tiny gold mining town of Chitina. The Full Trip or Lower River Trip will continue down the river to Cordova. The trip is highlighted by a float past the mile-wide Childs Glacier, where you'll watch mammouth icebergs calve into the river. Founded in 1979. Includes: Transportation from Anchorage, 2 nights hotel, all meals, guiding, group equipment. Dates: July and August. Length of trip: 8–15 days. Group size: 12–15 (maximum). Cost: $1,200–$1,995. Special requirements: $400–$700 advance deposit required; no skill level required—but good health is necessary.

Far Flung Adventures
P.O. Box 31
Terlingua, TX 79852
915-371-2489   *AK/Copper*

Beginning in the Wrangell Mountains near Valdez, Far Flung Adventures takes you through the Chugach Range and floats into deltalands near Controller Bay, an inlet of the Gulf of Alaska at Cordova—about one hundred fifty miles. Along the route, you'll camp at a safe distance from the Miles and Childs glaciers, and have a chance to watch as these icy titans put on their show. National Park Service and Bureau of Land Management licensed, seven years of service. Includes: Guides, gear, safety equipment, waterproofing, tentage, food and preparation of food, ground and air transportation. Dates: July through September. Length of trip: 10 to 14 days. Group size: 9 to 12. Cost: $1,000. Special requirements: Deposit of $200 per person; personal health information and liability waiver, foul weather gear (listed on brochure); sleeping bag, eating kit.

KOBUK RIVER (Class II)

Cradled by the Baird and Waring Mountains, the Kobuk flows from Walker Lake to Kotzebue Sound. For hundreds of years, it has served as a major transportation artery for coastal and inland Eskimos. Here you are truly in the land of the Midnight Sun—since the river lies above the Arctic Circle, there's twenty-four hours of daylight during the summer. Grizzly and black bear, moose, lynx and osprey are frequently sighted along the shores.

In addition to rewarding rafters with superb whitewater, the river offers outstanding fishing. At times, the Kobuk becomes a flurry of motion, as salmon make their fateful way to their upstream spawning beds. And trophy-sized shellfish—up to sixty pounds—have been caught.

Echo: The Wilderness Company
6529 Telegraph Avenue
Oakland, CA 94609
415-652-1600   *AK/Kobuk*

Beginning at Walker Lake, near the headwaters of the Kobuk, you'll float for eleven days and travel 125 miles through magnificent Kobuk Canyon and past the Schwatka Mountains. The scenery alternates between spruce forest and tundra, and the water is "clear as gin." Eighth season of running Brooks Range trips. Includes: Guides, river gear, food, bush flights. Dates: July. Length of trip: 11 days. Group size: 6–12. Cost: $1,498. Special requirements: Capable of walking through tundra and sedge tussocks, able to cope with cool nights and some rain. $150 deposit per person.

James Henry River Journeys
P.O. Box 807
Bolinas, CA 94924
415-868-1836   *AK/Kobuk*

Starting from Walker Lake, you'll kayak (in two-person Kleppers) and raft downstream through the exquisite landscape of birch, spruce and tundra, passing beaches strewn with jasper and jade. You'll also have contact with native Eskimo groups. In business ten years. Licensed by Idaho Outfitters and Guides Association, Alaska Association of Mountain and Wilderness Guides. Includes: All river rafting equipment, guides, meals provided, transportation from points of embarkation to point of debarkation. Dates: August. Length of trip: 12 days. Group size: 16–30. Cost: $1,475.

NOVA Riverrunners
P.O. Box 444
Parkgate Building, 2nd Floor
Eagle River, AK 99577
907-694-3750
Telex 090-26659   *AK/Kobuk*

Arctic whitewater will confront you early on this expedition, since the first boulder-strewn stretch is only a few miles out of Walker Lake. (At very high water, this stretch may need to be portaged.) More whitewater will also be encountered in the Lower Kobuk River Canyon. Along the way, you'll have plenty of time to fish for whitefish, salmon and sheefish. NOVA has been operating river raft trips for over nine years, member of Alaska Association of Mountain and Wilderness Guides, most guides are EMT trained. Includes: All inclusive tour package round trip Anchorage to Anchorage, all scheduled air flights and air charter, ground transportation, guides and equipment, all meals, rubber boots, and lifejackets. Dates: July through August. Length of trip: 12 days, 11 nights. Group size: 5 to 12 persons. Cost: $2,250. Special requirements: No skills necessary.

LIONSHEAD

NOVA Riverrunners
P.O. Box 444
Parkgate Building, 2nd Floor
Eagle River, AK 99577
907-694-3750
Telex 090-26659   *AK/Lionshead*

If you're looking for a heart-stopping thrill, LionsHead is the answer, rated at Class IV and V on the International scale. Be prepared to get wet! NOVA has been operating river raft trips for over nine years. Member of Alaska Association of Mountain and Wilderness Guides; most guides are EMT trained. Includes: Raft trip, rainsuit, rubber boots, lifejackets, transportation from Anchorage and lunch. Dates: June through August. Length of trip: 1 day (approximately 4 hours). Group size: 4 to 50 (maximum) persons. Cost: $89. Special requirements: For guided trips no skill necessary, only good health. For unguided trips—physical stamina. Deposit of $25 required for reservations.

MATANUSKA RIVER

NOVA Riverrunners
P.O. Box 444
Parkgate Building, 2nd Floor
Eagle River, AK 99577
907-694-3750
Telex 090-26659   *AK/Matanuska*

Try the oars on this exciting day trip only an hour and a half drive from Anchorage. You'll enjoy a scenic float amidst the Chugach and Talkeetna mountains, running a number of easily-negotiated rapids. Glimpses of bald eagle and moose occur occasionally as you drift fifteen miles of this historic waterway. NOVA has been operating river raft trips for over nine years. Member of Alaska Association of Mountain and Wilderness Guides, most guides are EMT trained. Includes: Raft trip, rainsuit, rubber boots, lifejackets, transportation from Anchorage and lunch. Dates: May through September, daily. Length of trip: 1 day trip (approximately 4½ hours). Group size: 4 to 50 (maximum) persons. Cost: $89. Special requirements: For guided trips—no experience necessary. For unguided trips—some physical stamina. Deposit of $25 required for reservation.

NOATAK RIVER (Class II)

Margaret E. Murie, author of "Two in the Far North," perhaps described the Noatak best: "The breeze, the birdsong, the fragrance of myriad brave burgeoning mosses and flowers—all blend into one clear entity, one jewel. It is the Arctic world in its unbelievably accelerated summer life . . . The heart of the whole region is, of course, the river."

Considered by many as the most pristine of Arctic Alaskan rivers, the Noatak flows gently from the glaciers of the Central Brooks Range and gracefully sweeps 435 miles to the Arctic waters of Kotzebue Sound. In summer, the days are long, sunsets endless and the nights ablaze with stars and northern lights. Along the way, you might encounter Dall sheep, grizzly bear or bald eagles—plus an amazing assortment of smaller critters like ptarmigan, pipits and whistling swans. All are cast upon a stage of stunning beauty—spruce and fir forests, tundra expanses aglow with wildflowers, and the towering presence of the Brooks Range.

Far Flung Adventures
P.O. Box 31
Terlingua, TX 79852
915-371-2489 *AK/Noatak*

From Bettles, you'll fly to the Noatak's headwaters near the slopes of Mt. Igikpak. Traveling a 160-mile course entirely within the Arctic Circle, you'll journey to the Cutler River confluence, surrounded by unmatched vistas of the Brooks Range. National Park Service and Bureau of Land Management licensed; seven years of experience. Includes: Guides, gear, safety equipment, waterproofing, tentage, food and preparation of food, ground and air tansportation. Dates: July. Length of trip: 14 days. Group size: 9 to 12. Cost: $1,300. Special requirements: Deposit of $200 per person, personal health information and liability waiver, foul weather gear (listed in brochure), sleeping bag, eating kit.

James Henry River Journeys
P.O. Box 807
Bolinas, CA 94924
415-868-1836 *AK/Noatak*

After an easy backpacking trip into one of the Noatak's upper-tributary valleys, you'll travel by raft and two-person Klepper, following a serene, meandering course interspersed with dancing rapids. Licensed by Idaho Outfitters and Guides Association; Alaska Association of Mountain and Wilderness Guides. Includes: All river rafting equipment, guides, meals provided, transportation from points of embarkation to points of debarkation. Dates: August and September. Length of trip: 15 days. Group size: 16–30. Cost: $1,700.

TATSHENSHINI RIVER (Class III)

The Tatshenshini is glaciers, grizzlies, bergs, forests, waterfalls, mountains, wildflowers and wildlife.

Beginning in the interior of British Columbia, the river carves its way through the rugged St. Elias Range to the Gulf of Alaska. Along its banks, wildflowers splash a rainbow of colors—a startling contrast to the gray granite cliffs in the background. Between the peaks, iridescent blue glaciers edge towards the valleys, frequently calving ice with a thundering roar. Overhead, eagles and hawks soar in dizzying flight.

As John Muir wrote in his "Travels in Alaska" (1875): "It seemed inconceivable that nature could have anything finer."

Alaska Discovery
P.O. Box 26
Gustavus, AK 99826
907-697-3431 *AK/Tatshenshini*

Beginning in Juneau, Alaska's capital, the trip travels into interior British Columbia, Canada, for the put-in. You'll have a full eleven days of shooting the rapids, with plenty of time to explore the glaciers and icebergs in Alsek Bay. Twelve years' experience; American Association of Mountain and Wilderness Guides certified outfitter; certified guides with EMT training. Includes: All rafting and camping gear, food, insurance, hotel at beginning of trip, all ground and charter airplane transportation, guides. Dates: Late July through end of August. Length of trip: 12 days. Group size: 12–15. Cost: $1,350.

James Henry River Journeys
P.O. Box 807
Bolinas, Ca 94924
415-868-1836   *AK/Tatshenshini*

Glacier walks, glacier calvings, munching wild edibles and unwinding in a river sauna are all part of this adventure. Paddle option available. Licensed by Idaho Outfitters and Guides Association; Alaska Association of Mountain and Wilderness Guides. Includes: All river rafting equipment, guides, meals provided, transportation from points of embarkation to points of debarkation. Dates: July and August. Length of trip: 12 days. Group size: 16–30. Cost: $1,390.

Sobek Expeditions
Angeles Camp, CA 95222
209-736-2661
800-344-3284 except HI, AK, CA
Telex 172746   *AK/Tatshenshini*

On this twelve-day trip, highlights include a full-day layover at Alsek Bay, where you'll have a chance to watch as giant chunks of ice calve into the water from the seven-mile face of the Alsek glacier. The trip also features spacious campsites and meals occasionally embellished with edible wild plants. Trip leader experienced river and mountain guide, photographer. Dates: July and August. Length of trip: 12 days. Group size: 6. Cost: $1,390. Special requirements: $300 deposit, moderate difficulty.

Wind Over Mountain
410 Highland
Boulder, CO 80302
303-444-8028   *AK/Tatshenshini*

After meeting in Haines, Alaska, you'll have twelve days of whitewater rafting, passing more than twenty glaciers, plus grizzlies, forests, waterfalls and wildflowers. In business since 1974. Includes: Double-occupancy hotel in Haines before and after trip, all meals while on the river, group farewell dinner, all river equipment including life jackets. Dates: July. Length of trip: 12 days. Group size: 16 plus crew. Cost: $1,390.

YUKON AND CHARLEY RIVERS

NOVA Riverrunners
P.O. Box 444
Parkgate Building, 2nd Floor
Eagle River, AK 99577
907-694-3750
Telex 090-26659   *AK/Yukon, Charley*

The historic gold rush years set the background for this ten-day adventure on the Yukon and Charley rivers. You'll journey some seventy-five miles of the Charley in the newly-established Yukon-Charley National Preserve. This preserve is also range for the Forty Mile Caribou herd, and the trips are timed to allow glimpses of the animals. The North's most historic waterway, the Yukon originates in Canada and flows 2,100 miles to the Bering Sea; you'll cover about sixty miles of its beauty on this journey. Mountain goats and Dall sheep browse on the many cliffs surrounding the river, and fishing opportunities abound for grayling, char, pike and salmon. NOVA has been operating river raft trips for over nine years. Member of Alaska Association of Mountain and Wilderness Guides; most guides are EMT trained. Includes: All inclusive tour package and round trip Anchorage to Anchorage. All scheduled air flights and air charter, helicopter flight, ground transportation, guides and equipment, all meals, rubber boots and life jackets. Dates: June through August. Length of trip: 10 days, 9 nights. Group size: 5–12 persons. Cost: $1,675. Special requirements: No experience necessary.

Arizona

COLORADO RIVER—The Grand Canyon
(Class IV–V)

Bright moon peering over black canyon walls . . . tumbling springs and cascading waterfalls . . . smooth, opaque water and booming rapids with dancing jets of spray . . . the broken tops of the big waves or haystacks . . . this is river rafting in the Grand Canyon of the Colorado.

Here in the northwestern corner of Arizona, the Colorado River has carved out one of the greatest natural wonders of the world: 277 miles long, a mile deep and alive with color—from pure white to blazing red and inky black. Everything exists on a monumental scale—like Red Wall Cavern, a natural ampitheater carved in the side of Marble Gorge, said to be large enough to seat fifty thousand people. Yes, the Grand Canyon is guaranteed to give you a new sense of proportion.

In 1869, John Wesley Powell, a one-armed veteran of the Civil War, became the first white man to traverse the Canyon. By 1949, only one hundred people had retraced Powell's river route. Today, increasingly skilled boatmen and women, and advances in raft design, have made the canyon accessible to just about everybody. About fourteen thousand people floated their way down the Colorado in 1983.

The Colorado River is known as one of the most challenging whitewater runs in North America. On the river from Lee's Ferry to Diamond Creek, there are thirty-seven major rapids Class IV and above, including some of whitewater's awesome legends—Badger Creek, Sockdolager, Grapevine, Hance, Hermit, Crystal. And the incomparable Lava Falls. Also known as Vulcan's Rapid, Lava Falls is the fiercest rapid on the Colorado, with mammoth holes, exploding foam and humongous waves, twenty to thirty feet from crest to trough.

The river has an introspective side too—with hidden places like Vasey's Paradise, Havasu Canyon (aquamarine waters . . . great for swimming) and Silver Grotto. As you travel the river, you'll also be journeying through time, being able to touch and climb rocks billions of years old. On short hikes along the river, you'll observe prehistoric Indian sites, plus the permanent residents of the canyon—big horn sheep, deer, birds, and reptiles. And during the entire trip, there's the constant contrast of vegetation—from desert cactus on the canyon slopes to cottonwoods and ferns beside waterfalls and creeks in the side canyons.

Depending on how much time you have, you can run all 280 miles or so of the canyon (about eleven to eighteen days), or a portion of it (five to eight days). How much you cover depends on the pace of the trip and type of craft (motorized rafts go faster than oar/paddle-propelled ones).

Here are the most common runs:

Lee's Ferry to Phantom Ranch (Bright Angel Trail): eighty-nine river miles. This is the "upper end" of the run, known for its short hikes, narrow rapids and crystal-clear water. Includes such famous runs as Badger Creek, Soap Creek and Sockdolager Rapids, plus Vasey's Paradise, Stanton's Cave and Redwall Cavern.

Phantom Ranch (Bright Angel Trail) to Diamond Creek: 136 river miles. Includes some of the classics—Crystal Rapids, Deer Creek Falls and Lava Falls. Although the river continues on, most trips pull out at Diamond Creek (just below Lava Falls) to avoid the forty miles of still water on Lake Mead.

Whitmore Canyon to Pierce Ferry (Lake Mead): Whitmore Canyon is just below Lava Falls. The startling beauty of the Grand Canyon is always present, and there are many noteworthy attractions on this stretch—Travertine Canyon, a magnificent series of waterfalls tumbling down a travertine mountain; Spencer Canyon, with its green pools; and Pumpkin Springs, a colorful hot sulfur spring on the edge of the river. Although you will encounter several good rapids on this portion of the river, the major runs occur above Lava Falls.

When planning your trip, remember that the Grand Canyon is, of course, a canyon—about a mile or so deep. Check how the tour operator will transport you from the canyon rim down to the river and back up again: hike, helicopter or via horse and mule. This may depend on which portions of the river you run.

Arizona Raft
P.O. Box 697
Flagstaff, AZ 86002
602-526-8200   *AZ/Colorado*

Arizona Raft Adventures gears its trips to participation in the river experience—from actively rowing or paddling, to relaxing on the boats, adrift with the current, to hiking up to a hidden side canyon waterfall. A variety of oar, motor and all-paddle trips are available, from Lee's Ferry to Diamond Creek. Many years' experience. Includes: Food, waterproof storage of gear, full or partial transportation to and from Colorado River/Flagstaff, sleeping gear on trips including a hike in or out of canyon. Dates: April through October. Length of trip: 6 to 15 days. Group size: 18–23 participants. Cost: $600–$1,200. Special requirements: No experience needed. $200 per person deposit confirms reservation.

Expeditions, Inc.
Route 4, Box 755
Flagstaff, AZ 86001
602-774-8176
602-779-3769   *AZ/Colorado*

"We feel the river has a soul and we like to expose our customers to the entirety of its being," say Dick and Susan McCallum, owners of Expeditions, Inc. They personally guide as many of their river trips as possible. All their trips are oar-powered. Company has thirteen years' experience. Includes: Transportation from Flagstaff and back, sleeping gear, waterproof bags and ammo can, meals and everything but personal gear. Dates: April through October. Length of trip: 5–20 days. Group size: 20. Cost: $500–$1,200. Special requirements: $200 deposit.

Friends of the River
P.O. Box 1115
Flagstaff, AZ 86002
602-774-0130   *AZ/Colorado*

Raft, paddle or kayak the Grand Canyon—and help protect the Colorado River as well. Friends of the River offers a variety of expeditions through the Grand Canyon, at special low prices, as part of its fundraising efforts. Grand Canyon charters operated by Arizona Raft Adventures, an authorized concessioner of the National Park Service. Includes: All boats and equipment, guides, food, transportation package, waterproof duffel, camping gear available (included on partial trips). Dates: Spring through fall. Length of trip: 1 to 21 days. Group size: Small. Cost: $1,055 raft or paddle, $798 kayak. Special requirements: Class III to IV skill level for kayakers.

GRAND
CANYON   **Grand Canyon Dories**
DORIES   **P.O. Box 3029**
                  Stanford, CA 94305
                  415-851-0411   *AZ/Colorado*

Grand Canyon Dories runs the only rigid (non-inflated) boats on public trips through the Grand Canyon. In these graceful, capable dories specifically developed for running the Colorado, you'll have room to sit or lounge, and all the duffel is stowed away, leaving the decks clear. They offer a variety of trips from Lee's Ferry to Grand Wash—covering the full 277 miles of the Canyon. Grand Canyon Dories have been running the Grand Canyon with rigid boats longer than any other present outfitter, and is the only outfitter using rigid boats in the Grand Canyon. Licensed and recommended by the National Park Service, and has a faultless safety record. Includes: Motor transportation from Hilton Inn at St. George, Utah, to Lee's Ferry, Arizona, beginning point of the Grand Canyon. Oar-powered boat trip through Canyon for 188 miles, with all meals, etc. Return to St. George by muleback and airplane. Dates: Mid-April through October. Length of trip: 14 days, Sunday–Saturday. Group size: 20 to 24. Cost: $1,296. Special requirements: No skill needed but boating skills may be used by those who wish. 25% deposit with reservation. 10% youth discount for those under 16.

O.A.R.S.
P.O. Box 67
Angels Camp, CA
209-736-4677
Telex 172746 STO   *AZ/Colorado*

O.A.R.S. runs trips of various lengths through the Canyon—from Lee's Ferry to Diamond Creek—using small (seventeen-foot) inflatable oar-powered rafts. Fourteen years' rafting experience in the Grand Canyon, as well as on twenty-six Western rivers. Includes: Meals from lunch on the first day to lunch on the last day; all rafting equipment including waterproof packs and water-tight ammo cans; experienced, friendly guides who row your rafts, cook your meals and give you unique and personal insights into the Canyon they love. Dates: April through October. Length of trip: 5 to 13 days. Group size: 16 passengers. Cost: $645–$1,295 per person. Special requirements: If the reservation is made prior to February 1st of the year the trip occurs, the deposit is $125 per person. If it occurs after February 1st of the year the trip occurs the deposit is $500 per person for 8- and 13-day trips and $400 per person for 5-day trips.

Outdoors Unlimited
P.O. Box 22513-T
Sacramento, CA 95822
916-452-1081   *AZ/Colorado*

Operating river trips for eleven years, Outdoors Unlimited offers a variety of expeditions from Lee's Ferry to Diamond Creek. Permit issued by National Park Service. Includes: On 5- and 8-day trips they provide all camping gear, food, river equipment. On full trip (12 days) camping gear can be rented for $35 per person. Special trips available offering extended hiking, paddle rafting, and advanced kayaking instruction. Dates: Mid-May through end of September. Length of trip: 5, 8 and 12 days. Group size: 18–20. Cost: $525–$960.

Western River Expeditions
7258 Racquet Club Drive
Salt Lake City, UT 84121
801-942-6669 (in Utah)
800-453-7450   *AZ/Colorado*

A variety of programs are offered through the Canyon, from Lee's Ferry to Whitmore Canyon, just below Lava Falls, plus a four-day trip from Whitmore Canyon to Pierce Ferry on Lake Mead. Includes: Professional river guide service and first class meal preparation, all meals while on the river, tents, camping equipment, ground transportation. Dates: May through September. Length of trip: 4 or 7 days. Cost: $495–$975.

California

AMERICAN RIVER

North Fork: (Class IV and V)—Roaring out of the Sierra's Desolation Wilderness, The North Fork offers the most challenging whitewater on the American. Since the river is free-flowing, with no dams controlling it, it can vary dramatically in water volume. The North Fork has been included in the California Wild and Scenic River system—and with rapids with names like Chamberlin Falls, Staircase and Widow Maker, it's easy to figure out why.

South Fork: (Class III)—Flowing down the western slope of the Sierra Nevada Mountains just east of Sacramento, the South Fork of the American blends relaxing calms with thrilling rapids. Moving first among big, rounded foothills and later through a steep granite canyon, the river initially struts out quick and strong, then eases serenely, before rushing in headlong climax through the fabled American River Gorge, where one rapid follows another in dizzying succession. Six miles downstream from Chili Bar, the river flows past the historic township of Coloma, where James Marshall discovered gold—sparking the California Gold Rush.

Middle Fork: (Class IV)—Challenging whitewater and a unique Gold Rush Heritage make this an exciting river adventure . . . you can even raft through an old mining tunnel. A century ago, the river turned sharply at Horseshoe Bend. But eager prospectors altered the course of the river by blasting a tunnel through the hillside. Now the river rampages down Tunnel Chute, a craggy confine hewn by dynamite, then breezes through an underground tunnel with plenty of headroom. Afterwards, the river relaxes a bit—before plummeting through the awesome Ruck-A-Chucky rapids.

Access to Adventure
P.O. Box 500
Lotus, CA 95651
916-626-5042 _CA/American_

Rafts the South Fork of the American from Chili Bar to Folsom Lake. Twelve years' experience; member American River Recreation Association, American Guides Association, Klamath Canyon River Outfitters, Friends of the River, Pacific River Outfitters and Guides Association, Western River Guides. Includes: Camping, meals, rafts, life jackets, paddles, dry bags, all special river gear, shuttle transportation at the river. Dates: April through October. Length of trip: 1 or 2 days. Group size: 1–120. Cost: $30–$150. Special requirements: $30 per person deposit. Balance due 30 days prior to trip.

Action Adventures Wet 'n' Wild
P.O. Box 1500
Woodland, CA 95695
916-662-5431 _CA/American_

South, Middle and North Forks. Twenty-five years without a single personal injury claim to their insurance company; charter member of American Guides Association. Includes: Intermediate area transportation, food, safety and sanitary equipment, group camp gear (everything except personal gear). Dates: April through October. Length of trip: ½ to 2 days. Group size: Varies. Cost: $35 to $140 per day.

All-Outdoors Adventure Trips
2151 San Miguel Drive
Walnut Creek, CA 94596
415-932-8993 _CA/American_

South, Middle and North Forks of the American. Participants will indeed participate— learning about river navigation, safety techniques and equipment. All-paddle or oar-paddle options are available. Fifteen years' experience. Operate under appropriate United States Government agency permits. Includes: All rafting equipment, food, local transportation, guide. Dates: May through September. Length of trip: 1, 2 or 3 days. Group size: 10–25. Cost: $58–$195. Special requirements: Deposit $15 per day. Participant supplies own sleeping bag (rental available at nominal charge).

Epic Adventures
550 South 1st Street
San Jose, CA 95113
408-294-5676   *CA/American*

You'll be an active, paddling crew member on these paddle boat runs on the South Fork of the American. Under the direction of a skilled guide, you and your boatmates will power the raft around rocks, over waves and through exciting rapids. On the North Fork, the rapids are long, technical and powerful. Here guides use oar frames for extra power and control. However, for good and experienced paddlers, Epic may also run a paddle boat crew. Six years' whitewater experience. Includes: All meals, all rafting equipment, river shuttle, skilled guides, swimming, camp area. Dates: April through October. Length of trip: 1 or 2 days. Group size: 6 to 50 persons. Cost: $45–$65 per day. Special requirements: Ages 8 to 89, no special requirements.

James Henry River Journeys
P.O. Box 807
Bolinas, CA 94924
415-868-1836   *CA/American*

South, Middle and North Forks. In business ten years. Licensed by Idaho Outfitters and Guides Association and Alaska Association of Mountain and Wilderness Guides. Includes: All river rafting equipment, guides, meals provided, transportation from point of embarkation to point of debarkation. Dates: All year. Length of trip: 1, 2 or 3 days. Group size: 16–30. Cost: $58–$215. Special requirements: Varies with trips—usually novices' conditioning program required on more strenuous trips—river experience required for more advanced rivers.

Little Switzerland's Wet Fantasies
P.O. Box 11583
Tahoe Paradise, CA 95708
916-577-5646   *CA/American*

Four years' experience. Includes: Equipment on the river, trained guides, meals. Dates: Mid-April through September. Length of trip: ½ day thru 4 days. Group size: Varies. Cost: $35–$250. Special requirements: Full payment 7 days before departure. No previous experience required.

Mariah Wilderness Expeditions
P.O. Box 1384
El Cerrito, CA 94530
415-527-5544   *CA/American*

South, Middle and North Forks. Mariah Wilderness also features several "special trips" which include mother/daughter, father/son raft trips, gourmet trips, all-women trips, 3-day raft clinics and mountain-river wilderness training. In winter, cross-country hut and chalet ski trips take place in the ski resort of Bear Valley, on the western slopes of the California Sierras. Owners/operators have been in the business of rafting for eight years. Licensed. Includes: equipment, food, guides, camp fees. For ski trips: lodging meals, trail fees, instruction, guides. Dates: February through October. Length of trip: 1–5 days. Group size: 1–60. Cost: $50–$400.

O.A.R.S.
P.O. Box 67
Angels Camp, CA 95222
209-736-4677
Telex 172 746 STO   *CA/American*

O.A.R.S. rafts the seventeen-mile section of the American River (Middle Fork) upstream of Auburn, including the old mining tunnel. Since the gradient is forty feet per mile, the white-water is intense. Fourteen years of rafting experience on twenty-six Western rivers. Includes: Meals from lunch the first day through lunch the 2nd day; all rafting equipment including life jackets; and experienced, knowledgeable guides. Dates: May through September. Length of trip: 2 days, 1 night. Group size: 20 maximum, 4–6 per boat. Cost: $155. Special requirements: Minimum age 12, $30 per person deposit.

Turtle River Rafting
507 McCloud Avenue
Mt. Shasta, CA 96067
916-926-3223   *CA/American*

Eight years' experience. Includes: Food, equipment, guide service. Dates: May and June. Length of trip: 1 to 5 days. Group size: 6–24. Cost: $58 per day. Special requirements: A deposit is required to reserve a space.

Whitewater Voyages
P.O. Box 906
El Sobrante, CA 94803
415-222-5994   *CA/American*

The tour operator offers both one- and two-day excursions on the South Fork of the American. Author of *Whitewater Rafting* and *The Guide's Guide*, William McGinnis has led trips on rivers throughout the world. He has owned and operated Whitewater Voyages for eight years. Includes: Fully outfitted whitewater rafting trip with professional guides captaining each paddle crew and oar boat; meals and refreshments; shuttle transportation to and from the rendezvous northwest of Placerville. (Personal camping gear not included.) Dates: May through October. Length of trip: 1 and 2 days. Group size: 1–30 (no maximum). Cost: $78–$154. Special requirements: No previous experience necessary.

**White Water West
2 Virginia Gardens
Berkeley, CA 94702
415-548-0782**   *CA/American*

White Water West runs all three forks of the American, including a North/South two-day combination. Fully licensed, insured, five years in business. Includes: Guide service, all equipment, gourmet meals. Dates: April through October, daily. Length of trip: 1 or 2 days. Group size: 1–50. Cost: From $50 1-day to $135 2-day (approximate). Special requirements: No experience necessary for South Fork trip; participants on North and Middle Fork journeys must have previous paddling experience. 50% deposit.

**Wild Water Whitewater Trips
P.O. Box 431
Suisun City, CA 94585
707-425-1431**   *CA/American*

Trips include the North, Middle and South Forks of the American River. Seven years' experience as professional outfitter; member: American River Recreation Association, El Dorado Professional Outfitters, American River Guides Association. Includes: Either wilderness or resort camping, all meals, transportation, Coast Guard approved equipment, safety instructions and campfire entertainment. Dates: May through October. Length of trip: 1, 2, or 3 days. Group size: 16 to 50 people. Cost: Approximately $60 per day. Special requirements: Minimum age 8 years old, good physical condition. $30 per person deposit, final payment 30 days prior to trip date.

CARSON RIVER

East Fork: (Class II)—The Carson flows swiftly out of the eastern Sierras from an elevation of 5,500 feet at Markleeville (just south of Lake Tahoe) into the deserts of Nevada. Although it runs fast and continuous with many small rapids, there are few major rapids to run, and the scenery and mountain atmosphere provide a relaxing escape. You'll glide past desert canyons of sculptured rock, pine trees and cottonwood groves. Along the route, there are remnants of old homesteads and Washo Indian sites. And after a day's rafting, the soothing waters of the nearby mineral hot springs will feel warm and relaxing.

**Access to Adventure
P.O. Box 500
Lotus, CA 95651
916-626-5042**   *CA/Carson*

In addition to a two-day raft trip on the East Carson, Access to Adventure offers a combination horsepack/float trip. You'll ride remote trails which long ago were the hunting grounds of the Washo Indians ... camp near hot springs under a canopy of stars ... then enjoy a thrilling raft trip down the river. Twelve years' experience. Member American River Recreation Association, American Guides Association, Klamath Canyon River Outfitters, Friends of the River, Pacific River Outfitter & Guides Association, Western River Guides. Includes: Camping, meals, rafts, life jackets, paddles, dry bags, all special river gear, shuttle transportation at the river. Dates: May through July. Length of trip: 2 days. Group size: 1–120. Cost: $125–$155. Special requirements: $30 per person deposit—balance due 30 days prior to trip.

**All Outdoors
2151 San Miguel Drive
Walnut Creek, CA 94596
415-932-8993**   *CA/Carson*

All-paddle or oar-paddle options available on the East Carson. Fifteen years' experience. Operate under appropriate United States Government agency permits. Includes: All rafting equipment, food, local transportation, guide. Dates: April through mid-July. Length of trip: 1–2 days. Group size: 10–25. Cost: $52–$126. Special requirements: Deposit $15 per day. Participant supplies own sleeping bag (rental available at nominal charge).

**Epic Adventures
550 South 1st Street
San Jose, CA 95113
408-294-5676**   *CA/Carson*

Choose from paddle boats, oar boats or inflatable kayaks for a run on this river. Six years' whitewater experience. Includes: All meals, all rafting equipment, river shuttle, skilled guides, swimming, campfires. Dates: April through July. Length of trip: 2 days. Cost: $115–$135. Special requirements: Ages 8 to 80. No special requirements.

**James Henry River Journeys
P.O. Box 807
Bolinas, CA 94924
415-868-1836**   *CA/Carson*

Paddle and oar boats available. In business ten years. Licensed by Idaho Outfitters and Guides Association, Alaska Association of Mountain and Wilderness Guides. Includes: All river rafting equipment, guides, meals provided, transportation from points of embarkation to points of debarkation. Dates: May through mid-June. Length of trip: 2 days. Group size: 16–30. Cost: $115–$135. Special requirements: Varies with trips—usually novices' conditioning program required on more strenuous trips. River experience required for more advanced rivers.

Little Switzerland
P.O. Box 11583
Tahoe Paradise, CA 95708
916-577-5646   *CA/Carson*

East Fork of the Carson. Four years' experience. Includes: Equipment on the river, trained guides, meals. Dates: Mid-April through September. Length of trip: 1–2 days. Group size: Open. Cost: $39–$99 per person. Special requirements: Full payment 7 days before departure.

Turtle River Rafting
507 McCloud Avenue
Mt. Shasta, CA 96067
916-926-3223   *CA/Carson*

To encourage a more personal experience, everyone is involved in paddling, boat preparation and camping activities. Eight years' experience. Includes: Food, equipment, guide service. Dates: May and June. Length of trip: 1 to 5 days. Group size: 6–24. Cost: $58 per day. Special requirements: A deposit is required to reserve a space.

Wild Water White Water
P.O. Box 431
Suisun, CA 94585
415-921-5020   *CA/Carson*

With Wild Water White Water, you can either paddle yourself or let your skilled guide row you down the Carson's East Fork. Seven years as professional outfitter. Member: American River Recreation Association, El Dorado Professional Outfitters, American River Guides Association. Includes: All meals, transportation, Coast Guard-approved rafting gear, safety instruction, and on-river entertainment. Dates: April through July. Length of trip: 2 days. Group size: 24. Cost: $150. Special requirements: $30 per person deposit. Final payment 30 days before trip date.

EEL RIVER

Middle Fork: (Class II–IV)—The Middle Fork of the Eel combines exciting rafting with coastal mountain scenery. As California's longest navigable wilderness run, with no public access, the Eel meanders through lush grassy meadows covered with a fantastic array of wildflowers—as well as sheer-walled canyons with thundering rapids that may border on the unrunnable in spring. The Eel has a superb reputation for wildlife (especially during the salmon season) and beaver, otter, muskrat, deer, herons, ducks, osprey and a variety of other birds may be observed.

James Henry River Journeys
P.O. Box 807
Bolinas, CA 94924
415-868-1836   *CA/Eel*

Paddle and oar options on the Middle Fork, with special natural history trips available. In business ten years. Licensed by Idaho Outfitters and Guides Association, Alaska Association of Mountain and Wilderness Guides. Includes: All river rafting equipment, guides, meals provided, transportation from points of embarkation to points of debarkation. Dates: April and May. Length of trip: 3–4 days. Group size: 16–30. Cost: $240–$315. Special requirements: Varies with trips—usually novices' conditioning program required on more strenuous trips. River experience required for more advanced rivers.

Wild Water White Water
P.O. Box 431
Suisun, CA 94585
415-921-5020   *CA/Eel*

Paddle yourself or relax and let a guide row you down the Middle Fork. Seven years as professional outfitter. Member: American River Recreation Association, El Dorado Professional Outfitters, American River Guides Association. Includes: All meals, transportation, Coast Guard-approved rafting gear, safety instruction, and on-river entertainment. Dates: April through July. Length of trip: 2 days. Group size: 24. Cost: $150. Special requirements: $30 per person deposit. Final payment 30 days before trip date.

KERN RIVER

Upper Kern: (Class IV–V)—If you crave whitewater adventure—but only have one day to spare—the Upper Kern offers plenty of Class IV and V thrills. Particularly in late spring and early summer, its extreme gradient, big waves and tricky drops pack in a lot of excitement.

Lower Kern: (Class IV)—One of the few Class IV runs that is great for beginners and veterans alike, the Kern starts mild and steadily builds to a walloping crescendo. Close to Southern California in Sequoia National Forest, the lower Kern charges down a steep, convoluted gorge lined with smooth white boulders. There are jungle-like stretches lined by maze-like tunnels of lush foliage—and galloping rapids of ever-increasing intensity.

Forks of the Kern: (Class V)—In this breathtaking canyon of solid granite deep within Sequoia National Forest, the Kern River pirouettes through one of the finest stretches of raftable whitewater in North America. Dropping at the rate of sixty feet per mile, the river tumbles through a nearly continuous series of Class IV and V rapids and waterfalls. Awesome drops, mammoth holes and towering waves follow in quick-fire tempo.

Chuck Richards
P.O. Box W. W. Whitewater
Lake Isabella, CA 93240
619-379-4685   *CA/Kern*

Both paddle and oar options available on the Upper, Lower and Middle Fork of the Kern. Original outfitter and only continuously-permitted outfitter on the Kern since 1975. Permits from Sequoia National Forest. Includes: All meals, all equipment, guides, private river camp. Dates: All year. Length of trip: 1–5 days. Group size: Maximum 25. Cost: $60 per day and up.

Special requirements: Trips and classes for all levels of passengers, including Class V (extreme) sections for experienced veterans. 25% deposit within 7 days of booking; balance 45 days prior to trip.

Outdoor Adventures
3109 Fillmore Street
San Francisco, CA 94123
415-346-8700   *CA/Kern*

Middle and Forks of the Kern. Thirteen years of operation in California. Permitted by United States Department of Agriculture Forest Service, fully insured. Includes: All on-river meals, all necessary rafting equipment, wetsuit rental. Dates: April through September. Length of trip: 2 and 3 days. Group size: 15–25. Cost: $174–$395. Special requirements: $50 or $75 deposit depending on trip, balance due 45 days before trip.

Whitewater Voyages
P.O. Box 906
El Sobrante, CA 94803
415-222-5994   *CA/Kern*

Whitewater Voyages offers a variety of trips on the Lower Kern and Forks of the Kern. William McGinnis, author of *Whitewater Rafting* and *The Guide's Guide*, has led trips on rivers throughout the world. He has owned and operated Whitewater Voyages for eight years. Includes: Fully outfitted whitewater rafting trip with professional guides, all river equipment, meals and refreshments, shuttle transportation to and from the rendezvous north of Kernville. (Personal camping gear NOT included.) Dates: May through August. Length of trip: 2–4 days. Group size: 15 maximum. Cost: $340–$490. Special requirements: The Forks of the Kern trip demands extensive paddling experience, while no previous experience is necessary for Lower Kern trip.

KLAMATH RIVER

With over two hundred tributaries, the Klamath is the largest of California's whitewater rivers. This is Sasquatch country, home of Bigfoot. Quiet sections of the river are often punctuated by roaring rapids. Various stretches of the river each have their own spectacular attractions.

Lower Klamath: (Class III)—A lively, bouncy, leisurely river, the Klamath's warm waters are ideal for swimming. If you listen carefully in the quiet of summer evenings, you might hear Bigfoot stomping across the timbered Siskiyou mountainsides. If Bigfoot proves shy, there are also great blue heron, osprey, bald eagle, ringtail cat, beaver, otter and bear.

Hell's Corner Canyon: (Class IV+)—Hold on tight! Long, turbulent rapids intertwine with high, abrupt drops—over forty major rapids pepper the run—making this a spray-soaked, breathless dash. In places, particularly near the beginning and end of the run, the river has its quiet moods—where it whispers swiftly past park-like meadows thick with oak, Douglas fir, Ponderosa pine and incense cedar. Hell's Canyon also retains an Old West flavor—abandoned settler cabins are visible on the banks, and waterfalls and rapids are known by names like Old Hooch, Gunsmoke, Jackass and Ol' Bushwacker.

Access to Adventure
P.O. Box 500
Lotus, CA 95651
916-626-5042   *CA/Klamath*

Both oar-powered and paddle trips on Lower Klamath and Hell's Corner Gorge. Twelve years' experience. Member American River Recreation Association, American Guides Association, Klamath Canyon River Outfitters, Friends of the River. Includes: Camping, meals, rafts, life jackets, paddles, dry bags, all special river gear, shuttle transportation at the river. Dates: April through October. Length of trip: 2, 3 and 5 days. Group size: 1–20. Cost: $155–$360. Special requirements: $30 per person deposit, balance due 30 days prior to trip.

Action Adventures
P.O. Box 1500
Woodland, CA 95695
916-662-5431   *CA/Klamath*

Hell's Corner Gorge, Middle and Lower Klamath. Twenty-five years without a single personal injury claim to their insurance company, charter member of American Guides Association. Includes: Intermediate area transportation, food, safety and sanitary equipment, group camp gear (everything except personal gear). Dates: April through October. Length of trip: 2, 3 and 6 days. Group size: Any size—depends on trip. Cost: $150–$300.

All Outdoors Adventure Trips
2151 San Miguel Drive
Walnut Creek, CA 94596
415-932-8993   *CA/Klamath*

Lower Klamath plus Hell's Corner Gorge. Fifteen years' experience. Operate under appropriate United States Government agency permits. Includes: All rafting equipment, food, local transportation, guide. Dates: May through September. Length of trip: 1, 2 and 3 days. Group size: 10–25. Cost: $50–$100 per day. Special requirements: Deposit $15 per day. Participant supplies own sleeping bag (rental available at nominal charge).

Epic Adventures
550 South 1st Street
San Jose, CA 95113
408-294-5676   *CA/Klamath*

Paddleboat and oarboat adventures on the Upper and Lower Klamath, including Hell's Corner Gorge. Six years' whitewater experience. Includes: All meals, all rafting equipment, river shuttle, skilled guides, swimming, campfire. Dates: April through October. Length of trip: 1

or 2 days. Group size: 6 to 50 persons. Cost: $45–$65 per day. Special requirements: Ages 8 to 80, no special requirements.

James Henry River Journeys
P.O. Box 807
Bolinas, CA 94924
415-868-1836   *CA/Klamath*

Hell's Corner Gorge and Lower Klamath. Accompanied by a naturalist as well as river-raft guides. In business ten years. Licensed by Idaho Outfitters and Guides Association, Alaska Association of Mountain and Wilderness Guides. Includes: All river-rafting equipment, guides, meals, transportation from point of embarkation to point of debarkation. Dates: May through July. Length of trip: 2, 3 and 5 days. Group size: 16–30. Cost: $170–$390. Special requirements: Varies with trip—usually novices' conditioning program required on more strenuous trips—river experience required for more advanced rivers.

Little Switzerland
P.O. Box 11583
Tahoe Paradise, CA 95708
916-577-5646   *CA/Klamath*

Four years' experience. Includes: Equipment on the river, trained guides, meals. Dates: Mid-April through September. Length of trip: 4 days. Group size: Open. Cost: $250. Special requirements: Full payment 7 days before departure, no previous experience required.

Klamath River Trips
P.O. Box 1077
335 Indian Creek Road
Happy Camp, CA 96039
916-493-2976   *CA/Klamath*

Inflatable kayaks are used on the Lower Klamath; large, durable aluminum oar boats on the Upper. Ten years' experience. Includes: Meals, transportation to and from put-in and take-out points. Coast Guard-approved life jackets. Dates: May through September. Length of trip: 3 days. Group size: 3 to 25. Cost: $245. Special requirements: $25 deposit per person.

Mariah Wilderness Expeditions
P.O. Box 1384
El Cerrito, CA 94530
415-527-5544   *CA/Klamath*

Mariah Wilderness also features several "special trips" which include mother/daughter, father/son raft trips, gourmet trips, all-women trips, three-day raft clinics and mountain-river wilderness training. In winter, cross-country hut and chalet ski trips take place in the ski resort of Bear Valley, on the western slopes of the California Sierras. Owners/operators have been in the business of rafting for eight years. Licensed. Includes: Equipment, food, guides, camp fees. For ski trips: Lodging, meals, trail fees, instruction, guides. Dates: February through October. Length: 1–5 days. Group size: 1–60. Cost: $50–$400.

Outdoors Unlimited
P.O. Box 22513-T
Sacramento, CA 95822
916-452-1081   *CA/Klamath*

Runs the Klamath near Happy Camp (Middle and Lower Klamath.) Operated here for fifteen years. Permitted by United States Forest Service. Includes: All meals on trip, river equipment, shuttle back to car at end of trip. Paddle option available. Dates: Mid-June through end of August. Length of trip: 3 and 6 days. Group size: 20. Cost: $230–$405.

Turtle River Raft
507 McCloud Avenue
Mt. Shasta, CA 96067
916-926-3223   *CA/Klamath*

Lower, Middle and Upper Klamath. Everyone is involved in paddling, boat preparation and camping activities. On the Upper Klamath, Turtle River runs oar/paddle combination boats—and paddle boats for the more adventurous . . . and experienced. Eight years' experience. Includes: Food, equipment, guide service. Dates: May and June. Length of trip: 1 to 5 days. Group size: 6–24. Cost: $58 per day. Special requirements: A deposit is required to reserve a space.

Whitewater Voyages
P.O. Box 906
El Sobrante, CA 94803
415-222-5994   *CA/Klamath*

Runs both Lower Klamath and Hell's Corner Canyon. William McGinnis, author of *Whitewater Rafting* and *The Guide's Guide*, has owned and operated Whitewater Voyages for eight years. Includes: Fully outfitted whitewater rafting trip with professional guides; all river equipment, meals and refreshments, shuttle transportation to and from the rendezvous northwest of Eureka. (Personal camping gear is NOT included.) Dates: July through September. Length of trip: 5 days. Group size: 20 maximum. Cost: $410. Special requirements: Daring souls recommended! No previous experience necessary.

White Water West
2 Virginia Gardens
Berkeley, CA 94702
415-548-0782   *CA/Klamath*

White Water West runs the Upper and Lower Klamath, including Hell's Corner Gorge. You'll tackle the rapids in paddle rafts or inflatable kayaks, while an escort van carries gear between riverside campsites. Fully licensed, insured, five years in business. Includes: Guide service, all equipment, gourmet meals. Dates: June through October. Length of trip: 2 days. Group size: 1 to 25. Cost: $150. Special requirements: No experience necessary. 50% deposit.

Wild Water Whitewater
P.O. Box 431
Suisun City, CA 94585
415-921-5020   *CA/Klamath*

Paddling or oar-raft adventure on the Lower Klamath; oar-rigged rafts only through Hell's Corner. Seven years as professional outfitters. Member American River Recreation Association. Includes: All meals, transportation, Coast Guard-approved rafting gear, on-river entertainment and safety instruction. Dates: April through October. Length of trip: 2 or 3 days. Group size: 24. Cost: $75 per day. Special requirements: Have had previous rafting experience for Upper Klamath. $30 per person deposit, final payment 30 days before trip date.

MERCED RIVER (Class IV)

Pure Sierra snowbelt, the Merced slips out of Yosemite National Park below the awesome cataracts of El Portal. Tumbling quick and clear, it explodes into rapids up to a quarter of a mile long. After a portage around a twenty-foot waterfall, the Merced makes its way to Lake McClure. With a backdrop of California poppies in the springtime and the intrigue of old abandoned railroad trestles and gold mines, this trip offers an intense whitewater experience. Bring wet suits in April and May.

Access to Adventure
P.O. Box 500
Lotus, CA 95651
916-626-5042   *CA/Merced*

Both oar-powered and paddle rafting (previous experience necessary for paddle rafters). Twelve years' experience. Member American River Recreation Association, American Guides Association, Klamath Canyon River Outfitters, Friends of the River. Includes: Camping, meals, rafts, life jackets, paddles, dry bags, all special river gear, shuttle transportation at the river. Dates: May through August. Length of trip: 2 days. Group size: 1–120. Cost: $165. Special requirements: $30 per person deposit, balance due 30 days prior to trip.

Action Adventures
P.O. Box 1500
Woodland, CA 95695
916-662-5431   *CA/Merced*

Twenty-five years without a single personal injury claim to their insurance company; charter member of American Guides Association. Includes: Intermediate area transportation, food, safety and sanitary equipment, group camp gear (everything except personal gear). Dates: April through October. Length of trip: 1–2 days. Group size: Varies. Cost: $100–$190.

All Outdoors Adventure Trips
2151 San Miguel Drive
Walnut Creek, CA 94596
415-932-8993   *CA/Merced*

Fifteen years' experience. Operates under appropriate United States Government agency permits. Includes: All rafting equipment, food, local transportation, guide. Dates: April through July. Length of trip: 1–2 days. Group size: 10–25. Cost: $50–$100 per day. Special requirements: Previous advanced whitewater experience required. Wet suits strongly advised in April and May.

James Henry River Journeys
P.O. Box 807
Bolinas, CA 94924
415-868-1836   *CA/Merced*

Oar boats are available for the inexperienced, but some river experience is preferred. In business ten years. Licensed by Idaho Outfitters and Guides Association, Alaska Association of Mountain and Wilderness Guides. Includes: All river rafting equipment, guides, meals, transportation from point of embarkation to point of debarkation. Dates: April through June. Length of trip: 2 days. Group size: 16–30. Cost: $135–$155. Special requirements: Varies with trip—usually novices' conditioning program required on more strenuous trips—river experience required for more advanced rivers.

Outdoor Adventures
3109 Fillmore Street
San Francisco, CA 94123
415-346-8700   *CA/Merced*

Thirteen years' experience in California; permits from Bureau of Land Management, fully insured. Includes: All on-river meals, all necessary rafting equipment. Dates: May through July. Length of trip: 2 days. Group size: 25. Cost: $198. Special requirements: $50 deposit, balance due 45 days before trip.

Outdoors Unlimited
P.O. Box 22513-T
Sacramento, CA 95822
916-452-1081   *CA/Merced*

Operated here for ten years. Permitted by United States Forest Service. Includes: All meals on trip, river equipment, shuttle from car to river and back. Dates: May through August. Length of trip: 2 days. Group size: 24. Cost: $155–$175. Special requirements: Previous river experience preferred.

SACRAMENTO RIVER

Turtle River Rafting Company
507 McCloud Avenue
Mt. Shasta, CA 96067
916-926-3223   *CA/Sacramento*

Few people have rafted the headwaters of the Sacramento—California's largest river. The Upper Sacramento cascades through a steep canyon, creating continuous action and excitement. Beginning and experienced rafters alike will enjoy the rapids, clean pools and beautiful scenery. This lively river is runnable only in the spring (May–June). Eight years' experience. Includes: Food, equipment, guide service. Dates: May–June. Length of trip: 1 to 5 days. Group size: 6–24. Cost: $58 per day. Special requirements: A deposit is required to reserve a space.

SALMON RIVER (Class IV and V)

In the early spring, the Salmon River, a tributary of the Klamath in northwestern California, provides some of the most challenging whitewater around. Runoff from the Marbale Mountains and the Salmon-Trinity Wilderness areas swells the river into a wild and charging torrent. Confined between narrow canyon walls, the Salmon is a constant series of sharp drops, long and violent rapids, huge holes and midstream boulders. It also abounds in fish, birds, bear, deer and otter. Another hallmark of the run is the water quality . . . it is truly exceptional. Wooley Creek, its major tributary, is reputed to be the clearest stream in the state; and the Salmon can't be far behind.

Access to Adventure
P.O. Box 500
Lotus, CA 95651
916-626-5042   *CA/Salmon*

Twelve years' experience; member American River Recreation Association, American Guides Association, Klamath Canyon River Outfitters, Friends of the River, Pacific River Outfitter and Guides Association, Western River Guides. Includes: Camping, meals, rafts, life jackets, paddles, dry bags, all special river gear, shuttle transportation at the river. Dates:

April through June. Length of trip: 2 days. Group size: 1–120. Cost: $180. Special requirements: $30 deposit per person, balance due 30 days prior to trip.

Action Adventures
P.O. Box 1500
Woodland, CA 95695
916-662-5431   *CA/Salmon*

Twenty-five years without a single personal injury claim to their insurance company, charter member of American Guides Association. Includes: Intermediate area transportation, food, safety and sanitary equipment, group camp gear (everything except personal gear). Dates: April through October. Length of trip: 2–3 days. Group size: Varies. Cost: $245–$345.

All Outdoors
2151 San Miguel Drive
Walnut Creek, CA 94596
415-932-8993   *CA/Salmon*

Fifteen years' experience. Operate under appropriate United States Government agency permits. Includes: All rafting equipment, food, local transportation, guide. Dates: April through mid-July. Length of trip: 1, 2 and 3 days. Group size: 10–25. Cost: $50–$100 per day. Special requirements: Deposit $15 per day. Participant supplies own sleeping bag (rental available at nominal charge).

O.A.R.S.
P.O. Box 67
Angels Camp, CA 95222
209-736-4677
Telex 172 746 STO   *CA/Salmon*

Fourteen years of rafting experience on twenty-six western rivers. Includes: Meals from lunch first day through lunch the last day; all rafting equipment, including life jackets and waterproof gear bags, and experienced, informative guides. Note: May trips include lodging at the rustic Otter Bar Lodge. Dates: May and June. Length of trip: 2–3 days. Group size: 16 maximum, 4–6 per boat. Cost: $245–$345. Special requirements: Prior rafting experience recommended; minimum age 12; $60 per person deposit.

Turtle River Raft
507 McCloud Avenue
Mt. Shasta, CA 96067
916-926-3223   *CA/Salmon*

Oar/paddle and paddle boats available on the Lower Salmon, continuing into the Klamath for a day through the "Ikes" to Orleans. Eight years' experience, professional guide for ten years. Includes: Food, equipment, guide service. Dates: April through June. Length of trip: 1 to 5 days. Group size: 6–24. Cost: $58 per day. Special requirements: A deposit is required to reserve a space.

White Water West
2 Virginia Gardens
Berkeley, CA 94702
415-548-0782   *CA/Salmon*

Fully licensed, insured, five years in business. Includes: Guide service, all equipment, gourmet meals. Dates: April to July. Length of trip: 2 or 3 days. Group size: 1 to 25. Special requirements: Prior rafting experience recommended but not required. 50% deposit.

Wild Water Whitewater
P.O. Box 431
Suisun City, CA 94585
415-921-5020   *CA/Salmon*

Seven years as professional outfitter. Member American River Recreation Association. Includes: All meals, transportation, Coast Guard-approved rafting gear, on-river entertainment and safety instruction. Dates: April through October. Length of trip: 2 or 3 days. Group size: 24. Cost: $75 per day. Special requirements: Previous rafting experience necessary. $30 per person deposit, final payment 30 days before trip date.

TUOLUMNE RIVER (Class IV–V)

Located near Yosemite National Park, the Tuolumne (pronounced too-WAL-ah-me) tumbles at a gradient of forty feet per mile through seventeen miles of clear pools, frothing whitewater and spectacular canyon scenery.

It is one of the last few stretches of wilderness water left in California, and it packs in over fifty major rapids.

More like a giant creek than a river, the Tuolumne features crystalline waters, colorful wildflowers and many tricky, rock-dotted steep passages—making it one of the most exhilarating rivers in the west.

The "T" also offers you an intimate river experience: because of government regulations, the number of commercial trips is limited to two per day, with a maximum trip size of eighteen guests.

Action Adventures
P.O. Box 1500
Woodland, CA 95695
916-662-5431   *CA/Tuolumne*

Twenty-five years without a single personal injury claim to their insurance company, charter member of American Guides Association. Includes: Intermediate area transportation, food, safety and sanitary equipment, group camp gear (everything except personal gear). Dates: April through October. Length of trip: 1, 2 and 3 days. Group size: Varies. Cost: $200–$345.

All Outdoors
2151 San Miguel Drive
Walnut Creek, CA 94596
415-932-8993   *CA/Tuolumne*

Fifteen years' experience. Operates under appropriate United States Government agency permits. Includes: All rafting equipment, food, local transportation, guide. Dates: March through November. Length of trip: 1, 2 and 3 days. Group size: 10–25. Cost: $90–$260. Special requirements: Deposit $15 per day. Participant supplies own sleeping bag (rental available at nominal charge).

Outdoors Unlimited
P.O. Box 22513-T
Sacramento, CA 95822
916-452-1081   *CA/Tuolumne*

Have operated river trips here for twelve years. Permit issued by United States Forest Service. Includes: Meals on trip, all river equipment, shuttle from car to river and back. Paddle option available. Dates: April through October. Length of trip: 1, 2 and 3 days. Group size: 18. Cost: $200–$345. Special requirements: Passengers should have prior whitewater experience.

NORTH YUBA RIVER (Class IV and V)

The North Yuba combines advanced whitewater, exquisite wilderness scenery and solitude—an uncrowded, special run. At its headwaters (Sierra City to Goodyear's Bar), the North Yuba offers radical Class V rafting—narrow, bouldery and steep, with an average gradient of ninety feet per mile. From Goodyear's Bar down, the river packs in plenty of Class IV thrills. Since the river runs best in spring, you can look forward to green hillsides with a variety of different wildflowers.

All Outdoors
2151 San Miguel Drive
Walnut Creek, CA 94596
415-932-8993   *CA/North Yuba*

Fifteen years' experience. Operate under appropriate United States Government agency permits. Includes: All rafting equipment, food, local transportation, guide. Dates: April through July. Length of trip: 1 or 2 days. Group size: 10–25. Cost: $63–$148 per day. Special requirements: Deposit $15 per day. Participant supplies own sleeping bag (rental available at nominal charge).

White Water West
2 Virginia Gardens
Berkeley, CA 94702
415-548-0782   *CA/North Yuba*

Fully licensed, insured, five years in business. Includes: Guide service, all equipment, gourmet meals. Dates: April to July. Length of trip: 2 or 3 days. Group size: 1 to 25. Special requirements: Prior rafting experience recommended but not required. 50% deposit.

Colorado

ARKANSAS RIVER

Colorado Adventure Network
194 South Franklin Street
Denver, CO 30209
303-722-6482   *CO/Arkansas*

Colorado Adventure Network emphasizes paddle trips, to encourage teamwork and total participation in the rafting experience. The fast narrow stretches of the Arkansas River will thrill you with Class V rapids. On the trips you will be part of a paddling team learning to read and respond to the variety of water a river presents. You will be able to explore remote canyons, spot wildlife and archeological sites, and safely enjoy the thrills of a stretch of river still "wild and free." Colorado Adventure Network also runs a Rio Grande River through Taos Box Canyon, which will challenge and reward you with its quiet isolation and breathtaking beauty. The tour operator has guided river raft trips for the last ten years in Colorado; he has been the staff trainer for Outward Bound. Includes: Sleeping bags, pad, all food, cooking equipment, eating utensils, shuttle of vehicles, rafts, and experienced guides. Dates: April through September. Length of trip: 1, 2 and 3 days. Group size: Minimum 10. Cost: $50–$75 day. Special requirements: 50% deposit, balance due 15 days before multi-day trips.

Ultimate Escapes
2506 West Colorado Avenue, Dept. S
Colorado Springs, CO 80904
303-578-8383
Telex 499 2665 OLD COLO CITY   *CO/Arkansas*

Ultimate Escapes' "Surf & Turf" adventure combines wildwater rafting on the Arkansas River (Class V) and horsepacking into the Sangre de Cristo Range. You'll start off with three days on horseback, climbing switchbacks, crossing mountain meadows bright with alpine flowers, and camping lakeside. Then it's on to two days' rafting on the Arkansas. Includes: Round-trip transportation Cold Springs; 13 meals, tents, rafts, horses and all necessary equipment; 2 nights at the Superior Monarch Ski Resort Lodge with jacuzzi, health club, pool; 3-day horse trip, 2-day river trip. Dates: Every Monday, June through September. Length of trip: 5 days, 4 nights. Group size: 4 to 12. Cost: $449. Special requirements: Suitable for anyone in good health and moderately good condition. No previous experience necessary.

COLORADO RIVER

Range Tours
1540 South Holly Street
Denver, CO 80222
303-759-1988
800-525-8509
Telex 910 931 0574   *CO/Colorado*

The Upper Colorado River near Vail alternates sections of great whitewater with mellow scenic touring. The rapids in Gore Canyon, Red Gorge and Christmas Canyon present exhilarating rafting—all with the Gore Range and Flat Tops areas of the Rockies as the panoramic backdrop. Range Tours offers a variety of programs on this section of the Colorado, featuring riverside campsites and hearty, Old West-style meals. The rafts are oar-powered or paddle-powered. Includes: Rafting, camping, round-trip transportation from Vail to the river, meals from lunch the first day through lunch on the last, group equipment, experienced boatmen and guides, Coast Guard-approved life jackets. Dates: Most days May through September. Length of trip: 1 to 4 days. Group size: 15–20 passengers. Cost: $43–$250. Special requirements: No previous experience required.

DOLORES RIVER

Outlaw River Expeditions
P.O. Box 790-M
Moab, UT 84532
801-259-8241   *CO/Dolores*

The Dolores River is a small, swift river, runnable only in the spring and early summer. You'll begin in the colorful state of Colorado and wind through narrow, deep canyons where early prospectors scaled the sheer sandstone walls in their efforts to mine gold. "The Narrows" bring you nearly a mile of superb whitewater—some of the most thrilling you'll encounter anywhere. Blond sand beaches, auburn Mule deer peering from serene willows, majestic great blue heron wading the shallows—all are just a part of what you'll see on this beautiful stretch of river. You'll pass beneath the majestic upthrust of the snow-capped LaSal Mountains, through rugged primitive Gateway Canyon until joining the mighty Colorado River. Licensed, insured, federally-permitted river outfitter. Fifteen years' experience running southwestern rivers. Includes: Transportation to river put-in, and back from take-out to the point of published departure (Moab or Grand Junction). All camping and sleeping gear, waterproof bags and boxes, all meals, wine with dinners, and cold beer. Dates: May through September. Length of trip: 3 days. Group size: 5 to 30. Cost: $334. Special requirements: ⅓ of fare to hold space.

GREEN RIVER

"After dinner we pass through a region of wildest desolation," wrote Major John Wesley Powell of his 1869 expedition. "The canyon is very tortuous, the river very rapid, and many lateral canyons enter on either side. Crags and tower-shaped peaks are seen everywhere, and above them long lines of broken cliffs . . . We are minded to call this the Canyon of Desolation."

Today, the primitive character of Desolation and Gray canyons, which seemed forbidding to Powell, draws knowledgeable river runners for the Green River of Colorado and Utah.

Perhaps the least well-known, the Green River is one of the most scenic, colorful and historic of all Western rivers. Riffles and rapids—over sixty of them—gradually increase in difficulty downriver. The rapids alternate with calm, swift stretches of water, offering a perfect change of pace. White sandy camping beaches are plentiful and offer opportunities for swimming and hiking side canyons.

Highlights along the route include historic McPherson Ranch, an occasional way-station for Butch Cassidy's Wild Bunch when they needed grub or fresh horses; Desolation Canyon, with its steep red walls and pinon and juniper on the talus slopes, and Gray Canyon. Through the Lodore Canyon area, canyons are deep and exciting with heavy vermilion colors. Trips on the Green can often be combined with expeditions on the Yampa and Colorado rivers.

Don Hatch
P.O. Box C
Vernal, UT 84078
801-789-4316   *CO/Green*

Don Hatch runs the Green River through Lodore Canyon and the Green/Yampa combination. The Green/Yampa is best run on spring and early summer high water, when volume often exceeds that of the Colorado River. Don Hatch is one of the pioneers of the commercial river running industry, with forty-three years and three generations of river experience. Over the years, their notable guests have included: Lowell Thomas, Sir Edmund Hillary, Lawrence Rockefeller, Paul Mellon, John Glenn, the Robert and Ted Kennedy families and others. Hatch is a fully bonded and licensed outfitter. Includes: Boats, experienced guides, life jackets, all whitewater-related equipment, all meals and meal preparation, transportation from base point to river and return, vehicle parking, airport and motel pickup and delivery, special arrangements for birthdays, anniversaries, etc. Dates: May through September. Length of trip: 3, 4, and 5 days. Group size: Average 15 with 25 maximum. Cost: $305. Special requirements: No skill requirements. Deposit of $100 required if booking in advance.

Moki Mak
P.O. Box 21242
Salt Lake City, UT 84121
801-943-6707
Telex 381 528 HQ SLC   *CO/Green*

Hike, swim, raft and ride in the Utah wilderness on Moki Mak's combination trail ride and float trip down the Green River. The owners of Moki Mak, Bob, Clair and Richard Quist, have been running rivers for twenty-nine years. Includes: All food on the trip, eating utensils, use of 2 waterproof bags for personal gear, watertight container for camera, and Coast Guard-approved life jacket; transportation from Green River, UT and return (option, transportation from Grand Junction, CO and return $50 extra). Dates: June through September. Length of trip: 6 days, 5 nights. Group size: 8 to 15. Cost: $549. Special requirements: $100 per person deposit, balance due 30 days prior to trip departure.

On some trips, you can combine horsepacking with river rafting for double adventure.
(MOKI MAC RIVER EXPEDITIONS)

Outlaw River Expeditions
P.O. Box 790-M
Moab, UT 84532
801-259-8241

CO/Green

With Outlaw River Expeditions, you can enjoy a leisurely-paced oar-powered raft trip through Desolation Canyon—or man your own sportyak. The company also offers a Green/Colorado River combination trip through Cataract Canyon and Canyonlands National Park. Licensed, insured, federally permitted river outfitter. Fifteen years' experience running Southwestern rivers. Includes: Transportation to the river put-in, and back from take-out to the point of published departure (Moab or Grand Junction). All camping and sleeping gear, waterproof bags and boxes, all meals, wine with dinners, and cold beer. Dates: May through September. Length of trip: 4–7 days. Group size: 5 to 30. Cost: $459 to $689. Special requirements: ⅓ of fare to hold space.

Western River Expeditions
7258 Racquet Club Drive
Salt Lake City, UT 84121
801-942-6669
800-453-7450 in Utah

CO/Green

Western River Expeditions offers both paddle and oar-boat expeditions on the Green River, as well as a week-long adventure that combines a two-day outing at a working cattle ranch with a five-day trip on the river. Includes: Flight from Grand Junction, Colorado, to Tavaputs Ranch; scenic plane ride from ranch to river launch site; bus trip from Green River, Utah to Grand Junction at end of trip. Sightseeing, meals, accommodations at Tavaputs Ranch, all meals while on the river, tents on river, professional river guide service and first-class meal preparation. Dates: June through August. Length of trip: 5–7 days. Cost: $495–$685.

Georgia/South Carolina

CHATTOOGA RIVER (Class V)

The Chattooga may be America's best-known river, having "starred" in the movie "Deliverance." Spawned in the North Carolina highlands at the crest of the Appalachian Mountains, the Chattooga works its way along the Georgia/South Carolina border over fifty miles of the most primitive, exciting and spectacular country in the East. Forming a gorge of sheer rock cliffs, it falls many times as rapidly as the Colorado; harboring waterfalls, blistering rapids, lovely pools, exotic plants and wildlife.

Section III of the river traverses some of its most beautiful sections and includes a run through fabled Bull Sluice Rapid as well as several rapids featured in "Deliverance."

Section IV of the Chattooga is the steepest section of river currently being rafted on a commercial basis in the East. Sheer cliffs rise above the foaming waters, and large waterfalls drop into the riverbed, feeding the ever-growing torrent. Famous portions include Seven Foot Falls, Raven Rock Rapids, Corkscrew, Jawbone and Sock-Em-Dog.

Nantahala Outdoor Center
U.S. 19 West, Box 41
Bryson City, NC 28713
704-488-9221 *GA, SC/Chattooga*

Runs Sections III and IV of the river. Founded 1972; licensed with United States Forest Service and founding member of the Eastern Professional River Outfitters Association (EPRO). Includes: All equipment (including wet suits if necessary), lunch, transportation to and from the river, experienced guides. Dates: May through October. Length of trip: 1 day. Cost: $32–$45.

Wildwater Limited Outdoor Adventures
Long Creek, SC 29658
803-647-9587 *GA, SC/Chattooga*

Runs both Sections III and IV of the river. Founded 1971. Licensed; Member of American Whitewater Affiliation and Eastern Professional River Outfitters Association. Includes: Full day trip, with lunch, all equipment, shuttle and guides. Dates: March through October. Length of trip: 1 day. Group size: Varies. Cost: $30–$50. Special requirements: Age minimum 12 years.

Idaho

SALMON RIVER (Class III +)

They call it "River of No Return."

Discovered by Lewis and Clark, the Salmon flows through the second-deepest gorge in North America. Because of its rollercoaster waves and mile-high mountainsides, early explorers called it impassable. But today, the Salmon's thrilling rapids make it a premier outdoor vacation.

Along the Salmon you'll see many remnants of how the West was won—mining claims, tattered homesteads, Indian caves with beautiful petroglyphs. Because of the untamed nature of this rugged country, sometimes the river provides the only access to remote canyons and gorges. Many forms of wildlife make their homes here—deer, elk, bear, mountain sheep as well as smaller animals and birds, including golden and bald eagles.

Middle Fork: (Class III+)—The Salmon's Middle Fork rips through 105 miles of some of the most inaccessible, primitive country in the world, running hard with an average drop of twenty-five feet per mile. Designated a Wild and Scenic River, the Middle Fork is free of dams. Among its famous rapids are Velvet Falls, Water Wheel, Rubber Rapids and Tappan Falls. During late summer and early fall, the Middle Fork is renowned for its trout fishing. It's also known for natural hot springs, where you can unwind at the end of the day.

Main Salmon: (Class III)—Flowing for some ninety or so miles, the Main Salmon cuts the second deepest canyon in North America and bisects Idaho's vast Primitive area—the largest undeveloped land mass in the contiguous United States. The river offers a varied rhythm of dramatic rapids and lazy calms, rock-walled gorges and forested slopes. Riverside hikes may reward adventurers with the discovery of an abandoned cabin or Indian cave painting.

Lower Salmon: Hot sun. Warm water. Crashing waves. White beaches. Steep canyons. This is the lower Salmon Gorge. Below Whitebird, Idaho, the Salmon flows for fifty-two miles before joining the mighty Snake—which then continues nineteen miles to the confluence with the Grande Ronde.

Barker-Ewing
P.O. Box 1243
Jackson, WY 83001
307-733-3410   *ID/Salmon*

On the Main Salmon, runs comfortable and commodious sweep-rigged rafts, with paddle rafts also available. Twenty years' experience. Includes: Round-trip transportation from Jackson, Wyoming or Idaho Falls, Idaho for trips when water levels permit jetboat ride back up the river, usually until August. Meeting in Jackson, a ten-mile scenic float with breakfast on the Snake River prior to trip departure for Salmon. All meals beginning with morning of the Salmon River trip, all transportation. Dates: July and August. Length of trip: 5 days, 4 nights, camping. Group size: 12–24 persons. Cost: Adults $700, child $600. Special requirements: $100 per person upon booking (non-refundable). Sleeping bag rental available.

Custom River Tours
Box 7071
Boise, ID 83707
208-343-3343   *ID/Salmon*

On the Middle Fork, Custom River Tours offers both twelve-foot paddle boats and seventeen-foot oar boats. Ken Masoner, operator, has been floating since '64. He's the second generation running this family-owned outfit. Includes: Waterproof containers for gear, roomy tents—everything but your toothbrush; excellent and personable guides. Dates: June (high-water) and September (fishing and rapids). Length of trip: 6 days. Group size: 24 guests maximum. Cost: $800 per person. Special requirements: $200, 60 days in advance. Age limit depends on water level and nature of party. Some trips are adult-only, others are family-oriented. Wet suits for spring nature trips.

Echo: The Wilderness Company
6529 Telegraph Avenue
Oakland, CA 94609
415-652-1600   *ID/Salmon*

Echo runs the Main Salmon, with a paddleboat normally available on all trips. Twelve years of whitewater river-running experience. Member of Western River Guides Association, Oregon Guides and Packers. Includes: Guides, river gear, food, six days of Idaho wilderness whitewater and wildlife. Dates: June through September. Length of trip: 6 days. Group size: 6 to 25. Cost: $660. Special requirements: Reasonable physical condition. Deposit of $100 per person required, full payment 60 days before trip begins.

Don Hatch River Expeditions, Inc.
P.O. Box C
Vernal, UT 84078
801-789-4316   *ID/Salmon*

Runs the Middle Fork of the Salmon, allowing plenty of time for on-shore activities, such as hiking to spectacular waterfalls and Indian petroglyphs. Don Hatch has forty-three years and three generations of river experience. Notable guests have included Sir Edmund Hillary and the Rockefeller and Kennedy families. Includes: Boats, guides, all whitewater-related equipment, all meals, transportation from Sun Valley to river. Dates: Mid-June through August. Length: 6 days. Group size: Average 20, maximum 24. Cost: $589. Special requirements: Minimum age 11; advance reservations with deposit.

High Adventure River Tours
P.O. Box 1434
Twin Falls, ID 83301
208-324-2962   *ID/Salmon*

Oar-powered raft trips on the Middle Fork. Randy L. Stone (managing agent) has twelve years' guiding experience on the Middle Fork of the Salmon River, and has logged over twelve thousand miles on the river. Includes: Everything except sleeping bag and pad plus personal gear. Dates: Late June to mid-September. Length of trip: 6 days. Group size: 24 guests, 6 guides. Cost: $795. Special requirements: Deposit of $200 is needed to secure a reservation.

James Henry River Journeys
P.O. Box 807
Bolinas, CA 94924
415-868-1836   *ID/Salmon*

Middle Fork and Main Salmon. Paddle and oar trips are available, plus inflatable kayaks on trips later in the season. In business ten years. Licensed by Idaho Outfitters and Guides Association, Alaska Association of Mountain and Wilderness Guides. Dates: June through August. Length of trip: 6 days. Cost: $645–$750.

Middle Fork River Expeditions
(June–August)
P.O. Box 199
Stanley, ID 83278
208-774-3659

(September–May)
1615 21st East
Seattle, WA 98112
206-324-0364   *ID/Salmon*

Oar-powered raft trips on the Middle Fork. You'll spend about six hours a day on the river—leaving plenty of time for hiking, swimming, fishing and photography. Middle Fork River Expeditions is a licensed and bonded outfitter with the State of Idaho; member of Idaho's Outfitters and Guides Association; employs experienced and licensed boatmen. Includes: Six-day, five-night float trip, gourmet food including black tie champagne brunch at take-out and gala farewell banquet; ground transportation to and from river; experienced and licensed boatmen; life jacket, first aid supplies, tents, cooking and eating utensils, waterproof containers for personal gear and cameras. Dates: June to September. Length of trip: 6 days (ask about shorter trips). Group size: 2–24 people. Cost: $750 per person for adults; $625 for children under 12 years. Special requirements: They welcome first-timers and old-timers, 8–90 years old, non-swimmers and swimmers. A deposit of $200 is required to hold your reservation firm.

Northwest Adventures
North 8884 Government Way, Suite B
Hayden Lake, ID 83835
208-772-7531
800-635-1379   *ID/Salmon*

Includes: Transfers from airport—meals on the river. Dates: May through October. Length of trip: 4–6 days. Group size: 2–200. Cost: $300–$490. Special requirements: Deposit of $100 or 25% whichever is more.

Outdoor Adventures
3109 Fillmore Street
San Francisco, CA 94123
415-346-8700   *ID/Salmon*

Runs the Main Salmon and its Middle Fork. Thirteen years' experience in Idaho, licensed by State of Idaho, permitted by United States Department of Agriculture Forest Service, fully insured. Includes: All on-river meals, trip origin in Stanley and trip end in Salmon, all necessary rafting equipment, waterproof duffels. Dates: Late June through early September. Length of trip: 6 days. Group size: 24. Cost: $750. Special requirements: $100 deposit, balance due 45 days before trip.

RANGE TOURS

Range Tours
1540 South Holly Street
Denver, CO 80222
303-759-1988
800-525-8509 toll free
Telex 91 0931 0574   *ID/Salmon*

Range Tours run oar-powered raft trips on the Main Salmon and Middle Fork. Includes: Rafting, camping, meals, major group equipment and supplies, and round-trip transportation from Salmon, Idaho to river. Dates: June through August. Length of trip: 6 days, 5 nights. Group size: 15–20. Cost: $634. Special requirements: Must be in good physical condition.

River Odysseys West
East 320 17th Avenue
Spokane, WA 99203
509-624-7317   *ID/Salmon*

Oar and paddle trips on the Lower Gorge of the Salmon. River Odysseys West is a small, family outfit owned by two brothers—one or the other of whom goes along on every trip. They emphasize gourmet cooking and personalized service. Fully-licensed and bonded guides and outfitters in Oregon and Idaho. Includes: Food, equipment, guides, black bags, life jackets, tents (everything except clothes and sleeping bags). Dates: July through September. Length of trip: 4–5 days. Group size: 8–24 people. Cost: $385–$445. Special requirements: $100 deposit with reservation.

Rocky Mountain River Tours
P.O. Box 126
Hailey, ID 83333-0126
208-788-9300   *ID/Salmon*

Oar-powered raft trips on the Middle Fork are designed to allow you plenty of time off-river for hiking, fishing, birdwatching, sunbathing and swimming. David Mills and Rocky Mountain River Tours are licensed and bonded by the State of Idaho. David Mills has fourteen years of extensive river running experience with a background in recreation management. Sheila Mills is the author of Rocky Mountain Kettle Cuisine and has twelve years' whitewater experience. Their guides have minimum ten years' guiding experience and science education backgrounds. Includes: Round-trip transportation from meeting point, licensed guides, small oar-powered rafts, life jackets, food, waterproof personal gear bags and camera bags, camping equipment. Dates: June through August. Length of trip: 5 nights, 6 days. Group size: 8 to 24. Cost: From $450. Special requirements: No experience necessary, $150 per person deposit.

Teton Expeditions
P.O. Box 218
Rigby, ID 83442
208-745-6476   *ID/Salmon*

On both the Main and Middle Fork of the Salmon, Teton Expeditions runs different-sized rafts—from smaller, "let 'em buck" types to larger rafts for a greater feeling of security. Teton Expeditions is an "all in the family" company, started over thirty years ago by the Fosters. Licensed through State of Idaho, permittee of United States Forest Service, member of Idaho Outfitters and Guides Association, bonded through the State. Includes: Food, tents, waterproof bags, complete guide service, transportation from Boise or Stanley to trip start and back to point of beginning from trip end. Dates: June through August. Length of trip: 5 days, 4 nights. Group size: 24 maximum. Cost: $625. Special requirements: Reservation by $150 deposit.

SNAKE RIVER (Class III–IV)

Running through a canyon a mile and a half deep, the Snake River has a history and lore nearly as exciting as its pulsating fifteen-foot waves. Deserted homesteads—rusty farm implements still intact—recall the efforts of white settlers to coax a living out of this land, while Indian petroglyphs and rock dwellings remind you of the canyon's earliest inhabitants. The surrounding area had been the home of the inventive Nez Perce Indians, who domesticated animals, bred the Appaloosa horse, and ventured as far as the Great Plains to hunt buffalo.

The Snake's Hell's Canyon is the deepest gorge in North America, with vertical basalt walls towering nearly seven thousand feet in height. Gradually the Snake grows more gentle, and the rugged walls give way to grassy slopes, cactus meadows, beaches, shady fern-lined sidestreams and cooling waterfalls. The water is warm enough for swimming but cold enough for black bass, trout, chinook—and six-foot-long sturgeon have been caught. Meanwhile, osprey and eagles circle above.

Not as rough or primitive as the Salmon, the Snake is ideal for newcomers to rafting and extended camping, while major rapids like Wild Sheep, Granite Creek and Waterspout keep things interesting for river veterans.

Echo: The Wilderness Company
6529 Telegraph Avenue
Oakland, CA 94609
415-652-1600   *ID/Snake*

Runs the Hell's Canyon portion of the Snake. Twelve years of whitewater and wilderness river touring experience. Includes: Guides, gear, food, shuttle from Boise to river and return to Boise. Dates: May through September. Length of trip: 6 days. Group size: 6–25. Cost: $660. Special requirements: Camping skills, enthusiasm for outdoors and wildlife; deposit of $100 required per person, full payment 60 days before trip starts.

James Henry River Journeys
P.O. Box 807
Bolinas, CA 94924
415-868-1836   *ID/Snake*

Paddle, oar and inflatable kayak expeditions through Hell's Canyon of the Snake. In business ten years. Licensed by Idaho Outfitters and Guides Association, Alaska Association of Mountain and Wilderness Guides. Includes: All river rafting equipment, guides, meals provided, transportation from points of embarkation to points of debarkation. Dates: July and August. Length of trip: 6 days. Group size: 16–30. Cost: From $475. Special requirements: Varies with trips—usually novices' conditioning program required on more strenuous trips.

Northwest Adventures
North 8884 Government Way, Suite B
Hayden, ID 83835
208-772-7531
800-635-1379   *ID/Snake*

Includes: Transfers from airport—meals on the river. Dates: May through October. Length of trip: 1–3 days. Group size: 2–200. Cost: $35–$225. Special requirements: Deposit of $100 or 25%, whichever is more.

Snake River Outfitters
811 Snake River Avenue
Lewiston, ID 83501
208-746-2232
208-743-7288   *ID/Snake*

Trip puts in directly below Hell's Canyon Dam and runs the eighty-six miles through the gorge. Guides licensed through Idaho Outfitter and Guides Board; United States Forest Service Permit. Includes: Transportation to launch and from take-out point back to Lewiston, life jackets, tents, meals, waterproof gear bags, water-tight hand cases. Sleeping bags with pads and fishing gear available to rent. Dates: June through September. Length of trip: 5 days. Group size: 10–25. Cost: $495 per person. Special requirements: 25% deposit, full payment 30 days prior to float.

UPPER OWYHEE RIVER

River Odysseys West
East 320 17th Avenue
Spokane, WA 99203
509-624-7317   *ID/Upper Owyhee*

River Odysseys West is a small, family outfit run by two brothers—one or the other of whom accompanies every trip. Due to the fragility of the desert ecosystem of the Owyhee, they are allowed to conduct only two trips per season on the river. It is a small river in an extraordinary wilderness, requiring the use of shorter, thirteen-foot rafts, each carrying one guide and two passengers. Portaging or lining of some rapids is occasionally required. Fewer than two hundred people float this section each year. Includes: Food, equipment, guides, black bags, life jackets, tents (everything except clothes and sleeping bags). Dates: April and May. Length of trip: 6 days. Group size: 8–24 people. Cost: $795. Special requirements: $100 deposit with reservation.

Kentucky

CUMBERLAND RIVER

Cumberland Outdoor Adventures
Route 6, Box 372-B
Corbin, KY 40701
606-523-0629; if no one answers in winter:
704-689-5228   *KY/Cumberland*

Spend a day rafting the whitewater of the Cumberland River near Cumberland Falls, Kentucky. You will leave all signs of civilization behind as you float down the river between towering bluffs. This eight-mile, seven-hour trip is an adventure the entire family can enjoy. Cumberland also runs raft trips on Tennessee's Obed River, Daddy's Creek, and Big South Fork Gorge; and offers canoe camping in Big South Fork National Park. Includes: Rafts, paddles, life jackets, lunch, trained guides, transportation to and from river. Dates: Daily June through Labor Day; Thursday, Saturday, and Sunday during May, September and October; other dates by arrangement. Length of trip: Approximately 7 hours. Group size: 50. Cost: Adults $29; children $19.

Maine

DEAD RIVER (Class III–IV)

The Dead River can be run only in springtime, when special high water releases from Central Maine Power turn this river into sixteen miles of continuous, churning whitewater.

In addition to offering challenging rafting, the Dead River wilderness area encompasses some of Maine's wildest and most rugged terrain. Moose sightings are by no means rare, and deer and bear are often seen.

Due to the coldness of spring water temperatures, wet suits are generally required.

Saco Bound
P.O. Box 113 (Route 302)
Center Conway, NH 03813
603-447-3002   *ME/Dead*

Runs paddle rafts on the Dead River at high water levels—generally only two weeks a year. Fully licensed, professional rafting company licensed by the State of Maine. Includes: Rafting equipment, transportation in the area, guide in each raft, steak-fry lunch on the river. Dates: Mid-May through June 1 (approximate). Length of trip: 1 day. Group size: Maximum 80. Cost: $60–$72.50. Special requirements: Wet suits required (can be rented from operator). Participants must be at least 16 years old.

Unicorn Rafting
P.O. Box 50
West Forks, ME 04985
207-663-2258   *ME/Dead*

Runs the Dead River at high water. Wet suits can be rented from operator. Includes: All gear, meals, professional guide, lobster dinners. Dates: May. Length of trip: 1–9 days. Group size: Up to 80 per trip. Cost: $70. Special requirements: None.

KENNEBEC RIVER (Class IV–V)

The Kennebec River drains Moosehead Lake, the largest body of fresh water in New England. As the river plummets through majestic Kennebec Gorge, it is transformed into one of the most challenging continuous whitewater runs in the East. Rapids like the Three Sisters, Goodbye, Alleyway and Magic Falls test the skills of raft and crew.

As the river leaves the gorge, it broadens and slows. Rafters can enjoy a swift but pleasant swim through the lower rapids. And if conditions permit, you can hike into Moxie Falls, a ninety-foot waterfall with a foaming pool.

Saco Bound
P.O. Box 113 (Route 302)
Center Conway, NH 03813
603-447-3002   *ME/Kennebec*

Saco Bound runs paddle day-trips on the Kennebec. They also offer a two-day package with Sugarloaf Inn, which includes lodging and meals in addition to the rafting. Fully licensed, professional rafting company licensed by the State of Maine. Includes: Rafting equipment, transportation in the area, guide in each raft, steak-fry lunch on the river. Dates: Mid-May through June 1 (approximate). Length of trip: 1 day. Group size: Maximum 80. Cost: $60–$72.50. Special requirements: Must be at least 12 years old.

Unicorn Rafting
P.O. Box 50
West Forks, ME 04985
207-663-2258   *ME/Kennebec*

Unicorn offers one- and two-day trips on the Kennebec. Includes: All gear, meals, professional guide, lobster dinners. Dates: May. Length of trip: 1–9 days. Group size: Up to 80 per trip. Cost: $70. Special requirements: None.

PENOBSCOT RIVER—West Branch
(Class IV–V)

The West Branch of the Penobscot River drains one of the most scenic portions of Maine. Flowing through the heart of Thoreau country in the embrace of mile-high Mount Katahdin, the river offers beautiful surroundings, boiling rapids and varied wildlife, such as moose, bald eagles and beavers.

The upper portion of the Penobscot—from the Ripogenus Gorge to the Big Eddy—features some of the wildest whitewater in the East, including the Exterminator and Staircase rapids. Here, the river tumbles swiftly out of the mountains, dropping over seventy feet per mile. In the quiet stretches between rapids, there's time to admire the splendor of Ripogenus' sheer granite walls. Below the gorge, the river bursts loose into the Class V Cribwork—hailed as the most technical big water run in the East.

On the fourteen-mile run from Big Eddy to Pockwockamus Falls, the river alternates between calm scenic pools and sharply churning rapids, including breathtaking Nesowdnehunk Falls, a nine-foot drop into a boiling sousehole.

Saco Bound
P.O. Box 113 (Route 302)
Center Conway, NH 03813
603-447-3002   *ME/Penobscot*

Offers paddle raft trips on both sections of the Penobscot. Fully licensed, professional rafting company licensed by the State of Maine. Includes: Rafting equipment, transportation in the area, guide in each raft, steak-fry lunch on the river. Dates: Mid-May through June 1 (approximate). Length of trip: 1 day. Group size: Maximum 80. Cost: $60–$72.50. Special requirements: Participants must be at least 12 years of age; 14 years old for the gorge section.

Unicorn Rafting
P.O. Box 50
West Forks, ME 04985
207-663-2258   *ME/Penobscot*

Runs day trips including Ripogenus Gorge, plus an overnight adventure that also features the Class V Debsconeag Falls. Includes: All gear, meals, professional guide, lobster dinners. Dates: May. Length of trip: 1–9 days. Group size: Up to 80 per trip. Cost: $70. Special requirements: None.

Maryland

YOUGHIOGHENY RIVER

Precision Rafting Expeditions
P.O. Box 185
Friendsville, MD 21531
301-746-5290   *MD/Youghiogheny*

The sport of whitewater is pushed to its technical limits on the challenging Upper Youghiogheny River in the mountains of western Maryland. The "Upper" drops a nonstop 120 feet per mile, dashing down through a "Wild and Scenic" canyon with over twenty Class IV and V rapids. It's a day of rafting unequalled in excitement by any other eastern river. Drops with names like "Zinger," "Meat Cleaver" and "Double Pencil Sharpener" will thrill even the most experienced rafters. Three adventurers and one guide travel in each four-man raft; a safety kayaker also accompanies each trip. Twenty years' combined experience in commercial rafting from Canada to Peru. All guides are expert kayakers as well as highly experienced raft guides. Includes: All the transportation to and from river. All safety equipment, rafts, experienced guides, safety kayaker and river lunch. Dates: May through October. Length of trip: 10.5 miles—about 5–6 hours. Group size: 12 or smaller. Cost: $100. Special requirements: Good physical condition. You should have at least a little whitewater experience. $20 deposit.

Montana

MISSOURI, SMITH AND YELLOWSTONE RIVERS

**Great Adventures West
820 Central Avenue
Great Falls, MT 59401
406-761-1677**   *MT/Missouri, Smith, Yellowstone*

Great Adventures West's float trips take you to some remote and beautiful reaches on Montana's Missouri, Smith and Yellowstone Rivers. You'll be able to view wildlife and fauna in the most ideal and natural conditions. You can see deer, antelope, mink, beaver, hawks, eagles, ducks and geese all on one river trip. Whether you want whitewater excitement, fishing or tranquil scenic floats, Great Adventures West's guides are ready to get you there and back safely and enjoyably. Both paddle and oar-powered trips are available. Member, Montana Outfitters and Guides Association; Western River Guides Association; Fishing and Floating Association of Montana. Includes: Food, camping gear, boats, saunas; everything except personal items. Dates: May through October. Length: 1–7 days. Group size: 1–50. Cost: Approximately $75 per day per person. Special requirements: $100 deposit for extended trips; advance payment for day trips.

New York

HUDSON RIVER (Class V)

In the High Peak region of the Adirondack Mountains in northern New York lies the source of the mighty Hudson River.

To catch the Hudson at its peak levels in spring is to experience one of the great whitewater rivers of them all. The Hudson is not dam-controlled at all and it offers magnificent scenery. Towering canyon walls, pure mountain streams one can drink from and thrilling long rapids like Blue Ledge, the Narrows and Harris's Rift characterize this beautiful wilderness area.

**Bark Eater Lodge
Alstead Mill Road
Keene, NY 12942
518-576-2221**   *NY/Hudson*

Combine a one-day raft trip on the Hudson with a relaxing stay at Bark Eater Lodge—a historic old country inn located in the Lake Placid region. Twenty years' experience in outfitting. Includes: Food, lodging, guided rafting, wet suit. Dates: April and May. Length of trip: 1–3 days. Group size: 8–10 per boat. Cost: $84–$108.

Unicorn Rafting
P.O. Box 50
West Forks, ME 04985
207-663-2258   *NY/Hudson*

Offers day and overnight trips on the Hudson. Includes: All gear, meals, professional guide, lobster dinners. Dates: April and May. Length of trip: 1–2 days. Group size: Up to 80 per trip. Cost: $55–$130. Special requirements: No previous experience necessary.

Wilderness Tours
P.O. Box 89
Beachburg, Ontario
Canada K0J 1C0
613-582-3351   *NY/Hudson*

One of the largest rafting outfitters in Canada, Wilderness Tours originated Ottawa river rafting in 1975, and has had nine years of experience. Includes: Rafting equipment, experienced guide, life vest, applicable meals, overnight camping on two-day trips, sand beach, sauna, showers, sailboards, canoes, kayaks, organized games, campfire entertainment. Dates: April through mid-May. Length of trip: 1 or 2 days. Group size: From 1 to 300. Cost:

They've made it past a huge "haystack"—and now this rafting team paddles around a churning sousehole. (WILDERNESS TOURS)

$50–$124 US. Special requirements: Minimum age 14 years, participants should be capable swimmers, 50% deposit for individuals, 25% for groups of 12 or more.

MOOSE RIVER

Unicorn Rafting Expeditions
P.O. Box 50
West Forks, MA 04985
207-663-2258   *NY/Moose*

Have you rafted the Hudson, Kennebec and Penobscot—and are you looking for something more challenging? The Moose River, flowing out of the high peaks of the Adirondacks in Old Forge, New York, is best described as a highly exciting and DANGEROUS river. Unicorn Rafting Expeditions believes that there is a place for high-risk rafting, provided individuals know exactly what they are getting into. Quite simply, the Moose River is a dangerous river, and the chances of an injury or accident occurring while rafting are great. Although the company takes every precaution possible, this river pulls all the plugs on excitement. Includes: All gear, meals, professional guide, lobster dinners. Dates: April through October. Length of trip: 1–9 days. Group size: up to 80 per trip. Cost: $55–$80 per day. Special requirements: Previous rafting experience.

Oregon

GRANDE RONDE (Class II)

Despite their stunning beauty, the canyons of the Grande Ronde remain little known. The course through the Blue Mountains runs between high stairstep canyon walls of lava mellowed with grasses, flowers and woods.

No dam mars the beauty and the river runs fast and deep in spring. In May and June in particular, new life bursts from every nook and cranny, displaying natural gardens of wild roses, buttercups and yellow snow lilies set among bizarre lava pinnacles. Wildlife sightings are excellent. Once the home of Chief Joseph and the Nez Perce, the Grande Ronde Canyon is now inhabited by deer, bear, mink and roaming elk herds.

This is a superb trip for first-time river runners and families with young children. The river flows quickly but does not have any difficult rapids.

Access to Adventure
P.O. Box 500
Lotus, CA 95651
916-626-5042   *OR/Grande Ronde*

Twelve years' experience; Member American River Recreation Association, American Guides Association, Friends of the River. Includes: Camping, meals, rafts, life jackets, paddles, dry bags, all special river gear, shuttle transportation at the river. Dates: May through July. Length of trip: 5 days. Group size: 1–120. Cost: $300. Special requirements: $30 per person deposit, balance due 30 days prior to trip.

**River Odysseys West
East 320 17th Street
Spokane, WA 99203
509-624-7317** *OR/Grande Ronde*

Paddle, oar and inflatable kayak trips. They also offer a Grande Ronde float and horseback combination, journeying into the rugged Wenaha River country. Fully licensed and bonded guides and outfitters in Oregon and Idaho. Includes: Food, equipment, guides, black bags, life jackets, tents; everything except clothes and sleeping bags. Dates: June and July. Length of trip: 3–5 days. Group size: 8–24 people. Cost: $245–$320 ($595 for horsepack combo). Special requirements: $100 deposit with reservation.

OWYHEE RIVER (Class III)

Called the Grand Canyon of the Northwest, the Owyhee, which traverses southeastern Oregon, is known for its spectacular, colorful canyons in the high desert. Because of its extreme remoteness, few people have visited this basalt canyonland of pinnacles and spires, where ancient Indians, pre-dating any known tribe, lived in caves and left petroglyphs for river runners of today to ponder.

Because this is a dry and barren land, all life revolves around the river—including a large concentration of wildlife. Otter, mink, beaver, coyotes, rabbits and badger live within the canyon, while antelope roam the rims above.

This canyon, where eagles soar and antelope bound through side gorges, where old rustlers' cabins lie abandoned, is a paradise for rockhounds looking for thundereggs of agate and petrified wood. During spring run-off, the river is at its best, and the desert blossoms with brilliant wildflowers. You'll camp on pristine sand beaches, each offering excellent hiking possibilities.

Lower Owyhee

This section of the river has whitewater of moderate difficulty and is suitable for beginning and experienced rafters alike. Stopping below towering canyon walls, you can bathe in the pools of several hot springs ranging in temperature from 100°–107°. You can also stop to look at several sites of petroglyphs—native American rock carvings—and there are unlimited opportunities for hiking.

Middle Owyhee

The Middle Owyhee is an incredible wilderness whitewater experience with the most challenging whitewater of the entire river. Rapids such as Bombshelter, Raftflip Drop, the Ledge and the Widowmaker make this one of the most thrilling whitewater runs in the country. Although there are no hot springs as on the Lower Owyhee, there are native American rock carvings to see and good hikes to take.

**James Henry River Journeys
P.O. Box 807
Bolinas, CA 94924
415-868-1836** *OR/Owyhee*

Paddle, oar and inflatable kayaks on the Owyhee during the best of the spring run-off. Trips are accompanied by John Kipping, naturalist. In business ten years. Licensed by Idaho Outfitters and Guides Association and Alaska Association of Mountain and Wilderness Guides. Includes: All river rafting equipment, guides, meals, transportation from points of embarkation to points of debarkation. Dates: May. Length of trip: 5 days. Group size: 16–30. Cost:

$450. Special requirements: Varies with trips—usually novices' conditioning program required on more strenuous trips—river experience required for more advanced rivers.

River Odysseys West
East 320 17th Avenue
Spokane, WA 99203
509-624-7317 *OR/Owyhee*

Paddle and oar-powered trips on Oregon's Middle and Lower Owyhee, as well as the Upper Owyhee in Idaho. Fully licensed and bonded guides and outfitters in Oregon and Idaho. Includes: Food, equipment, guides, black bags, life jackets, tents; everything except clothes and sleeping bags. Dates: April through June. Length of trip: 4–8 days. Group size: 8–24 people. Cost: $360–$645. Special requirements: $100 deposit with reservation.

Turtle River Rafting
507 McCloud Avenue
Mt. Shasta, CA 96067
916-926-3223 *OR/Owyhee*

Turtle River Rafting believes that participation enhances the river experience, so everyone gets involved in paddling, boat preparation and camping on these trips. Eight years' experience. Includes: Food, equipment, guide service. Dates: April through June. Length of trip: 1–5 days. Group size: 6–24. Cost: $58 per day. Special requirements: A deposit is required to reserve a space.

ROGUE RIVER (Class III)

One of the original wild rivers protected by the 1967 Wild and Scenic River Act, the Rogue cascades through a canyon of stunning loveliness in Oregon's Siskiyou National Forest. Lush woods of ponderosa pine, Douglas fir and native cedar oak create a paradise of vibrant green. Pounding, raft-tossing whitewater alternates with long, warm pools perfect for swimming. The thundering of Rainie Falls reverberates up and down the canyon, while in Mule Creek Canyon, smooth, vertical cliffs pinch the river into a tumultuous, twisting raceway at times only eighteen feet wide.

The place is enchanted. Sculpted boulders hunker in midstream like giant talismans. Echoing grottos thick with rhododendron and maidenhair fern combine with idyllic plunge pools carved in stone ... while tantalizing side-canyon waterfalls like Flora Dell work irresistible magic on all who see them. Swimming is absolutely the BEST, warm and wonderful—jump overboard and float in your buoyant life jacket or take a cooler dip in one of the many side creeks.

Under the cool overhangs of the forests, you can observe deer browsing, bear scrambling along a hillside, or blue heron and osprey catching fish. In September, the Rogue is especially fine, with warm weather, abundant wildlife and excellent fishing for steelhead.

Access to Adventure
P.O. Box 500
Lotus, CA 95651
916-626-5042 *OR/Rogue*

Twelve years' experience; Member American River Recreation Association, American Guides Association, Friends of the River. Includes: Camping, meals, rafts, life jackets, paddles, dry bags, all special river gear, shuttle transportation at the river. Dates: May through October. Length of trip: 4–5 days. Group size: 1–120. Cost: $280–$360. Special requirements: $30 per person deposit, balance due 30 days prior to trip.

Action Adventures
P.O. Box 1500
Woodland, CA 95695
916-662-5431   *OR/Rogue*

Paddle, oar or inflatable kayak expeditions. During spring and summer, three-day raft trips with overnights in wilderness lodges available. Twenty-five years without a single personal injury claim to their insurance company, charter member of American Guides Association. Includes: Intermediate area transportation, food, safety and sanitary equipment, group camp gear (everything except personal gear). Dates: April through October. Length of trip: 1–4 days. Group size: Varies. Cost: $60–$360.

Echo: The Wilderness Company
6529 Telegraph Avenue
Oakland, CA 94609
415-652-1600   *OR/Rogue*

Twelve years' experience running the rivers of the west, Alaska, Yugoslavia, Peru, Mexico and Africa. Includes: Guides, river gear, food, forty-five miles of wild and scenic river, including bear, ospreys, eagles, hawks, salmon, deer, otter and the colorful history of the area. Dates: May through September. Length of trip: 3–5 days. Group size: 6–20. Cost: $345–$415. Special requirements: Generally physically fit. Deposit of $100 per person required. Full payment 60 days before trip.

James Henry River Journeys
P.O. Box 807
Bolinas, CA 94924
415-868-1836   *OR/Rogue*

You'll have ample time to savor this river, since James Henry includes a layover day near some fascinating hiking trails. Trips are by paddle, oar or inflatable kayak. In business ten years. Licensed by Idaho Outfitters and Guides Association and Alaska Association of Mountain and Wilderness Guides. Includes: All river rafting equipment, guides, meals, transportation from points of embarkation to points of debarkation. Dates: June through September. Length of trip: 4–5 days. Group size: 16–30. Cost: $315–$540. Special requirements: Varies with trips—usually novices' conditioning program required on more strenuous trips; river experience required for more advanced rivers.

Mariah Wilderness Expeditions
P.O. Box 1384
El Cerrito, CA 94530
415-527-5544 *OR/Rogue*

Mariah Wilderness also features several "special trips" which include mother/daughter, father/son raft trips, gourmet trips, all-women trips, three-day raft clinics and mountain-river wilderness training. Owners/operators have been in the business of rafting for eight years. Licensed. Includes: Equipment, food, guides, camp fees. For ski trips: Lodging, meals, trail fees, instruction, guides. Dates: February through October. Length: 1–5 days. Group size: 1–60. Cost: $50–$400.

Outdoors Unlimited
P.O. Box 22513-T
Sacramento, CA 95822
916-452-1081 *OR/Rogue*

Oar or paddle trips. Outdoors Unlimited has operated here for fifteen years. Permit issued by Bureau of Land Management. Includes: Meals on trip, river equipment. Paddle option available. Dates: Mid-June through end of August. Length of trip: 5 days. Group size: 20. Cost: $385.

Whitewater Voyages
P.O. Box 906
El Sobrante, CA 94803
415-222-5994 *OR/Rogue*

Oar, paddle and inflatable kayak expeditions. During the spring, their three-day trips stay in comfortable wilderness lodges, and trip members savor the comforts of hearty, home-cooked meals, a warm hearth and luxurious beds. Author of *Whitewater Rafting* and *The Guide's Guide*, William McGinnis has led trips on rivers throughout the world. He has owned and operated Whitewater Voyages for eight years. Includes: Fully outfitted whitewater rafting trip with professional, conscientious, and informative guides captaining each paddle crew and oar boat; meals and refreshments, shuttle transportation to and from the rendezvous in Grants Pass. (Personal camping gear NOT included.) Dates: May through September. Length of trip: 4 days. Group size: 20 maximum. Cost: $340. Special requirements: No previous experience required.

Pennsylvania

LEHIGH RIVER

Whitewater Challengers
P.O. Box 8
White Haven, PA 18661
717-443-9532 *PA/Lehigh*

Whitewater Challengers offers outdoor fun and adventure in Pennsylvania's Pocono Mountains. Whitewater rafting tours on the Lehigh River combine exciting rapids, dazzling scenery and high excitement for first-time rafters and veterans alike. You can also take advantage of fine Outdoor Center programs, including bicycling, kayaking, canoeing, hiking, climbing, camping and more. Includes: one- and two-day whitewater rafting tours include all equipment, guides, instruction, transportation to and from the river, and use of our convenient and comfortable base facilities. Nine years of experience. Includes: Guides, shuttle, equipment. Dates: March through November. Length of trip: 1–2 days. Cost: $35 per day.

Tennessee

OCOEE RIVER

**Wildwater, Limited
Outdoor Adventures
Long Creek, SC 29658
803-647-9587 (Reservations for all trips)**   *TN/Ocoee*

The Ocoee has rapidly become a popular whitewater river in the South, and no wonder! Pouring out of a mist-covered sluiceway at the top of Tennessee's Cherokee National Forest, the Ocoee is the most continuous, tumultuous, non-stop, roller-coaster five-mile stretch of river in the east. Rapids named Slingshot, Tablesaw, Hell's Hole and Double Trouble pulse with power. And because the river is dam-controlled, you can enjoy its big waves and giant holes long after other rivers have dried up. The Ocoee runs so fast, the outfitter can run two trips a day. Includes: Equipment, guides and shuttle. Dates: April through September. Length of trip: Half-day trips. Cost: $16–$22. Special requirements: Age minimum 13 years.

Texas

RIO GRANDE (Lower Rio Grande)
(Class III–IV+)

Wild and untamed like the Old West itself, the Lower Rio Grande (below Big Bend National Park) cuts through desert as primitive as it was a century ago. Spires, arches, natural bridges and sheer walls stretch a thousand feet overhead. The most amazing thing about this area is its variety—travelers can spend from four days to four weeks exploring the side canyons, encountering everything from languid calms to churning whitewater. Rapids with names like Burro Bluff and Horseshoe Falls provide plenty of diversion, and then there's the famous Rockslide—which often needs to be portaged in highwater. For relaxation, plunk into a soothing warm spring at the end of the day.

**Far Flung Adventures
P.O. Box 31
Terlingua, TX 79852
915-371-2489**   *TX/Rio Grande*

Oar and paddle trips through the Santa Elena area; Colorado Canyon; and the lower canyons, including Horse Canyon, Las Vegas de las Ladrones ("Outlaw Flats") and sixty miles of the lower canyon cliffs. National Park Service and Bureau of Land Management licensed, seven years of experience, professional guides trained in advanced first aid and rescue. Member Western River Guides Association. Includes: Guides, gear, safety equipment, waterproofing, tentage for foul weather, food and preparation of food, ground transportation. Dates: Year-round. Length of trip: 1–7 days. Group size: 6 minimum, 24 maximum. Cost: $45–$65 per day. Special requirements: Deposit of $25 per person for all trips; except Lower Canyons, deposit of $100 per person. Floaters need personal sleeping bags, eating utensils, and other personal gear.

Ultimate Escapes
2506 West Colorado Avenue (Dept. S)
Colorado Springs, CO 80904
303-578-8383
Telex 499 2665 Old Colo City   *TX/Rio Grande*

Oar and paddle trips on the Lower Rio Grande, with plenty of time to explore side canyons, photograph historic sites and study the geology of this larger-than-life frontier. Includes: All meals, group equipment, tents, rafts, etc. Round-trip transportation from Midland, Texas; choice of paddle or oar rafting; extensive instruction in river running. Dates: November through May. Length of trip: 7 days, 6 nights. Group size: 10–20. Cost: $525. Special requirements: No previous experience necessary—good health.

Utah

COLORADO RIVER

Born in the Wind River Range in Wyoming, and the Never-Summer-Mountains of Colorado, the Colorado winds its way for 1,440 miles to the Gulf of California. Although its most famous stretch is, of course, the 277 miles of the Grand Canyon, the river also provides other opportunities for memorable river rafting.

Westwater Canyon (Class IV–V)

Westwater Canyon is often called "The Little Grand Canyon of the Colorado." Located deep in the sandstone cliffs northeast of Moab, Westwater Canyon is graced with beautiful and contrasting scenery. Black igneous rock has intruded into the towering red and pink sandstone cliffs and the narrow canyon constricts the river into a series of exciting rapids challenging experienced boatmen and first-time river runners. Since this is a free-flowing river, water levels vary greatly, and it may be completely unrunnable at spring high water.

Cataract Canyon (Class IV–V)

You'll find big water galore in Cataract Canyon, whose rapids equal or exceed those of Grand Canyon in power and difficulty, especially in June. More moderate rapids are experienced for the remainder of the season. Above the confluence of the Green and Colorado rivers, the rafting is leisurely and easy, but below the confluence the canyon deepens to two thousand feet and explodes into an all-day fury of twenty-eight whitewater rapids. The granddaddy of them all is definitely Big Drop—a series of three nasty rapids that demand precise technical maneuvering.

Don Hatch River Expeditions, Inc.
P.O. Box C
Vernal, UT 84078
801-789-4316   *UT/Colorado*

Fully bonded and licensed outfitter. Includes: All equipment; meals; transportation from Moab to river and return. Dates: April through August. Length: 3 and 4 days. Group size: Average 20. Cost: $374 (3 days), $466 (4 days). Special requirements: $100 deposit.

Outlaw River Expeditions
P.O. Box 790-M
Moab, UT 84532
801-259-8241   *UT/Colorado*

Licensed, insured, federally permitted river outfitter. Includes: Transportation to the river put-in, and back from take-out to the point of departure (Moab or Grand Junction); all camping and sleeping gear; waterproof bags and boxes; all meals, wine, beer. Dates: May through September. Length: 2 and 5 days. Group size: 5–30. Cost: Westwater Canyon (2 days): $291; Cataract Canyon (5 days): $559. Special requirements: ⅓ of fare to hold space.

Western River Expeditions
7258 Racquet Club Drive
Salt Lake City, UT 84121
801-942-6669
800-453-7450   *UT/Colorado*

Includes: Round-trip transportation from Grand Junction, Colorado; all meals while on river; tents; guide. Dates: May through August. Length: 3 and 4 days. Cost: Westwater Canyon (3 days): $275; Cataract Canyon (4 days): $450–$490. Special requirements: $100 deposit.

SAN JUAN RIVER

Canyonland Tours
P.O. Box 460, Dept. STI
Flagstaff, AZ 86002
602-774-7343 AZ, AK, HI
800-841-7317
Telex 172-029 SPX SRFL   *UT/San Juan*

Adventure and scenic wonder combine on this trip across the Navajo Indian Reservation to world-famous Monument Valley and the San Juan River. Spend an afternoon touring the backcountry of Monument Valley, site of massive sandstone buttes, spires and monuments. See and meet the people who inhabit the Valley. Enjoy a cook-out dinner, and then overnight in a motel. The next day, begin a two-day rafting trip on the San Juan River. Visit Indian ruins and rock art sites. Float through incredible geologic upheavals and meanders. Ride this fast-flowing river and run its lively rapids. Patrick and Susan Conley, owners-operators, each have over twelve years' experience in guiding and outfitting in the Southwest. Their company, Canyonland Tours, was established in 1965. All their guides have been chosen for their competence, and ability to run safe, happy, educational trips. Includes: Direct trip transportation; meals en route; guide service; river equipment; park entry fees; sleeping bags, foam pad, ground cloth, tent (double occupancy); motel (double occupancy). Dates: April through October. Length of trip: 3 days, 2 nights. Group size: 20 guests maximum (unless chartered). Cost: $395 per person. Special requirements: None; $100 per person deposit necessary to confirm reservation; full fare due 45 days prior to departure.

O.A.R.S., Inc.
P.O. Box 67
Angels Camp, CA 95222
209-736-4677
Telex 172746 STO   *UT/San Juan*

O.A.R.S., Inc. offers both a four-day and a five-day trip on the San Juan. Using small inflatable, oar-powered seventeen-foot rafts, the five-day trip puts-in each Monday at Sand Island, just a few miles west of your meeting place in Bluff, Utah. The second day, after traveling twenty-eight miles, you'll stop at Mexican Hat, Utah to pick up those people wishing to take the four-day trip. Your adventure then continues for fifty-five miles, taking-out of the river at Clay Hills Crossing on an arm of Lake Powell. Passengers are returned to Bluff. O.A.R.S. has fourteen years of rafting experience on twenty-six Western rivers. Includes: Meals from lunch on the first day to lunch on the last day; all rafting equipment including life jackets; two waterproof packs to store your gear in; a water-tight ammo can; experienced, friendly guides who row your rafts, cook your meals, and offer unique and personal insights into the river's geology and history. Dates: April through early July. Length of trip: 4 or 5 days. Group size: 24 passengers. Cost: $370–$440 per person. Special requirements: A deposit of $125 per person is required when the reservation is made.

Washington, D.C.

POTOMAC RIVER

Rio Bravo, Inc.
P.O. Box 6004
McLean, VA 22101   *DC/Potomac*

Your adventure begins on the Virginia side with a look at the thundering Great Falls of the Potomac, an impressive river-wide cataract. The river put-in lies just below the falls. The action starts immediately with the big waves of Observation Deck Rapids, continues with the whirlpools of S-Turn Rapids and the waves of Rocky Island and Wet Bottom Rapids, and culminates with one of the three chutes of Difficult Run. In between rapids, you get to enjoy the scenery of this steep-walled gorge. As the river slows, you might glimpse wildlife such as deer or turkey. Passing the riffles of Yellow and Stubblefield Falls, you'll arrive at your take-out near Lock 10 on the Maryland side. Eight years' commercial rafting experience. Includes: Professional rafts, life jackets, guides. Dates: April through October. Length of trip: 4 hours. Group size: 1–60 passengers. Cost: $30 (weekend); $20 (weekday).

West Virginia

NEW RIVER (Class III–V)

Formidable—that's the best way to describe the New River. Called by Indians "the river of death," it's probably the best-known whitewater river in the East. The lower section of the New River provides Class V whitewater that verges on the unrunnable at high water. This section—the "Grand Canyon of the East"—is strictly for experts only. Perhaps the meanest rapids on the river—the infamous Keeney Brothers—tripleheader rapids that flow one into the next, cramming in stoppers, souseholes and drops! Upstream from this major whitewater is a gentler Class III section suitable for beginning and intermediate rafters. A pleasant bonus—the water temperature in summer is a warm seventy degrees. If you have time, explore the surrounding area, which is rich with colorful history. The Hatfield and McCoy feud broke out in the vicinity, and the town of Thurmond, midpoint in the run, was so wild and lawless at the turn of the century that upstanding citizens said, "The only difference between Hell and Thurmond was that a river ran through Thurmond."

GAULEY RIVER (Class V–VI)

Impressed with the above description of the New River? Good. Because the Gauley is even tougher—probably the finest, wildest whitewater in the Eastern United States. The Gauley is only runnable in fall, when the Summersville Dam releases an adequate water supply. At high water, the river is completely unrunnable. With over sixty rapids Class III or higher, the river powers treacherously past huge boulders, holes and gargantuan waves. Only rafters with considerable experience can tackle this one, whose notorious rapids include Lost Paddle, Five Boat Hole and Pure Screaming Hell.

Class VI River Runners, Inc.
P.O. Box 78 SPT
Lansing, WV 25862
304-574-0704   *WV/New, Gauley*

Member, Eastern Professional River Outfitters; West Virginia license. Includes: All equipment; guide; food. Dates: April through November. Length: 1–5 days. Group size: 1–150. Cost: $40–$200.

Mountain River Tours
Box 88 ST Sunday Road
Hico, WV 25854
304-658-5014   *WV/New, Gauley*

Licensed by State of West Virginia; Member Eastern Professional River Outfitters. Fully insured. Includes: Guides; meals; all safety gear; transportation to and from the river from office. Dates: March through November. Length: 1–3 days. Group size: 1–215. Cost: $40 up. Special requirements: Ability to swim.

West Virginia Whitewater, Inc.
Route 1 Box 447
Fayetteville, WV 25840
304-574-0871   *WV/New, Gauley*

Includes: Equipment; transportation to and from river; meals on the river. Dates: April through October. Length: 1–2 days. Group size: 1–125. Cost: $45–$125. Special requirements: Minimum age 14. Rafting experience required for the Gauley. 30% deposit.

Wyoming

NORTH PLATTE RIVER

Richard Brothers, Inc.
2215 Rangeview Lane
Laramie, WY 82070
307-742-7529   *WY/North Platte*

The North Platte River is one of the last free-flowing, truly wild rivers left in the west. A portion of this river has been recommended for National Wilderness protection by the United States Forest Service. The Wyoming Game and Fish commission has rated the North Platte as a Class I wild, blue ribbon trout fisheries; a status awarded few rivers. Wildlife abounds in an equally wild setting. Bighorn sheep, elk, deer, black bear, bald and golden eagles are some of the species often seen from a silently drifting boat. Richard Brothers, Inc. pioneered whitewater rafting on the North Platte River thirteen years ago. They have outfitted trips for the Sierra Club, the Wilderness Society, National Audubon Society, the American Wilderness Alliance. Oar and paddle trips available. Includes: Everything except personal gear, like sleeping bags. They furnish tents; all camping gear and cooking/eating utensils; all river accessories—dry bag, life jacket, etc. Dates: Mid-May through mid-July. Length of trip: 1–7 days. Group size: 25 maximum. Cost: $55–$65 per day. Special requirements: For paddle trip, prior experience recommended before doing North Gate Canyon.

SNAKE RIVER

Barker-Ewing Float Trips
P.O. Box 1243
Jackson, WY 83001
307-733-3410   *WY/Snake*

This eight-mile whitewater trip through the Snake River Canyon originates near Jackson at West Table Creek. Between rapids, exceptional geological formations are apparent as the Snake River cuts westward through the southern extremity of the Teton Range. This trip will appeal to adventurous persons who wish to sample the kind of river experience offered on more rugged and remote sections of the Snake or Salmon. At the end of the float trip you return to Jackson with a round-trip time of three-and-a-half to four hours. Over twenty years of safe, interpretive, professional float trips for over four hundred thousand people; perfect safety record. Includes: Round-trip transportation from Jackson; professional guides; all equipment. Dates: May through September. Length of trip: 4 hours (approximate). Group size: Up to 80 persons. Special requirements: Reservations. No special requirements. Minimum age 6, higher during high water season.

Parklands Expeditions, Inc.
P.O. Box 3055
Jackson Hole, WY 83001
307-733-3379   *WY/Snake*

Combine the excitement of the swift-moving Snake River with the serenity of Jackson Lake on this five-day raft adventure. You launch on the river just south of Yellowstone National Park and move quickly downstream. Every twist and bend in the river reveals a new vista. After sweeping onto Jackson Lake in Grand Teton National Park, you'll cruise along the western wilderness shoreline at the foot of the magnificent Teton Range, going ashore frequently to explore hidden waterfalls. For three nights, you camp on the lakeshore at beautiful wilderness sites. Day four finds you back on the Snake River. Your guides skillfully maneuver the rafts through rapidly changing channels and help you spot bald eagles, ospreys, otters, perhaps even a grazing moose. The final campsite at river's edge gives you a breathtaking view of the Teton sunset. Concessionaire in Grand Teton National Park and Teton National Forest. Over twenty years' experience. Includes: All meals, transfers and equipment except for personal sleeping gear which may be rented. Dates: June through September; Sunday, Monday, Tuesday. Length of trip: 5 days, 4 nights. Group size: 10–12. Cost: $585.

INTERNATIONAL

Australia

Wilderness Expeditions
P.O. Box 755 Cooma
NSW 2630 Australia
(0648) 21 587

Raft the wild waters of Australia's many rivers. No previous experience is necessary—Wilderness Expeditions teaches you everything you need to know and provides you with a guide and all equipment stowed in waterproof drums. Some of the available rivers are the Snowy River, in spectacular Snowy River National Park; the Murray, powered by melting snow and gushing through the Murray Gates Gorge; and beautiful Murrumbidgee River. The exceptional thing about the Murrumbidgee is the birds. You are watched by cockatoos, swans, ibis and more as you paddle your raft past rock outcroppings and tree-lined shores. In the evening, keep an eye out for a surfacing platypus or toss in a line for a fresh trout dinner. Licensed and insured leaders. Includes: All rafting gear, tents, meals, camping gear, guides and instructor. Dates: September through April. Length of trip: 1–8 days. Group size: 3–8. Cost: $55 per day. Special requirements: Swimming ability.

Canada

COPPERMINE RIVER

Arctic Waterways
R. R. 2
Stevensville, Ontario
Canada L0S 1S0
416-382-3882

Arctic Waterways does NOT offer whitewater thrills. Their safe, large, non-motorized inflatables are a means of exploring the arctic wilderness, otherwise inaccessible to all but the hardiest of adventurers! They take you into total wilderness for a two-week adventure on the Coppermine River, north of the Arctic Circle in Canada's Northwest Territories. Here you can peek into the aeries of gyrfalcons and eagles; photograph moose and caribou and experience the incredible beauty of the arctic tundra in full bloom! Fish for the roughest fighter of them all, the Arctic char, or cast your fly at beautiful Arctic grayling in teeming waters! You can also join Arctic Waterways on the remote, beautiful Horton and Anderson rivers. Operating arctic tours since 1976. Licensed by Government of North-West Territories. Includes: All-inclusive from Yellowknife, Northwest Territory. Dates: July through mid-August. Length of trip: 2 weeks. Group size: 10 guests, 2 rivermen. Cost: $1,400 US. Special requirements: Deposit 20% with booking.

FRASER RIVER

Canadian River Expeditions, Ltd.
845 Chilco Street
Vancouver, British Columbia
CANADA V6G 2R2
604-926-4436

This long-distance, fly-in expedition shows off British Columbia at her spectacularly unspoiled best. From Vancouver, you'll sail aboard a 76-foot yacht through the Inside Passage and up the mountain-walled Bute Fjord. Then a Mallard float plane takes you over the coastal Rockies to jewel-like Chilko Lake, where you'll camp for two days. Next comes the whitewater fun—220 miles down the Chilko, Chilcotin and Fraser rivers. You'll run the French Bar Rapids, Chisholm Canyon and the granite gorges of 2,000-foot deep Moran Canyon. In business since 1972 under the same ownership/management. Includes: Virtually everything—bus, yacht, plane, raft, railway transportation; all food, beer, cocktails; all equipment needed for the trip. Dates: Mid-June through mid-September. Length: 11 days. Group size: 22–24. Cost: $1,450. Special requirements: Reasonable physical condition; no age limit.

HARRICANAW RIVER

New World River Expeditions
5475 Pare, Suite 221
Montreal, Quebec H4P 1P7 Canada
514-733-7166

Located in Northern Quebec, the mighty Harricanaw River offers fantastic opportunities for the person seeking a five-day rafting vacation. An original route of the fur traders, the Harricanaw today remains as pristine a wilderness as it was over two hundred years ago. Otter aircraft departs from the town of Matagami and heads north where the seventy-five-mile journey begins. Each day you descend downstream through rugged gorges and whopping rapids, such as "The Big Drops," "The Maze" and "Satan's Falls." With dynamic rapids such as these, your trip becomes a whitewater extravaganza—a once-in-a-lifetime thrill complete with expert guides and gourmet food. Although the pace is relaxed and you'll have time for fishing, birdwatching and swimming, you must be ready to paddle through the demanding rapids. Outfitters on the Harricanaw since 1976. Includes: 5 days' rafting on the Harricanaw River, 5 nights' camping facilities (including tents), 3 meals per day, return air transportation to Matagami (400 miles north of Montreal), all equipment, a New World guide. Dates: July. Length of trip: 5 days. Cost: $495 (Canadian). Special requirements: Ages 14 and over. No experience necessary. Deposit of $100 Canadian to secure your reservation.

OTTAWA RIVER

The Ottawa is a world-class waterway with spectacular scenery and big wild rapids. It offers a unique combination of warm temperatures and powerful rapids all through the season.

Ottawa River Whitewater Rafting, Ltd.
P.O. Box 179
Beachburg, Ontario
Canada K0J 1C0
416-883-1818

In business for seven years. Includes: Camping; meals; guide; equipment; transportation from cap to put-in point. Dates: May through September. Length: 1–2 days. Group size: 1–250. Cost: $50 Canadian–$145 Canadian. Special requirements: Ability to swim. 50% deposit.

Wilderness Tours
P.O. Box 89
Beachburg, Ontario
Canada K0J 1C0
613-582-3351

In business since 1975. Includes: all equipment; guide; some meals. Dates: May and June. Length: 1–2 days. Group size: 1–300. Cost: $50–$124 US. Special requirements: Minimum age 14; deposit.

ROUGE RIVER

The Upper Rouge (between Eagle Lake and L'Annonciation) features twenty-one miles of untamed wilderness and spectacular rapids. Due to the seclusion of the river in the Rouge-Matawin Reserve, rafters are flown in. At the beginning of the descent, three major gorges toss the raft into a bed of swirling rapids. The Lower Rouge (between Kilmar and Calumet) flows downstream through canyons and gorges, offering a variety of rapids sure to thrill the novice as well as the expert rafter.

New World River Expeditions
5475 Pare, Suite 221
Montreal, Quebec
Canada H4P 1P7
514-733-7166

Includes: All equipment; some meals; guide. Dates: April through October. Length: 1–2 days. Group size: 1 or more. Cost: $45 Canadian–$135 Canadian. Special requirements: Minimum age 14. $15 Canadian deposit.

Wilderness Tours
P.O. Box 89
Beachburg, Ontario
Canada K0J 1C0
613-582-3351

In business since 1975. Includes: all equipment; guide; some meals. Dates: May and June. Length: 1 day. Group size: 1–300. Cost: $42–$51 US. Special requirements: Minimum age 14; deposit.

SNAKE RIVER

Yukon Fishing Safaris, Ltd.
P.O. Box 5209
Whitehorse, Yukon Territory
Canada Y1A 4Z1
403-668-2287 summer
604-785-2394 winter

Mayo, a small mining town in the Northern Yukon, is your destination for this trip. From here you board a Dehaviland Otter aircraft for your flight over the mountains to the head of the Snake River in the Wernecke Mountains. After portaging the gear from a lake to the river, you begin your float through the rugged terrain of the Snake River. Moose, grizzly bear and caribou are frequent companions along the riverbank. As you gaze skyward you will frequently spot the sleek white forms of Dall sheep dotting the mountainside. Peregrine and gyr falcons are often seen soaring above or nesting in some of the magnificent canyons en route. Several times during the trip you can stop to study and photograph the awe-inspiring rock formations and wildlife. Fifteen years' wilderness experience on varying degrees of water ensuring a safe, enjoyable and educational experience. Includes: Everything except sleeping bags, mattress, personal gear and round-trip airfare to Gateway City. Fishing tackle and waders provided if requested prior to trip. Excellent fishing, photography and hiking as part of the trip. Dates: April through May and July through October. Length of trip: 10 days. Group size: 12 maximum. Cost: $260 per person per day. Special Requirements: ⅓ deposit is required to confirm a booking.

TASEKO RIVER

Thompson Guiding, Ltd.
Highway 20
Riske Creek, B.C. V0L 1T0, Canada
604-659-5635

Translated literally from the native Chilcotin language the word "taseko" means "stream that wanders in the wilderness." There is no better way to describe this river. From very frequent wildlife encounters to the raw, natural, untouched landscapes, the Taseko continually displays its wild surroundings. You begin at Taseko Lake, nestled in the lee side of the Coast Range. The river then flows north for ninety miles dropping to meet the Chilko and then the Chilcotin rivers in the Chilcotin Plateau. Although scenery is the premier attribute of the Taseko, it offers its share of exciting whitewater. There are many spirited rapids, highlighted by the Taseko Falls and four other major drops. Thompson Guiding is one of Canada's oldest and most experienced non-motorized river outfitters, specializing in wilderness rivers. They have done the initial exploration and started commercial rafting on most of the rivers they run. Includes: All meals (gourmet fare); return transportation from Williams Lake, BC; river equipment, guides, waterproof duffel. Dates: June through September. Length of trip: 4 days. Group size: Maximum 30. Cost: $395 US. Special requirements: $250—60 days in advance.

Chile

BIO-BIO RIVER

The Rio Bio-Bio in the Chilean Andes is whitewater at its finest; big water roaring through lava rock canyons, past tumultuous tributaries, limestone spires and smoking volcanoes. And you can descend the wild and powerful Bio-Bio as it plunges through rugged wilderness . . . in your own kayak or in large, oar-rigged inflatable rafts manned by guides for those participants without whitewater experience. With majestic Callaqui Volcano in the background, you'll pass through one of the most spectacular whitewater canyons in the world where the Bio-Bio is at its pulsing, pounding, throbbing best. In between thrills and spills, fish for trout, soak in natural hot springs and explore side canyons and alpine lakes.

Nantahala Outdoor Center
U.S. 19 West, Box 41
Bryson City, NC 28713
704-488-9221

Nantahala Outdoor Center was founded in 1972. Includes: Meals, lodging, rafting equipment, transportation while in Chile, guides. Dates: January to March. Length of trip: 15 days. Group size: 12–15. Cost: $1,600. Special requirements: Boaters must be experienced paddlers. Rafters must be unafraid of executing whitewater. Camping experience helpful.

Steve Currey Expeditions
P.O. Box 1574
Provo, UT 84603
801-224-6797

Trip includes hike to Volcano Callaquiz. Twenty years of whitewater experience in Western United States. Includes: Deluxe hotels; train rides; 8 days on the river; all equipment; meals; guides. Dates: January and February. Length: 10 days. Group size: 12. Cost: $1,795. Special requirements: Good physical condition; $250 deposit.

Costa Rica

RIO CHIRRIPO (Class III–IV)

Tumbling from its source on Mt. Chirripo, the Rio Chirripo offers exciting whitewater in a rich tropical environment. It has over one hundred Class III and IV rapids in the first forty miles. With a water temperature of about 70°, Chirripo is ideal for beginning paddle rafters or intermediate kayakers.

RIO PACUARE (Class IV–V)

The Pacuare, one of the most beautiful rivers in the tropics, cuts through the virgin jungle of Costa Rica. Waterfalls drop out of the jungle one hundred feet straight into the river.

Costa Rica Expeditions
Apartado 6941
San Jose
Costa Rica, C.A.
23-99-75
Telex 2917 CREAR

Includes: Ground transportation, lodging, some meals, all rafting and community camping equipment. Dates: All year, depending on river. Length: 6–7–11 days. Group size: 14. Cost: $452–$497–$796.

Wildwater, Ltd.
Outdoor Adventures
Long Creek, SC 29658
803-647-9587

Includes: Round-trip airfare from Miami, all local transportation, 3 days of whitewater rafting, guides, equipment, meals on river, 4 nights' lodging, double occupancy, most meals, Pacific Island Cruise, Paos Volcano trip. Dates: November and December. Length: 1 week. Group size: Maximum 20. Cost: $795–$895. Special requirements: Minimum age 12.

Mexico, Central America

RIO USUMACINTA

Libra Expeditions
11017 Sevenhills Drive
P.O. Box 310
Tujunga, CA 91042
213-353-7469

Once the heart of the Maya Empire, the Usumacinta—"river of ruins"—links some of the most important—and least-visited—archeological sites in Central America. Your trip begins with a visit to Palenque, a beautiful restored complex set like a jewel in the verdant forest. The next two ruins are inaccessible by road; the river carries us to their overgrown, wildlife-rich locations. Yaxchilan features bas-relief stonework and undeciphered hieroglyphics, and Piedras Negras is obscured by jungle until you stumble onto its unexplored riches. Scarlet macaws screech overhead, howler monkeys roar in the night, iguanas and turtles scurry from beaches as you approach, and the lush variety of the rain forest unfolds like a living scroll as you float by. This trip is a birder's delight, with many rare birds visible including the solitary eagle. Outfitter was designer of Campways rafting equipment 1974–1980. Has run Rio Usumacinta since 1981; fourth year in business as commercial whitewater rafting company. Includes: Everything from first day of trip including airport pick-up, food, rafting gear, guides, and transportation to the river and return. Dates: February and March. Length of trip: 10 days. Group size: 20 people maximum. Cost: $990. Special requirements: None. A trip for all ages 12–80. Deposit of 20% upon making reservation. Balance due 60 days before trip.

Nepal

InnerAsia
2627 Lombard Street
San Francisco, CA 94123
415-922-0448
Telex 278716 TIGER

Although Nepal is a country of few roads, it has mighty rivers that penetrate to the remote peoples and villages of this exotic kingdom. InnerAsia offers a wide variety of river trips lasting from one to eight days which are operated by Himalayan River Exploration. All three major systems of Nepal are used—the Narayani, the Karnali and the Sapt Kosi. Many of the river journeys end at the Tiger Tops Jungle Lodge, the famous wildlife lodge set in the heart of the Chitwan National Park, home of many endangered species. Includes: Tents, sleeping bags, food, transportation between Kathmandu and trek or raft start/finish point, trek permit, documentation, park fees, porter insurance. Dates: September through July. Length of trip: 3 to 25 days. Group size: 15 maximum. Cost: Varies with duration. Special requirements: A spirit of adventure, good health, and some outdoor experience.

**PEREGRINE
EXPEDITIONS**

Peregrine Expeditions
343 Little Collins Street, Suite 710, 7th Floor
Melbourne, VIC 3000, Australia
60 1121
60 1122
Telex 31380

The Trisuli River rises in Tibet and runs through the mountains of the Mahabarat Range. It is joined by the Kali Gandaki and the Seti Khola to form the Narayani River which flows through Chitwan National Park. This is an excellent introduction to river-running through some incredibly beautiful and serene parts of Nepal, and certainly adds another dimension to an already fascinating country. Each raft is guided by an experienced boatman and two experienced crew (who also set up camp and cook excellent meals). There are rapids and you do get wet—but it is all good fun! The outfitter also operates a five-day program which includes an extra day's rafting (and more rapids!), commencing from Flishting Tar, one day above Mugling. Includes: Full board, all transfers and services of guides, etc., from Kathmandu to Kathmandu, life jackets, safety helmets, sleeping bags, etc. Dates: October through May. Length of trip: 3 days. Group size: 6 per raft. Cost: $462 Australian. Special requirements: $50 deposit, balance 60 days prior to trip.

In Nepal, you can combine whitewater adventure with an elephant safari to the Royal Chitwan National Park. (PEREGRINE EXPEDITIONS)

Kashmir

Kashmir Himalayan Expeditions
Boulevard Shopping Complex
P.O. Box 168
Srinagar, Kashmir, India
190001
78698/73913

This adventure combines trekking with a run down one of the world's highest, most remote rivers—the Zanskar—where sheer cliffs of amber rock rise thousands of feet from the water's edge, merging into snowy peaks. First you'll acclimate among the forests, pastures and Hindu villages of the Kulu Valley before driving along Rhotany Pass to Darcha, starting point for the expedition. Rafts, paddles and equipment are loaded on mules and the trek begins. Slowly you'll ascend the Shingola Pass (5,100 meters), an ancient trade route between India and Tibet. You'll have superb views of the Himalaya and Zanskar ranges on the way to Padam, put-in point for the rafts. Now get ready for ten thrilling days on the river, with its awesome gorges and brilliant white beaches that provide perfect campsites. The rapids become more challenging as you move down river, culminating in high grade whitewater for the last two days. No prior rafting knowledge is required, since each raft is captained by an experienced boatman. However, everyone will have a paddle and will help maneuver the boats through the rapids. In operation since 1970. Includes: Varies. Write for information. Dates: August and September. Length of trip: 36 days. Group size: Varies. Cost: $1,260.

New Guinea

WATUT RIVER

Sobek Expeditions
Angels Camp, CA 95222
209-736-2661
800-344-3284 (except HI, AK, CA)
Telex 172746

The wildest river run in the Pacific, brimming with rapids and rich in history and culture, the Watut River drains the razorback peaks of central New Guinea. It begins with a deceptively hushed glide through gold country, then explodes through the Kuper Mountains, roaring along one hundred major rapids for a water rodeo wrapped in glistening jungle. You'll visit native villages, sing in the showers of tributary waterfalls, and pluck coconuts at the river's edge. The Watut is offered by itself or in combination with other aspects of this fascinating island. Advanced Class III–V whitewater. Operator has more than ten years' experience. Includes: Everything, except airfare. Dates: September. Length: 6 days. Group size: 5–15. Cost: $795.

Peru

Rio Bravo, Inc.
P.O. Box 6004
McLean, VA 22101

Thrill to the superb whitewater in spectacular Apurimac Canyon—a mile-deep, tropical gorge in the heart of the Andes. This action adventure combines trekking with rafting on the source river of the Amazon. First, you hike to Inca ruins hanging above the roaring waters of the Apurimac. Then you descend to a tropical Shangri-La where the river adventure begins. You'll raft exciting rapids such as Rocket and Wholy Holy between the steep walls of the canyon. Passing mountainside cascades, look for otter, deer, and signs of puma. Camps are on beautiful sandy beaches. The fishing is outstanding and so is the eating. Your river journey ends near Thornton Wilder's "Bridge of San Luis Rey." Rio Bravo also runs rafting expeditions on Peru's Rio Tambopata and Urubamba River. Eight years' experience on Peruvian rivers. Includes: All transportation, meals and lodging (clients provide their own tents), Cusco to Cusco, plus professional rafts, life jackets, river guides, and waterproof storage. Dates: All year. Length of trip: 9 days (May through October); 5 days (November through April). Group size: 1–15 passengers. Cost: 9 days: $650–$900; 5 days: $440–$500.

Zambia

Sobek Expeditions
Angels Camp, CA 95222
209-736-2661
800-344-3284 except CA, AK, HI
Telex 172746

In October 1981, Sobek made the first navigation of the Zambezi from the base of Victoria Falls to Lake Kariba. Sobek considers the route one of the most magnificent river corridors ever explored, with rapids better than those of the famed Bio-Bio. Now adventurers can retrace this original route. Besides the rousing rapids, the Zambezi offers exotic wildlife, from crocodiles to hippos to shoreline antelopes. The fishing is superb—the river abounds with bream and tiger fish. Friendly fishermen dwell along the banks in thatched huts, and welcome your unusual passage with friendly waves. This stretch of the Zambezi also boasts two spectacular waterfalls, where the river drops over twenty-foot basalt cliffs. (The two falls are beautiful to behold, but they also necessitate portages. Fortunately the portages are short, causing little delay or hardship.) The sixth night is spent camping on the shores of Lake Kariba in the Zimbabwen town of Deka, a small, quiet resort which attracts fishermen in search of the feisty tiger fish. Here you'll have the opportunity to enjoy a good hotel meal, and quaff cold drinks from the well-stocked bar. Trip leader has fifteen years' experience as mountain and river leader. Includes: Everything except airfare, off-river meals and hotels. Dates: August through November. Length of trip: 7 days. Group size: 5–18 people. Cost: $990. Special requirements: Ages 14–70; Class VI whitewater; $300 deposit.

Sailing •
Windjamming •
Sailing Schools •

In this book, we've differentiated between sailing and yacht charter in that on a sailing voyage: 1) the boats are crewed and usually larger, accommodating more than just you and your friend(s); 2) the itineraries are normally determined by the operator. The voyages you'll find listed here are a diversified lot—from cruises aboard tall ships (windjammers)—to flotilla sailing, where you captain your own ship in company with several other boats led by a fleet master. We've also included sailing schools which offer both basic sailing courses as well as courses in advanced cruising lasting up to several weeks.

SECTIONS OF RELATED INTEREST

Cruises
Diving
Research Expeditions
Yacht Charter

Adrift Adventures, Ltd.
P.O. Box 577, Dept. K
Glenwood Springs, CO 81602
303-945-2281   *Hawaii*

If you desire a bit of adventure and the romance of Pacific trade winds while sailing among tropical islands, then Adrift Adventures' Hawaii Sun and Sail program is just for you. Year-round, weekly departures from Mamele Harbor, Lanai allow you to choose the tropical season best suited to your plans. The sleek thirty-five-foot sloops glide lazily over beautiful coral formations surrounded by butterflies, damsel and parrot fish. Evenings, you anchor in quiet coves and enjoy fresh seafood and native dishes, bunking down on deck or in a comfortable berth below. You awake to a swim in warm crystal-clear waters, snorkeling, sunbathing and relaxing under the tropical sun. You may also visit ports and remote anchorages, explore ancient temples and petroglyphs, and observe dolphins and humpback whales. Adrift Adventures' skippers and boats are United States Coast Guard-licensed. Includes: Transportation from airport to harbor and return, gourmet meals, and accommodations. Dates: All year.

Length of trip: 6 days, Sunday to Saturday. Group size: 6 per yacht. Cost: $695. Special requirements: $100 deposit.

Amante Sail Tours
P.O. Box 51, Orcas Island
Deer Harbor, WA 98243
206-376-4231   *Washington*

How would you like to cruise the 172 San Juan Islands on the thirty-three-foot crewed sloop "Amante"? Skipper Don Palmer is a United States Coast Guard licensed skipper who has conducted sailing groups through the San Juan Islands for almost twenty years. Join him on an exploration where you will view the sea and bird life of the islands. The sheltered waterways are safe and ideal for sailing, with sand and rock beaches perfect for sunning, swimming, hiking and discovering marine life. Every night, the ship has a different moorage, sometimes in a remote cove, sometimes at a tiny island; the Palmers' many island friends give them access to a variety of private locations not open to tourists and occasional yachtsmen. Sailing experience is not required, but experienced sailors can help sail and navigate. Instruction is offered to the novice who wishes to learn. Or you can just relax and sightsee. Excellent meals are prepared aboard by the skipper. Three- or five-day stays at the Palmers' Chart House on Orcas Island before or after your sailing trip can be arranged at additional cost. Includes: Lodging aboard ship, meals, sailing and sightseeing. Dates: June through August. Length of trip: 4 days. Group size: 4. Cost: $200 per person. Special requirements: ½ of fee due at time of reservation.

Blue Sky Adventures
P.O. Box 126, Milton Road
Oak Ridge, NJ 07438
201-697-7233   *Caribbean*

The Brigantine "Romance" provides an ideal setting for an exciting exploration of the natural world of the Caribbean . . . a living classroom environment with colorful, unspoiled coral reefs, tropical flora and fauna, diverse island cultures, historic places of interest. Cooperation, understanding, and compromise is a must; this is not a luxury cruise ship. Part of the tour's charm is having to duck to avoid a beam; pumping the "head"; using a rope ladder when transferring to and from the skiff; lending a hand with the sails. And what magnificent sails they are—sixteen sails including the studding sails that give the picturesque broad spread of canvas to the clippers. Ports of call (depending on trip date) can include: Nevis, St. Kitts, St. Barts, St. Martin, Saba, Virgin Gorda, Peter Island, the Baths, Marina Cay, Spanish Town, the wreck of the "Rhone," and the Great Barrier Reef at Gorda Sound. Your skipper, Captain Arthur M. Kimberly is a graduate of the United States Merchant Marine Academy at Kings Point and holds dual Master's papers; all tours are led by professionals in their field; scientists, naturalists, biologists, etc. Includes: Round-trip transfers to ship; all meals while on board; berth; all shore excursions; full-time naturalist(s)/leader(s); all lectures, field trips, etc. Dates: January and November. Length of trip: 8 days, 7 nights. Group size: 16 maximum. Cost: $650 (projected). Special requirements: No special skills necessary; should be in good health, agile, and enjoy sailing; $200 deposit, reservations deadline 45 days before departure.

Coastal Cruises
P.O. Box 798
Camden, ME 04843
207-236-2750

Join the schooner "Mary Day" for a windjammer cruise off the coast of Maine. Exciting sailing, a variety of weather and beautiful scenery make this a unique adventure. You'll visit out-of-the-way places like Frenchboro, Isle Au Haut, Matincus, and Monhegan, unreachable by car. The "Mary Day" carries no engine, so passengers lend a hand to hoist sails, coil halyards, cat the anchor and hoist the yawl-boat. The yawl-boat, a small power boat, is used to push the schooner when there is no wind. The "Mary Day" is eighty-three feet long with 4,500 square feet of sail. Her hull is entirely of oak, deck and cabins are native cedar and pine, masts are Douglas fir from the West Coast. The main cabin features an open fireplace and an old-fashioned organ for musical evenings. The ship's Captain, Havilah S. Hawkins, is in his thirtieth season of windjamming. Includes: All meals, accommodations and a lobster feast. Dates: May through September. Length of trip: 6 days. Group size: 1–28. Cost: $395 per person. Special requirements: Minimum age is 15. $100 deposit is necessary.

Great Expeditions, Inc.
2956 West 4th Avenue
Vancouver, B.C., Canada V6K 1R4
604-734-4948   *Greece*

Imagine cruising the crystal-blue waters of the Aegean—sailing from the island of Kithnos to Siphnos, or Delos to Patmos—visiting islands inhabited by only a handful of people—and exploring the magnificence of Rhodes and Crete. On this leisurely two-week voyage, you'll also have time for swimming in the languid waters—sunning on the pearly white beaches—drinking ouzo in vine-covered taverns and sampling the local stuffed grape leaves and roasted lamb in a simple little restaurant set in a flower-laden courtyard. Accommodating up to eight passengers, your sailboat is a comfortable cruising vessel. Your guide will be knowledgeable in the history, archeology and culture of Greece, and will take you to unusual places. Established in 1977, member of Pacific Area Travel Association. Includes: Sailboat, most meals, guide, some local excursions. Dates: Fall. Length of trip: 14 days. Group size: Maximum 15 people. Cost: $1,150. Special requirements: $300 deposit.

| Guides
for
All
Seasons |

Guides for All Seasons
P.O. Box 97
Carnelian Bay, CA 95711
916-583-8475 Call Collect   *Greece*

Spend two weeks in Greece sailing among the islands and exploring interesting spots along the way. The trip starts in Athens where you'll spend a few days sightseeing in this fascinating and ancient city. A week of sailing on a chartered yacht will be the next phase of your trip. You'll travel through the Cyclades at an unhurried pace—usually sailing in the morning and sunning, swimming or hiking in the afternoons. In Piraeus, board a steamer for Crete, the final destination. Famous for the maze at Knossos, Crete is also well-known for fantastic beaches and the gorge of Samaria. During the unhurried itinerary, you'll be eating good Greek food, drinking retsina and dancing to excellent Greek bouzouki music. Includes: All lodging, ground transportation, chartered yacht, captain, breakfasts and lunches, guides. Dates: Summer. Length of trip: 16 days. Group size: Maximum 20. Cost: $1,450.

Himalayan Travel, Inc.
P.O. Box 481
Greenwich, CT 06836
800-243-5330
Telex 4750032   *Maldive Islands*

The Maldives encompass more than 1,900 islands, a coral archipelago of nineteen atolls, lying off the west coast of India. Less than two hundred of these beautiful islands are inhabited. It's a true tropical paradise—where pristine white sandy beaches are topped by gentle swaying coconut palms and surrounded by crystal-clear waters containing some of the very best coral reefs in the world. The Maldivians travel in Dhonis, a traditional sailing craft, very similar in design to the Arabian Dhow, from which it is modeled. It is in these Dhonis that you'll travel from island to island as the winds and your inclinations take you. You will experience seven days of Maldivian serenity exploring these fabulous tropical islands, meeting their peoples, learning their history and enjoying the fruits and fish. You help sail and you help fish—and you can expect to be asked to dance with the sailors and villagers around the evening fire! Six years' experience arranging adventure vacations on the Indian subcontinent. Includes: Use of sailboat and crew, meals, trip leaders, some equipment. Dates: November through April. Length of trip: 8 days. Group size: Maximum 15. Cost: $595.

Islands in the Sun (Ted Cook Tours, Inc.)
2814 Lafayette Street
P.O. Box 1398
Newport Beach, CA 92663
714-675-8100
800-854-3413 Nationwide
800-432-7080 California
Telex 685 615 ISLANDS-NPBH   *Tahiti*

Dreaming of graceful sailing ships gliding through tropical waters . . . clear blue skies . . . brilliant sunsets . . . soft, steady breezes and warm, star-filled nights? For the adventurous traveler desiring "out-of-the-way" islands accessible only by boat, here's a fourteen-day sailing vacation in French Polynesia. Sail aboard the fifty-eight-foot ketch, "Danae III," hosted by Claude and Claudine Goche and their two sons. They're all competent sailors and will add to the enjoyment of your adventure. Enjoy sailing in the warm trade winds, and water sports in the crystal-clear lagoons . . . but most of all, experience the authentic "Tahitian way of life" found only on these beautiful unspoiled and remote outer islands. Complimentary activities include the use of water sport equipment such as windsurfer, dinghy, fishing gear, snorkeling and scuba diving equipment. Eighteen years' experience. Includes: Round-trip airfare from Los Angeles; accommodations aboard yacht and in hotels; all meals while on board yacht "Danae III"; transfers; sports equipment on board yacht. Dates: Year-round. Length of trip: 14 days. Group size: Maximum 8 passengers. Cost: $1,979 per person.

Marine Sciences Under Sail
P.O. Box 3994
Hollywood, FL 33083
305-983-7015   *Bahamas, Florida*

Enjoy a week of gunkholing in the Florida Keys or the Bahamas. Marine Sciences Under Sail offers study-cruises and gunkholing (sailing on protected waters among islands, shoals and coral reefs) in the warm waters of the Keys and the Caribbean Sea. The atmosphere is relaxed and the easy-paced activities allow you to become directly involved in the operation of the boat while you sail with certified instructors. You'll visit relatively undisturbed regions, jungle rivers, and uninhabited islands. For those with coastal sailing experience who wish to expand their seamanship knowledge, Marine Sciences Under Sail gives an Open Ocean Crossing program between the Keys and Honduras or Belize. This trip features ocean cruising routines and instruction in navigation and safety procedures. Both programs offer excellent opportunities to study and photograph whales, seabirds, flying fish, sea turtles and dolphin, as well as snorkel and swim. Marine Sciences Under Sail is United States Coast Guard-licensed. Includes: Instruction in sailing, snorkeling and various disciplines related to the ocean. Dates: Fall, winter and spring. Length of trip: Varies. Group size: 4 or more. Cost: $48 per day. Special requirements: ⅓ of the total fee as a deposit.

North Shore Sailing School
1601 Granville Street
Vancouver, B.C.
Canada V6Z 2B3
604-669-0840   *British Columbia, Hawaii*

North Shore Sailing offers vacation courses combining a relaxed atmosphere and pleasant surroundings with intensive sailing lessons. They give courses for novices, advanced, and "seamasters"; each course dovetailing into the next. The beginners' program, a five-day "Cruise and Learn" package, is offered on twenty-seven to thirty-three-foot sloops around the beautiful Gulf Islands of British Columbia. Navigation and sailing instructions are given en route. The second course is also five days; the "Advanced Coastal Cruising" program is aboard a forty to forty-two-foot sloop or ketch cruising the Gulf Islands and the Georgia Straits. The course features extensive navigation, spinnaker and sea rescue drills. The Canadian Yachting Association (CYA) Advanced Coastal Cruiser certification is awarded to students successfully completing the course and a two-part exam. The third and most stringent course is a four-week "Seamaster" offshore trip from British Columbia to Hawaii. This trip is on modern forty to fifty-foot vessels. Students learn celestial navigation; monitor weather reports; watch duty, maintenance, and all aspects of running the ship. Upon completion students may receive Canadian Yachting Association Offshore certification. The course is also offered on the Hawaii to British Columbia return route. All North Shore instructors are fully certified by Canadian Yachting Association. Includes: All meals, accommodations, and instructions. Dates: Spring, summer and fall. Length of trip: Courses I and II—5 days. Course III—4 weeks. Group size: 3–6. Cost: Course I—$565. Course II—$695. Course III—$2,790. Special requirements: Prior sailing experience for courses II and III.

Ocean Voyages
1709 Bridgeway
Sausalito, CA 94965
415-332-4681
Telex 470-561 SAIL UI *Aegean Islands, Turkey*

Voyage among the legendary islands of the Aegean Sea and along the largely undiscovered Turkish coast. Homer's Aegean is a world of historic significance and treasured archeological sites . . . where both ancient and contemporary structures contrast with sunswept landscapes, ethereal skies and turquoise waters. Ocean Voyages' sailing programs run out of Rhodes, with Bodrum (once Halicarnassus), Kos, Marmaris among the ports and islands that may be visited. With these programs, you can enjoy the feeling of having your own yacht, with skipper and crew. You can also learn to improve your sailing, with expert skippers who know the area well. A cook cares for your needs, and the crew introduces you to the insider's places to visit: secluded beaches, lively restaurants, etc. All skippers highly experienced sailors; and are personally selected by Mary T. Crowley, director of Ocean Voyages. Includes: All-inclusive for time on the boat. Sailing, accommodations, sail training; except liquor. Dates: April through October. Length of trip: 10 and 14 days; or as long as wanted. Group size: 2, 4, 6, 8, and upwards. Cost: 10 days, $1,375. 14 days, $1,875. Rates for longer charters on request. Special requirements: $200 deposit; sense of adventure and good spirit.

Ocean Voyages
1709 Bridgeway
Sausalito, CA 94965
415-332-4681
Telex 470-561 SAIL UI *Tahiti*

Ready to be a lotus eater in Paradise? Ocean Voyages runs sailing programs through the Leeward Islands of French Polynesia: Huahine, Raiatea, Tahaa, Bora Bora. This is a perfect cruising area: sailing for the most part with the wind, you'll reach the remote bays, motus (islets), beaches and villages that elude most visitors. The water is warm and clear, giving superb snorkeling on the coral; good sailing, with sail training for those who want to start or gain more sailing experience. Plus other delights—like island exploration, snorkeling in the lagoon of Bora Bora, sitting on deck watching the tropical sunset, and dining on fresh-caught mahi-mahi. Ocean Voyages has been running sail programs worldwide for four years. Includes: All-inclusive for time on the boat: sail training, food, accommodations, snorkel equipment, windsurfer, etc.; except liquor. Dates: Year-round. Length of trip: 8 and 14 days; as wished. Group size: 2, 4, or more. Cost: 8 days $875. 14 days $1,475. Special requirements: $200 deposit; sense of adventure, good spirit.

Ocean Voyages
1709 Bridgeway
Sausalito, CA 94965
415-332-4681
Telex 470-561 SAIL UI *Ecuador, Galapagos Islands*

The Galapagos Islands fascinate visitors with their remarkable flora and fauna, flightless cormorants, blue-footed boobies, penguins, flamingos, iguanas and, of course, the magnificent leathery galapagos—giant tortoises. All are relatively free of fear of man, making close observation possible. Ocean Voyages' programs are conducted in small groups, giving maximum access to the different islands. You'll cruise aboard either sail or power yachts. The skippers are all long-term residents of the islands, who love to share their remarkable home with participants, who are guests, not tourists. All programs are accompanied by a naturalist guide trained at the Darwin Station. Ideal for photographers, nature enthusiasts, bird- and animal-watchers, and the adventurous and interested. Fifteen-day programs give a comprehensive view of the islands; twenty-two-day programs reach more remote areas, such as climbing the Alcedo volcano and diving in underwater caverns. Ocean Voyages has been coordinating programs to the Galapagos for the last five years. Includes: All-inclusive for time on the boat, i.e., food, accommodations, skipper, guide from Darwin Station, etc.; except for liquor. Dates: November through September. Length of trip: 15 days. Group size: Up to 35. Cost: $1,425. Special requirements: Reasonable health.

Ocean Voyages
1709 Bridgeway
Sausalito, CA 94965
415-332-4681
Telex 470-561 SAIL UI   *Caribbean*

The Caribbean is justly famous for having some of the finest sailing in the world. The trade winds blow consistently and the myriad islands and cays offer spectacular anchorages. Ocean Voyages has a variety of ships in the Caribbean, based in many islands. Participation is encouraged on all the vessels, and the experienced skippers and crews are ready to give sail training, whatever your level of experience. Island exploration, relaxation, enjoying the local cultures are also key points of the voyages. Group sizes vary: from two to a small flotilla of boats carrying a large group. Vessels include: "Water Pearl," sixty-eight-foot schooner; "William H. Albury," seventy-foot schooner; "Morva," fifty-seven-foot classic English cutter; "Westerner," forty-four-foot Alden cutter; "Chrisaldy," seventy-two-foot ketch. Bahamas, St. Maarten/St. Martin, Martinique, the delightful Grenadines, United States Virgin Islands/British Virgin Islands, etc., are potential ports to explore and enjoy, on your own yacht. All skippers are experienced sailors, happy to give sail training and navigation instruction. Includes: All-inclusive for time on the boat; sail instruction, food, accommodations, windsurfing on some boats, etc.; except liquor. Dates: Year-round. Length of trip: 8 days on. Group size: 2 or more. Cost: From $575. Special requirements: $200 deposit.

Royal Palm Tours, Inc.
P.O. Box 06079
Ft. Myers, FL 33906
813-489-0344
Telex 523046   *Florida*

Toast seven glorious sunsets after cruising with dolphins, rays and tarpon on this flotilla sailing adventure. Both seasoned salts and non-sailors are welcome. For eight days, you'll be cruising in flotilla on board twenty-six-foot Commodore sloops. Although the itinerary is planned and directed by a Fleetmaster, there is plenty of time to free sail, exploring tropical barrier islands, estuaries and inlets—most inhabited only by gulls, pelicans and man o'war birds. You'll also be able to snorkel for live shells and fish for red snapper. Sailing out of Ft. Myers beach, the eight-day itinerary includes the islands of Sanibel, Captiva, Cabbage Key, Cayo Costa and Lovers' Key, up to the mouth of the Peace River. With two to four passengers per boat, you'll tie up at some of the finest resorts and marinas on the Gulf Coast, where you'll enjoy breakfasts and dinners in the dining rooms. Licensed Florida Receptive Tour Operator. Includes: 7 nights' berth on board, 7 breakfasts and dinners in dining rooms, 6 lunches provisioned, dock fees, ice, sea bag, T-shirt, airport transfers, tips, taxes. Dates: Year-round. Length of trip: 8 days, 7 nights. Group size: 2–4. Cost: From $540 per person. Special requirements: $50 non-refundable deposit.

Special Odysseys
P.O. Box 37
Medina, WA 98039
206-455-1960
Telex TWX 910-443-2366   *Fiji Islands*

Discover the magic of Fiji's remote islands. Your yacht is crewed by a native skipper and cook. They'll sail, or you can man the helm, and with rail down feel your ship drive ahead. And safely inside the barrier reef every night, enjoy the romance of the South Pacific Islands with all that contributes to their mystique: the warm, gracious people who will welcome you; roasted sea foods that will delight the gourmet. In addition, you'll get a good look at the culture of Fiji, since these islands are closed to regular tour groups. For convenience and economy of utilizing the best schedules and fares, this trip starts and ends in Nandi, Fiji. Experienced—references available. Includes: Airfare from Nandi, Fiji. Length of trip: 7 days, 6 nights. Group size: 2–6. Cost: $495 per person (party of 6); $915 per couple. Special requirements: Good health, $500 deposit.

Viking Yacht Cruises
230 Spruce Street
Southport, CT 06490
203-259-6030
212-221-6788
Telex 4750086 DAYL   *Caribbean*

The best cure for winter is sailing among the palm-tree isles of the French West Indies and the British Windwards on a three-masted schooner with fourteen sails in full rig. The "Godewind" is a floating first-class hotel that offers passengers comfortable living quarters

Discover the romance of windjamming aboard a luxury barquentine built for royalty.
(WINDJAMMER BAREFOOT CRUISES)

combined with the adventure of a genuine windjammer. With the wind blowing through your hair you'll meander by empty coves ... discover white sandy beaches ... and the world's most swimmable waters. Your ports of call include the tropical isles of Martinique ... Santa Lucia ... St. Vincent ... Mustique ... and lots of other paradises surrounded by the crystal blue waters of the Caribbean. Viking Yacht Cruises is a family-run business with seven years' cruise experience. Includes: Sailing as per program; all meals. Dates: Year-round. Length of trip: 7 day cruises. Group size: 24 maximum. Cost: $730 per person. Special requirements: 25% deposit upon confirmation, full payment 35 days prior to sailing.

Windjammer Barefoot Cruises, Ltd.
P.O. Box 120
Miami Beach, FL 33119-0120
800-327-2600
Telex 515729   *British Virgin Islands*

Windjammer Barefoot Cruises, Limited, with world's largest privately-owned fleet of Tall Ships, has regular sailings in the Bahamas, British Virgin Islands and West Indies for "old salts" and "landlubbers" with a yearning for adventure and a desire to "get away from it all" at remote tropical islands. Year-round weekly sailings may be combined for longer adventures ... or if you have more time, there's a nine-month 'Round-the-World Expedition. You may lend a hand or leave the sailing to a full professional crew. Includes: Accommodations, all meals and a daily ration of grog. Dates: Every Tuesday—year-round. Length of trip: 6 days. Group size: Varies. Cost: From $425. Special requirements: $125 per person deposit, balance due 45 days prior to sailing.

Cross-Country Ski •

Cross-country skiing, also known as ski-touring, is a sport that has recently exploded with popularity. The reasons are as varied as the trails you'll find when you take up this sport.

On top of the list is expense. While the price of lift tickets and equipment for Alpine skiing has sky-rocketed, cross-country expenses have remained modest, with the added attraction of no lengthy lift lines to endure. The cross-country skier's equipment is simple, effective and not subject to the popularity swings that make an Alpine skier's brand-new boots or skis outdated almost immediately.

Cross-country skiing is also great exercise. Doctors consider it an ideal tune-up for the muscles as well as the cardiovascular system—there's little physical risk in the sport, unlike downhill which is a minefield of dangerous moments.

But best of all, cross-country is fun for everyone, from small children to grandma and grandpa. There's nothing like the feeling of gliding along some snow-covered trail, enjoying the beauty of the virgin snow and feeling at peace with the world. The wintery countryside crackles with cold and little puffs of moisture constantly leave your mouth as you perfect your flowing kick-and-glide motion across the white ground.

The Scandinavians love to say that "If you can walk you can cross-country ski," but it's a good idea for the beginner to take a few lessons. Then start to explore all the wonderful trails for cross-country skiing. Wherever there's snow, there will be chances for cross-country skiing. There's a wide range of opportunities for all levels of skiers—from easy, gentle excursions through the countryside to the fast-paced exhilaration of downhill backcountry skiing. Usually at the start of each trail system there will be a warming hut which offers equipment for rent and sale, handles repair jobs and has a staff to advise and give lessons.

An offshoot of cross-country skiing is that it can be combined with other winter activities—glacier travel, snowcamping, snowshoeing and dog sledding.

The tours in this chapter will take you skiing all over the world, but there are a few common points to keep in mind:

1. Will you be using a lodge as a base? Camping out? Skiing inn-to-inn (or hut-to-hut)?
2. Are tours self-guided, or will you travel with a guide and group?
3. Will there be someone available to give you lessons if need be?
4. If traveling inn-to-inn, find out if the tour operator provides lunch for your rucksack.
5. If traveling inn-to-inn, how do you get your car back? Is there a shuttle service or do you ski back to your point of origin?
6. How far do you ski each day? And over what kind of terrain? Who chooses the route? Is the skiing for your level?
7. What kind of trails do you prefer? Blazing your own or groomed? What kind will you encounter on this tour?
8. Are rentals available? If so, can you reserve in advance? (On those perfect snow weekends, everyone wants to ski and the equipment goes fast.) If equipment can be reserved, send a deposit to make sure you get what you want.
9. If you'll be camping out, ask who carries the gear (sleeping bags, food, etc.)—you or the operator.
10. Ask the tour operator to provide a list of recommended clothing and equipment. Is any specialized equipment required (over-boots or climbing skins)?

Alaska Discovery
P.O. Box 26
Gustavus, AK 99826
907-697-3431   *Alaska*

A good introduction to snowcamping and glacier travel, this trip combines miles of excellent cross-country skiing on the spectacular Juneau icecap with patient instruction. By helicoptering high onto the icecap, you can benefit from the long hours of Alaskan daylight and summer temperatures, while enjoying some of the finest spring skiing conditions anywhere. Although some skiing experience (either Alpine or Nordic) is required, you don't have to be an expert. The trip cost includes lessons in flatland skiing with a pack and telemark skiing on the virgin slopes and bowls around camp. Your glacier guide is a certified professional ski instructor. Twelve years' experience, Alaska Association of Mountain and Wilderness Guides certified outfitter, certified Alaskan Guides. Includes: Completely outfitted, includes cross-country skis, boots, poles, all camping and cooking equipment, all food, ground transportation, charter helicopters, guides and insurance. Dates: May through July. Length of trip: 5 nights, 6 days. Group size: 4–8. Cost: $625 (approximate). Special requirements: Intermediate Nordic or Alpine skiing skills.

Alaska River and Ski
1801 Sunrise Drive
Anchorage, AK 99504
907-276-3418
Telex 25147   *Alaska*

Spend the sunny days of the Alaskan spring high on the slopes of Mt. McKinley and the Ruth Glacier. At six thousand feet you'll glide over untouched glaciers, marvel at the towering granite peaks, and enjoy one breathtaking vista after another. Perfect for skiers of all levels. This trip offers comfortable heated cabins, and plenty of fun activities on the side, such as sled racing. Both beginners and experts will also thrill at the chance to ski through the Chugach, Kenai and Talkeetna Mountains. Enjoy ski touring by day and warm, friendly Alaskan roadhouses by night . . . complete with good food, saunas and hot tubs. Or for the more adventuresome—come out for an overnight snowcamp. Member of Alaska Association of Mountain and Wilderness Guides and Professional Ski Instructors of America. Includes: All-inclusive. Dates: November through May. Length of trip: 4–5 days. Group size: 4. Cost: $625. Special requirements: Good health.

Churchill House Inn
R.D. 3
Brandon, VT 05733
802-247-3300   *Vermont*

Scenic central Vermont is the setting for this inn-to-inn cross-country ski tour. Experienced skiers will find a variety of terrain and distance to challenge them on this self-guided trip. People with limited skiing experience can enjoy touring centers at or near each inn. Along the way, four historic inns offer warm hospitality and excellent food ranging from home cooking to gourmet meals. Includes: 5 nights' lodging, all meals, maps, car shuttle. Dates: Sunday through Thursday, mid-January through mid-March. Length of trip: 5 nights, 4 days.

Group size: Up to 12. Cost: $325. Special requirements: Intermediate skiing level, $100 non-refundable deposit.

Crooked Creek Ski Touring
P.O. Box 3142
Vail, CO 81658
303-949-5682   *Colorado*

Whether it's the longing call of a coyote or the quiet sound of snow and skis coming together, the sights and sounds of this secluded back-country adventure will rejuvenate you. Spend your days cross-country skiing the untracked powder between Crooked Creek and Aspen. Spend your nights in lodges and huts located along the way—feasting on home-cooked meals and soaking in an outdoor jacuzzi as you take in the panoramic view. Participants should be able to snowplow, use step turns for changing direction and be able to herringbone or side-step up hills. All guides are certified Rocky Mountain Ski Instructors Association mountain ski touring guides with EMT medical training. Crooked Creek Ski Touring is owned by Buck and Holly Elliott who have organized wilderness ski-touring trips for the past ten years. Includes: All food, lodging, transportation from local airport, to and from trailhead. Equipment list sent at time of reservation. Dates: January through April, or anytime on a private basis. Length: 5–6 days. Group size: 9 persons. Cost: $330 per person. Special requirements: 40% deposit, full payment due 2 weeks prior to trip.

Liberty Bell Alpine Tours
Star Route
Mazama, WA 98833
509-996-2250   *Washington*

Cross-country ski in the North Cascade Mountains of Washington State! Stay at Mazama Country Inn, a rustic, converted ranch house that offers twenty miles of spectacular groomed trails, certified instructors, and a full ski shop for rentals and repairs. Or you can learn to ski downhill on cross-country skis. For those with some cross-country skiing experience, Liberty Bell teaches a five-day course on back-country skiing that will have you swooping down the trails in no time. "Inn-to-inn" tours as well as overnights in mountain huts can be arranged. For downhill powder enthusiasts, there is also helicopter skiing. Ten years' experience. Member, Professional Ski Instructors of America; American Professional Mountain Guides Association. Includes: Accommodations, ranch-style, home-cooked meals and packed lunches for all-day excursions; instruction, transportation during the program; and any specialized equipment needed. Ski rentals available. Dates: November through May. Length of trip: 1–5 days. Group size: 4–12. Cost: $35–$150 a day. Special requirements: Transportation from Seattle can be arranged; $100 deposit.

Mountaineering School at Vail, Inc.
P.O. Box 3034
Vail, CO 81658
303-476-4123   *Colorado*

Learn cross-country skiing on the famous slopes of Vail, Colorado. Whatever your level of skill, here's an opportunity to spend a day being taught by friendly, experienced ski instructors, while enjoying the beautiful mountain scenery. Small groups, no more than eight people in each, allow for a great deal of individualized instruction. Guided tours include a trip through White River National Forest, famous for its captivating silence and extraordinary wintertime scenery. Operating under a United States Forest Service permit since 1970. Includes: All-inclusive. Dates: November through April. Length of trip: 1 day. Group size: 8 students. Cost: $28.

**Nantahala Outdoor Center
U.S. 19 West, Box 41
Bryson City, NC 18713
704-448-9221** *Wyoming*

Picture a magical land where geysers produce mushroom clouds of mist that rise many times their summer height. Moving through this wintry landscape are frosty, snow-covered animals—and you—the cross-country skier who has discovered the wonder of Yellowstone National Park in winter. Under the quiet hush of heavy snow, the park becomes a paradise for cross-country skiers—Old Faithful, the Mallard Lake Trail as it winds through a lodgepole pine forest, and Shoshone Lake with the finest back-country geyser basin in the park . . . all with the magnificent Grand Tetons in the background. Includes: Lodging in the Snow Lodge at Old Faithful, most meals. Dates: March. Length of trip: 7 days. Cost: $725. Special requirements: Previous cross-country ski experience required; however, there are a variety of tracks in the area suitable for skiers of all levels.

**Pacific Adventures
P.O. Box 5041
Riverside, CA 92517
714-684-1227** *California*

The only sound will be the squeak and slide of your skis on the virgin snow as you pass the largest of all living things—the Sequoia redwoods, over three thousand years old. Pacific Adventures offers a choice of cross-country ski excursions in the wilderness regions of Southern California. Spend three days exploring Sequoia National Park—Morro Rock, Crescent Meadow, and of course, groves of giant sequoias. For beginners, Pacific Adventures offers a ski trip to Mt. San Jacinto. Here you'll learn the basic skills amid the beautiful pine-covered slopes and snow-covered meadows. Guide for seven years. Includes: Ski equipment, instruction, lodging, most meals and ground transportation. Dates: January–March. Length of trip: 1–3 days. Group size: 6–20 people. Cost: $69–$249.

**Sun Valley Trekking Company
P.O. Box 2200
Sun Valley, ID 83353
208-726-9595** *Alaska, British Columbia, Idaho*

When the snow falls, put on your cross-country skis because there's something for everyone to enjoy—whether it's criss-crossing Sun Valley by day, listening to the snow crunch during a night excursion . . . or using mountain huts as your base for an extended tour into the Sawtooth Wilderness. Try the excitement of helicopter skiing in the Canadian Rockies during a fifteen-day ski extravaganza including Alpine and Nordic skiing. Sun Valley Trekking also offers a back-country ski journey through Yellowstone. And for the seekers of the unusual, there's an ice field summer ski tour in Alaska coupled with a float trip. You can select a tour that's already put together, or one that's just right for you—the cross-country adventurer. All personnel professionally certified and licensed; Professional Ski instructors of America and Idaho Outfitters and Guides Board. Includes: Varies with trip, everything from guide service and instruction only (plus facility use if a hut tour), to the deluxe trip which includes food, all equipment and a French chef. Dates: December 1 through May 15th. Length: ½ day to 1 month. Group size: 5–11 people. Cost: $50–$2,300. Special requirements: $150 non-refundable deposit, balance 30 days in advance of trip.

Weber-Alyeska Wilderness Guides
P.O. Box 10-1663
Anchorage, AK 99511
907-345-2081   *Alaska*

Nestled in the shadows of Mt. McKinley, Kroto Lake is the center of hundreds of square miles of superb skiing terrain. Your base is a rustic but comfortable log chalet just outside Denali state and national parks. Here, snow depths average over six feet and the snow often lasts into May. Temperatures from February on are comparable to Montana or Idaho and are very conducive to cross-country skiing. Snow vehicles pull the cargo sled and function as tracksetters for skiers. On longer trips, the traditional European hut-skiing concept is used, with overnights in trappers' cabins or heated wall tent camps. Also on the longer ski packages, you'll sample one or more days of dog sledding; on shorter tours, dog sledding is optional as is Denali (McKinley) flightseeing. The Kroto Lake Hut is also a staging point for ski mountaineering into the McKinley Range mountains. Twenty-five years' experience as a professional ski-instructor and ski-school director. Includes: Ground transportation (5-day stay or longer), baggage transportation, lodging, all meals, sauna, daily guided trips, trail grooming. Optional: flightseeing, charter flights, dog mushing. Dates: February through April. Length of trip: 2 days and up. Group size: Up to 16. Cost: $85 and up. Special requirements: Must be at least a beginning skier; 25% deposit with reservation.

Wilderness Expeditions
P.O. Box 755 Cooma
New South Wales 2630 Australia
(0648) 21 587   *Australia*

Join Wilderness Expeditions for exhilarating skiing in the untouched areas of New South Wales, Australia. The company offers several options, including a beginner's overnight tour teaching the basics of cross-country skiing and snowcamping. Other courses cover cross-country and snowcraft, advanced snowcraft, and advanced overnight skills. There are also day trips, mountain tour-leader courses and various workshops in Kosciusko National Park. In addition, Wilderness Expeditions offers a classic ski tour: a one-hundred-kilometer trip from the historic Gold Rush town of Kiandra to the highest point in Australia, Mt. Kosciusko. Fit and experienced skiers are invited to come along on this ten-day trip across Alpine plains, windswept mountain passes and valleys of gnarled snowgums. The flexible itinerary allows for downhill skiing at Mt. Jagungal, the Grey Mares and Mt. Townsend. The last leg touches the highest summits in Australia before telemarking back down to civilization. All instructors and teachers are certified by the Australian Ski Federation. Includes: Ski gear, meals, camping gear and instruction. Dates: June through October. Length of trip: 1–10 days. Group size: 9 maximum. Cost: $30–$55 per day.

Wilderness Expeditions
P.O. Box 755 Cooma
New South Wales 2630 Australia
(0648) 21 587   *Japan*

Spend your vacation skiing in Japan with Wilderness Expeditions. The trip begins on Hokkaido amid snow-covered rice paddies of the Asahikawa Valley. This time of year the mountains are covered with "fwa fwa yuki"—powder snow so dry it squeaks. The first week is spent taking day trips from your lodge nestled among the pines of Daisetsuzan National Park. The untouched slopes and extensive forests of Hokkaido's highest mountain, Asahi Dake (2290 meters), offer plenty of excitement for the downhill cross-country skier. Evenings are filled with relaxing baths in natural hot springs in the true Japanese tradition and by sightseeing and shopping in nearby Asahikawa. For those so inclined, there will also be time to join the 3,500 participants in the Vasa Ski Race. Instructors are certified by the Australian Ski Federation. Includes: Accommodations, meals, and instruction. Dates: March. Length of trip: 22 days. Group size: 15 maximum. Cost: $1,718 (airfare not included).

Yukon Mountain & River Expeditions, Ltd.
P.O. Box 5405
Whitehorse, Yukon Y1A 4Z2 Canada
403-668-2513
403-399-3131 (home)   *Canada*

This trip begins with a flight over Kluane National Park onto the tip of the Lowell Glacier in Yukon's huge St. Elias Range. An ascent of this glacier takes you towards Mt. Kennedy, 13,905 feet, with its spectacular North Ridge dominating the first few days of skiing. The views of the glaciers and peaks are breathtaking as you ascend an eight-thousand-foot pass close to Pinnacle Peak and emerge onto the plateau of ice at the head of the South Arm Glacier. The descent from here towards the main Kaskawulsh Glacier is through a range of smaller peaks, with magnificent tributary glaciers flowing in from either side. A ski or walk out along the Slims River to the Alaska Highway pick-up point will complete the eighty-mile trip. Terrain is mixed, with some steeper sections, but suitable for light skis. Ten years' guiding/instructing experience. Includes: Transportation, air charter, food, mountain equipment, camping equipment, full guiding service. Dates: April and May. Length of trip: 10 days–2 weeks. Group size: Maximum 8. Cost: $950 Canadian. Special requirements: Mountain skiing ability, top-line personal clothing and equipment, $200 deposit.

Volcano Tours •

The awesome sight of dormant and active volcanoes can be found in all the far-flung corners of the world—from such distant points as lush Martinique with Mount Pel'ee ... to the grandeur of the Hawaiian volcanoes ... or the magnificence of the "Valley of ten thousand smokes," far from civilization in the Alaskan wilderness.

Touring of these eruptors of fire and molten lava can mean traveling to seldom-visited corners of a country, as in the volcano tour to Alaska outlined in this chapter. Also be prepared for a good deal of walking once you get to any volcano site—cars and jeeps can usually travel only so far, then it's up to you and your feet for further exploring.

For other tours that include volcanoes, refer to the index at the back of this book. There will be listings for the Caribbean, Dominica, Costa Rica, Hawaii and Krakatoa—all involving tours of volcanoes as part of their program.

Exploration Holidays & Cruises
1500 Metropolitan Park Building
Seattle, WA 98101
800-425-0600
206-624-8551 in WA and Canada
Telex 32 96 36   *Alaska*

The most violent volcanic eruption in the history of man formed the "land of Katmai" in 1912. Today both active and dormant volcanoes make this a dynamic landscape. Brooks Lodge is where visitors will stay, situated on the shores of Naknek Lake. This tour is for the real out-of-doors lover; away from the crowds and the typical routine. The first day you'll fly from Anchorage to King Salmon, where you board an Alaskan bush plane for a twenty-minute hop to Brooks Lodge. The second day includes an all-day excursion by bus to the "Valley of Ten Thousand Smokes" with a Park Service naturalist. The Valley road is twenty-three miles long and provides an opportunity to see nature's untouched magnificence. A hiking trail leads to the valley where you actually walk on the pumice and ash bases of the volcano itself. The third day includes a visit to the old Eskimo village site before returning via bush plane to King Salmon to connect with the Anchorage flight. Includes: Air transportation from Anchorage to Brooks Lodge; airport transfers; guided bus tours to the "Valley of Ten Thousand Smokes" with lunch and hotel accommodations. Dates: July through September. Length of trip: 3 days, 2 nights. Cost: $489.

Covered Wagons •

A hundred years ago it was common to hear "wagons ho" and see a long line of sturdy, covered Conestoga wagons set off for the long journey cross-country to the Western plains. Now you can relive that pioneer spirit and discover what life on the prairie was like for our forebears. You'll follow the paths of the early settlers, riding under the same cloudless skies, over the same rolling hills and across the same streams.

These are journeys for the adventure-seeker—where pleasure is found astride a horse or atop the wagon seat, where a long day in the saddle makes you hungry for the family-style meals cooked over an open fire. As you prepare for a night's sleep under the stars, while listening to some good old-fashioned fiddle music accompanied by chirping crickets, you'll heartily regret the invention of the car.

Since traveling by covered wagon is such a novel vacation idea, you should carefully look into all the details:

1. Get a clear idea of the wagon train's route, particularly the start and end points. Will you need a car before and after the journey or are transfers provided?
2. The tour operator will supply a list of what to bring. Check whether you'll need to bring your own sleeping bag.
3. Once you've started, do you ride in the wagon all the time, or is there horseback riding also available? Is there an extra charge to ride full time?
4. Is there time to explore and are side trips available?
5. How much is expected of you when it comes time to set up camp each night? Can you hike, swim or ride—or will you be expected to pitch in? Are you willing to pitch in if asked to?
6. What are some typical menus on the trip? If you have special eating requirements, will the tour operator accommodate you?
7. Fishing is a favorite pastime for many. Will there be time to fish en route? Is a fishing license necessary if you want to catch breakfast? Who supplies the fishing gear?

The following wagon trips cover a lot of territory and should bring out the pioneering spirit in everyone.

Thrill to the feel of a good team of gentle horses at the end of the reins as you try your hand. (WAGONS WEST)

334

Haggerty's Tour and Travel Service
Baken Park Shopping Center
Rapid City, SD 57701
605-348-1434   *South Dakota*

Relive the great pioneer migration to the American West! Travel by covered wagon, following the paths of the early settlers while experiencing the open skies and rolling grasslands of the Dakotas ranges. Ford rivers, square dance to fiddle music, enjoy hearty outdoor meals and sleep under the stars beside a warm campfire surrounded by the circled wagons. Learn to drive the horses and mule-drawn wagons or ride horseback along the train. Includes: Transportation by wagon, all meals, tents and gear; experienced wagon boss and trail crew; luggage handling; state and local taxes. Dates: June through August. Length of trip: 3 to 7 days. Group size: 10–40. Cost: $210–$420.

L. D. Frome, Outfitter
RFD
Afton, WY 83110
307-886-5240   *Nevada, Wyoming*

Journey by wagon train through the panoramic foothills of the Tetons in Wyoming or the Sonoran Desert of Nevada. You can travel atop the wagon seat or ride tall in the saddle on a gentle trail horse. Frequent rest stops provide ample time to enjoy the natural splendor of these wild areas of the West. Special guided horseback rides into the surrounding mountains are also available. In the early afternoon the wagon circle is formed and there is plenty of time to hike, fish, ride and relax before supper. The chuckwagon serves up family-style fare around the campfire. At night, sleep comfortably in the wagon, in a tepee or under the stars. Summer treks take place in the Tetons near Jackson, Wyoming. Fall, winter and spring treks are in the Sonoran Desert Foothills near Las Vegas, Nevada. Eighteen years' experience. Includes: Everything except sleeping bag (rental fee: $10). Full-time horseback riding is $15 per day extra. Dates: June through August in the Tetons; September through May in Nevada. Length of trip: 2, 4 and 6 days. Group size: Maximum 50. Cost: $160, $280, $390 for adults; children under 16 less. Special requirements: $25 deposit.

Parklands Expeditions, Inc.
P.O. Box 3055
Jackson Hole, WY 83001
307-733-3379   *Wyoming*

"Roll the wagons!" The call rings out in the clear mountain air. The team horses lean into their harness. The trail dust rises beneath their hooves and the Conestoga wagons line out in the deep pine forest. Explore the awesome Teton Wilderness perched high atop a wagon seat or astride a mountain-savvy horse. Sleep under the stars or in the wagon after an evening meal cooked on the open fire and served from the chuckwagon. The second half of this adventure travels by raft on the Snake River through Jackson Hole Valley and Grand Teton National Park, where the sky-high Tetons rise majestically from flower-bright meadows on the river bank. At night the boatmen turn into gourmet chefs and prepare hearty Western meals with all the trimmings. Over twenty years in business. Includes: Meals, all equipment for horses, wagons, rafts, camping (except sleeping gear which may be rented). You can horseback ride at least half the time at no extra charge, full-time riding costs $15 per day extra. Dates: June through September. Length: 4 days. Group size: 10–12 river, 20–25 wagons. Cost: $380.

Whalewatch •

A forty-five-ton body hurls out of the water and lands in a spectacular belly flop that reverberates like a clap of thunder. This is called breaching, and whales love to be gymnasts for an appreciative audience. They swim, breathe enormous spouts of water into the air and raise their massive triangular heads out of the water until their eyes are above the surface to check out what's happening, in a movement called spy-hopping.

The time to catch all this whale action is during their annual migrations. Whales travel the five thousand to six thousand miles between their winter and summer feeding and breeding grounds in approximately ten to twelve weeks, swimming as much as seventy miles a day and sleeping very little.

On North America's West Coast, for example, gray whales head south from the arctic waters of the Chukchi and Bering seas around September, having spent summer months gorging themselves on small fish. By December, the grays begin arriving off Baja California, their numbers peaking in mid-January and extending through April. Four placid lagoons are the Baja bedrooms for the grays where they court, mate and give birth to fifteen- to sixteen-foot babies.

On the East Coast, the whales follow a similar pattern, summering off the shores of Eastern Canada, then migrating south for the winter.

Once these gentle giants arrive at their destinations, the whalewatchers flock to the area for tantalizing sights of them at play. The whale's tolerance for human spectators is amazing. Even more surprising is the willingness of the extremely protective mother whale to have her calf be touched by humans. At times she actually seeks out people for petting and back-scratching.

When you decide to go whalewatching, there are a variety of ways to observe them—from cruise ships, kayaks or land. Whalewatching demands common sense and sensitivity, and proper boating techniques are essential. Whichever method you choose, ask if there will be a guide or naturalist on hand to explain what's happening. To get a better view of the action, bring binoculars, and photographers should bring a zoom or telephoto lens.

Whalewatching tours with different emphasis—like kayaking or scientific research expeditions—appear elsewhere in this book as well. Consult the comprehensive index at the end of the book, or check out these additional chapters:

SECTIONS OF RELATED INTEREST

Cruise
Kayak
Nature Trips
Research Expeditions

Blue Sky Adventures
P.O. Box 126 Milton Road
Oak Ridge, NJ 07438
201-697-7233   *Massachusetts*

See a humpback whale up close when this gentle giant notices your ship and swims over for a look. Seek out the humpback, finback and minke whales off the coast of Massachusetts, where these mighty cetaceans feed and play along the Stellwagon Banks. This whalewatching excursion emphasizes the collection of scientific data by the fine staff of research biologists aboard the boat. You'll learn how to identify individual humpbacks, study whale behavior and gain environmental and oceanographic information. Includes: Accommodations, lecture with slides, two 4-hour cruises, breakfast and wine party. Dates: May and September on Friday through Sunday. Length of trip: 3 days, 2 nights. Group size: 40 maximum. Cost: $200. Special requirements: $50 deposit, good health.

Nature Expeditions International
474 Williamette Avenue
Box 11496
Eugene, Oregon 97440
503-484-6529   *Mexico*

Nature Expeditions presents a gray whale expedition to the west coast of Baja California. Aboard the vessel "Qualifier 105," you'll visit San Benito, Cedros and San Martin Islands and the San Ignacio Lagoon. From late December through March, the wildlife activity is at its peak. The gray whales bear their young, elephant seals pup and breed, sea lions frolic in the surf and the Guadalupe fur seals swim and bask among volcanic rocks and cliffs. In addition, the migratory shorebirds and waterfowl are in their greatest numbers and killer whales and dolphins are there to be observed. There are a variety of environments to study including mangrove swamps, fog pine forests, beaches, estuaries and islands. This exceptional setting provides a unique classroom for the naturalist and nature photographer alike. Twelve years' experience in whalewatching tours. Includes: Meals and accommodations on ship. Dates: December, February, March. Length: 9 days. Group size: 34 maximum. Cost: $1,090.

Pacific Sea Fari Tours
530 Broadway, Suite 1224
San Diego, CA 92101
619-226-8224   *Mexico*

Imagine being so close to a gray whale that you're literally showered as "Thar She Blows"! This adventure will take you as far south as the world-famous San Ignacio Lagoon, winter quarters of the magnificent California gray whale. To and from the Lagoon, you will explore the islands of Todos Santos, San Benitos, Cedros and San Martin. Fifteen years' experience, professional naturalists, licensed crew, United States Coast Guard-certified vessels. Includes: All meals, accommodations, Mexican permits. Dates: December through April. Length of trip: 8 days. Group size: 20 to 38. Cost: $1,080.

Wilderness Alaska/Mexico
Bissel Road, Dept. STB
Hunters, WA 99137
509-722-3263 *Mexico*

Situated along the west coast of Baja California, Scammons Lagoon is the winter home for hundreds of great gray whales. From your camp, explore the bays, estuaries and desert countryside. Stable two-person kayaks permit easy observation of these magnificent marine mammals as they cavort, breach and play. The Lagoon also plays host to thousands of birds: black brant feed on plentiful eel grass; cormorants roost on the sandy shoals and pelicans are frequently seen. In addition, on-shore walks will enable you to explore the unusual flora and fauna of the Vizcanio Desert. Five years' experience. Includes: Air transport to and from San Diego, food and cooking gear, kayak gear, guides, tents. Dates: February and March. Length: 5 days. Group size: 7. Cost: $775. Special requirements: $200 deposit, camping experience.

WILDLIFE SAFARIS •

> *"Out on the Safaris, I had seen a herd of Buffalo, one hun-*
> *dred and twenty-nine of them, coming out of the morning*
> *mist under a copper sky ... I had seen a herd of Elephant*
> *travelling through dense Native forest ... pacing along as if*
> *they had an appointment at the end of the end of the world*
> *... I had time after time watched the progression across the*
> *plain of the Giraffe, in their queer, inimitable, vegetative*
> *gracefullness."*
>
> ISAK DINESEN
> *Out of Africa*

Africa is a continent of ultimates. Here you can find the tallest animal on earth (giraffe—eighteen feet), the heaviest (elephant—six tons) and fastest (cheetah—seventy miles per hour). Throughout Africa's twelve million square miles, geological wonders abound. There's the two-thousand-mile-long Great Rift Valley, which sprawls from the Red Sea to Mozambique, marking where the continent is drifting apart. And Ngorongoro Crater—a ten-mile-wide caldera (collapsed volcano), whose lush grassy plain sustains herds of wildebeest and zebra. Africa has the world's longest river, the Nile ... the vastest desert, the Sahara ... and the second largest lake, Lake Victoria. In Africa, you can find the very beginnings of mankind itself. At Tanzania's dusty, sun-baked Olduvai Gorge, Drs. Louis and Mary Leakey found human remains two million years old.

Safari. The word means journey in Swahili—and today, it is an adventure accessible to everyone.

WHAT TO EXPECT

When Teddy Roosevelt set off on safari at the turn of the century, he was accompanied by one hundred porters, professional hunters and enough provisions to last for several months. (Most travelers spent the first six months of their trip just assembling supplies.) Today, you'll be able to travel much lighter and easier.

You can choose from accommodations ranging from simple, self-service hotels to comfortable, tented camps (complete with floors, electricity, private toilet and shower) to luxury game lodges (like South Africa's Mala Mala, with marble bathrooms and a ratio of two servants to every guest). And bring your bathing suit—many lodges have refreshing swimming pools.

Travelers today rarely hike through the bush, despite the image of safaris created by Hollywood films. In most game parks, visitors ride in comfortable minibuses, with roofs that slide open for game viewing and photography. Sturdy Land Rovers also are used frequently. Because the animals come so close, no one is allowed outside the vehicles. But if you want to track wild animals on foot, many parks do permit walking safaris; check the tour operator listings for details.

While on safari, you'll generally enjoy two "game runs" a day into the surrounding areas—early morning and late afternoon, when the animals tend to be most active. Some parks also offer "hides"—sheltered viewing areas near a choice site, such as a forest glade, salt lick or river pool—where animals congregate. At famous game-viewing lodges like Treetops or the Ark, you don't go to the animals—they come to you, to snack on specially prepared food or quench their thirst at a nearby water hole. Viewing lodges offer particularly good opportunities to see nocturnal animals like giant forest hogs and bushbucks.

Here are some pointers that can help you get the most out of your safari:

1. About wet and dry seasons. Most areas of Africa follow fairly predictable
   patterns of wet and dry seasons. During the dry season, no rain may fall

for months at a time; while during the wet season, the rainfall comes down in buckets. Non-stop.

In general, the dry season affords the best opportunities for game viewing, since animals concentrate around the few permanent water holes. The dry season also facilitates transportation. Many game parks do not have paved roads, so rainy season visitors may end up wallowing in a sea of mud. (If you do go during the heavy rains, make sure you will travel by four-wheel-drive vehicle.)

But each season offers unique advantages. The onset of the rains often coincides with the calving season—enabling travelers to observe the antics of newborn springbok, hippos or elephant. And the light (or intermittent) rainy season gives travelers pleasant relief from the thick dust and strong sunshine of the dry months.

Because Africa is so enormous, seasons vary throughout the continent. The following chart indicates the approximate weather conditions for some of the most popular safari destinations. But be aware that the start of the seasons can fluctuate widely.

Hv=Heavy Rain Lt=Light Rain (Intermittent)	Jan	Feb	Mar	Apr	May	Jun	Jul	Aug	Sep	Oct	Nov	Dec
BOTSWANA	Hv	Hv	Hv									Hv
KENYA				Hv	Hv						Lt	Lt
NAMIBIA	Hv	Hv	Hv	Hv								
RWANDA			Hv	Hv	Hv						Lt	Lt
SO. AFRICA	Lt	Lt	Lt							Lt	Lt	Lt
TANZANIA												
North				Hv	Hv						Hv	Hv
Central & South	Lt	Lt	Lt	Lt	Lt							Lt
ZAIRE												
North						Hv	Hv	Hv	Hv			
Central & South		Hv	Hv	Hv						Hv	Hv	
ZAMBIA	Hv	Hv	Lt	Lt							Lt	Lt

2. Check migratory patterns. With the change of the seasons, animals seek out new food and water sources—creating the vast animal migrations across Africa. Africa's largest and most spectacular migration occurs in the Serengeti, where from December through March, over one-and-a-half million wildebeest, zebra and Thomson's gazelle ("Tommies") march south across the grasslands of Tanzania. From June through September, the pattern reverses itself—the herds head back north to Kenya's Masai Mara game reserve.

Find out about the migratory patterns in the game parks you plan to visit. During some months, the movements might take the animals out of the reserves you plan to visit and into another country. As a rule of thumb, the migrations occur with the changeover from dry to rainy season and rainy to dry.

3. Check closing season. Because of weather conditions, some parks are not open all year. Namibia's Etosha closes from the end of October until March—to take some strain off the wildlife during the worst of the dry season. Meanwhile, Mikumi in Tanzania closes during the height of the rainy weather, when roads become impassable.

4. Choose game reserves offering a wide variety of habitats, so you can see many different kinds of animals. Africa encompasses three basic types of environments, each favorable for different species.

Savanna—Although savannas may be either open plains or thick woodlands, they share a common denominator—extreme variability of climate, particularly rainfall. Savannas are home to the principal migratory animals—including zebra, wildebeest and gazelle—and their main predators—lions and cheetahs. Giraffe, warthog and rhino also prefer these regions.

Wetlands—Rivers, lakes, swamps and marshes support different animals—hippopotamus, crocodile, otter—plus colorful birds—cranes, ibis and flamingos. On large lakes, flamingo flocks can number over one million birds.

Forests—Some of Africa's forests are millions of years old and can contain trees over 180 feet tall. Chief forest dwellers are the elephants (who can uproot trees and munch them like blades of grass) and the primates—monkeys, baboons and gorillas.

5. About climate. Although Africa straddles the Equator, temperatures in many areas tend to be moderate—even cool. Throughout Africa, the main factor affecting climate is altitude. For example, Nairobi is located at about 5,500 feet and evening temperatures drop into the fifties. Since many of the famous game reserves are located at over five thousand feet, expect to find cool nights there as well. You'll experience hotter weather and greater humidity along the coast.

6. Check passport and visa requirements. Some African nations have fairly stringent passport requirements. For Kenya and Tanzania, passports must be valid for six months after date of entry; for South Africa, they must be valid for one year. Contact the individual consulate or the tour operator for the latest information.

ABOUT PHOTOGRAPHY

Since photography is a very important part of many people's African safaris, here are some special tips for capturing wild animals—on film.

1. Bring lots of film. The average amateur photographer shoots about six hundred still photos during a two-week safari. Film is nearly always cheaper and fresher if you buy it in the United States—although most major film brands are sold in large African cities.

2. Recommended film speeds: ASA 64 for daylight photos; ASA 400 or 1,000 for dawn, dusk and nighttime pictures.

3. Bring extra camera batteries. With all the photography you'll be doing, camera batteries will run down fast. Take along extra batteries from home, because replacements to fit your camera model may not be available abroad . . . at any price.

4. A telephoto lens is essential for terrific animal pictures. It can also double as binoculars. A 200 or 300 mm lens is best. Larger lenses get wobbly, and tripods are impractical during game runs—when you do all your photography from safari vehicles.

5. Your worst enemy on safari is dust. Take plenty of plastic bags to protect your camera, along with dust remover and lens tissue. Protect your camera lens with appropriate filters.

6. For photographing spectacular mountains, like Kilimanjaro or Mt. Kenya, the early morning hours just after sunrise are best. Later in the day, clouds shroud the peaks.

SECTIONS OF RELATED INTEREST

Nature Expeditions
Photography
Research Expeditions

Born Free Safaris
12504 Riverside Drive
North Hollywood, CA 91607
800-423-2883
213-877-0657 collect in CA   *Africa*

Born Free Safaris offers a complete program of exciting wildlife safaris throughout Africa. Pursue adventure in the tradition of Hemingway and Roosevelt on a "Classic Tented Photographic Safari" in Kenya's Masai Mara, Samburu, and Amboseli game reserves. At Tanzania's Serengeti National park, visit the Olduvai Gorge, site of anthropologist Louis Leakey's discovery of the Zinjanthropus man, humanity's ten-million-year-old ancestor. For lovers of adventure, freedom and nature, Born Free has "Camping Safaris" to South Africa, Namibia and Botswana, including Etosha and Kalahari Parks. "Walking Safaris" in Zambia afford unique game viewings along the banks of the Luangwa River. Accompanied by an experienced armed ranger and safari leader, you can learn different ways of tracking animals by spoors and footprints. Many options are available on the Born Free tours including hot air ballooning in the Masai Mara and whitewater rafting on the Zambezi River. Born Free has been operating safaris in Africa for ten years. Includes: All meals on safaris, accommodations, sightseeing. Dates: Year-round. Length of trip: 17–25 days. Group size: 5–15. Cost: $1,989–$3,699.

Camera Safaris, Inc.
936 South Avenue West
Westfield, NJ 07090
201-233-4555   *Botswana, Namibia*

Observe game few people have ever seen . . . kudu, wildebeest, springbok. Listen to the cry of the jackal or the roar of the lion. Camera Safaris offers two tented safaris to South Africa. Highlights include Kalahari Gemsbok National Park—home of bushmen who frequently serve as trackers on safari. Here, you'll encounter true desert conditions and plentiful game

Land Cruiser with roof-hatch for easy gameviewing. (CAMERA SAFARIS, INC.)

viewing—including the famous black-maned Kalahari lion. You can also visit Namibia's Etosha—"The Place of Dry Water." In this beautiful and cruel environment, animals must meet a daily test for survival of the fittest. Another safari explores the Okavango Delta—a rich area of waterway, reedbed and forest. Traveling in part by dugout canoe, you'll see zebra and cape buffalo . . . elephants, hippo and crocodile. Safaris are led by Mr. Syd Youthed, Botswana conservationist, naturalist and Registered Professional Guide. Includes: Accommodations, meals, drinks, staff gratuities on safari portion. Video tape of safari available to participants after the expeditions (complimentary). Airfare additional. Dates and Costs: Kalahari to Etosha, 25 days, $3,990 per person, July through October. Kalahari to Okavango, 18 days, $2,985 per person, May through October. Group size: 10 people. Special requirements: Deposit of $350 at time of booking. Very good health. Children under 14 not accepted unless it is a private safari.

Forum Travel International
2437 Durant Avenue
Berkeley, CA 94704
415-843-8294
EXPLORE Telex 9103667092   *Madagascar*

See the earth as it might have appeared fifty million years ago. Madagascar, the fourth largest island in the world, is a living museum of ancient environments. Nine out of ten species of plants and animals native to Madagascar are found nowhere else on earth. Among the indigenous animals are the lemurs, close relatives of the ancestral primates that evolved into monkeys, apes . . . and ourselves. Graceful animals resembling monkeys with bright, catlike eyes, lemurs range in size from the lesser mouse lemur—two can fit in your hand—to the three-foot-tall indri of the eastern rain forest. Civets, genets, and mongoose species also abound as well as 170 species of colorful birds—including blue and crested couas, banded kestrel and the velvet asity. Tour members visit the Berenty Lemur Reserve, Perinet Reserve, many wildlife sanctuaries, and the islands of Nossi Be, Nossi Komba, and Nossi Tonikely. Though this trip is primarily nature-oriented, you'll be able to get to know the Malagasy people—the world's only Afro-Asian culture. Forum Travel, in operation since 1965, is one of the few operators running tours to Madagascar. Includes: Land transportation, boat excursions, all domestic airfare, accommodations, all meals, transfers, guide. Dates: June and October. Length of trip: 2 weeks. Group size: 4–20. Cost: $1,998.

Forum Travel International
2437 Durant Avenue, Suite 208
Berkeley, CA 94704
EXPLORE 415-843-8294   *Kenya, Seychelles*

Explore Kenya's wild kingdom, then relax on the beautiful beaches of the Seychelles Islands. This Forum tour begins in the Northern Serengeti (Masai Mara, Kenya), at the Mara Buffalo camp. Travelers stay right on the Mara River in two-bed tents or huts equipped with private bath, shower, and hot and cold water. Daily game safaris are taken to the surrounding wildlife areas. From the Mara, visitors travel to the Seychelles Islands—known for its gently sloping beaches with fine white sand and crystal-clear warm waters. Enjoy diving, fishing, sailing, yachting and swimming—or just admire this lush island paradise with its easygoing, friendly people. Optional diving, deep-sea fishing and yachting excursions are also available. Founded in 1965, Forum now operates over three hundred programs worldwide. Other Forum programs in Africa include Tanzania, Rwanda, Botswana, Namibia, Ethiopia, Zaire and Zambia. Includes: Varies with safari. Might include airfare from New York, accommodations, all meals, transfers, activities. Dates: Year-round. Length of trip: 17–31 days. Group size: 2–20. Cost: From $1,356. Special requirements: Good health.

Fun Safaris, Inc.
P.O. Box 178
Bloomingdale, IL 60108
312-893-2545
800-323-8020   *Kenya*

This deluxe safari features the finest accommodations at Kenya's most famous game reserves, including Samburu, Amboseli, and Tsavo, where you'll enjoy nocturnal game viewing at an illuminated waterhole just yards from the lodge. Also included in this deluxe tour is a stay at the luxurious Mt. Kenya Safari Club, meeting place of the world's wealthy and elite. Founded by actor William Holden, the club features its own outdoor heated swimming pool, sauna, nine-hole golf course, horseback riding, a bowling green and tennis courts. From there, continue to famous Masai Mara game reserve. Observe the "Big Five" (elephant, buffalo, rhino, lion and leopard), watch hippos lolling in the Mara River, and enjoy the wonderful birdlife of the riverine forest. Fun Safaris has operated successfully in East Africa for eight years. Includes: All transportation, accommodations, sightseeing, game viewing, entrance fees, most meals. Dates: Year-round. Length of trip: 18 days. Group size: 20 maximum. Cost: $3,200.

Fun Safaris, Inc.
P.O. Box 178
Bloomingdale, IL 60108
312-893-2445
800-323-8020
Telex 910-291-3542   *Botswana*

This program takes you on a great wildlife adventure in Botswana. Driving through the Moremi Game Reserve, you can watch black-maned lions, photograph leopards and cheetahs, and see the scavengers—hyenas and vultures. From your camp on the banks of the Okavango River in the Moremi Game Reserve, you'll make trips into the delta with its great variety of wild game and birds. The delta's beautiful lagoons, pools and streams with gin-clear water are perfect for swimming. In the Savuti Channel, you'll view and photograph large herds of hippos at close range. The Chobe National Park is famous for its herds of elephants, which can be observed in the late afternoon when they come down to water. Among other species calling Chobe their home are waterbuck, buffalo, impala and Chobe busbuck. The tour also includes the fabulous Victoria Falls and a possible extension into the magnificent Wankie Game Reserve of Zimbabwe. Specialist in zoological safaris for past ten years. Includes: All transportation, accommodation, sightseeing, game viewing, most meals. Dates: April through October, annually. Length: 22 days. Group size: Maximum 18 persons. Cost: $4,000 per person.

GEO Expeditions
P.O. Box 27136-STB
Oakland, CA 94602
415-530-7211   *Tanzania*

Tanzania's Serengeti is home to one of the greatest concentrations of wildlife in Africa. On this safari, you'll view wildebeest, zebra, giraffe, gazelle, hippo, elephant, cheetah, and lions, as well as numerous other animals and birdlife. In addition to the vast Serengeti, you'll visit Lake Manyara, Olduvai Gorge and Lake Natron in the Rift Valley—a shallow soda lake that's a breeding place for flamingos. At the lush wildlife area of Ngorongoro Crater, you'll stay at a comfortable private campsite on the crater floor—an excellent starting place for game runs to view lions, hyenas and the carefully protected population of rare black rhino. GEO designs its safaris for the keen naturalist with emphasis on wildlife observation and photography. Safaris are led by a professional biologist; special ornithology safaris are also scheduled. An optional seven-day ascent of Mt. Kilimanjaro is offered for which no technical experience is necessary. Includes: Accommodations, land transport, all meals, expert leadership. Dates: Year-round. Length of trip: 18 days. Group size: 15 maximum. Cost: $1,450. Special requirements: $200 deposit.

Lindblad Travel, Inc.
P.O. Box 912
8 Wright Street
Westport, CT 06881
203-226-8531
Telex 221412 (Lind Ur)   *Kenya*

Air travel is ideally suited to East Africa, where distances are often great, and where some of the most fascinating places are difficult to reach by road. Lindblad's Wing Safari is surely an ultimate in safari travel. You'll cruise in a comfortable multi-engined light aircraft across the Great Rift Valley, the forests of the Aberdares, past the snow-capped peaks of Mount Kenya and Mount Kilimanjaro. The Wing Safari allows you the maximum time "on safari" in the most interesting places. Your pilots all know the country thoroughly. They—together with the safari leaders—will provide you with an intimate and rounded view of Kenya and its wildlife that is not available to land-based travelers. On the ground you will view game from specially-designed safari vehicles offering each participant a window seat, and stay in the best accommodations that Kenya has to offer. Operating tours to Kenya for twenty-five years. Includes: Full breakfast Nairobi, all meals on safari, all flights between game reserves by private plane, experienced tour escort plus driver/guide on land portions, private barbeque briefing at home of Resident Manager. Dates: June through March. Length of trip: 18 days. Group size: Maximum 25 persons. Cost: $2,750.

Safariworld
40 East 49th Street
New York, NY 10017
212-486-0505
800-221-4737
Telex 144594   *Kenya*

Photograph a towering giraffe silhouetted against a sunset sky. Capture the iridescent plumage of a Bird of Paradise in his exotic dance of love. Or simply relax at poolside and enjoy the warm African sun. On this sixteen-day deluxe wildlife safari, you will see, study and photograph an infinite variety of African fauna and flora in their natural habitat. Game viewing is done in the mornings and the afternoons and you will see free-roaming gazelles, elephants and lions, hippos and cheetahs and more. Your journey is by modern minibus with pop-up roof for close-up photography. English-speaking driver/guides who know the habits and habitats of the animals will take you on the game runs. The tour covers nine major sites in Kenya and you'll stay in the best safari lodges and hotels—located right in the center of each reserve. Highlights include Keekorok Lodge in the Masai Mara and Mt. Kenya Safari Club. Includes: Round-trip airfare from New York, deluxe safari lodges and hotels for thirteen nights; all meals on safari, entrance fees; window seats on the safari vans, 7 persons per van; game drives. Dates: Year-round. Length of trip: 16 days. Group size: Up to 25. Cost: $1,995.

EXPLORE

Special Interest Travel
2437 Durant Avenue
Berkeley, CA 94704
415-843-8294   *Africa*

Hike into the montane rain forest in Central Africa and see mountain gorillas in their natural habitat. Explore the plains, forest, and swamplands of Akegera National Park. Experience the beauty of lowland rain forests, visit fascinating pygmy villages, view Lake Kivu in western Rwanda, and a gold mine. Take a five-day extension to Zaire and trek through Virunga National Park. In addition, you can go on gorilla-tracking expeditions in hilly, densely vegetated country in Rwanda's Volcanoes National Park and hike up Bisoke Volcano. Company operating since 1967 as a division of Forum International, founded in 1965. Includes: All land transportation and accommodations on full board within Rwanda, transfers, services of guides. Dates: Monthly. Length: 6–15 days. Group size: 2–20 people. Cost: From $949. Special requirements: Very good health.

The African Experience
7 Cherry Street
Lexington, MA 02173
617-862-2165
Telex 923-348   *Zambia*

A dreamworld for photography buffs and animal lovers, South Luangwa National Park in Zambia is also a virtual paradise for sixty thousand elephants and two thousand rhino. The major feature of this safari is the ability to track and observe the animals on their level—by foot. You'll enjoy the comfort of both lodges and tented camps—and thrill to spectacular night game safaris by Land Rover, allowing you to observe nocturnal animals. Nine years in business; founded 1974. Extensive experience on African continent. Includes: Hotels/lodges, all meals except in Lusaka, 2 walking tours daily with safari guide. Dates: Dry season, June through October. Length: 10 days. Group size: No minimum participation. Cost: $1,400.

The African Experience
7 Cherry Street
Lexington, MA 02173
617-862-2165
Telex 923-348   *Tanzania*

When you visit the Selous Game Reserve in Tanzania, you'll experience true African bush. The area has only tented camps and very limited accommodations so that the number of tourists who visit the area is very small. It is a vast unspoiled wilderness with excellent game-viewing possibilities. You track the animals by foot, Land Rover, or by boat, without the feeling that civilization is just around the corner. You can combine this trip with a safari to the Serengeti Plain. Nine years in business. Includes: 2 nights Dar es Salaam, 1 night Indian Ocean, 4 nights Mbuyu Camp Selous. All meals except in Dar, game viewing by Land Rover, foot or boat daily in Selous, expert local guide, all local transportation. Dates: Year-round from Dar es Salaam. Length of trip: 8 days. Group size: Minimum participation 2 persons. Cost: $2,200.

The African Experience
7 Cherry Street
Lexington, MA 02173
617-862-2165
Telex 923-348   *Rwanda*

Come track the vanishing mountain gorilla. According to estimates, less than two hundred exist in the wild today. Volcano National Park in Rwanda is one of the last homes of this rare creature. Led by experienced guides—all members of a gorilla protection unit—you'll have an excellent chance of sighting and observing the gorillas at close range. Be in shape because this safari involves plenty of hiking through high altitudes and jungle terrain. Once you view the gorillas close up in their natural habitat you'll be glad you made the effort. Nine years in business; founded 1974. Includes: 1 night in Kigali and 3 nights in Gisenyi; all meals included (except in Kigali) and transportation; 2 full days gorilla trekking. Dates: All year. Length: 5 days. Group size: Minimum 2 persons. Cost: $1,475. Special requirements: Must be in good physical condition; will customize programs for groups and individuals.

Ventures Extraordinaire, Inc.
940 Emmett Avenue, Suite 12
Belmont, CA 94002
415-592-2629   *Kenya*

Go on safari first class with Ventures Extraordinaire. Over twenty different safari itineraries within Kenya are offered and Ventures Extraordinaire, Inc. also arranges custom itineraries of any length for parties of four or more. Visit the magnificent game parks of Masai Mara, Amboseli, Tasavo, Salt Lick and Aberdare. At Samburu, you can observe abundant giraffes and zebras, while at Meru, you can visit the home of the Born Free lions and search for the rare white rhino. Ventures Extraordinaire, Inc. tours feature first class hotels and game lodges (such as Mt. Kenya Safari Club), as well as English-speaking guides and drivers. This all-service safari combines thirteen years of safari experience with eight years of safari operations in Kenya. Includes: Accommodations, safari, guides, drivers, all meals on safari, fees and taxes. Dates: Year-round. Length of trip: From 12 days. Group size: 7 maximum. Cost: From $895 per person, 12 days. Special requirements: $300 deposit, balance due 45 days prior to departure.

Wilderness Travel
1760-HB Solano Avenue
Berkeley, CA 94707
417-524-5111   *Kenya*

Enjoy a comprehensive tour of Kenya from its snow-capped mountains to the sprawling savanna and sparkling Indian Ocean. You'll explore Aberdare (staying overnight at the famous Ark with its elephant watering hole); Mt. Kenya; Samburu; Lake Nakuru with its flamingo spectacle; and the Masai Mara. A special feature is a stay at an extraordinary private reserve where, accompanied by an expert tracker, you'll go out on game walks—something not allowed in the national parks. At night, sleep in comfortable tented camps, experiencing the timeless and primeval quality of the African savanna. From the game parks, travel by train on the famous "Lunatic Express" to the Indian Ocean sea coast. Here the crystal-clear waters of the Malindi Marine Park offer fine snorkeling among beautiful coral reefs. The excursion ends with a visit to the exotic island of Lamu where traditional Moslem Shirazi architecture and ways of life are preserved. Includes: Accommodations, land transportation, round-trip charter flights to Lamu Island, all meals, park entry fees, guides. Dates: March. Length of trip: 22 days. Group size: 5–15. Cost: $2,190. Special requirements: $200 reservation deposit plus $400; 2nd deposit 4 months prior to departure.

Wine and Spirits •

Any occasion becomes more festive, any meal more elegant, and any shared experience more memorable when the moment is enhanced with a bottle of wine or other fine spirits.

The world of wines and spirits can be as complex or as simple as you choose to make it. If you like, you can keep your repertoire of favorites to a few low-keyed, inexpensive brews that will fill the need for any occasion, or you can pursue exciting new vineyards and fine brands with total dedication and often times a great deal of money. However, most people find themselves somewhere in the middle, with a lifestyle that includes alcoholic beverages of all levels of sophistication, tastes and expense.

The world of wines and spirits is full of new adventure and experience—there's always a new wine not yet tasted, a vineyard to sample, a brand of scotch or vodka to discover.

Special tasting tours can heighten enjoyment of your favorite potions. Plan an excursion to the Napa Valley of California . . . the world-famous vineyards of the Loire Valley, Burgundy and Bordeaux regions in France; the Rhine and Moselle areas of Germany, or visit the celebrated malt whiskey distillers of Scotland. Wherever your tasting adventures take you, you'll discover new sensations and increased knowledge that will increase your drinking pleasures.

When you pick a tasting tour, keep several points in mind:

1. What is the specific theme of the tour? Is it tasting? Or is it wine making, manufacturing, brewing or distilling? What do you want to learn more about?
2. How many tastings are included and of how many different labels? Of what caliber?
3. Check carefully what tour price includes—meals? lodging?
4. Will you be accompanied by a knowledgeable guide who will pass along interesting facts about the beverages you're sampling?

Forum Travel International
2437 Durant Avenue, #208
Berkeley, CA 94704
415-843-8294

Europe

Forum Travel features several in-depth tours of Bordeaux, center of the world's largest vineyard of fine wines. The programs have several themes—initiation to testing, wines and gastronomy, and bordeaux and cognac. Along the way, you'll enjoy winetasting; visit cellars and famous vineyards such as Mouton-Rothschild, Chateau Margaux and Chateau Yquem; tour medieval cities and enjoy the delectable foods the region is known for. Forum Travel also runs a ten-day, three-country vineyard tour through France, Germany and Switzerland. Forum Travel has been in operation since 1965. Includes: All land transportation, accommodations, most meals, guiding, visits to wineries. Dates: Spring, summer and fall. Length: 4–21 days. Group size: 2–20. Cost: $378 and up.

Forum Travel International
2437 Durant Avenue, #208
Berkeley, CA 94704
415-843-8294   *South America*

Get to know the wines of South America—some of the finest and least-known wines in the world. For two weeks, you can immerse yourself in the wine country of both Chile and Argentina. There will be in-depth tours and tastings at fine wineries such as Cousino-Macul, Concha y Toro, and San Pedro in Chile, and Flichman in Argentina. You will meet the owners, be given a chance to taste young wines in the barrel, and enjoy the finest cuisine of both countries, accompanied by their best wines. In addition, four days will be spent in the indescribably beautiful Lake Country of Southern Chile. Forum Travel has been in operation since 1965. Includes: Accommodations, most meals, guides, ground transportation, visits to wineries and cantinas. Dates: November through May (approx.)—spring and summer in the respective hemisphere. Length: 4–21 days. Group size: 2–20. Cost: On request.

Napa Valley Heritage Tours
1512 Fourth Street
Napa, CA 94559
707-253-8687   *California*

The robust burgundy tingles on your tongue. The wine has such an unusual flavor, you want the taste to never end. This is what it's like on a custom-designed winetasting tour of the Napa Valley—where you learn about and experience some of America's finest wines—and what it takes for a fine bottle of wine to reach your dinner table. Tours cover small exclusive cellars to large, renowned wineries . . . leaving no bottle uncorked. All tour guides are local Napa Valley residents with extensive knowledge of area wineries, etc. Owner is fifteen-year resident with eight years of tour operation experience. Includes: Custom-designed winetasting itinerary, tour guide, air-conditioned van transportation, lunch on all-day tour. Dates: All year. Length: ½ to several days. Group size: 4–9 people. Cost: $20–$60 per person per day. Special requirements: Reservations, deposits for meals and accommodations.

Voyages Sans Frontieres, U.K.
Travel Concepts
191 Worcester Road
Princeton, MA 01541
617-464-2933   *Europe*

Voyages Sans Frontieres offers leisurely-paced tours of Europe that emphasize a region's history, art, cuisine and wine. In France and Germany, visit some of the world's greatest chefs. Tours in France include the following areas: Burgundy; Bordeaux and Cognac; the Loire Valley; Alsace; Provence; and Champagne. In Germany, spend a week in the Rhine wine resort town of Rudesheim and explore the Rhine and Moselle regions. In England, combine a stay in London with a tour of some of the country's prettiest villages and best country inns. Fifteen years' experience in specialty group travel. Includes: Transatlantic air transportation, first-class accommodation, sightseeing, transfers, breakfasts and gastronomic meals, vineyard visits; full-time courier/lecturer. Dates: Year-round. Length of trip: 10–15 days. Group size: 20. Cost: From $1,400.

Voyages Sans Frontieres, U.K.
Travel Concepts
191 Worcester Road
Princeton, MA 01541
617-464-2933   *Scotland*

This nine-day program spends three nights in Edinburgh plus four days in the Highlands of Scotland. You'll follow the sixty-two-mile-long Whiskey Trail, visiting the malt whiskey distilleries of such famous names as Glenfiddich and Glenlivet. At the distilleries you'll see just how the "water of life" is made—and probably be offered a free dram! You'll also visit some of the region's famous castles and spend time in Aviemore, Ft. William, and Inverness. Fifteen years' experience in specialty group travel. Includes: Transatlantic air transportation, first-class accommodations, transfers, sightseeing, breakfasts and dinners, full-time courier/lecturer, entrances to all distilleries and castles. Dates: Spring, summer and fall. Length of trip: 9 days. Group size: 20–30. Cost: $1,200.

Wine Stains
P.O. Box 285
Ithaca, NY 14850
607-273-6071   *Worldwide*

Wine Stains' tours visit the best wineries, restaurants and hotels in famous wine districts throughout California, New York and Central Europe. Emphasis is on calibrating the senses, the language of taste, and exploring the quality factors that make each region unique. You will meet the wine makers, visit vat rooms and vineyards, and taste more than two hundred wines! The California tour leads you off the beaten path to San Luis Obispo, Paso Robles, Edna Valley, Santa Maria, Santa Barbara, Temecula and Estrella. You'll meet Ely Callaway of Callaway Winery, Marshall Ream of Zaca Mesa Winery and Jim Lawrence of Lawrence Winery. There will also be trips to the mission at San Juan Capistrano, the Hearst Castle at San Simeon, and a champagne ride along the spectacular Pacific Coast. Wine Stains also offers tours of New York's Finger Lakes region and the European wine districts. Craig Goldwyn, tour leader, is editor of *Vinophile* magazine, director of the American Wine Competition and President of the Beverage Tasting Institute. He teaches wine appreciation at Cornell University and is a frequent judge at major wine competitions. Includes: Surface transportation, accommodations, 5 luncheons, 2 dinners, wine tastings, taxes and tips. May be deductible for wine and food professionals. Dates: Summer. Length: 7 days. Group size: 20–25. Cost: $895–$1,095.

Yacht Charter •

Imagine yourself tanned and relaxed after a day's sail, watching the sunset from the deck of your yacht. You are anchored in a small cove off a postcard-perfect island and the only other signs of civilization are a few other yachts moored nearby, gently bobbing in the water, halyards lazily slapping against the masts. In the galley, the crew is preparing dinner. All day, you sailed, fished, and snorkeled right off the boat; then sunned yourself on deck while your yacht cut through the blue waters, your captain at the tiller.

Chartering a yacht for your vacation offers you an exciting alternative to staying at a resort hotel or taking a trip on a cruise liner. And the price is right—frequently a luxury yacht charter costs less per person than a hotel room on terra firma.

Whether you select a crewed or bareboat (you're the captain) charter, you will have opportunity to enjoy a variety of beaches, islands and anchorages of your own choosing and engage in your favorite watersport—right off your own boat and when you want to do it. Every day will be a new experience—and you might even keep your food bill down by catching your own dinner.

The options for a yacht charter are many: sailing or motor yachts from about thirty feet to several hundred feet in length, with or without crew. The larger yachts are usually crewed chartered only, while you can generally captain the smaller to medium-sized ones yourself, if you like—and if you have sufficient sailing experience. You can dream hours away on the teak deck of a classic wooden schooner, take the helm of a racing sloop or party in the wide salon of a motor yacht.

As for sailing locations, the possibilities are endless: You can island-hop the crystal-clear waters of the Bahamas or United States and British Virgin Islands—or cruise off the French Riviera, putting into St. Tropez, Cannes and other fashionable Mediterranean ports. How about the Aegean, where two thousand Greek islands can provide you with superb cruising and picturesque island harbors—complete with tavernas, beaches and ancient ruins. Australia's Queensland coast offers year-round sailing with spectacular diving on the Great Barrier Reef. Other cruising areas in the warm South Pacific include New Zealand, Hawaii and Tahiti. Nearer home, you can cruise the New England coast, the Florida Keys, Washington's San Juan Islands. Just set your course.

CHARTERING THE RIGHT BOAT FOR YOU

Most charter boats are represented by charter companies, some of which handle a large number of boats worldwide, both sail and power, crewed and bareboat. Some companies specialize in one cruising area, e.g. the Virgin Islands. When you have decided where to charter, give the company(ies) specifics like dates, number of people in your party, sailing experience (for bareboat charter), special interests (fishing, snorkeling, etc.), and the company will match you up with the right boat.

In choosing a boat, use also your own judgment. Be realistic about the number of people who can stay comfortably on board, especially if you're going out for a week or more. Since space and privacy can become prized commodities, be sure to have enough room for everybody and their gear. (Soft duffels store away better than valises.)

Check carefully with the charter company to see what comes with the yacht. Many will have windsurfers, snorkel gear and fishing rods on board. Confirm that it's all in working order. Also find out what the charter price covers—sometimes the companies charge separately for captain and crew; fuel generally costs extra. Remember too that it is customary to tip at the end of the voyage.

If you are a novice sailor or have little experience cruising, you may want to start out with a crewed charter. This way you leave the responsibility, and work of docking, anchoring and sailing to the crew. Depending on the size of the boat, the crew will consist of a captain and one or more mates, who will do the cooking and other chores on board. On your request, the crew will also buy provisions for the trip, which is practical if you are chartering a boat far from home.

PREPARING FOR THE TRIP

The charter company will provide you with a list of what you should pack for the trip, which may vary according to climate and season. The boats are normally fully equipped with everything else needed for cruising—linens, pots and pans . . . even complete stereo systems, video cassette recorders or color television sets on the real luxury boats. All you need to do if you are not going by car is have your travel agent make the travel arrangements to get you to the point of embarkation.

Charter Cruise Company
P.O. Box 3730
Auckland 1 New Zealand
734-557   *New Zealand*

Be a modern-day Captain Cook as you explore New Zealand's hundreds of miles of spectacular coastline, innumerable offshore islands and warm clear waters teeming with marine life. Charter Cruise Company offers crewed and bareboat charters. Both novice and experienced sailors will feel at home on the comfortable vessels equipped with excellent cooking, toilet and washing facilities, and plenty of space in the refrigerator to keep the wine cool. Bring your own tapes for the stereo system. Cruising highlights include Bay of Islands, a magnificent region of harbors, inlets and secluded bays; and Havraki Gulf, with its profusion of verdant islands. Company is in its sixth year of operation; all vessels comply with New Zealand marine department regulations and are inspected annually. Includes: Yacht, crew, all food, some liquor. Dates: October through May. Length of trip: 3, 7, or 14 days. Group size: 1–6. Cost: $NZ 100 per day.

Compu*Charter, Inc.
153 South Main Street
Wallingford, CT 06492
800-243-0022   *Worldwide*

Once a luxury affordable by only the very rich, yacht cruising vacations are today available to fit your budget. Compu*Charter is a computerized charter yacht listing, locator and booking service. Crewed or bareboat, sailing or motor yacht, from the Caribbean to the Pacific, Compu*Charter will match your requirements of vessel size, dates and location with available vessels. Includes: Varies from bareboat (yacht only) to yacht, crew, provisions and bar. Dates: Year-round. Length: From 1 day, most common is 1 week. Group size: 1–20. Cost:

According to yacht. Special requirements: Sailing experience needed for bareboat charter. Deposit required to reserve date.

**Crewed Charters
6 Long Bay Road
St. Thomas, VI 00802
809-774-4811
Telex 3470088** *Virgin Islands*

This company specializes in crewed charters for the United States and British Virgin Islands. They will carefully choose the right yacht and crew for you for your needs—i.e., number of people in the party, expectations and sailing experience. The crew will do all the sailing, cleaning and cooking, securing of provisions, etc., for the charter. You can participate in the sailing and navigating to the degree you want. Company has five years in business; member Charter Yacht Brokers Association, Marine Association of St. Thomas and St. John. Includes: Yacht, food, beverages, bar; water sports; discount on air fare. Dates: Year-round. Length: 1 week or more. Group size: 1 or more. Cost: $500–$1,000 per person per week. Special requirements: 50% deposit at time of booking; children should be able to swim.

**Emerald Star Line
St. James Gate
Dublin 8, Ireland
720244**

or

**U.S. Agent: Patrick Henry International
3530 Forest Lane
Dallas, TX 75234
800-527-5750** *Ireland*

Watch quiet villages and lush green countryside pass by as you cruise Ireland's peaceful Shannon River. On the river, Emerald Star Line operates 170 cruisers, ranging in length from twenty-seven to forty-two feet. Cruisers are fully equipped and "bare boat"; the company provides full navigation maps and gives personal instruction to each crew. The Shannon is navigable for 160 miles and is a preserved nature area with numerous moorings inviting you to explore along the way. A subsidiary of Guinness Brewing Company, Emerald Star Line is recommended by the Irish Tourist Board. Includes: River cruiser, tuition and film instruction on boat handling, maps. Dates: April through October. Length of trip: 1–2 weeks. Group size: 2–8. Cost: Varies.

**Fraser Charters, Inc.
3471 Via Lido
P.O. Box 2268
Newport Beach, CA 92663
714-673-5252** *Worldwide*

Wherever in the world and whatever your sailing interest, Fraser Charters has a crewed yacht for your next vacation. The majority of their fleet are modern, recreational cruising yachts of every size and design imaginable—some small enough for one couple, others large enough to accommodate as many as eight to ten guests in complete privacy. For racing enthusiasts, there are fully-equipped Swans, and for traditionalists, classic wooden ships with histories that read like a swashbuckling novel. And if you're a "moss back" (an endearing term for scuba diver), Fraser has a selection of yachts that specialize in diving vacations—complete with tanks, air compressors, underwater camera gear . . . even dive platforms. Kay Parker, manager, has been a licensed yacht and charter broker for over twenty-five years. Includes: Yacht, crew, food, liquor, watersports equipment. Dates: Year-round. Length of trip: Varies. Group size: Varies. Cost: Varies. Approximately from $600 to $800 per person per week.

G.P.S.C.
600 H Street, Andrews Road
Philadelphia, PA 19118
215-247-3903
Telex 831540   *Greece, Turkey*

Sailing in perfect Mediterranean weather . . . mooring in picturesque Greek island harbors . . . snorkeling in crystal-clear water . . . cruising aboard the finest motor yachts, motorsailers and sailing yachts. What more could any yachtsman ask for? G.P.S.C., an international organization with offices in America and Greece, cooperates with a group of three companies in order to deal with every aspect of yachting—chartering, lease-back programs, naval design and architecture. G.P.S.C. owns or exclusively represents a wide selection of yachts and acts as agents for all other sizes and types. Founded in 1977. Includes: Yachts completely equipped for charterers. Dates: Late March through early November. Length: Minimum 7 days. Group size: 1 or more. Cost: According to yacht. Special requirements: Bareboat charterers must have sufficient sailing skills. Deposit according to yacht.

International Charter Association
1278 Glenneyre
Laguna Beach, CA 92651
714-494-3411
800-227-1617
800-772-3545 (CA)   *Worldwide*

From Australia to Greece, Trinidad to Tahiti—International Charter Association represents some of the finest crewed charter yachts available. From modest budget to ultra-luxury, International Charter Association offers both power and sailing yachts, from thirty-six to 240 feet in length, specializing in parties from one to sixteen per yacht. You will enjoy sunning and swimming, spearfishing and scuba diving, snorkeling and windsurfing, waterskiing, underwater photography and learning to sail and navigate. Includes: Crewed yacht fully equipped for cruising. Dates: Year-round. Length: Varies. Group size: 1–16. Cost: According to yacht.

Lynn Jachney Charters
P.O. Box 302
Marblehead, MA 01945
800-223-2050   *Worldwide*

Cruise the waters of the Mediterranean, New England, Greece, Turkey, the South Pacific or the Caribbean on a crewed yacht vacation tailored especially for you. Every yacht and captain is personally known to Lynn Jachney Charters enabling them to match you with the right yacht for your trip. Offering yacht charters since 1968. Includes: Yacht and crew, may

also include food and liquor. Dates: Year-round. Length of trip: Varies. Group size: Varies.
Cost: Varies.

Robin Brandon Charters, Ltd.
Place du Marche
83360 Port Grimaud, France
(010-33) (94) 561314   *Mediterranean*

Based at Port Grimaud situated at the head of the Golfe de St. Tropez, a small fleet of high
class yachts—Nicholsons and Swans—awaits the experienced sailor. The area offers much to
the day sailor—famous harbors, beautiful offshore islands and peaceful anchorages; and is
within one or two days' sailing of Corsica, Sardinia, the Baleric Islands, Spain and Italy for
those wishing to explore further afield. Each yacht is fully equipped to standards in excess of
those recommended by the Royal Yachting Association and Yacht Charterers' Association.
Includes: Fully-equipped yacht. Dates: Spring, summer and autumn. Length of trip: 1, 2 or 3
weeks. Group size: Varies. Cost: $600–$2,000 per week. Special requirements: Skipper and
two crew members must have good sailing experience.

SailAway Yacht Charter Consultants
P.O. Box 14702, Dept. ST184
Chicago, IL 60614
312-935-9791   *Virgin Islands*

Escape from crowded seaside hotels and cruise liners. Charter a crewed yacht and pick your
pleasure—diving for lobster dinner, taking a turn at the wheel, snorkeling, or lazing on a secluded beach. SailAway, a yacht charter brokerage representing over one hundred crewed
yachts in the United States Virgin Islands, offers yachts in a variety of sizes and price ranges
to accommodate almost anyone's needs and pocketbook. A sample of one of their favorites—the "Satori"—a fifty-seven-foot gaff-rigged schooner built, owned and crewed by Ed
and Gay Thompson. It features spacious teak decks for sunbathing, a stained-glass skylight
and beautiful hand-crafted hardwood interiors. Yachting specialists since 1978, SailAway
has inspected all the yachts it recommends. Includes: Yacht, crew, food, liquor, watersports
equipment. Dates: Year-round. Length of trip: 7 nights, 8 days. Group size: 2–18. Cost:
$80–$125 per person per day.

Valef Yachts, Ltd.
7254 Fir Road
Ambler, PA 19002
215-641-1624   *Greece*

Combine Greek mythology, the ruins of vanished civilizations, picturesque fishing villages
and spectacular island scenery and you have a cruise among the Greek Islands. Valef Yachts
owns and manages the largest fleet of charter yachts in Europe. Their fully-crewed yachts
range in size from forty to two-hundred feet carrying four to twenty-six people in comfort
and luxury among Greece's two thousand islands. Includes: Yacht, crew, food, liquor. Dates:
March through October. Length of trips: Minimum 7 days. Cost: $100–$200 per person per
day.

Ventura Yacht Services, Inc.
15 Orchard Beach Boulevard
Port Washington, NY 11050
516-944-8415
800-645-6308   *Worldwide*

Ventura Yacht Services represents many excellent sailing and motor yachts—complete with captain and crew eager to give you a fantastic cruise. You can sail the Caribbean from the beautiful Virgin Islands down to the Grenadines; Florida; the Bahamas; the New England coast from New York to Maine; explore the classic traditions of the Greek Islands and the Turkish coast; or the western Mediterranean Sea. You'll anchor in secluded coves, swim in blue-green waters, and enjoy haute cuisine aboard your chartered yacht. Five years' experience; continuous personal inspection of yachts and crews. Includes: Varies. Contact for information. Dates: Year-round. Length: 1 week or longer. Group size: 2–12, plus. Cost: According to yacht.

Virgin Islands Water Safaris
P.O. Box 9997
St. Thomas, U.S. Virgin Islands 00801
800-524-7676   *Virgin Islands*

Virgin Islands Water Safaris offers private yacht charters (crewed, bareboat to experienced sailors) for groups of two, four, six, eight or more. Most charters begin in St. Thomas, sail through the American and British Virgin Islands and return to St. Thomas after a week aboard. Or if you're looking for a different site for your business seminar, Virgin Islands Water Safaris can arrange special group seminar charters, on a sail-in-tandem basis, for tax-deductible qualifications. Includes: Yacht, crew, food, liquor and watersports equipment. Dates: Year-round. Length of trip: 1 week. Group size: Varies. Cost: $750 per person per week.

Windward Leeward Sailing Tours
680 Beach Street, Suite 494
San Francisco, CA 94109
415-441-1334   *Worldwide*

Why let the rich have all the fun? Windward Leeward Sailing is a professional yacht charter agency offering sailing opportunities throughout the world—the Caribbean, Tahiti, Australia, New Zealand, Greece and the Mediterranean. They represent a wide variety of yachts, both sail and power, with or without crew to suit your cruising needs. Ten years' experience. Includes: Yacht with or without crew, food, watersports equipment. Dates: Year-round. Length of trip: 7 days minimum, no maximum. Group size: 2–8. Cost: $100–$125 per day with crew, $40–$65 per day without crew.

Yacht Holidays International
23241 Ventura Boulevard, Suite 216
Woodland Hills, CA 91364
213-702-0111
Telex 658211   *Caribbean*

Yacht charter is an ideal adventure for active, fun-loving people who appreciate the good things in life. Imagine the thrill of sailing on your own, private, world-class yacht, with your own professional crew in attendance, dining on elegantly-served meals, and enjoying the many activities awaiting you in the always-warm waters of the Caribbean. Over fourteen years' general travel experience. Includes: Luxury yacht, professional crew, gourmet meals, open bar, watersports (windsurfing, snorkeling, fishing, sailing, waterskiing, scuba diving). Dates: Year-round. Length: 7–14 days. Group size: 2–8 or more. Cost: From $699 per person per week. Special requirements: "C" card if scuba diving.

Yachting World Yacht Charters
680 Beach Street, #498
San Francisco, CA 94109
415-928-4480
Telex 278396   *Australia*

First sailed by Captain Cook on his voyage of discovery in 1770, the Great Barrier Reef stretches for over twelve hundred miles off Australia's Queensland coast. It offers ideal year-round cruising in the protected area between the Outer Reef and the mountainous coast. The tropical waters are warm and clear and teem with marine life of almost infinite variety—corals, anemones, shells, clams, turtles and fish. The cruising area of over one thousand square miles incorporates seventy-four uninhabited national park islands and six island resorts. Surrounded by fringing coral reefs and white beaches, they feature deep bays with many safe anchorages. The charter fleet, available bareboat or with a crew (skipper and cook), consists of the NAUT 33 and 40, all fully equipped for cruising. Includes: Yacht, with provisions and crew optional. Dates: All year. Length of trip: 7 day minimum. Group size: 2 minimum. Cost: According to yacht, averages $60 per person per day for four on a NAUT 33. Special requirements: Some sailing experience.

Foreign Government • Tourist Offices

Arab Information Center
747 Third Avenue
New York, NY   10017
(212) 838-8700

Australian Tourist Commission
1270 Avenue of the Americas
New York, NY   10020
(212) 489-7550

Austrian National Tourist Office
545 Fifth Avenue
New York, NY   10017
(212) 697-0651

Bahamas Islands Tourist Office
30 Rockefeller Plaza
New York, NY   10020
(212) 757-1611

Barbados Board of Tourism
800 Second Avenue
New York, NY   10017
(212) 986-6516

Belgian National Tourist Office
745 Fifth Avenue
New York, NY   10151
(212) 758-8130

Bermuda Department of Tourism
630 Fifth Avenue
New York, NY   10111
(212) 397-7700

Bhutan Travel Agency
120 East 56th Street
New York, NY   10022
(212) 838-6382

Consulate General of Bolivia
10 Rockefeller Plaza
New York, NY   10022
(212) 586-1607

Bonaire Tourist Information Office
1466 Broadway
New York, NY   10027
(212) 838-1797

Brazilian Tourism Authority
(Embratur)
230 Park Avenue
New York, NY   10169
(212) 286-9600

British Tourist Authority
680 Fifth Avenue
New York, NY   10019
(212) 581-4700

British Virgin Island Tourist Board
370 Lexington Avenue
New York, NY   10017
(212) 371-6759

Bulgarian Tourist Office
161 East 86th Street
New York, NY   10028
(212) 722-1110

Canadian Government Office of Tourism
1251 Avenue of the Americas
New York, NY   10020
(212) 757-4917

Caribbean Tourism Association
20 East 46th Street
New York, NY   10017
(212) 682-0435

Colombian Government Tourist Office
140 East 57th Street
New York, NY   10022
(212) 688-0151

Cook Islands Tourist Authority
7833 Haskell Avenue
Van Nuys, CA   91406
(213) 988-6898

Costa Rica Tourist Board
200 S. E. 1st Street
Miami, FL   33131
(800) 327-7033 out-of-stae
(305) 358-2150

Cyprus Tourism Organization
13 East 40th Street
New York, NY   10016
(212) 686-6016

CEDOK-Czechoslovak Travel Bureau
10 East 40th Street
New York, NY   10016
(212) 689-9720

Danish Tourist Board
75 Rockefeller Plaza
New York, NY   10019
(212) 582-2802

Dominican Tourist Information Center
485 Madison Avenue
New York, NY　10022
(212) 826-0750

Eastern Caribbean Tourist Association
220 East 42nd Street
New York, NY　10017
(212) 986-9370

Egyptian Government Tourist Office
630 Fifth Avenue
New York, NY　10111
(212) 246-6960

Tourist Information Section
Fiji Mission to the United Nations
One United National Plaza
New York, NY　10017
(212) 355-7316

Finland National Tourist Office
75 Rockefeller Plaza
New York, NY　10019
(212) 582-2802

French Government Tourist Office
610 Fifth Avenue
New York, NY　10020
(212) 757-1125

German National Tourist Office
747 Third Avenue
New York, NY　10017
(212) 757-8570

Ghana Tourist Office
445 Park Avenue
New York, NY　10022
(212) 832-1300

Greek Nation Tourist Information
574 Fifth Avenue
New York, NY　10036
(212) 421-5777

Grenada Mission & Information Office
141 E. 44th Street
New York, NY　10017
(212) 599-0301

Guatemala Tourist Commission
P.O. Box 523850
Miami, FL　33152
(305) 358-5110

Haiti Government Tourist Bureau
1270 Avenue of the Americas
New York, NY　10020
(212) 757-3517

Hong Kong Tourist Association
548 Fifth Avenue
New York, NY　10036
(212) 947-5008

IBUSZ Hungarian Travel Bureau
630 Fifth Avenue
New York, NY　10111
(212) 582-7412

Government of India Tourist Office
30 Rockefeller Plaza
New York, NY　10112
(212) 586-4901

Indonesian Tourist Promotion Board
323 Geary Street
San Francisco, CA　94102
(415) 981-3585

Irish Tourist Board
590 Fifth Avenue
New York, NY　10036
(212) 246-7400

Israel Government Tourist Office
350 Fifth Avenue
New York, NY　10018
(212) 560-0650

Italian Government Tourist Office
(E.N.I.T.)
630 Fifth Avenue
New York, NY　10111
(212) 245-4822

Ivory Coast Tourist Bureau
c/o Air Afrique
1350 Avenue of the Americas
New York, NY　10019
(212) 841-7488

Jamaica Tourist Board
2 Dag Hammarskjold Plaza
New York, NY　10017
(212) 688-7650

Japan National Tourist Organization
630 Fifth Avenue
New York, NY　10111
(212) 757-5460

Kenya Tourist Office
60 East 56th Street
New York, NY　10022
(212) 486-1300

Mexican National Tourist Council
405 Park Avenue
New York, NY　10022
(212) 755-7212

Moroccan National Tourist Office
521 Fifth Avenue
New York, NY　10175
(212) 421-5771

Netherlands National Tourist Office
576 Fifth Avenue
New York, NY　10036
(212) 245-5320

New Zealand Government Tourist Office
63 Fifth Avenue
New York, NY   10111
(212) 586-0060

Consulate General of Nigeria
575 Lexington Avenue
New York, NY   10022
(212) 935-6100

Norwegian-Swedish National
Tourist Office
75 Rockefeller Plaza
New York, NY   10019
(212) 582-2802

Pacific Area Travel Association
228 Grant Avenue
San Francisco, CA   94108
(415) 986-4646

Panama Government Tourist Bureau
19 West 44th Street
New York, NY   10036
(212) 246-5841

Peruvian Tourism Promotion Board
7833 Haskell Avenue
Van Nuys, CA   91406
(213) 902-0726

Philippines Ministry of Tourism
556 Fifth Avenue
New York, NY   10036
(212) 575-7915

Portuguese National Tourist Office
548 Fifth Avenue
New York, NY   10036
(212) 354-4403

Puerto Rico Tourism Company
1290 Avenue of the Americas
New York, NY   10104
(212) 541-6630

Romanian National Tourist Office
573 Third Avenue
New York, NY   10016
(212) 697-6971

Republic of Seychelles
Permanent Mission to the UN
820 Second Avenue
New York, NY   10017
(212) 687-9766

Singapore Tourist Promotion Board
342 Madison Avenue
New York, NY   10017
(212) 687-0385

South Africa Tourist Corporation
610 Fifth Avenue
New York, NY   10020
(212) 245-3720

Spanish National Tourist Office
665 Fifth Avenue
New York, NY   10022
(212) 759-8822

Sri Lanka Tourist Board
609 Fifth Avenue
New York, NY   10017
(212) 935-0369

Swiss National Tourist Office
608 Fifth Avenue
New York, NY   10020
(212) 757-5944

Tahiti Tourist Board
366 Madison Avenue
New York, NY   10017
(212) 989-0360

Taiwan Visitors Association
210 Post Street
San Francisco, CA   94108
(415) 989-8677

Tanzania Tourist Corporation
201 East 42nd Street
New York, NY   10017
(212) 986-7124

Tourism Authority of Thailand
5 World Trade Center
New York, NY   10048
(212) 432-0433

Togo Information Service
1625 K Street NW
Washington, DC   20006
(202) 659-4330

Trinidad & Tobago Tourist Board
400 Madison Avenue
New York, NY   10017
(212) 838-7750

Turkish Tourism & Information Office
147 West 42nd Street
New York, NY   10036
(212) 687-2194

U.S. Virgin Islands
Division of Tourism
1270 Avenue of the Americas
New York, NY   10020
(212) 582-4520

U.S.S.R. Company for Foreign Travel
Intourist
630 Fifth Avenue
New York, NY   10111
(212) 757-3884

Venezuela Government Tourist Bureau
450 Park Avenue
New York, NY   10022
(212) 355-1101

Yugoslav National Tourist Bureau
509 Madison Avenue
New York, NY   10022
(212) 757-2801

Zambia National Tourist Board
235 East 52nd Street
New York, NY   10155
(212) 758-9450

Zimbabwe Tourist Board
35 East Wacker Drive
Chicago, IL   60601
(800) 621-2381 out-of-state
(312) 332-2601

State Tourism • Offices

Alabama Tourism Office
532 South Perry Street
Montgomery, AL   36104
(800) 252-2262 outside Alabama except Hawaii and Alaska
(800) 392-8096 in AL outside Montgomery
(205) 832-5510

Alaska Division of Tourism
Pouch E
Juneau, AK   99811
(907) 465-2010

Arizona Office of Tourism
3507 N. Central Avenue
Phoenix, AZ   85012
(602) 255-3618

Arkansas Dept. of Parks & Tourism
One Capitol Mall
Little Rock, AR   77201
(501) 371-1219

California Office of Tourism
1030 13th Street, Suite 200
Sacramento, CA   95814
(916) 322-2881
(916) 322-1396

Colorado Office of Tourism
1313 Sherman, Room 500
Denver, CO   80203
(303) 866-3045

Connecticut Office of Tourism
210 Washington Street
Hartford, CT   06106
(203) 566-3336
(800) 842-7492 in CT
(800) 243-1685 Maine to VA, eastern seaboard

Convention and Visitors Association
1575 "I" Street NW, Suite 250
Washington, DC   20005
(202) 789-7000

Delaware State Travel Service
99 Kings Highway
P.O. Box 1401
Dover, DE   19901
(302) 736-4271
(800) 228-8667 in Delaware
(800) 441-8846

Florida Divison of Tourism
Room 505 Collins Building
107 West Gaines Street
Tallahassee, FL   32301
(904) 488-5605

Georgia Department of Industry and Trade
Tourism Division
P.O. Box 1776
Atlanta, GA   30301
(404) 656-3553

Hawaii Visitors Bureau
2270 Kalakaua Avenue
Honolulu, HI   96815
(808) 923-1811

Idaho Tourism
Room 108, Capitol Building
Boise, ID   83720
(208) 334-2470
(800) 635-7820

Illinois Office of Tourism
310 South Michigan Avenue
Chicago, IL   60604
(312) 793-4732
(217) 782-7139
(618) 997-4371

Indiana Tourism Development Division
Indiana Department of Commerce
One North Capitol, Suite 700
Indianapolis, IN   46204
(317) 232-8860
(800) 622-4464

Iowa Development Commission
Tourism and Travel Division
250 Jewett Building
Des Moines, IA   50309
(515) 281-3100

Kansas Department of Economic Development
503 Kansas Avenue, 6th Floor
Topeka, KA   66603
(913) 296-2009

Kentucky Office of Tourism Development
Capital Plaza Tower
Frankfort, KY   40601
(502) 564-4930

Louisiana Office of Tourism
P.O. Box 44291
Baton Rouge, LA   70804
(504) 925-3850

The Maine Publicity Bureau
97 Winthrop Street
Hallowell, ME   04347
(207) 289-2423

Maryland Office of Tourism Development
1748 Forest Drive
Annapolis, MD   21401
(301) 269-2686

Massachusetts Department of Commerce
Division of Tourism
100 Cambridge Street
Boston, MA   02202
(617) 727-3201

Michigan Department of Commerce
P.O. Box 30226
Lansing, MI   48909
(517) 373-0670
(800) 292-2520 in-state
(800) 248-5700 out-of-state

Minnesota Tourism Division
419 North Robert Street
St. Paul, MN   55101
(612) 296-2755
(612) 296-2756

Mississippi Office of Tourism
P.O. Box 849
Jackson, MS   39205
(601) 359-3414
(800) 647-2290 out-of-state
(800) 962-2346 in-state

Missouri Division of Tourism
P.O. Box 1055
Jefferson City, MO   65102
(314) 751-4133

Montana Promotion Bureau
1424 9th Avenue
Helena, MT   59620
(406) 449-2654
(800) 548-3390

Nebraska Travel and Tourism Division
Box 94666
301 Centennial Mall South
Lincoln, NE   68509
(402) 471-3794
(800) 228-4307
(800) 742-7595 in-state

Nevada Office of Tourism
DED
Capitol Complex
Carson City, NV   89710
(702) 885-4322

New Hampshire Office of Vacation Travel
105 Loudon Road
Concord, NY   03301
(603) 271-2666

New Jersey Division of Travel and Tourism
CN 384
Trenton, NJ   08625
(609) 292-2470

New Mexico Tourism & Travel Division
C&ID
Bataan Memorial Building
Sante Fe, NM   87503
(800) 545-2040

New York State Department of Commerce
230 Park Avenue, Room 866
New York, NY   10169
(212) 949-9321

North Carolina Division of Travel & Tourism
430 North Salisbury Street
Raleigh, NC   27611
(919) 733-4171

North Dakota Office of Tourism
Capitol Grounds
Bismarck, ND   58505
(701) 224-2527

Ohio Office of Travel & Tourism
P.O. Box 1001
Columbus, OH   43216
(614) 466-8844
(800) BUCKEYE in state only

Oklahoma Marketing Services Division
500 Will Rogers Building
Oklahoma City, OK   73105
(405) 521-2406

Oregon Travel Information Section
Salem, OR   97310
(503) 378-6309
(800) 547-7842 out-of-state

Pennsylvania Department of Commerce
416 Forum Building
Harrisburg, PA   17120
(717) 787-5453
(800) 237-4363
(800) A-FRIEND

Rhode Island Dept of Economic Development
7 Jackson Walkway
Providence, RI   02903
(401) 227-2601
(800) 556-2484 Me through VA; No. Ohio
  except RI

South Carolina Dept of Parks, Recreation &
   Tourism
1205 Pendleton Street
Columbia, SC   29201
(803) 758-2536
(803) 758-8570

South Dakota Division of Tourism
221 South Central
Pierre, SD   57501
(605) 773-3301
(800) 843-1930
(800) 952-2217 in-state

Tennessee Tourist Development Office
P.O. Box 23170
601 Broadway
Nashville, TN   37202
(615) 741-2158

Texas Office of Tourism
Box 12008, Capitol Station
Austin, TX   78711
(512) 475-4326
(512) 475-4327
(512) 475-4328

Utah Office of Tourism
Council Hall/Capitol Hill
Salt Lake City, UT
(801) 533-5681

Vermont Travel Division
134 State Street
Montpelier, VT   05602
(802) 828-3236

Virginia State Travel Service
202 North Ninth Street
Richmond, VA   23219
(804) 786-2051

Washington Travel Development Division
101 General Administration Building
Olympia, WA   98504
(800) 541-WASH

West Virginia Travel Development Program
1900 Washington Street East
Charleston, WV   25305
(304) 348-2286
(800) 624-9110

Wisconsin Division of Tourism
P.O. Box 7970
123 West Washington Avenue
Madison, WI   53707
(608) 266-2147

Wyoming Travel Commission
1–25 College Drive
Cheyenne, WY   82002
(307) 777-7777
(800) 443-2784

N. Marianas Office of Tourism
P.O. Box 861
Saipan, CM   96950
67325
67327

Puerto Rico Tourism Company
P.O. Box 3072
San Juan, PR   00903
(809) 721-2400

Virgin Islands Division of Tourism
P.O. Box 6400
St. Thomas SUVI   00801
(809) 774-8784

Clubs and •
Associations

BACKPACKING

Appalachian Trail Conference
P.O. Box 807
Harpers Ferry, WV   25425-0807

International Backpackers Association
P.O. Box 85
Lincoln Center, ME   04458

National Campers and Hikers Association
7172 Transit Road
Buffalo, NY   14221

National Hiking and Ski Touring Association
P.O. Box 7421
Colorado Springs, CO   80933

National Trail Council
1824 Tatum Street
St. Paul, MI   49068

Sierra Club
530 Bush Street
San Francisco, CA   94108

Walking Association
4113 Lee Highway
Arlington, VA   22207

BALLOONING

Balloon Federation of America
P.O. Box 346
Indianola, IA   50125

Highamerica Balloon Club
Box 87
Rochester, MI   48063

BICYCLE TOURING

International Bicycle Touring Society
2115 Paseo Dorado
LaJolla, CA   92037

Tandem Club of America
84 Durand Drive
Rochester, NY   14622

United States Cycling Federation
1750 East Boulder Street
Colorado Springs, CO   80909

CANOEING, KAYAKING, RIVER RAFTING

American Canoe Association
P.O. Box 248
Lorton, VA   22079

American Rivers Conservation Council
323 Pennsylvania Avenue SE
Washington, DC   20003

American Whitewater Affiliation
Box 1483
Hagerstown, MD   21740

Eastern Professional
River Outfitters Association
P.O. Box 119
Oak Hill, WV   25901

Western River Guides Association
994 Denver Street
Salt Lake City, UT   84111

CAVING

National Caves Association
Rt. 9, Box 106
McMinnville, TN   37110   USA

National Speleological Society, Inc.
Cave Avenue
Huntsville, AL   35810   USA

DIVING

National Association of Underwater Instructors
Box 630
Colton, CA   92324

Underwater Photography Instruction Association
Key Largo Diving Headquarters
Rt. One, Box 293
Key Largo, FL   33037

DOG SLEDDING

International Sled Dog Racing Association
RFD 2 Box 4004
Farmington, ME   04938

HANG GLIDING, SOARING

Hang Glider Association
Box 1860
Santa Monica, CA   90406

United States Hang Gliding Association
P.O. Box 66306
Los Angeles, CA   90066

Soaring Society of America
P.O. Box 66071
Los Angeles, CA   90066

MOUNTAINEERING

American Alpine Club
113 East 90th Street
New York, NY   10028
PACK TRIPS

Trail Riders of the Wilderness
American Forestry Association
1319 18th St. NW
Washington, DC   20036

RUNNING/JOGGING

National Jogging Association
2420 K Street, NW
Washington, DC   20006

SKI TOURING

United States Ski Association
1750 East Boulder
Colorado Springs, CO   80909

Index of •
Tour Operators

High Adventure River Tours
P.O. Box 1434
Twin Falls, ID 83301
High Adventure Tours
4000 Mass. Avenue NW
#1426
Washington, DC 20016
Himalaya, Inc.
1802 Cedar Street
Berkeley, CA 94703
Himalayan Rover Trek
P.O. Box 24382
Seattle, WA 998124
Himalayan Travel, Inc.
P.O. Box 481
Greenwich, CT 06836
Homemade Holidays
Bankside, Cox Green
Rudgwick RH12 3DD
England
Hugh Glass Backpacking
P.O. Box 110796
Anchorage, AK 99511
I.T.G., Inc.
175 Fifth Avenue
New York, NY 10010
Inland Waterway Cruises
Preston Brook, Runcorn
Cheshire WA7 3AL
England
Innerasia
2627 Lombard Street
San Francisco, CA 94123
Interlocken
RD 2 Box 165-B
Hillsboro, NH 03244
International Alpine School
P.O. Box 333
Eldorado Springs, CO
80025
International Charter
1278 Glenneyre
Laguna Beach,
CA 92651
International Friends
5819 Green Oak Drive
Los Angeles, CA 90068
International Photographic
Tours
2230 N. University Park-
way
Provo, UT 84604
International School of
Mountaineering
Club Vagabond
Leysin, Vaud
Switzerland 1854
Intimate Glimpses
P.O. Box 6091
San Diego, CA 92106

Islands in the Sun
P.O. Box 1398
Newport Beach, CA
92663
Jamaica Camping & Hiking
Association
P.O. Box 216
Kingston 7
Jamaica
Jamaica Centre
8951 SW 196 Drive
Miami, FL 33157
James Henry River Journeys
P.O. Box 807
Bolinas, CA 94924
Journeys International
P.O. Box 7545-ST
Ann Arbor, MI 48107
KAO International
1007 Broxton Avenue
Los Angeles, CA 90024
Karpes & Pugh Company
P.O. Box 5152
Whitehorse, YT
Canada YIA 2S3
Kashmir Himalayan Expedi-
tions
P.O. Box 168
Srinagar-Kashmir
India
Kichatna Guide Service
P.O. Box 219
Chugiak, AK 99567
Klamath River Outdoor
Experiences
P.O. Box 1077
Happy Camp, CA 96039
Koksetna Camp
P.O. Box 69
Iliamna, AK 99606
L. D. Frome Outfitter
RFD
Afton, WY 83110
La Mer Diving Seafari, Inc.
823 UN Plaza, #810
New York, NY 10017
La Sonrisa Institute
2629 Sixth Street
Santa Monica, CA
90405
Ladatco Tours
2220 Coral Way
Miami, FL 33145
Las Ventanas de Osa
P.O. Box 820
Yellowknife, NWT
Canada X1A 2N6
Liberty Bell Alpine Tours
Star Route
Mazama, WA 98833

Libra Expeditions
P.O. Box 310
Tujunga, CA 91042
Lindblad Travel, Inc.
P.O. Box 912
Westport, CT 06881
Little Switzerland's Wet
Fantasies
P.O. Box 11583
Tahoe Paradise, CA 95708
LJA, Inc.
P.O. Box 19537
Portland, OR 97219
Logos Enterprises, Inc.
P.O. Box 704
New York, NY 10013
Lost Coast Llama Caravans
77321 Usal Road
Whitehorn, CA 95489
Lucullan Travels, Ltd.
402 29th Street
Des Moines, IA 50312
Lynn Jachney Charters
P.O. Box 302
Marblehead, MA 01945
Lyon Travel Services
1031 Ardmore Avenue
Oakland, CA 94610
MacKenzie River Cruises
P.O. Box 65
Fort Simpson, NWT
X0E 0N0 Canada
Mainstream Outfitters
Box 51
Canton, CT 06019
Marathon Tours, Inc.
1430 Mass. Avenue
Cambridge, MA 02138
Mariah Wilderness Expedi-
tions
P.O. Box 1384
El Cerrito, CA 94530
Marine Environmental Re-
search
P.O. Box 1167
Monterey, CA 93942
Marine Sciences Under Sails
P.O. Box 3994
Hollywood, FL 33083
Maupintour, USA East
P.O. Box 807
Lawrence, KS 66044
Mayflower Charters, Ltd.
Maison Eclusiere 61
Chatel Censoir
France 89660
McGee Creek Pack Station
Rt 1-Box 162
Mammoth Lakes, CA
93546

Geographical •
Index

AFRICA
Ballooning, 343
Religion, 241–242
River rafting, 343
Wildlife safaris, 344–345
Central Africa
Wildlife safaris, 347
Southern Africa
Wildlife safaris, 343
Southwest Africa
Trekking, 163
Wildlife safaris, 163
West Africa
Art, 26–27
Trekking, 144
Algeria
Camel expeditions, 195
Botswana
Wildlife safaris, 345
Egypt
Archeology, 23
Ethiopia
Trekking, 162, 169
Ghana
Culture, 110
Kenya
Horse riding, 178
Photography, 346
Wildlife safaris, 343–346, 348–349
Madagascar
Wildlife safaris, 344
Morocco
Culture, 112
Horse riding, 178
Rwanda
Hiking, 348
Wildlife safaris, 348
South Africa
Art, 28
Botany, 68
Wildlife safaris, 343–344
Tanzania
Birdwatching, 346
Wildlife safaris, 345–346, 347
Tunisia
Archeology, 21
Zaire
Trekking, 347
Zambia
River rafting, 317
Photography, 347
Wildlife safaris, 347

Zimbabwe
Archeology, 23
Birdwatching, 66

ASIA
Railway trips, 237–238, 239
Southeast Asia
Photography, 234–235
Bhutan
Religion, 240
Trekking, 151–152
China
Bicycle touring, 47, 51–52
Birdwatching, 65
Crafts, 101
Culture, 109–110, 113, 119
Trekking, 150, 153, 159
Walking, 145
India
Archeology, 19
Birdwatching, 157
Bicycle touring, 59
Cruises, 106–107
Culture, 110, 112, 115
Kayaking, 86
Photography, 231, 234
Religion, 241, 242
River rafting, 157, 166, 316
Sailing, 321
Skiing, cross-country, 157
Skiing, downhill, 157
Trekking, 142, 144, 157–158, 163–164, 166
Walking, 157
Indonesia
Culture, 114, 119–120, 121
History expeditions, 120
Nature expeditions, 220
Japan
Crafts, 100
Culture, 111–112, 116–117
Gourmet, 96
Language study, 191–192
Photography, 234
Skiing, cross-country, 332
Trekking, 142, 148–149
Walking, 154
Malaysia
Religion, 241
Trekking, 146–147